Exploring Themes of Social Justice in Education

Readings in Social Foundations

JOAN H. STROUSE
Portland State University

Merrill,
an imprint of Prentice Hall
Upper Saddle River, New Jersey   *Columbus, Ohio*

Library of Congress Cataloging-in-Publication Data

Strouse, Joan.
   Exploring themes of social justice in education : readings in social foundations / Joan
H. Strouse.
     p. cm.
   Includes bibliographical references (p.) and index.
   ISBN 0-13-442237-6 (pbk.)
   1. Educational sociology. 2. Educational anthropology. 3. Social justice—Study and
teaching. I. Title.
   LC191.S754 1997
   370.19—dc20   96-23111
                               CIP

Cover art: *Reproduction:* ©1996 Jay Mallin; *Original:* Library of Congress, Prints and
  Photographs Division, FSA/OWI Collection, LC-USF34-25378-D
Editor: Debra A. Stollenwerk
Production Editor: Louise N. Sette
Design Coordinator: Julia Zonneveld Van Hook
Text Designer: Ed Horcharik
Cover Designer: Susan E. Frankenberry
Production Manager: Deidra M. Schwartz
Electronic Text Management: Marilyn Wilson Phelps, Matthew Williams, Karen L. Bretz,
  Tracey Ward
Director of Marketing: Kevin Flanagan
Advertising/Marketing Coordinator: Julie Shough

This book was set in Revival 565 by Prentice Hall and was printed and bound by Quebecor
Printing/Book Press. The cover was printed by Phoenix Color Corp.

© 1997 by Prentice-Hall, Inc.
Simon & Schuster/A Viacom Company
Upper Saddle River, New Jersey 07458

Printed in the United States of America

10 9 8 7 6 5 4 3 2 1

ISBN: 0-13-442237-6

Prentice-Hall International (UK) Limited, *London*
Prentice-Hall of Australia Pty. Limited, *Sydney*
Prentice-Hall of Canada, Inc., *Toronto*
Prentice-Hall Hispanoamericana, S. A., *Mexico*
Prentice-Hall of India Private Limited, *New Delhi*
Prentice-Hall of Japan, Inc., *Tokyo*
Simon & Schuster Asia Pte. Ltd., *Singapore*
Editora Prentice-Hall do Brasil, Ltda., *Rio de Janeiro*

With Love For
My Life Partner,
Bill Greenfield

My Parents,
Bette Wolf Strouse
1922–1989
Lawrence Klein Strouse
1918–1991

My Niece and Nephew,
Jessica Strouse
David Strouse

You have taught me so much

Preface

The aim of this book is to help teachers become critically informed about the process of teaching and schooling in the United States. This book is designed to actively engage students in the process of developing a personal perspective for themselves of the function of schooling in our society, and of the special responsibilities teachers have to consider the broader implications of the enterprise of formal education as it occurs in this country. Whether they are prospective teachers or more experienced educators, readers will find much here to challenge their assumptions about schools and teaching. And, it is hoped, in coming to personal terms with the perspectives offered here, both groups will approach their responsibilities with a new sensitivity to the social justice challenges and complexities of teaching.

THE RATIONALE FOR THIS BOOK

Teaching is very demanding work, work that is not well understood or appreciated by the public at large. Public education, as the social bedrock supporting virtually all other occupations and institutional structures in our society, depends increasingly on teachers' willingness to commit themselves to serving the public good, believing that they *can* make an important difference in the lives of children, particularly the growing numbers of children representative of those in U.S. society who have been marginalized by virtue of their social class, gender, and/or linguistic, racial, or cultural heritage. If teachers are to be *good* teachers, they need to understand the roots of our system of public schooling, the assumptions upon which it rests, and the degree to which it is intended to serve all children equitably and effectively. This book's purpose is to help teachers develop a personally meaningful understanding of the foundations of U.S. education and their implications for their effectiveness as professional educators.

WHAT'S "SUBJECT MATTER" GOT TO DO WITH TEACHING?

If all teachers had to do was teach subject matter content, their work would be challenging, of course, but nevertheless relatively simple compared to what they actually find themselves doing. The prevailing approach to both preservice and inservice teacher education is usually grounded in such an assumption, requiring that teachers "complete" certain subject-matter courses and college majors. They learn how to design lesson plans, manage classrooms, and use specific teaching techniques, and are generally required to demonstrate a minimum level of proficiency at these tasks under the guidance of a supervising teacher in their local public school system. Indeed, in many states teachers are even now required to demonstrate subject-matter proficiency on national tests and there is a strong movement afoot to increase emphasis in subject-matter expertise and content learned as standards of proficiency for teachers and for students in schools. There is no doubt that both can be important. However, what too often gets ignored both by teacher-educators (as well as by pundits telling educators how to improve our country's public school system) is that children and the communities in which they live are tremendously diverse and becoming increasingly so.

Exploring Themes of Social Justice in Education: Readings in Social Foundations doesn't deny the need for teachers to be grounded in the subject matter of their teaching specialty, classroom management techniques, and good pedagogical practices. There is no question that these are important to good teaching. However, what is often missing in the education of teachers in general, and in the perspectives teachers bring to their daily work, is a personalized understanding of the broader function of school in society, the principles upon which it was founded, the rhetoric on which it is sustained, and the unintended but nevertheless negative consequences of our system of schooling for those whom it exists to serve, and who are most in need of what formal education can make possible in our society.

The readings in this book encourage beginning and experienced teachers alike to examine the present system and its effects on children and the broader social structure, and to challenge themselves to develop their capacity to make a real difference in the lives of children. Schools offer the possibility of social justice—and teachers themselves are the critical link in that equation. What are the issues of social justice that confront teachers daily in their classrooms? What are teachers' commitments to teaching in ways that are responsive to the life experiences of the children in their classrooms?

PERSPECTIVES ON SCHOOLING IN AMERICA

This book offers prospective as well as experienced teachers a unique opportunity to read original source materials written by authors representing divergent points of view and a broad historical spectrum in the field of education. It introduces students to this broader view of education, enabling them to understand the roots of many of the challenges confronting contemporary educators and providing them with the basis for developing a personal philosophical perspective on the work of teaching, the function of schools in our society, and the relationships between education, productivity, community, and the changing social, cultural, linguistic, and ethnic landscape of our society and its impact on schools, children, and teaching. While a number of the articles selected for inclusion might seem "old" to many readers, their message is of enduring importance to understanding the challenges faced by contemporary educators.

KEY THEMES

Several key themes integrate the readings. These are reflected in questions such as:

- What are the relationships between culture, society, and education?
- What are the dynamics of daily life in schools as institutions in particular organizational and community contexts?
- In what ways are gender, language, culture, race, social class, and the relationship between school and work important to our education?

STRUCTURE OF THE TEXT

The book is divided into six parts: Education as Cultural Transmission, Social Structure and Education, Socialization and Progress, Legitimation and Reproduction, School Life, and Education and Societal Inequality: Race, Gender, Class, and Ethnicity. Each part contains two or three contributions by distinguished and well-recognized educators of historical and contemporary significance. An introduction highlights the key ideas and issues reflected in the readings. At the end of the readings are a series of questions intended to guide the reader in examining the critical issues and to stimulate discussion of the ideas and their implications for contemporary teaching and schooling. The six parts are briefly reviewed below.

Education as Cultural Transmission

What are the values embedded in school curricula, the roles of teachers and students, social relations within the school, and the way the classroom and the school are organized and governed? Practices usually thought of as "normal," because they are so much a part of our experience and accepted ways of doing things, often are not examined or questioned. Yet it is these very practices which are, in subtle and informal ways, the primary means by which schools transmit and embed culture in our society. Given deliberate consideration, what values can teachers point to that are transmitted by the curriculum and other aspects of the ways in which we conduct schooling in our society? While many would have us believe that schools and teaching are "value free," they simply are not. What values should (and should not) be promulgated by our public schools? What are teachers' rationales for their perspectives regarding this crucial function of schooling?

Social Structure and Education

Because the success of one's effort in formal education is believed by most Americans to be based on achieved rather than ascribed attributes like race, class, native language, or gender, it is assumed by the public at large, including most legislators as well as most public educators, that the availability of a free public education gives every citizen an equal chance to advance and to become satisfied and productive citizens reaping all of the social and economic benefits of being *fully American*. Is this truth or fiction? The readings in this section engage students in an examination of how societal, school, and teacher expectations often have the effect of undermining the rhetoric that sustains our belief in schools as the great "leveler" in our society. What are the *functionalist principles* upon which public schools in the United States are grounded, and do these serve all citizens well? Often left out of the picture are the devastating effects of intergenerational poverty, poor health, a climate of violence, social neglect, and family and community turmoil. Do schools serve mainly to perpetuate the existing class structures and divisions in our society? If race, class, and gender *do* make a critical difference, what about teachers' expectations of children? What are teachers' perspectives on children of color, non-English speakers, or poor children? What difference do their expectations of children make in U.S. schools?

Socialization and Progress

What is the role of school in society? Is it the purpose of our nation's public schools to train the next work force generation, to shape the moral development of children, to teach the academic skills needed to pursue higher education, or to be agents of social change, as has been tried in the desegregation of schools and the teaching of safer sexual practices? While it is clear that schools are major influences on the moral and technical socialization of children, and teachers are critical socializing agents, to what ends should the efforts of schools be directed? The readings in this part encourage teachers to reflect on their beliefs about what children should learn in school and who should be making this decision.

Legitimation and Reproduction

The readings in this part lead teachers to examine the role of schools in maintaining and legitimizing the existing social structure in the United States. The readings offer both theoretical and concrete examples of how schools function as instruments of class domination. By encouraging a critical examination of whose interests are being served by schools, who gets ahead and why, the readings challenge teachers to consider how they will either reinforce or work to change the status quo. Exploring radically different ways of thinking about schools and education, and about the functions of school in society, invites teachers to entertain the potential of significantly different models of schooling and their implications for curriculum, the roles of teachers and students, and the interplay of school and community.

School Life

Excerpts from two ethnographies of schooling and a discussion of education in a multicultural society comprise the readings in this part. They illustrate how influential the teacher is, and how often teachers and students are on different wavelengths in terms of their understandings of rules, roles, and expectations; in other words, how different the cultures are that are shaping children and the cultures of schooling in the United States. What is life in schools like from the student's perspective? What dilemmas must teachers face as they struggle to balance their efforts to meet the needs of both low- and high-achieving students: Should the teacher give a lot to a few or a little to many? What kind of knowledge counts most for teachers—and why is this form of knowing so alien to so many students? What teachers do to enable themselves to keep abreast of the continuously changing reality of school life can make a tremendous difference for them as they search for the best way to be fair and effective as teachers. These readings examine the assumptions and stereotypes teachers have of children, particularly children of color and children of the poor, and help us understand how influential teachers can be in helping (or hindering) student learning and development.

Education and Societal Inequality: Race, Gender, Class, and Ethnicity

Despite the tremendous strides that have been made during this century, much work remains to make schools truly equitable places where all children can learn. U.S. demographics are changing rapidly, and teachers find themselves facing ever-increasing diversity in their classrooms—a diversity taking many forms, including ability, race, social class, language, and culture. Schools have always had difficulty succeeding with all students, particularly those who differ from the traditionally predominantly white, middle-class student body. While the vast majority of teachers in public schools reflect this historically dominant profile, the student profile is changing rapidly. Whether it be a learning disabled or physically or emotionally challenged student, a refugee whose native language is not English, or a student of color, the mix of students in contemporary classrooms presents teachers with a tremendous set of new challenges. The readings in this part will help new as well as experienced educators anticipate the changing classroom reality they face as contemporary teachers.

The increasingly culturally diverse communities that our public schools serve require that teachers be able to see beyond the latest teaching fad, the current curriculum or pedagogical controversy, or the school governance crisis of the moment. Teachers who do in fact see the bigger picture, who have a personally meaningful understanding of how teaching and schooling *can* make a difference in the lives of all children, *are* the teachers who will be most successful in serving our nation's students, particularly the ones from the historically marginalized groups least likely to benefit from traditional schooling. Teachers who have a historically rooted sense of their special role as a public educator will be the teachers most likely to succeed with children despite the odds against these students.

It is teachers such as these that this book seeks to inspire and encourage. Our profession needs to foster the development of a new kind of educator—one prepared to be thoughtful and reflective, and able to remind themselves and others of the historical and social significance of their work as public school teachers in a democratic society. The issues and dilemmas addressed in this book reflect the enduring challenges facing educators. Public school teachers who come to an early understanding of these broader issues will be better able than their contemporaries to teach and succeed in the emerging school milieu.

Reading and thinking about the implications of the ideas in this book will help teachers become more reflective about their practice—to think through the broader implications of the curriculum, the social relations that are fostered in schools, and the images of self, other, and society that are embedded and reinforced in traditional schooling practices. As a result of grappling at a personal level with the very real dilemmas inherent in our current system of public education, teachers will face the necessity to choose, for themselves, how they will practice their craft. Will they sustain the present system, or practice in ways that will enable schools to serve all students more equitably and effectively?

The purpose of this book is to heighten teachers' awareness of the bigger issues at stake and to stimulate them to reflect on their duty as professional educators to "educate" their students—that is, to prepare them to teach in a way that enables their students to benefit fully from their public schooling experience.

Study Questions

At the end of each part are a series of questions. These are not the sort of questions that have definitive answers. Rather, their purpose is twofold: to provide the reader with a preview of some of the major ideas to be explored in the readings, and to stimulate students to explore the implications of the readings as they discuss their thoughts and feelings with their classmates and with the instructor. Given the concerns their reflections on these questions yield, how might they orient themselves in the classroom, as a teacher? Would they have schools or the roles of teachers and students change in some respect? How, and why? Given what they have read, what are some alternative or competing perspectives? Questions in this section include both matters of primary concern to prospective or inexperienced teachers, as well as issues typically found to be of more interest to the experienced professional.

Field and Practicum Experiences

The book concludes by offering suggestions for field and practicum experiences. These obviously can be adapted to the particulars of any given instructional setting. These experiential, school and community-based components of learning can become a powerful supplement to the readings and class discussions in providing concrete examples of the ideas explored in this book.

The intention in having students participate in several different field experiences is to give them the opportunity to find out firsthand about life in schools beyond the pedagogical dimensions of classroom teaching. Whether a beginner or experienced in the classroom, spending some time talking deliberately with a teacher-colleague or principal about what it is like to be in that role can help provide a personal perspective on what it means, in a phenomenological sense, to be a teacher. The insights occasioned by a field experience will enable students to see the broader picture of teaching and schooling and the complex interplay between the community, school, and classroom that bear upon teaching and learning.

Similarly, a more extended experience, such as a practicum for the prospective teacher that involves the student in a concrete and recurring interaction with one or more children in a school or classroom setting, can be an especially enlightening learning experience. The primary purpose of the practicum is to enable prospective teachers to develop their awareness of the many factors influencing their work, to reflect on the effects of these influences on what occurs in a classroom, and perhaps to speculate about what courses of action a teacher might take to build on the positive influences and ameliorate those with negative effects. The equivalent for a more experienced teacher might be to arrange to "trade" teaching assignments with a colleague at another grade level or in a school that is culturally, racially, or socioeconomically different from one's usual or previous experience as a teacher.

Suggested Readings

At the end of the book is a bibliography of related readings that faculty and students may want to consider as they probe deeper into the ideas, theories, and concepts presented within this book.

SUGGESTIONS FOR INSTRUCTORS AND STUDENTS ABOUT USING THIS BOOK

The text is designed for a "Socratic" approach to teaching whereby the students assume a major responsibility for their learning, for engaging and exploring the ideas presented. The instructor's role is that of guide, facilitator, critical questioner, or devil's advocate. That is, the instructor supports students in helping them clarify their ideas, get beyond their taken-for-granted assumptions, and explore new terrain. This is a text that calls for active engagement by the students *and* the instructor in the material being explored. Because the issues explored by the readings are highly value-laden, and because there are no easy answers in any objective sense, the readings invite alternative and competing perspectives and interpretations.

This invitation to inquire into and consider such value-laden questions will be exciting to students, in the sense that it will get their "juices" flowing. It will also be scary and, for most, a first-time experience with authentic thinking and feeling in the context of their experience of formal schooling. Their experience will most likely have been that of passive vessel rather than active thinker. Thus it is important that the instructor encourage students to take personal risks in stating their feelings and expressing their thoughts about some very complex and important issues. Toward this end, it is important that the instructor be supportive and reinforcing as students seek to understand their thoughts and feelings and to give voice to them in a public arena like a classroom.

There is no special "magic" to the order in which the selections proceed. However, my 12 years' experience in teaching a course that uses these materials satisfies me that the current order "works" very well. Nevertheless, it may not work for every instructor, and I encourage you to rearrange the various parts into a sequence that fits with your logic of inquiry into these matters.

ACKNOWLEDGMENTS

My teaching career spans several decades. During this period I have "field tested" (with past and present students) several iterations of the text you now hold in your hands. I owe a great debt to my students, whom I hope are educating children and creating democratic classrooms in the spirit of these readings.

I want to thank my editor, Debbie Stollenwerk, who brought humor and reasonable deadlines to this work. I would also like to acknowledge the reviewers of this book: Carolyn Babione, Emporia State University; Kathleen A. Dolgos, Kutztown University; Oare' Dozier-Henry, Florida A. & M. University; Robert V. Farrell, Florida International University; JoAnn W. Haysbert, Hampton University; Carol P. Ramsay, Lake Erie College; and Stanley W. Rothstein, California State University–Fullerton.

I am fortunate to have friends, mentors, and colleagues who have supported me and my career in the three places I have called "home" (Denver, Madison, Portland). Thank you all so much. Special recognition and deep gratitude are given to those who have helped me as I wrote this: Richard Ruiz, Karen Brooks, Teri Venker, Amy Driscoll, Seema Kapani, Manya and Howard Shapiro, Leslie Rennie-Hill, Doug Sherman, Nina Saks, Mort and Sue Malter, Leslie McBride, Dan Wikler, Sue Weinstein, Ray DeMarco, Sabaii Dee, and Bill Greenfield, of course!

Manzanita, Oregon

Contents

Part 4
Legitimation and Reproduction   121

Part 5
School Life   159

Part 6
Education and Societal Inequality: Race, Gender, Class, and Ethnicity   221

Education as Cultural Transmission

The selections in Part 1 raise three basic questions for the reader:

- What are the key values reflected in U.S. culture?
- How is contemporary U.S. culture transmitted and maintained?
- What are the roles of schools and teachers in promulgating these values, attitudes, and beliefs, or in fostering changes in them in anticipation of our society's future needs?

The discussion by George Spindler provides a good introduction to the concept of culture and its transmission. It is especially useful because in his descriptions of the cultural practices and transmission processes of societies and groups unfamiliar to us, Spindler provides the reader with a perspective that is helpful in illuminating processes for cultural transmission and maintenance. What is especially difficult to understand about one's own culture is that the values, attitudes, and beliefs that constitute the culture are so familiar to us that they are hard to discern; they are "common sense," and so taken for granted as to remain hidden from us most of the time. Spindler's rich descriptions of cultural beliefs and practices not our own help one ask: How does U.S. society differ from those he describes? What similarities do they share? What are the ways educators shape the values, beliefs, and attitudes of children in the United States?

Similarly, the discussion by Conrad Arensberg and Arthur Niehoff is helpful to us in describing some of the more dominant U.S. cultural values. While these authors have written the piece to help readers understand how their values might differ from those of another culture, its importance to us is in focusing our attention on the key values associated with being American and being successful in our society today. While many other forces are shaping our values, beliefs, and attitudes, historically we have relied to a great extent upon our public schools as primary vehicles for transmitting and maintaining our culture. Schools socialize young children and adolescents to adopt orientations and dispositions that will enable them to contribute to maintaining and improving this society.

As a prospective teacher, you need to understand our core cultural values and how they are transmitted through public schooling. It also is important that you understand the special character of U.S. society and the challenges and opportunities that its increasingly heterogeneous population brings to the schoolhouse door. We are a society of multiple subcultural groups, and each group carries with it a natural desire to maintain its special heritage and identity, as reflected in different languages, races, religions, and cultural traditions. We are increasingly a multicultural society, and often the values and beliefs of divergent groups bubble up in the form of school curricula designed to celebrate and honor these differences, rather than seeking to homogenize them. What are our core cultural values? Are new cultural values emerging as these diverse cultural groups interact and influence one another? Are some traditional values becoming less central as society changes and evolves? What effects are mass communication and other highly advanced forms of technology having on our values, beliefs, and attitudes? What is the role of public education in transmitting and maintaining our society's core cultural values? Do public school teachers have a responsibility to help prepare young children and adolescents for a technologically sophisticated but largely unforeseeable future? What role does mass public education have in transmitting or changing our culture?

As you read and think about these issues, you should keep several key concepts in mind: culture; the management of cultural discontinuity and compression; cultural recruitment and maintenance; and cultural change. The idea of culture is easy enough to grasp: Many describe it as "the ideas, values, beliefs, and assumptions of a particular group or society." The culture of a particular group, especially one's own, is more difficult to understand because it is embedded in everything we do, in our notions of common sense, in what we take for granted as the way things are. The next two readings are designed to illustrate the meaning of culture, offer a framework for understanding U.S. cultural values, and focus attention on the historical role public schools have played as a primary source of cultural transmission and maintenance in our society.

The reading by Spindler offers examples of the ways culture is transmitted in different social groups. He examines the educational functions of initiation rites in small, homogeneous societies and shows how techniques like cultural discontinuity and compression come into play in transmitting and maintaining culture. He further illustrates the purpose of education in modern cultures for bringing about cultural change, showing us how schools serve both a recruitment function to maintain aspects of the culture, and how they also serve as agents of cultural discontinuity aimed at fostering cultural change and development.

Discontinuity in cultural transmission refers to the abrupt and often dramatic changes in roles that children and adolescents experience at certain stages in their journey to adulthood. Such transition points are of relatively brief duration in societies such as those described by Spindler. The discontinuity in cultural transmission of the sort Spindler describes has the effect of maintaining and validating the culture, thus resulting in cultural continuity. Spindler goes on to explain that the equivalent in developed Western society has a different effect. That is, a kind of cultural discontinuity occurs wherein traditional values and norms are not reinforced: Schools in part strive to recruit students to a cultural system that does not yet exist, or is emerging (Spindler, 1973, p. 304). To further paraphrase and extend Spindler's ideas to our contemporary situation in the United States, public schools function both to recruit people into the current system and to specific roles. It also strives to maintain the cultural system; to keep the system and roles working (Spindler, 1973, p. 303).

In a society like ours, what is the purpose of education? Can public schools effectively serve the purpose of maintaining our culture while introducing values and beliefs that challenge the accepted traditions in the effort to prepare us for the future? An example of such an effort is the 1954 *Brown v. Board of Education of Topeka, Kansas* Supreme Court decision aimed at providing access to equal educational opportunities for African Americans through school desegregation. Another example is the passage by Congress in 1972 of Title IX of the Education Amendments to the Civil Rights Act, which is intended to guard against discrimination on the basis of sex from participating in or benefiting from any education program or activity receiving federal assistance. These and other federal laws illustrate legislation that has had a profound impact on the nature of schooling in the United States and, ultimately, can be expected to have a sustaining influence on who our public schools serve, and upon the cultural values and beliefs that are promulgated as a result. In a marked departure from the past, more children today attend integrated schools, girls now are more likely than ever to play on a varsity sports team, and children with disabilities and limited English proficiency are more likely than in the past to be served in public schools. Because these changes challenge the cultural status quo, some communities have not accepted them easily. In this sense, as Spindler (1973) suggests, schools function as " . . . intentional agents of cultural discontinuity, a kind of discontinuity that does not reinforce the traditional values or recruit youngsters into the existing system" (p. 303).

A critical aspect of cultural transmission and maintenance, however, is that, as Spindler says, "People must believe in their system" (p. 303). The public school system is organized to foster recruitment into the existing cultural system. To ensure maintenance of the cultural system, the schools are organized to socialize students to the values, beliefs, and attitudes critical in maintaining the cultural system. Teachers, as crucial socialization agents, and as members of the profession our society has charged with responsibility for public schooling, have a moral duty to be deliberate in deciding what values, beliefs, and attitudes to cultivate through their teaching. It is entirely possible that a public school teacher may be asked to teach secular values or organizational attitudes (HIV education, life-skills, being a good "team player," being punctual and following rules, etc.) that are at odds with his or her personal beliefs (children should be encouraged to be spontaneous and creative; sex education is a parental responsibility).

What are U.S. cultural values, and what values, beliefs, and attitudes should public schools be teaching? Many argue that schools should not teach values. Often, what such advocates really mean is that schools should not be teaching values with which I disagree. This is a tough issue. Just what values should schools be teaching, and who gets to decide? Is it possible for a teacher to be neutral? Should a teacher even strive to be neutral?

While some cultural values are taught as an explicit goal of the school and are such that few would disagree with them (work hard, be honest, respect people and property), many cultural values are hidden within the curriculum, latent but nevertheless potent in their influence on young children and adolescents. Examples of these include habits of work, such as punctuality and persistence; habits of thought, such as don't be critical or questioning of authority; the idea that winning is what counts; the idea that only certain kinds of knowledge are important; the idea that some things are for "girls" and others are for "boys"; a hierarchical model of work; and so forth.

The second reading in this section, by Arensberg and Niehoff, offers a road map to our cultural values. Although the language used in their article is now dated, these are values that most mainstream Americans, from any part of the country, still subscribe to in their day-to-day lives and in their general cultural orientation. Among these are: the importance of material well-being; a propensity to classify acts as good or bad; the inclination to clearly differentiate work from play; the notion that time is money, and that time is scarce and worth saving; the belief that problems can be identified and overcome; the attitude that with enough effort, individuals can experience success; valuing of the pragmatic over the mystical; the idea that nature can be "harnessed"; and the belief that all people should have equal opportunities to achieve. These by no means reflect all the values that might be attributed to U.S. culture, nor are they necessarily the most central. As Arensberg and Niehoff propose, however, our history as a people has significantly influenced our character as a society and has left a distinctive cultural imprint.

The world view one brings to teaching is a product of one's education, experience, and personal background. As a teacher, you will approach that responsibility with a particular orientation, one reflecting your personal integration of the values you hold sacred, the secular values to which you subscribe as a member of the larger society, and the values you have been socialized to as a professional educator. What you teach, how you teach, and your view of and response to students will depend on this constellation of values. Your responsibility is to be aware of your values and of how they intrude into your work.

Students, too, will come to the classroom with their own special set of values: orientations that reflect their family upbringing, ethnic background, religious beliefs, social class, and childhood experiences. Sometimes the orientations of the children in your classroom will be compatible with your own attitudes, values, and beliefs; often they will differ. What is your duty as a teacher—to require the child to adapt, or to respond to the child as presented? Will the child suffer because he or she behaves in a culturally different (and by your standards, inappropriate) manner? Whose cultural values shall prevail?

As you read the next two selections, think of the purpose of public schooling in our society. Is it designed to maintain the cultural system as it presently exists, or to change certain aspects? Who decides what values count? As a teacher working with children and adolescents from diverse backgrounds, what is your responsibility relative to the transmission and maintenance of the cultural values required to sustain U.S. society? What cultural values will you strive to teach the children in your charge? Why?

The Transmission of Culture

George D. Spindler

This chapter is about how neonates become talking, thinking, feeling, moral, believing, valuing human beings—members of groups, participants in cultural systems. It is not, as a chapter on child psychology might be, about the growth and development of individuals, but on how young humans come to want to act as they must act if the cultural system is to be maintained. A wide variety of cultures are examined to illustrate both the diversity and unity of ways in which children are educated. The educational functions that are carried out by initiation rites in many cultures are emphasized, and the concepts of cultural compression, continuity, and discontinuity are stressed in this context. Various other techniques of education are demonstrated with selected cases, including reward, modeling and imitation, play, dramatization, verbal admonition, reinforcement, and storytelling. Recruitment and cultural maintenance are analyzed as basic educative functions. The chapter is not about the whole process of education but about certain parts of that process seen in a number of different situations.

WHAT ARE SOME OF THE WAYS THAT CULTURE IS TRANSMITTED?

Psychologists and pediatricians do not agree upon the proper and most effective ways to raise children. Neither do the Dusun of Borneo, the Tewa or Hopi of the Southwest, the Japanese, the Ulithians or the Palauans of Micronesia, the Turkish villagers, the Tiwi of North Australia, the people of Gopalpur, or those of Guadalcanal. Each way of life is distinctive in its outlook, content, the kind of adult personalities favored, and the way children are raised. There are also many respects in which human communities are similar that override cultural differences. All major human cultural systems include magic, religion, moral values, recreation, regulation of mating, education, and so forth. But the *content* of these different categories, and the ways the content and the categories are put together, differ enormously. These differences are reflected in the ways people raise their children. If the object of cultural transmission is to teach young people how to think, act, and feel appropriately this must be the case. To understand this process we must get a sense of this variety.

Source: "The Transmission of Culture" from *Education and Cultural Process: Towards an Anthropology of Education,* copyright 1973 by George D. Spindler. Reprinted by permission of author.

This Is How It Is in Palau

Five-year-old Azu trails after his mother as he walks along the village path, whimpering and tugging at her skirt. He wants to be carried, and he tells her so, loudly and demandingly. "Stop! Stop! Hold me!" His mother shows no sign of attention. She continues her steady barefooted stride, her arms swinging freely at her sides, her heavy hips rolling to smooth the jog of her walk and steady the basket of wet clothes she carries on her head. She has been to the washing pool and her burden keeps her neck stiff, but this is not why she looks impassively ahead and pretends not to notice her son. Often before she has carried him on her back and an even heavier load on her head. But today she has resolved not to submit to his plea, for it is time for him to begin to grow up.

Azu is not aware that the decision has been made. Understandably, he supposes that his mother is just cross, as she often has been in the past, and that his cries will soon take effect. He persists in his demand, but falls behind as his mother firmly marches on. He runs to catch up and angrily yanks at her hand. She shakes him off without speaking to him or looking at him. Enraged, he drops solidly on the ground and begins to scream. He gives a startled look when this produces no response, then rolls over on his stomach and begins to writhe, sob, and yell. He beats the earth with his fists and kicks it with his toes. This hurts and makes him furious, the more so since it has not caused his mother to notice him. He scrambles to his feet and scampers after her, his nose running, tears coursing through the dirt on his cheeks. When almost on her heel he yells and, getting no response, drops to the ground.

By this time his frustration is complete. In a rage he grovels in the red dirt, digging his toes into it, throwing it around him and on himself. He smears it on his face, grinding it in with his clenched fists. He squirms on his side, his feet turning his body through an arc on the pivot of one shoulder.

A man and his wife are approaching, the husband in the lead, he with a short-handled adz resting on his left shoulder, she with a basket of husked coconuts on her head. As they come abreast of Azu's mother the man greets her with "You have been to the washing pool?" It is the Palauan equiva-

lent of the American "How are you?"—a question that is not an inquiry but a token of recognition. The two women scarcely glance up as they pass. They have recognized each other from a distance and it is not necessary to repeat the greeting. Even less notice is called for as the couple pass Azu sprawled on the path a few yards behind his mother. They have to step around his frenzied body, but no other recognition is taken of him, no word is spoken to him or to each other. There is no need to comment. His tantrum is not an unusual sight, especially among boys of his age or a little older. There is nothing to say to him or about him.

In the yard of a house just off the path, two girls, a little older than Azu, stop their play to investigate. Cautiously and silently they venture in Azu's direction. His mother is still in sight, but she disappears suddenly as she turns off the path into her yard without looking back. The girls stand some distance away, observing Azu's gyrations with solemn eyes. Then they turn and go back to their doorway, where they stand, still watching him but saying nothing. Azu is left alone, but it takes several minutes for him to realize that this is the way it is to be. Gradually his fit subsides and he lies sprawled and whimpering on the path.

Finally, he pushes himself to his feet and starts home, still sobbing and wiping his eyes with his fists. As he trudges into the yard he can hear his mother shouting at his sister, telling her not to step over the baby. Another sister is sweeping the earth beneath the floor of the house with a coconut-leaf broom. Glancing up, she calls shrilly to Azu, asking him where he has been. He does not reply, but climbs the two steps to the threshold of the doorway and makes his way to a mat in the corner of the house. There he lies quietly until he falls asleep.

This has been Azu's first painful lesson in growing up. There will be many more unless he soon understands and accepts the Palauan attitude that emotional attachments are cruel and treacherous entanglements, and that it is better not to cultivate them in the first place than to have them disrupted and disclaimed. Usually the lesson has to be repeated in many connections before its general truth sinks in. There will be refusals of pleas to be held, to be carried, to be fed, to be cuddled, and to be amused; and for a time at least there will follow the same violent struggle to maintain control that failed to help Azu. For whatever the means, and regardless of the lapses from the stern code, children must grow away from their parents, not cleave to them. Sooner or later the child must learn not to expect the solicitude, the warm attachment of earlier years and must accept the fact that he is to live in an emotional vacuum, trading friendship for concrete rewards, neither accepting nor giving lasting affection (Barnett 1960:4–6).

Is culture being transmitted here? Azu is learning that people are not to be trusted, that any emotional commitment is shaky business. He is acquiring an emotional attitude. From Professor Barnett's further description of life in Palau (Barnett 1960) we know that this emotional attitude underlies economic, social, political, even religious behavior among adult Palauans. If this happened only to Azu we would probably regard it as a traumatic event. He might then grow up to be a singularly distrustful adult in a trusting world. He would be a deviant. But virtually all Palauan boys experience this sudden rejection (it happens more gradually for girls)—not always in just this particular way—but in somewhat the same way and at about the same time. This is a culturally patterned way of getting a lesson across to the child. This culturally patterned way of treating the child has a more or less consistent result—an emotional attitude—and this emotional attitude is in turn patterned, and fits into various parts of the Palauan cultural system. What is learned by Azu and transmitted by his mother is at once a pattern of child training (the mother had it and applied it), a dimension of Palauan *world view* (Palauans see the world as a place where people do not become emotionally involved with each other), a modal personality trait (most normal adult Palauans distrust others), and a pattern for behavior in the context of the many subsystems (economic, political, religious, and so forth), governing adult life.

Azu's mother did not simply tell him to stop depending upon her and to refrain from lasting emotional involvements with others. She demonstrated to him in a very dramatic way that this is the way it is in this life (in Palau at least). She probably didn't even completely rationalize what she did. She did not say to herself, "Now it is time for Azu to acquire the characteristic Palauan attitude that emotional attachments are not lasting and the best way to teach him this is for me to refuse to carry him." Barnett says that she "resolved not to submit to his plea." We cannot be sure that she even did this, for not even Homer Barnett, as well as he knows the Palauans, can get into Azu's mother's head. We know that she did not, in fact, submit to his plea. She may well have thought that it was about time for Azu to grow up. Growing up in Palau means in part to stop depending on people, even your very own loving mother. But maybe she was just plain tired, feeling a little extra crabby, so she acted in a characteristically Palauan way *without thinking about it* toward her five-year-old. People can transmit culture without knowing they do so. Probably more culture is transmitted this way than with conscious intent.

Discontinuity between early and later childhood is apparent in the Palauan case. Most cultures are patterned in such a way as to provide discontinuities of experience, but the points of time in the life cycle where these occur, and their intensity, differ widely. Azu experienced few restraints before this time. He did pretty much as he pleased, and lolled about on the laps of parents, kin, and friends. He was seldom if ever punished. There was always someone around to serve as protector, provider, and companion, and someone to carry him, usually mother, wherever he might go. Much of this changed for him after this day at the age of five. To be sure, he is not abandoned, and he is still shielded, guided, and provided for in every physical sense, but he finds himself being told more often than asked what he wants, and his confidence in himself and in his parents has been shaken. He no longer knows how to get what he wants. The discontinuity, the break with the ways things were in his fifth year of life, is in itself a technique of cultural transmission. We will observe discontinuities in the treatment of children and their effects in other cultures.

How Is It Done in Ulithi?

The Ulithians, like the Palauans, are Micronesians, but inhabit a much smaller island, in fact a tiny atoll in the vast Pacific, quite out of the way and fairly unchanged when first studied by William Lessa in the late forties (Lessa 1966). The Ulithians educate their children in many of the same ways the Palauans do, but differently enough to merit some special attention.

Like the Palauans, the Ulithians are solicitous and supportive of infants and young children.

> The infant is given the breast whenever he cries to be fed or whenever it is considered time to feed him, but sometimes only as a pacifier. He suckles often, especially during the first three to six months of his life, when he may average around eighteen times during the day and night. The great stress placed by Ulithians on food is once more given eloquent expression in nursing practices. Thus, if both the mother and child should happen to be asleep at any time and it seems to someone who is awake that the baby should be fed, both are aroused in order to nurse the baby. . . .
>
> The care of the baby is marked by much solicitude on the part of everyone. One of the ways in which this is manifested is through great attention to cleanliness. The infant is bathed three times a day, and after each bath the baby is rubbed all over with coconut oil and powdered with turmeric. Ordinarily, bathing is done by the mother, who, as she holds the child, rocks him from side to side in the water and sings:
>
> > Float on the water
> > In my arms, my arms
> > On the little sea,
> > The big sea,
> > The rough sea,
> > The calm sea,
> > On this sea.
> > [three sentences omitted]
>
> An infant is never left alone. He seems constantly in someone's arms, being passed from per-

son to person in order to allow everyone a chance to fondle him. There is not much danger that if neglected for a moment he will harm himself (Lessa 1966:94–96).

Unlike the Palauans, the Ulithians do not create any special discontinuities for the young child. Even weaning is handled with as little disturbance as possible.

> Weaning begins at varying ages. It is never attempted before the child is a year old, and usually he is much older than that. Some children are suckled until they are five, or even as much as seven or eight. Weaning takes about four days, one technique being to put the juice of hot pepper around the mother's nipples. Physical punishment is never employed, though scolding may be deemed necessary. Ridicule, a common recourse in training Ulithian children, is also resorted to. The child's reaction to being deprived of the breast often manifests itself in temper tantrums. The mother tries to mollify the child in a comforting embrace and tries to console him by playing with him and offering him such distractions as a tiny coconut or a flower (Lessa 1966:95).

Apparently this technique, and the emotional atmosphere that surrounds it, is not threatening to Ulithian children. We see nothing of the feelings of deprivation and rejection suffered by Azu.

> The reactions to weaning are not extreme; children weather the crisis well. In fact, a playful element may be observed. A child may quickly push his face into his mother's breast and then run away to play. When the mother's attention is elsewhere, the child may make a sudden impish lunge at the breast and try to suckle from it. After the mother has scolded the weaning, he may coyly take the breast and fondle it, toy with the nipple, and rub the breast over his face. A man told me that when he was being weaned at the age of about seven, he would alternate sleeping with his father and mother, who occupied separate beds. On those occasions when he would sleep with his father, the latter would tell him to say goodnight to his mother. The boy would go over to where she was lying and playfully run his

nose over her breasts. She would take this gesture good-naturedly and encourage him by telling him he was virtuous, strong, and like other boys. Then he would go back to his father, satisfied with his goodness (Lessa 1966:95).

We also see in the above account of Ulithian behavior that transmission of sexual attitudes and the permissiveness concerning eroticization are markedly different than in our own society. This difference, of course, is not confined to relations between young boys and their mothers, but extends through all heterosexual relationships, and throughout the patterning of adult life.

Given the relaxed and supportive character of child rearing in Ulithi, it is small wonder that children behave in a relaxed, playful manner, and apparently grow into adults that value relaxation. This is in sharp contrast with the Palauans, whom Barnett describes as characterized by a residue of latent hostility in social situations, and as subject to chronic anxiety (Barnett 1960:11–15).

Indeed, play is so haphazard and relaxed that it quickly melts from one thing to another, and from one place to another, with little inhibition. There is much laughter and chatter, and often some vigorous singing. One gains the impression that relaxation, for which the natives have a word they use almost constantly, is one of the major values of Ulithian culture (Lessa 1966:101).

Particularly striking in the transmission of Ulithian culture is the disapproval of unusually independent behavior.

The attitude of society towards unwarranted independence is generally one of disapproval. Normal independence is admired because it leads to later self-reliance in the growing individual, dependence being scorned if it is so strong that it will unfit him for future responsibilities. Ulithians talk a lot about homesickness and do not view this as improper, unless the longing is really for a spouse or sweetheart, the suspicion here being that it is really sexual outlet that a person wants. Longing of this sort is said to make a person inefficient and perhaps

even ill. Homesickness is expected of all children and not deprecated. I was greatly touched once when I asked a friend to tell me what a man was muttering about during a visit to my house. He said he felt sad that I was away from my home and friends and wondered how I could endure it. Ulithians do not like people to feel lonely; sociability is a great virtue for them (Lessa 1966:101).

The degree and kinds of dependence and independence that are inculcated in children are significant variables in any transcultural comparison of cultural transmission. Palauan children are taught not to trust others and grow to adulthood in a society where social relationships tend to be exploitative and, behind a facade of pleasantness, hostile. Palauans are not, however, independent, and tend to be quite dependent for direction upon external authority (Barnett 1960:13, 15–16). The picture is confused in Palau by the greater degree of acculturation (than at Ulithi) and the threatening situations that the Palauans have experienced under first German, then Japanese, and now American domination. In American society, middle-class culture calls for independence, particularly in males, and independence training is stressed from virtually the beginning of childhood. But adolescent and adult Americans are among the most sociable, "joiningest" people in the world. Ulithian children are not taught to be independent, and the individual who is too independent is the object of criticism. Palauan children are taught a kind of independence—to be independent of dependency upon other people's affection—by a sudden withdrawal of support at about five years of age. But which is really the more "independent" adult? Palauans are independent of each other in the sense that they can be cruel and callous to each other and exploitative in social relationships, but they are fearful of independent action and responsibility, are never originators or innovators, and are dependent upon authority for direction. Ulithians are dependent upon each other for social and emotional support, but do not exhibit the fearful dependency upon authority that Palauans do.

This does not mean that there is no predictable relationship between the training of children in dependency or independence and the consequences in adulthood. It does mean that the relationship is not simple and must be culturally contextualized if it is to make sense.

Every society creates some discontinuities in the experience of the individual as he or she grows up. It seems impossible to move from the roles appropriate to childhood to the roles appropriate for adulthood without some discontinuity. Societies differ greatly in the timing of discontinuity, and its abruptness. The first major break for Azu, the Palauan boy, was at five years of age. In Ulithi the major break occurs at the beginning of young adulthood.

> The mild concerns of ordinary life begin to catch up with the individual in the early years of adulthood and he can never again revert to the joyful indifference of his childhood.
>
> Attaining adulthood is marked by a ritual for boys and another for girls, neither of which is featured by genital operations. The same term, *kufar,* is used for each of the initiations. . . .
>
> The boy's *kufar* is much less elaborate and important. It comes about when he begins to show secondary sex characteristics and is marked by three elements: a change to adult clothing, the performance of magic, and the giving of a feast. All this occurs on the same day. . . .
>
> The outstanding consequence of the boy's ritual is that he must now sleep in the men's house and scrupulously avoid his postpubertal sisters. Not only must he not sleep in the same house with them, but he and they may not walk together, share the same food, touch one another's personal baskets, wear one another's leis or other ornaments, make or listen to ribald jokes in one another's presence, watch one another doing a solo dance, or listen to one another sing a love song (Lessa 1966:101–102).

Brother-sister avoidances of this kind are very common in human societies. There is a whole body of literature about them and their implications and consequences. The most important thing for us to note is that this is one of the most obvious ways in which restrictions appropriate to the young adult role in Ulithian society are placed on the individual immediately after the kufar. Transitional rites, or "rites of passage," as they are frequently termed, usually involve new restrictions of this sort. So, for that matter, do the events marking important transitions occurring at other times in the life experience. Azu lost the privilege of being carried and treated like an infant, and immediately became subject to being told what to do more often than demanding and getting what he wanted. One way of looking at Azu's experience and the Ulithian kufar is to regard them as periods of sharp discontinuity in the management of cultural transmission. Expressed most simply—what cultural transmitters do to and for an individual after the event is quite different in some ways from what they did before. Another way of looking at these events is to regard them as the beginning periods of cultural compression. Expressed most simply—cultural compression occurs when the individual's behavior is restricted by the application of new cultural norms. After the kufar, the Ulithian boy and girl cannot interact with their mature opposite-sex siblings except under very special rules. Azu cannot demand to be carried and is told to do many other things he did not have to do before.

In Ulithi the girl's kufar is much more elaborate. When she notices the first flow of blood she knows she must go immediately to the women's house. As she goes, and upon her arrival, there is a great hullabaloo in the village, with the women shouting again and again, "The menstruating one, Ho-o-o!" After her arrival she takes a bath, changes her skirt, has magic spells recited over her to help her find a mate and enjoy a happy married life, and is instructed about the many *etap* (taboos) she must observe—some for days, others for weeks, and yet others for years. Soon she goes to live in a private hut of her own, built near her parent's house, but she still must go to the menstrual house whenever her discharge begins (Lessa 1966:102–104).

The discontinuity and compression that Ulithian young people experience after the kufar are not limited to a few taboos.

Adolescence and adulthood obviously come rushing together at young Ulithians, and the attitude of the community toward them undergoes a rapid change. The boy and the girl are admitted to a higher status, to be sure, and they are given certain rights and listened to with more respect when they speak. But a good deal is expected of them in return. Young men bear the brunt of the heaviest tasks assigned by the men's council. For their own parents they must help build and repair houses, carry burdens, climb trees for coconuts, fish, make rope, and perform all the other tasks commonly expected of an able-bodied man. Young women are similarly called upon to do much of the harder work of the village and the household. Older people tend to treat these very young adults with a sudden sternness and formality lacking when they were in their childhood. The missteps of young people are carefully watched and readily criticized, so that new adults are constantly aware of the critical gaze of their elders. They may not voice strong objections or opinions, and have no political rights whatsoever, accepting the decisions of the men's and women's councils without murmur. Altogether, they are suddenly cut off from childhood and must undergo a severe transition in their comportment towards others about them. Only in the amatory sphere can they find release from the petty tyranny of their elders (Lessa 1966:104).

What Is It Like to Be Initiated in Hano?

Like the Hopi, with whom they are very close neighbors on the same mesa in Arizona, the Hano Tewa hold an initiation ceremony into the Kachina[1] cult at about nine years of age. In fact, the Tewa and Hopi share the same ceremony. Further examination of this occasion will be instructive. Up until that time Tewa children are treated about the way the Hopi children are. They are kept on a cradleboard at first, weaned

late, by middle-class American standards, and on the whole treated very permissively and supportively by mothers, mother's sisters, grandparents, fathers, older siblings, and other people in and about the extended family household, admonished and corrected by the mother's brother, and half scared to death from time to time when they are bad by the Kachinas, or the threat of Kachinas. Of course nowadays the continuity of this early period is somewhat upset because children must start in the government day school at Polacca when they are about seven, and the teachers' ideas of proper behavior are frequently at variance with those maintained by Tewa parents. Excepting for school, though, Tewa children can be said to experience a consistent, continuous educational environment through the early years.

Things change when the initiation takes place at about age nine. A ceremonial father is selected for the boy, and a ceremonial mother for the girl. These ceremonial parents, as well as the real parents and for that matter everyone in the pueblo, build up the coming event for the child so that he or she is in a tremendous state of excitement. Then the day comes. Edward Dozier reports the initiation experience of one of his informants.

We were told that the Kachina were beings from another world. There were some boys who said that they were not, but we could never be sure, and most of us believed what we were told. Our own parents and elders tried to make us believe that the Kachina were powerful beings, some good and some bad, and that they knew our innermost thoughts and actions. If they did not know about us through their own great power, then probably our own relatives told the Kachina about us. At any rate every time they visited us they seemed to know what we had thought and how we had acted.

---

[1]This word is sometimes spelled Katcina, sometimes Kachina. Voth, used as the source for the description of the Hopi ceremony, spells it Katcina. Dozier, used as the source for the Hano Tewa, spells it Kachina. Either is correct.

As the time for our initiation came closer we became more and more frightened. The ogre Kachina, the Soyoku, came every year and threatened to carry us away; now we were told that we were going to face these awful creatures and many others. Though we were told not to be afraid, we could not help ourselves. If the Kachina are really supernaturals and powerful beings, we might have offended them by some thought or act and they might punish us. They might even take us with them as the Soyoku threatened to do every year.

Four days before Powamu our ceremonial fathers and our ceremonial mothers took us to Court Kiva. The girls were accompanied by their ceremonial mothers, and we boys by our ceremonial fathers. We stood outside the kiva, and then two whipper Kachina, looking very mean, came out of the kiva. Only a blanket covered the nakedness of the boys; as the Kachina drew near our ceremonial fathers removed the blankets. The girls were permitted to keep on their dresses, however. Our ceremonial parents urged us to offer sacred corn meal to the Kachina; as soon as we did they whipped us with their yucca whips. I was hit so hard that I defecated and urinated and I could feel the welts forming on my back and I knew that I was bleeding too. He whipped me four times, but the last time he hit me on the leg instead, and as the whipper started to strike again, my ceremonial father pulled me back and he took the blow himself. "This is a good boy, my old man," he said to the Kachina. "You have hit him enough."

For many days my back hurt and I had to sleep on my side until the wounds healed.

After the whipping a small sacred feather was tied to our hair and we were told not to eat meat or salt. Four days later we went to see the Powamu ceremony in the kiva. As babies, our mothers had taken us to see this event; but as soon as we began to talk, they stopped taking us. I could not remember what had happened on Powamu night and I was afraid that another frightening ordeal awaited us. Those of us who were whipped went with our ceremonial parents. In this dance we saw that the Kachina were really our own fathers, uncles, and brothers. This made me feel strange. I felt somehow that all my relatives were responsible for the whipping we had received. My ceremonial father was kind and gentle during this time and I felt very warm toward him, but I also wondered if he was to blame for our treatment. I felt deceived and ill-treated (Dozier 1967:59–60).

The Hano Tewa children are shocked, angry, chagrined when they find that the supernatural Kachinas they have been scared and disciplined by all their lives up until then, and who during the initiation have whipped them hard, are really men they have known very well in their own community, their clans, their families. To be treated supportively and permissively all of one's life, and then to be whipped publicly (or see others get whipped) would seem quite upsetting by itself. To find out that the awesome Kachinas are men impersonating gods would seem almost too much. But somehow the experience seems to help make good adult Hano Tewa out of little ones.

If the initiate does not accept the spiritual reality of the Kachina, and will not accept his relatives' "cruel" behavior as necessary and good for him (or her), he can stop being a Tewa. But is this a real choice? Not for anyone who is human enough to need friends and family who speak the same language, both literally and figuratively, and whose identity as a Tewa Indian stretches back through all of time. Having then (usually without debate) made the choice of being a Tewa, one is a *good* Tewa. No doubts can be allowed.

There is another factor operating as well. Children who pass through the initiation are no longer outside looking in, they are inside looking out. They are not grown up, and neither they nor anyone else think they are, but they are a lot more grown up than they were before the initiation. Girls take on a more active part in household duties and boys acquire more responsibilities in farming and ranching activities. And it will not be long before the males can take on the role of impersonating the Kachinas and initiating children as they were initiated. The ceremonial whipping, in the context of all the dramatic ceremonies, dancing, and general community uproar, is the symbol of a dramatic shift in status-role. The shift starts with just being "in the know" about what really goes on in the kiva and who the Kachinas are, and continues toward more and more full participation in the secular and sacred life of the community.

Dorothy Eggan sums it up well for the Hopi when she writes:

> Another reorganizing factor . . . was feeling "big." They had shared pain with adults, had learned secrets which forever separated them from the world of children, and now they were included in situations from which they had previously been excluded, as their elders continued to teach intensely what they believed intensely; that for them there was only one alternative—Hopi as against Kahopi.
>
> Consistent repetition is a powerful conditioning agent and, as the youngsters watched each initiation, they relived their own, and by again sharing the experience gradually worked out much of the bitter residue from their own memories of it, while also rationalizing and weaving group emotions ever stronger into their own emotional core—"It takes a while to see how wise the old people really are." An initiated boy, in participating in the kachina dances, learned to identify again with the kachinas whom he now impersonated. To put on a mask is to "become a kachina" and cooperate actively in bringing about the major goals of Hopi life. And a girl came to know more fully the importance of her clan in its supportive role. These experiences were even more sharply conditioned and directed toward adult life in the adult initiation ceremonies, of which we have as yet only fragmentary knowledge. Of this one man said to me: "I will not discuss this thing with you only to say that no one can forget it. It is the most wonderful thing any man can have to remember. You know then that you are Hopi. It is the one thing Whites cannot have, cannot take away from us. It is our way of life given to us when the world began" (Eggan 1956:364–65).

In many ways the preadolescent and adolescent period that we have been discussing, using the Ulithian kufar and the Hano Tewa initiation ceremonies as representative cases, is the most important of all in cultural transmission. There is a considerable literature on this period, including

most notably the classic treatment given by Van Gennep (1960, first published in 1909) and the recent studies by Frank Young (1965), Yehudi Cohen (1964), Gary Schwartz and Don Merten (1968), and Whiting, Kluckhohn, and Albert (1958). Judith Brown provides a cross-cultural study of initiation rights for females (Brown 1963). But these studies do not emphasize the educational aspects of the initiation rites or rites of passage that they analyze.

One of the few studies that does is the remarkable essay by C. W. M. Hart . . . based upon a single case, the Tiwi of North Australia, but with implications for many other cases. Hart contrasts the attitude of cultural transmitters toward young children among the Tiwi to the rigorous demands of the initiation period.

> The arrival of the strangers to drag the yelling boy out of his mother's arms is just the spectacular beginning of a long period during which the separation of the boy from everything that has gone before is emphasized in every possible way at every minute of the day and night. So far his life has been easy; now it is hard. Up to now he has never necessarily experienced any great pain, but in the initiation period in many tribes pain, sometimes horrible, intense pain, is an obligatory feature. The boy of twelve or thirteen, used to noisy, boisterous, irresponsible play, is expected and required to sit still for hours and days at a time saying nothing whatever but concentrating upon and endeavoring to understand long intricate instructions and "lectures" given him by his hostile and forbidding preceptors. [sentence omitted] Life has suddenly become real and earnest and the initiate is required literally to "put away the things of a child" even the demeanor. The number of tabus and unnatural behaviors enjoined upon the initiate is endless. He mustn't speak unless he is spoken to; he must eat only certain foods, and often only in certain ways, at fixed times, and in certain fixed positions. All contact with females, even speech with them is rigidly forbidden, and this includes mother and sisters (1963:415).

Hart goes on to state that the novices are taught origin myths, the meaning of the sacred ceremonials, in short, theology, " . . . which in primitive society is inextricably mixed up with astronomy, geology, geography, biology (the mysteries of birth and death), philosophy, art, and music—in short the whole cultural heritage of the tribe"; and that the purpose of this teaching is not to make better economic men of the novices, but rather " . . . better citizens, better carriers of the culture through the generations . . . " (Hart 1963:415). In this view Hart agrees (as he points out himself) with George Pettit, who did a thorough study of educational practices among North American Indians, and who writes that the initiation proceedings were " . . . a constant challenge to the elders to review, analyze, dramatize, and defend their cultural heritage" (Pettit 1946:182).

Pettit's words also bring into focus another feature of the initiation rituals implicit in the description of these events for the Ulithians, Hano Tewa, and the Tiwi, which seems very significant. In all these cases dramatization is used as an educational technique. In fact a ceremony of any kind is a dramatization, sometimes indirect and metaphoric, sometimes very direct, of the interplay of crucial forces and events in the life of the community. In the initiation ceremonies dramatization forces the seriousness of growing up into the youngster's mind and mobilizes his emotions around the lessons to be learned and the change in identity to be secured. The role of dramatization in cultural transmission may be difficult for American readers to appreciate, because the pragmatization of American schools and American life in general has gone so far.

These points emphasize the view of initiation proceedings taken in this chapter—that they are dramatic signals for new beginnings and, at various times before and throughout adolescence in many societies, the intensification of discontinuity and compression in cultural transmission. Discontinuity in the management of the youngsters' learning—from supportive and easy to rigorous and harsh; compression in the closing in of culturally patterned demand and restriction as

the new status-roles attained by successfully passing through the initiation period are activated. Of course this compression of cultural demand around the individual also opens new channels of development and experience to him. As humans mature they give up the freedom of childhood for the rewards to be gained by observing the rules of the cultural game. The initiation ceremonies are dramatic signals to everyone that the game has begun in earnest.

What Happens in Gopalpur?

In the village of Gopalpur, in South India, described by Alan Beals, social, not physical, mastery is stressed.

> Long before it has begun to walk, the child in Gopalpur has begun to develop a concern about relationships with others. The period of infantile dependency is extended. The child is not encouraged to develop muscular skills, but is carried from place to place on the hip of mother or sister. The child is rarely alone. It is constantly exposed to other people, and learning to talk, to communicate with others, is given priority over anything else that might be learned. When the child does learn to walk, adults begin to treat it differently. Shooed out of the house, its training is largely taken over by the play group. In the streets there are few toys, few things to be manipulated. The play of the child must be social play and the manipulation of others must be accomplished through language and through such nonphysical techniques as crying and withdrawal. In the play group, the child creates a family and the family engages in the production of imaginary food or in the exchange of real food carried in shirt pockets (1962:19).

Children in Gopalpur imitate adults, both in the activities of play and in the attempts to control each other.

> Sidda, four years old, is playing in the front of his house with his cousin, Bugga, aged five. Sidda is sitting on the ground holding a stone and pounding. Bugga is piling the sand up like rice for the pound-

ing. Bugga says, "Sidda, give me the stone, I want to pound." Sidda puts the stone on the ground, "Come and get it." Bugga says, "Don't come with me, I am going to the godhouse to play." Sidda offers, "I will give you the stone." He gives the stone to Bugga, who orders him, "Go into the house and bring some water." Sidda goes and brings water in a brass bowl. Bugga takes it and pours it on the heap of sand. He mixes the water with the sand, using both hands. Then, "Sidda, take the bowl inside." Sidda takes the bowl and returns with his mouth full of peanuts. He puts his hand into his shirt pocket, finds more peanuts and puts them in his mouth. Bugga sees the peanuts and asks, "Where did you get those?" "I got them inside the house." "Where are they?" "In the winnowing basket." Bugga gets up and goes inside the house returning with a bulging shirt pocket. Both sit down near the pile of sand. Bugga says to Sidda "Don't tell mother." "No, I won't." Sidda eats all of his peanuts and moves toward Bugga holding his hands out. Bugga wants to know, "Did you finish yours?" "I just brought a little, you brought a lot." Bugga refuses to give up any peanuts and Sidda begins to cry. Bugga pats him on the back saying, "I will give you peanuts later on." They get up and go into the house. Because they are considered to be brothers, Sidda and Bugga do not fight. When he is wronged, the older Bugga threatens to desert Sidda. When the situation is reversed, the younger Sidda breaks into tears (Beals 1962:16).

In their play, Bugga and Sidda are faithful to the patterns of adult control over children, as they have both observed them and experienced them. Beals describes children going to their houses when their shirt pockets are empty of the "currency of interaction" (grain, bits of bread, peanuts).

This is the moment of entrapment, the only time during the day when the mother is able to exercise control over her child. This is the time for bargaining, for threatening. The mother scowls at her child, "You must have worked hard to be so hungry." The mother serves food and says, "Eat this. After you have eaten it, you must sit here and rock your little sister." The child eats and says, "I am going outside to play. I will not rock my sister." The child finishes its food and runs out of the house. Later, the child's aunt sees it and asks it to run to the store and buy some cooking oil. When it returns, the aunt says, "If you continue to obey me like this, I will give you something good to eat." When the mother catches the child again, she asks, "Where have you been?" Learning what occurred, she says, "If you bought cooking oil, that is fine; now come play with your sister." The child says, "First give me something to eat, and I will play with my sister." The mother scolds, "You will die of eating, sometimes you are willing to work, sometimes you are not willing to work; may you eat dirt." She gives it food and the child plays with its sister (1962:19).

This is the way the child in Gopalpur learns to control the unreliable world of other people. Children soon learn that they are dependent upon others for the major securities and satisfactions of life. The one with a large number of friends and supporters is secure, and they can be won and controlled, the individual comes to feel, through the use of food, but also by crying, begging, and working.

And Among the Eskimo?

Eskimo children are treated supportively and permissively. When a baby cries it is picked up, played with, or nursed. There are a variety of baby tenders about, and after the first two or three months of life older siblings and the mother's unmarried sisters and cousins take a hand in caring for it. There is no set sleeping or eating schedule and weaning is a gradual process that may not be completed until the third or fourth year.

How is it then that, as white visitors to Eskimo villages often remark, the Eskimo have managed to raise their children so well? Observers speak warmly of their good humor, liveliness, resourcefulness, and well-behaved manner. They appear to exemplify qualities that Western parents would like to see in their own children (Chance 1966:22). American folk belief would lead one to surmise that children who are treated so permissively would be "spoiled." Norman Chance describes the situation for the Alaskan Eskimo.

Certainly, the warmth and affection given infants by parents, siblings, and other relatives provide them with a deep feeling of well-being and security. Young children also feel important because they learn early that they are expected to be useful, working members of the family. This attitude is not instilled by imposing tedious chores, but rather by including children in the round of daily activities, which enhances the feeling of family participation and cohesion. To put it another way, parents rarely deny children their company or exclude them from the adult world.

This pattern reflects the parents' views of child rearing. Adults feel that they have more experience in living and it is their responsibility to share this experience with the children, "to tell them how to live." Children have to be told repeatedly because they tend to forget. Misbehavior is due to a child's forgetfulness, or to improper teaching in the first place. There is rarely any thought that the child is basically nasty, willful, or sinful. Where Anglo-Americans applaud a child for his good behavior, the Eskimo praise him for remembering. . . .

Regardless of the degree of Westernization, more emphasis is placed on equality than on super-ordination-subordination in parent-child relations. A five year old obeys, not because he fears punishment or loss of love, but because he identifies with his parents and respects their judgment. Thus he finds little to resist or rebel against in his dealing with adults. We will find rebellion more common in adolescents, but it is not necessarily a revolt against parental control.

By the time a child reaches the age of four or five, his parents' initial demonstrativeness has become tempered with an increased interest in his activities and accomplishments. They watch his play with obvious pleasure, and respond warmly to his conversation, make jokes with him and discipline him.

Though a child is given considerable autonomy and his whims and wishes treated with respect, he is nonetheless taught to obey all adults. To an outsider unfamiliar with parent-child relations, the tone of the Eskimo commands and admonitions sometimes sounds harsh and angry, yet in few instances does a child respond as if he had been addressed hostilely. . . .

After the age of five a child is less restricted in his activities in and around the village, although theoretically he is not allowed on the beach or ice without an adult. During the dark winter season, he remains indoors or stays close to the house to prevent him from getting lost and to protect him from polar bears which might come into the village. In summer, though, children play at all hours of the day or "night" or as long as their parents are up. . . .

Although not burdened with responsibility, both boys and girls are expected to take an active role in family chores. In the early years responsibilities are shared, depending on who is available. Regardless of sex, it is important for a child to know how to perform a wide variety of tasks and give help when needed. Both sexes collect and chop wood, get water, help carry meat and other supplies, oversee younger siblings, run errands for adults, feed the dogs, and burn trash.

As a child becomes older, more specific responsibilities are allocated to him, according to his sex. Boys as young as seven may be given an opportunity to shoot a .22 rifle, and at least a few boys in every village have killed their first caribou by the time they are ten. A youngster learns techniques of butchering while on hunting trips with older siblings and adults, although he is seldom proficient until he is in his mid-teens. In the past girls learned butchering at an early age, since this knowledge was essential to attracting a good husband. Today, with the availability of large quantities of Western foods, this skill may not be acquired until a girl is married, and not always then.

Although there is a recognized division of labor by sex, it is far from rigid at any age level. Boys, and even men, occasionally sweep the house and cook. Girls and their mothers go on fishing or bird-hunting trips. Members of each sex can usually assume the responsibilities of the other when the need arises, albeit in an auxiliary capacity (1966:22–26).

Apparently the combination that works so well with Eskimo children is support—participation—admonition—support. These children learn to see adults as rewarding and nonthreatening. Children are also not excluded, as they so often are in America, from the affairs of adult life. They do not understand everything they see, but virtually nothing is hidden from them. They are encouraged to assume responsibility appropriate to their age quite early in life. Children are participants in the flow of life. They learn by observing and doing. But Eskimo adults do not leave desired learning up to chance. They admonish, direct, remonstrate, but without hostility.

The Eskimo live with a desperately intemperate climate in what many white men have described as the part of the world that is the most inimical to human life. Perhaps Eskimo children are raised the way they are because a secure, good-humored, resourceful person is the only kind that can survive for long in this environment.

In Sensuron?

The people of Sensuron live in a very different physical and cultural environment than do the Eskimo. The atmosphere of this Dusun village in Borneo (not the Malaysian state of Sabah) is communicated in these passages from Thomas Williams' case study.

> Sensuron is astir an hour before the dawn of most mornings. It is usually too damp and cold to sleep. Fires are built up and the morning meal cooked while members of the household cluster about the house fire-pit seeking warmth. After eating, containers and utensils are rinsed off with water to "keep the worms off" and replaced in racks on the side of the house porch. Older children are sent to the river to carry water home in bamboo containers, while their mother spends her time gathering together equipment for the day's work, including some cold rice wrapped in leaves for a midday snack. The men and adolescent males go into the yard to sit in the first warmth of the sun and talk with male neighbors. The early morning exchange of plans, news, and recounting of the events of yesterday is considered a "proper way" to begin the day. While the men cluster in the yard center, with old shirts or cloths draped about bare shoulders to ward off the chill, women gather in front of one

house or another, also trading news, gossip, and work plans. Many women comb each other's hair, after carefully picking out the lice. It is not unusual to see four or more women sitting in a row down the steps of a house ladder talking, while combing and delousing hair. Babies are nursed while mothers talk and small children run about the clusters of adults, generally being ignored until screams of pain or anger cause a sharp retort of *kAdA!* (do not!) from a parent. Women drape spare skirts about their bare shoulders to ward off the morning chill. About two hours after dawn these groups break up as the members go off to the work of the day. The work tasks of each day are those to be done under the annual cycle of subsistence labor. . . .

Vocal music is a common feature of village life; mothers and grandmothers sing a great variety of lullabies and "growth songs" to babies, children sing a wide range of traditional and nonsense songs, while adults sing at work in the fields and gardens during leisure and social occasions and at times of ritual. Drinking songs and wedding songs take elaborate forms, often in the nature of song "debates" with sides chosen and a winner declared by a host or guest of honor on the basis of "beauty" of tone, humor, and general "one-upmanship" in invention of new verse forms. Most group singing is done in harmony. Adolescents, especially girls, spend much of their solitary leisure time singing traditional songs of love and loneliness. Traditional verse forms in ritual, and extensive everyday use of riddles, folktales, and proverbs comprise a substantial body of oral literature. Many persons know much ritual verse, and most can recite dozens of stylized folktales, riddles, and proverbs.

Village headmen, certain older males, and ritual specialists of both sexes are practiced speechmakers. A skill of "speaking beautifully" is much admired and imitated. The style used involves narration, with exhortation, and is emphasized through voice tone and many hand and body gestures and postures. Political debates, court hearings, and personal arguments often become episodes of dramatic representation for onlookers, with a speaker's phrase listened to for its emotional expressive content and undertones of ridicule, tragedy, comedy, and farce at the expense of others involved. The verse forms of major rituals take on dimensions of drama as the specialist delivers the lines with skillful impersonations of voices and mannerisms of disease givers, souls of the dead, and creator beings.

By late afternoon of a leisure day people in the houses begin to drift to the yards, where they again sit and talk. Fires are built to ward off the chill of winds rising off the mountains, and men and women circle the blaze, throwing bits of wood and bamboo into the fire as they talk. This time is termed *mEg-Amut*, after the designation for exchange of small talk between household members. As many as 20 fires can be seen burning in yards through Sensuron at evening on most leisure days and on many evenings after work periods. Men sit and talk until after dark, when they go into houses to take their evening meal. Women leave about an hour before dark to prepare the meal. Smaller children usually eat before the adults. After the evening meal, for an hour or more, the family clusters about the house firepit, talking, with adults often engaged in small tasks of tool repair or manufacture. By 8 or 9 P.M. most families are asleep; the time of retiring is earlier when the work days are longer, later on rest days (1965:78–79).

Children in Sensuron are, like Eskimo children, always present, always observers. How different this way of life is from that experienced by American children! Gossip, speech-making, folktale telling, grooming, working, and playing are all there, all a part of the stream of life flowing around one and with which each member of the community moves. Under these circumstances much of the culture is transmitted by a kind of osmosis. It would be difficult for a child *not* to learn his culture.

The children of Sensuron do not necessarily grow up into good-humored, secure, trusting, "happy" adults. There are several factors that apparently interact in their growing up to make this unlikely. In the most simple sense, these children do not grow up to be like Eskimo adults because their parents (and other cultural transmitters) are not Eskimo, Dusun cultural transmitters (anybody in the community that the child hears and sees) act like Dusun. But cultural

transmitters display certain attitudes and do certain things to children as well as provide them with models. In Sensuron, children are judged to be nonpersons. They are not even provided with personal names until their fifth year. They are also considered to be " . . . naturally noisy, inclined to illness, capable of theft, incurable wanderers, violent, quarrelsome, temperamental, destructive of property, wasteful, easily offended, quick to forget" (Williams 1965:87). They are threatened by parents with being eaten alive, carried off, damaged by disease-givers. Here are two lullabies sung to babies in Sensuron (and heard constantly by older children):

> Sleep, Sleep, baby,
> There comes the rAgEn (soul of the dead)
> He carries a big stick,
> He carried a big knife,
> Sleep, Sleep, baby,
> He comes to beat you!

or, as in this verse,

> Bounce, Bounce, baby
> There is a hawk,
> Flying, looking for prey!
> There is the hawk, looking for his prey!
> He searches for something to snatch up in
>   his claws,
> Come here, hawk, and snatch up this baby!
> (Williams 1965:88).

None of the things that the adults of Sensuron do to, with, or around their children is to be judged "bad." Their culture is different from Eskimo culture, and a different kind of individual functions effectively in it. We may for some reason need to make value judgments about a culture, the character of the people who live by it, or the way they raise children—but not for the purpose of understanding it better. It is particularly hard to refrain from making value judgments when the behavior in question occurs in an area of life in our own culture about which there are contradictory rules and considerable anxiety. Take, for instance, the transmission of sexual behavior in the village of Sensuron.

> In Sensuron people usually deal with their sex drives through ideally denying their existence, while often behaving in ways designed to sidestep social and cultural barriers to personal satisfaction. At the ideal level of belief the view is expressed that "men are not like dogs, chasing any bitch in heat," or "sex relations are unclean." Some of the sexuality of Dusun life has been noted earlier. There is a high content of lewd and bawdy behavior in the play of children and adolescents, and in the behavior of adults. For example, the eight-year-old girl in the house across from ours was angrily ordered by her mother to come into the house to help in rice husking. The girl turned to her mother and gave her a slow, undulating thrust of her hips in a sexual sign. More than 12 salacious gestures are known and used regularly by children and adults of both sexes, and there are some 20 equivalents of "four-letter" English terms specifically denoting the sexual anatomy and its possible uses. Late one afternoon 4 girls between 8 and 15 years, and 2 young boys of 4 and 5 years were chasing about our house steps for a half hour, grabbing at each other's genitals, and screaming, *uarE tAle!* which roughly translated means, "there is your mother's vulva!" Adult onlookers were greatly amused at the group and became convulsed with laughter when the four-year-old boy improvised the answer, "my mother has no vulva!" Thus, sexual behavior is supposed to be unclean and disgusting, while in reality it is a source of amusement and constant attention. . . .
>
> Children learn details of sexual behavior early, and sex play is a part of the behavior of four-to-six-year olds, usually in houses or rice stores while parents are away at work. Older children engage in sexual activities in groups and pairs, often at a location outside the village, often in an abandoned field storehouse, or in a temporary shelter in a remote garden (Williams 1965:82–83).

We can, however, make the tentative generalization that in cultures where there is a marked discrepancy between ideal and real, between the "theory" of culture and actual behavior, this conflict will be transmitted and that conflicts of this

kind are probably not conducive to trust, confidence in self and in others, or even something we might call "happiness." We are like the people of Sensuron, though probably the conflicts between real and ideal run much deeper and are more damaging in our culture. In any event, the transmission of culture is complicated by discrepancies and conflicts, for both the pattern of idealizations and the patterns of actual behavior must be transmitted, as well as the ways for rationalizing the discrepancy between them.

How Goes It in Guadalcanal?

Many of the comments that have been made about child rearing and the transmission of culture in other communities can be applied to the situation in Guadalcanal, one of the Solomon Islands near New Guinea. Babies are held, fondled, fed, never isolated, and generally given very supportive treatment. Weaning and toilet training both take place without much fuss, and fairly late by American standards. Walking is regarded as a natural accomplishment that will be mastered in time, swimming seems to come as easily. Education is also different in some ways in Guadalcanal. There is no sharp discontinuity at the beginning of middle childhood as in Palau, nor is there any sharp break at puberty as in Ulithi, or at prepuberty as among the Hano Tewa or Hopi. The special character of cultural transmission in Guadalcanal is given by Ian Hogbin:

> Two virtues, generosity and respect for property, are inculcated from the eighteenth month onward—that is to say, from the age when the child can walk about and eat bananas and other things regarded as delicacies. At this stage no explanations are given, and the parents merely insist that food must be shared with any playmate who happens to be present and that goods belonging to other villagers must be left undisturbed. A toddler presented with a piece of fruit is told to give half to "So-and-so," and should the order be resisted, the adult ignores all protests and breaks a piece off to hand to the child's companion. Similarly, although

sometimes callers are cautioned to put their baskets on a shelf out of reach, any meddling brings forth the rebuke, "That belongs to your uncle. Put it down." Disobedience is followed by snatching away the item in question from the child and returning it to the owner.

In time, when the child has passed into its fourth or fifth year, it is acknowledged to have at last attained the understanding to be able to take in what the adults say. Therefore, adults now accompany demands with reasoned instruction. One day when I was paying a call on a neighbor, Mwane-Anuta, I heard him warn his second son Mbule, who probably had not reached the age of five, to stop being so greedy. "I saw your mother give you those nuts," Mwane-Anuta reiterated. "Don't pretend she didn't. Running behind the house so the Penggoa wouldn't know! That is bad, very bad. Now then, show me, how many? Five left. Very well, offer three to Penggoa immediately." He then went on to tell me how important it was for children to learn to think of others so that in later life they would win the respect of their fellows.

On another occasion during a meal I found Mwane-Anuta and his wife teaching their three sons how to eat properly. "Now Mbule," said his mother, "you face the rest of us so that we can all see you aren't taking too much. And you, Konana, run outside and ask Misika from next door to join you. His mother's not home yet, and I expect he's hungry. Your belly's not the only one, my boy." "Yes," Mwane-Anuta added. "Give a thought to those you run about with, and they'll give a thought to you." At this point the mother called over the eldest lad, Kure, and placed the basket of yams for me in his hands. "There, you carry that over to our guest and say that it is good to have him with us this evening," she whispered to him. The gesture was characteristic. I noted that always when meals were served to visitors the children acted as waiters. Why was this, I wanted to know. "Teaching, teaching," Mwane-Anuta replied. "This is how we train our young to behave" (1964:33).

It appears that in Guadalcanal direct verbal instruction is stressed as a technique of cultural transmission. Hogbin goes on to describe the constant stream of verbal admonition that is directed at the child by responsible adults in almost every situation. And again and again the prime values, generosity and respect for property, are reinforced by these admonitions.

The amount of direct verbal reinforcement of basic values, and even the amount of direct verbal instruction in less crucial matters, varies greatly from culture to culture. The people of Guadalcanal, like the Hopi, keep telling their children and young people how to behave and when they are behaving badly. In American middle-class culture there is also great emphasis on telling children what they should do, explaining how to do it, and the reasons for doing it, though we are probably less consistent in what we tell them than are the parents of Guadalcanal. Perhaps also in our culture we tend to substitute words for experience more than do the people of Guadalcanal, for the total range of experience relevant to growing up appropriately is more directly observable and available to their children than it is to ours.

Girls go to the gardens regularly with their mother from about the age of eight. They cannot yet wield the heavy digging stick or bush knife, but they assist in collecting the rubbish before planting begins, in piling up the earth, and weeding. Boys start accompanying their father some two or three years later, when they help with the clearing, fetch lianas to tie up the saplings that form the fence, and cut up the seed yams. The men may also allocate plots to their sons and speak of the growing yams as their own harvest. The services of a youngster are of economic value from the time that he is pubescent, but he is not expected to take gardening really seriously until after he returns from the plantation and is thinking of marriage. By then he is conscious of his rights and privileges as a member of his clan and knows where the clan blocks of land are located. As a rule, he can also explain a little about the varieties of yams and taro and the types of soil best suited to earth.

At about eight a boy begins to go along with his father or uncles when the men set out in the evening with their lines to catch fish from the shore or on the reef. They make a small rod for him, show him how to bait his hook, and tell him about the different species of fish—where they are to be found, which are good to eat, which are poisonous. At the age of ten the boy makes an occasional fishing excursion in a canoe. To start with, he sits in the center of the canoe and watches, perhaps baiting the hooks and removing the catch; but soon he takes part with the rest. In less than a year he is a useful crew member and expert in steering and generally handling the craft. At the same time, I have never seen youths under the age of sixteen out at sea by themselves. Often they are eager to go before this, but the elders are unwilling to give permission lest they endanger themselves or the canoe (Hogbin 1964:39).

The children of Guadalcanal learn by doing as well as learn by hearing. They also learn by imitating adult models, as children do in every human group around the world.

Children also play at housekeeping. Sometimes they take along their juniors, who, however, do not remain interested for long. They put up a framework of saplings and tie on coconut-leaf mats, which they plait themselves in a rough-and-ready sort of way. Occasionally, they beg some raw food and prepare it; or they catch birds, bats, and rats with bows and arrows. Many times, too, I have seen them hold weddings, including all the formality of the handing-over of bride price. Various items serve instead of the valuables that the grownups use—tiny pebbles instead of dog's and porpoise teeth, the long flowers of a nut tree for strings of shell discs, and rats or lizards for pigs. When first the youngsters pretend to keep house they make no sexual distinction in the allocation of the tasks. Boys and girls together erect the shelters, plait the mats, cook the food, and fetch the water. But within a year or so, although they continue to play in company, the members of each group restrict themselves to the work appropriate to their sex. The boys leave the cooking and water carrying to the girls, who, in turn, refuse to help with the building (Hogbin 1964:37–38).

Children seem to acquire the culture of their community best when there is consistent rein-

forcement of the same norms of action and thinking through many different channels of activity and interaction. If a child is told, sees demonstrated, casually observes, imitates, experiments and is corrected, acts appropriately and is rewarded, corrected, and (as in the Tewa-Hopi initiation) is given an extra boost in learning by dramatized announcements of status-role change, all within a consistent framework of belief and value, he or she cannot help but learn, and learn what adult cultural transmitters want him or her to learn.

How Do They Listen in Demirciler?

In Demirciler, an Anatolian village in the arid central plateau of Turkey, a young boy, Mahmud, learns by being allowed in the room when the adult men meet at the Muhtar's (the village headman) home evenings to discuss current affairs.

Each day, after having finished the evening meal, the old Muhtar's wife would put some small earthenware dishes or copper trays filled with nuts or chick-peas about the room, sometimes on small stands or sometimes on the floor, and the old man would build a warm fire in the fireplace. Soon after dark the men would begin to arrive by ones or twos and take their accustomed places in the men's room. This was the largest single room in the village and doubled as a guest house for visitors who came at nightfall and needed some place to sleep before going on their way the next day. It had been a long time since the room had been used for this purpose, however, because the nearby growing city had hotels, and most of the modern travelers stayed there. However, the room still served as a clearing house for all village business, as well as a place for the men to pass the cold winter evenings in warm comfort.

The room was perhaps 30 by 15 feet in size, and along one side a shelf nearly 15 inches above the floor extended about 2 feet from the wall and covered the full 30 feet of the room's length. The old Muhtar sat near the center of the shelf, waiting for his guests to arrive. As the men came in, the oldest in the village would seat themselves in order of age on this raised projection, while the younger ones would sit cross-legged on the floor. No women were ever allowed to come into this room when the men were there. The Muhtar's wife had prepared everything ahead of time, and when additional things were occasionally needed during the evening, one of the boys would be sent out to fetch it. Opposite the long bench was a fireplace, slightly larger than those in the kitchen of the other village homes, in which a fire burned brightly spreading heat throughout the room. The single electric bulb lighted the space dimly and so the shadows caused by the firelight were not prevented from dancing about the walls.

Mahmud would have been happier if the electric bulb had not been there at all, the way it used to be when he had been a very small boy. Electricity had been introduced to the village only a year ago, and he remembered the days when only the glow of the fire lighted these meetings.

As the gatherings grew in size, Mahmud heard many small groups of men talking idly about all sorts of personal problems, but when nearly all of the villagers had arrived, they began to quiet down.

The Hoca posed the first question, "Muhtar Bey, when will next year's money for the mosque be taken up?"

"Hocam, the amount has not been set yet," was the Muhtar's reply.

"All right, let's do it now," the Hoca persisted.

"Let's do it now," the Muhtar agreed.

And Mahmud listened as the Hoca told about the things the mosque would need during the coming year. Then several of the older men told how they had given so much the year before that it had been hard on their families, and finally, the Muhtar talked interminably about the duty of each Moslem to support the Faith and ended by asking the head of each family for just a little more than he knew they could pay.

Following this request there were a series of discussions between the Muhtar and each family head, haggling over what the members of his family could afford to give. Finally, however, agreement was reached with each man, and the Hoca knew how much he could count on for the coming year. The Muhtar would see that the money was collected and turned over to the Hoca.

The business of the evening being out of the way, Mahmud became more interested, as he knew that what he liked most was to come now. He had learned that he was too young to speak at the meetings, because he had been taken out several times the year before by one of the older boys and told that he could not stay with the men unless he could be quiet, so he waited in silence for what would happen next. After a slight pause one of the braver of the teen-aged boys called to an old man.

"*Dedem*, tell us some stories about the olden times."

"Shall I tell about the wars?" the old man nearest the Muhtar asked.

"Yes, about the great war with the Russians," the youth answered.

"Well, I was but a boy then, but my father went with the army of the Sultan that summer, and he told me this story" (Pierce 1964:20–21).

Is there any situation in the culture of the United States where a similar situation exists? When America was more rural than it is now, and commercial entertainments were not readily available for most people, young people learned about adult roles and problems, learned to think like adults and anticipated their own adulthood in somewhat the same way the Mahmud did. Now it is an open question whether young people would want to listen to their elders even if there was nothing else to do. Possibly this is partly because much of what one's elders "know" in our society is not true. The verities change with each generation.

At the end of the "business" session at the Muhtar's home an old man tells a story. The story is offered as entertainment, even though it has been heard countless times before. Young listeners learn from stories as well as from the deliberations of the older men as they decide what to do about somebody's adolescent son who is eyeing the girls too much, or what to do about building a new road. Storytelling has been and still is a way of transmitting information to young people in many cultures without their knowing they are being taught. Any story has either a metaphoric application to real life, provides models for behavior, or has both features.

The metaphor or the model may or may not be translated into a moral. The elders in Demirciler do not, it appears, make the moral of the story explicit. In contrast, the Menomini Indians of Wisconsin always required a youngster to extract the moral in a story for himself. "You should never ask for anything to happen unless you mean it." "He who brags bites his own tail." A grandparent would tell the same story every night until the children could state the moral to the elder's satisfaction (Spindler 1971). People in different cultures vary greatly in how much they make of the moral, but stories and mythtellings are used in virtually all cultures to transmit information, values, and attitudes.

WHAT DOES CULTURAL TRANSMISSION DO FOR THE SYSTEM?

So far we have considered cultural transmission in cases where no major interventions from the outside have occurred, or, if they have occurred, we have chosen to ignore them for purposes of description and analysis. There are, however, virtually no cultural systems left in the world that have not experienced massive input from the outside, particularly from the West. This is the age of transformation. Nearly all tribal societies and peasant villages are being affected profoundly by modernization. One of the most important aspects of modernization is the development of schools that will, hopefully, prepare young people to take their places in a very different kind of world than the one their parents grew up in. This implies a kind of discontinuity that is of a different order than the kind we have been discussing.

Discontinuity in cultural transmission among the Dusun, Hopi, Tewa, and Tiwi is a process that produces cultural continuity in the system as a whole. The abrupt and dramatized changes in roles during adolescence, the sudden compression of cultural requirements, and all the techniques used by preceptors, who are nearly always

adults from within the cultural system, educate an individual to be committed to the system. The initiation itself encapsulates and dramatizes symbols and meanings that are at the core of the cultural system so that the important things the initiate has learned up to that point, by observation, participation, or instruction, are reinforced. The discontinuity is in the way the initiate is treated during the initiation and the different behaviors expected of him (or her) afterward. The culture is maintained, its credibility validated. As the Hopi man said to Dorothy Eggan, "I will not discuss this thing with you only to say that no one can forget it. It is the most wonderful thing any man can have to remember. You know then that you are Hopi [after the initiation]. It is the one thing Whites cannot have, cannot take from us. It is our way of life given to us when the world began.". . . . This Hopi individual has been *recruited* as a Hopi.

In all established cultural systems where radical interventions from outside have not occurred, the major functions of education are *recruitment* and *maintenance*. The educational processes we have described for all of the cultures in this chapter have functioned in this manner. Recruitment occurs in two senses: recruitment to membership in the cultural system in general, so that one becomes a Hopi or a Tiwi; and recruitment to specific roles and statuses, to specific castes, or to certain classes. We may even, by stretching the point a little, say that young humans are recruited to be male or female, on the terms with which a given society defines being male or female. This becomes clear in cultures such as our own, where sex roles are becoming blurred so much that many young people grow up without a clear orientation toward either role. The educational system, whether we are talking about societies where there are no schools in the formal sense but where a great deal of education takes place, or about societies where there are many specialized formal schools, is organized to effect recruitment. The educational system is also organized so that the structure of the cultural system will be maintained. This is done by inculcating the specific values, attitudes, and beliefs that make this structure credible and the skills and competencies that make it work. People must believe in their system. If there is a caste or class structure they must believe that such a structure is good, or if not good, at least inevitable. They must also have the skills—vocational and social—that make it possible for goods and services to be exchanged that are necessary for community life to go on. Recruitment and maintenance intergrade, as you can see from the above discussion. The former refers to the process of getting people into the system and into specific roles; the latter refers to the process of keeping the system and role functioning.

MODERNIZING CULTURES: WHAT IS THE PURPOSE OF EDUCATION?

In this transforming world, however, educational systems are often charged with responsibility for bringing about change in the culture. They become, or are intended to become, agents of modernization. They become intentional agents of cultural discontinuity, a kind of discontinuity that does not reinforce the traditional values or recruit youngsters into the existing system. The new schools, with their curricula and the concepts behind them, are future oriented. They recruit students into a system that does not yet exist, or is just emerging. They inevitably create conflicts between generations.

Among the Sisala of Northern Ghana, a modernizing African society, for example, there have been profound changes in the principles underlying the father-son relationship. As one man put it:

> This strict obedience, this is mostly on the part of illiterates. With educated people, if you tell your son something, he will have to speak his mind. If you find that the boy is right, you change your mind. With an illiterate, he just tells his son to do something. . . . In the old days, civilization was not so much. We obeyed our fathers whether right or wrong. If you

didn't, they would beat you. We respected our fathers with fear. Now we have to talk with our sons when they challenge us (Grindal 1972:80).

Not all of the Sisala have as tolerant and favorable a view of the changes wrought by education, however:

> When my children were young, I used to tell them stories about my village and about our family traditions. But in Tumu there are not so many people from my village and my children never went to visit the family. Now my children are educated and they have no time to sit with the family. A Sisala father usually farms with his son. But with educated people, they don't farm. They run around town with other boys: Soon we will forget our history. The educated man has a different character from his father. So fathers die and never tell their sons about the important traditions. My children don't sit and listen to me anymore. They don't want to know the real things my father told me. They have gone to school, and they are now book men. Boys who are educated run around with other boys rather than sitting and listening to their fathers (Grindal:83).

That these conflicts should flare up into open expressions of hostility toward education, schools, and teachers is not surprising. A headmaster of a primary school among the Sisala related to Bruce Grindal what happened when a man made a trip to a village outside Tumu.

> He parked his car on the road and was away for some time. When he returned, he saw that somebody had defaced his car, beaten it with sticks or something. Now I knew that my school children knew something about this. So I gathered them together and told them that if they were good citizens, they should report to me who did it and God would reward them. So I found out that this was done by some people in the village. When the village people found out their children told me such things, they were very angry. They said that the teachers were teaching their children to disrespect their elders. It is because of things like that that the fathers are taking their children out of school (Grindal:97–98).

The above implies that the new schools, created for the purposes of aiding and abetting modernization, are quite effective. Without question they do create conflicts between generations and disrupt the transmission of the traditional culture. These effects in themselves are a prelude to change, perhaps a necessary condition. They are not, however, the result of the effectiveness of the schools as educational institutions. Because the curricular content is alien to the existing culture there is little or no reinforcement in the home and family, or in the community as a whole, for what happens in the school. The school is isolated from the cultural system it is intended to serve. As F. Landa Jocano relates concerning the primary school in Malitbog, a barrio in Panay, in the middle Philippines:

> most of what children learn in school is purely verbal imitation and academic memorization, which do not relate with the activities of the children at home. By the time a child reaches the fourth grade he is expected to be competent in reading, writing, arithmetic, and language study. Except for gardening, no other vocational training is taught. The plants that are required to be cultivated, however, are cabbages, lettuce, okra, and other vegetables which are not normally grown and eaten in the barrio. [sentence omitted]
>
> Sanitation is taught in the school, but insofar as my observation went, this is not carried beyond the child's wearing clean clothes. Children may be required to buy toothbrushes, combs, handkerchiefs, and other personal items, and bring these to school for inspection. Because only a few can afford to buy these items, only a few come to school with them. Often these school requirements are the source of troubles at home, a night's crying among the children. . . . [sentence omitted] In the final analysis, such regular school injunctions as "brush your teeth every morning" or "drink milk and eat leafy vegetables" mean nothing to the children. First, none of the families brush their teeth. The toothbrushes the children bring to school are for inspection only. Their parents cannot afford to buy milk. They do not like goats' milk because it is *malangsa* (foul smelling) (Jocano 1969:53).

Nor is it solely a matter of the nonrelatedness of what is taught in the school to what is learned in the home and community. Because the curricular content is alien to the culture as a whole, what is taught tends to become formalized and unrealistic and is taught in a rigid, ritualistic manner. Again, among the Sisala of Northern Ghana, Bruce Grindal describes the classroom environment.

> The classroom environment into which the Sisala child enters is characterized by a mood of rigidity and an almost total absence of spontaneity. A typical school day begins with a fifteen-minute period during which the students talk and play, often running and screaming, while the teacher, who is usually outside talking with his fellow teachers, pays no attention. At 8:30 one of the students rings a bell, and the children immediately take their seats and remove from their desks the materials needed for the first lesson. When the teacher enters the room, everyone falls silent. If the first lesson is English, the teacher begins by reading a passage in the students' readers. He then asks the students to read the section aloud, and if a child makes a mistake, he is told to sit down, after being corrected. Variations of the English lesson consist of having the students write down dictated sentences or spell selected words from a passage on the blackboard. Each lesson lasts exactly forty minutes, at the end of which a bell rings and the students immediately prepare for the next lesson.
>
> Little emphasis is placed upon the content of what is taught; rather, the book is strictly adhered to, and the students are drilled by being asked the questions which appear at the end of each assignment. The absence of discussion is due partially to the poor training of the teacher, yet even in the middle schools where the educational standards for teachers are better, an unwillingness exists to discuss or explain the content of the lessons. All subjects except mathematics are lessons in literacy which teach the student to spell, read, and write.
>
> Interaction between the teacher and his students is characterized by an authoritarian rigidity. When the teacher enters the classroom, the students are expected to rise as a sign of respect. If the teacher needs anything done in the classroom, one of the students performs the task. During

lessons the student is not expected to ask questions, but instead is supposed to give the "correct" answers to questions posed to him by the teacher. The students are less intent upon what the teacher is saying than they are upon the reading materials before them. When the teacher asks a question, most of the students hurriedly examine their books to find the correct answer and then raise their hands. The teacher calls on one of them, who rises, responds (with his eyes lowered), and then sits down. If the answer is wrong or does not make sense, the teacher corrects him and occasionally derides him for his stupidity. In the latter case the child remains standing with his eyes lowered until the teacher finishes and then sits down without making a response (Grindal 1972:85).

The nonrelatedness of the school to the community in both the content being transmitted and the methods used to transmit it is logically carried into the aspirations of students concerning their own futures. These aspirations are often quite unrealistic. As one of the Sisala school boys said:

> I have in mind this day being a professor so that I will be able to help my country. . . . As a professor I will visit so many countries such as America, Britain, and Holland. In fact, it will be interesting for me and my wife. . . . When I return, my father will be proud seeing his child like this. Just imagine me having a wife and children in my car moving down the street of my village. And when the people are in need of anything, I will help them (Grindal: 89).

Or as another reported in an essay:

> By the time I have attained my graduation certificate from the university, the government will be so happy that they may like to make me president of my beloved country. When I receive my salary, I will divide the money and give part to my father and my wife and children. . . . People say the U.S.A. is a beautiful country. But when they see my village, they will say it is more beautiful. Through my hard studies, my name will rise forever for people to remember (Grindal: 89).

As we have said, the new schools, like the traditional tribal methods of education and schools everywhere, recruit new members of the community into a cultural system and into specific roles and statuses. And they attempt to maintain this system by transmitting the necessary competencies to individuals who are recruited into it via these roles and statuses. The problem with the new schools is that the cultural system they are recruiting for does not exist in its full form. The education the school boys and girls receive is regarded by many as more or less useless, though most people, like the Sisala, agree that at least literacy is necessary if one is to get along in the modern world. However, the experience of the school child goes far beyond training for literacy. The child is removed from the everyday routine of community life and from observation of the work rules of adults. He or she is placed in an artificial, isolated, unrealistic, ritualized environment. Unrealistic aspirations and self-images develop. Harsh reality intrudes abruptly upon graduation. The schoolboy discovers that, except for teaching in the primary schools, few opportunities are open to him. There are some clerical positions in government offices, but they are few. Many graduates migrate in search of jobs concomitant with their expectations, but they usually find that living conditions are more severe than those in the tribal area and end up accepting an occupation and life style similar to that of the illiterate tribesmen who have also migrated to the city. Those who become village teachers are not much better off. One Sisala teacher in his mid-twenties said:

> I am just a small man. I teach and I have a small farm. . . . Maybe someday if I am fortunate, I will buy a tractor and farm for money because there is no future in teaching. When I went to school, I was told that if I got good marks and studied hard, I would be somebody, somebody important. I even thought I would go to America or England. I would still like to go, but I don't think of these things very often because it hurts too much. You see me here drinking and perhaps you think I don't have any

sense. I don't know. I don't know why I drink. But I know in two days' time, I must go back and teach school. In X (his home village where he teaches) I am alone; I am nobody (Grindal:93).

The pessimist will conclude that the new schools, as agents of modernization, are a rank failure. This would be a false conclusion. They are neither failures nor successes. The new schools, like all institutions transforming cultural systems, are not articulated with the other parts of the changing system. The future is not known or knowable. Much of the content taught in the school, as well as the very concept of the school as a place with four walls within which teacher and students are confined for a number of hours each day and regulated by a rigid schedule of "learning" activities, is Western. In many ways the new schools among the Sisala, in Malitbog, and in many other changing cultures are inadequate copies of schools in Europe and in the United States. There is no doubt, however, that formal schooling in all of the developing nations of the world, as disarticulated with the existing cultural context as it is, nevertheless is helping to bring into being a new population of literates, whose aspirations and world view are very different than that of their parents. And of course a whole class of educated elites has been created by colleges and universities in many of the countries. It seems inevitable that eventually the developing cultures will build their own models for schools and education. These new models will not be caricatures of Western schools, although in places, as in the case of the Sisala or the Kanuri of Nigeria described by Alan Peshkin (Peshkin 1972), where the Western influence has been strong for a long time, surely those models will show this influence.

Perhaps one significant part of the problem and the general shape of the solution is implied in the following exchange between two new young teachers in charge of a village school among the Ngoni of Malawi and a senior chief:

The teachers bent one knee as they gave him the customary greeting, waiting in silence until he spoke.

"How is your school?"

"The classes are full and the children are learning well, Inkosi."

"How do they behave?"

"Like Ngoni children, Inkosi."

"What do they learn?"

"They learn reading, writing, arithmetic, scripture, geography and drill, Inkosi."

"Is that education?"

"It is education, Inkosi."

"No! No! No! Education is *very* broad, *very* deep. It is not only in books, it is learning how to live. I am an old man now. When I was a boy I went with the Ngoni army against the Bemba. Then the mission came and I went to school. I became a teacher. Then I was chief. Then the government came. I have seen our country change, and now there are many schools and many young men go away to work to find money. I tell you that Ngoni children must learn how to live and how to build up our land, not only to work and earn money. Do you hear?"

"Yebo, Inkosi" (Yes, O Chief) (Read 1968:2–3).

The model of education that will eventually emerge in the modernizing nations will be one that puts the school, in its usual formal sense, in perspective, and emphasizes education in its broadest sense, as a part of life and of the dynamic changing community. It must emerge if these cultures are to avoid the tragic errors of miseducation, as the Western nations have experienced them, particularly in the relationships between the schools and minority groups.

CONCLUSION

In this chapter we started with the question, What are some of the ways culture is transmitted? We answered this question by examining cultural systems where a wide variety of teaching and learning techniques are utilized. One of the most important processes, we found, was the management of discontinuity. Discontinuity occurs at any point in the life cycle when there is an abrupt transition from one mode of being and behaving to another, as for example at weaning and at adolescence. Many cultural systems manage the latter period of discontinuity with dramatic staging and initiation ceremonies, some of which are painful or emotionally disturbing to the initiates. They are public announcements of changes in status. They are also periods of intense cultural compression during which teaching and learning are accelerated. This managed cultural compression and discontinuity functions to enlist new members in the community and maintains the cultural system. Education, whether characterized by sharp discontinuities and culturally compressive periods, or by a relatively smooth progression of accumulating experience and status change, functions in established cultural systems to recruit new members and maintain the existing system. We then turned to a discussion of situations where alien or future-oriented cultural systems are introduced through formal schooling. Schools among the Sisala of Ghana, a modernizing African nation, and a Philippine barrio were used as examples of this relationship and its consequences. The disarticulation of school and community was emphasized. The point was made that children in these situations are intentionally recruited to a cultural system other than the one they originated from, and that the school does not maintain the existing social order, but, in effect, destroys it. This is a kind of discontinuity very different than the one we discussed previously, and produces severe dislocations in life patterns and interpersonal relations as well as potentially positive change.

REFERENCES AND FURTHER READING

Barnett, Homer G., 1960, *Being a Palauan*. CSCA. New York: Holt, Rinehart and Winston, Inc.

Beals, Alan R., 1962, *Gopalpur: A South Indian Village*. CSCA. New York: Holt, Rinehart and Winston, Inc.

Brown, Judith K., 1963, "A Cross-cultural Study of Female Initiation Rites," *American Anthropologist* 65:837–853.

Chance, Norman A., 1966, *The Eskimo of North Alaska*. CSCA. New York: Holt, Rinehart and Winston, Inc.

Cohen, Yehudi, 1964, *The Transition from Childhood to Adolescence*. Chicago: Aldine Publishing Company.

Deng, Francis Mading, 1972, *The Dinka of the Sudan*. CSCA. New York: Holt, Rinehart and Winston, Inc.

Dozier, Edward P., 1967, *Hano: A Tewa Indian Community in Arizona*. CSCA. New York: Holt, Rinehart and Winston, Inc.

Eggan, Dorothy, 1956, "Instruction and Affect in Hopi Cultural Continuity," *Southwestern Journal of Anthropology* 12:347–370.

Grindal, Bruce T., 1972, *Growing Up in Two Worlds: Education and Transition among the Sisala of Northern Ghana*. CSCA. New York: Holt, Rinehart and Winston, Inc.

Hart, C.W.M., 1963, "Contrasts Between Prepubertal and Postpubertal Education." In G. Spindler, ed., *Education and Culture*. Holt, Rinehart and Winston, Inc.

Henry, Jules, 1960. "A Cross-cultural Outline of Education," *Current Anthropology* 1, 267–305.

_____, 1963, *Culture Against Man*. New York: Random House.

Hogbin, Ian, 1964, *A Guadalcanal Society: The Kaoka Speakers*. CSCA. New York: Holt, Rinehart and Winston, Inc.

Jocano, F. Landa, 1969. *Growing Up in a Philippine Barrio*. CSEC. New York: Holt, Rinehart and Winston, Inc.

Lessa, William A., 1966. *Ulithi: A Micronesian Design for Living*. CSCA. New York: Holt, Rinehart and Winston, Inc.

Mead, Margaret, 1949, *Coming of Age in Samoa*. New York: Mentor Books (first published in 1928).

_____, 1953, *Growing Up in New Guinea*. New York: Mentor Books (first published in 1930).

_____, 1964, *Continuities in Cultural Evolution*. New Haven: Yale University Press.

Peshkin, Alan, 1972, *Kanuri Schoolchildren: Education and Social Mobilization in Nigeria*. CSEC. New York: Holt, Rinehart and Winston, Inc.

Pettit, George A., 1946, *Primitive Education in North America*. Publications in American Archeology and Ethnology, vol. 43.

Pierce, Joe E., 1964, *Life in a Turkish Village*. CSCA. New York: Holt, Rinehart and Winston, Inc.

Read, Margaret, 1968, *Children of Their Fathers: Growing Up Among the Ngoni of Malawi*. CSEC. New York: Holt, Rinehart and Winston, Inc.

Schwartz, Gary, and Don Merten, 1968, "Social Identity and Expressive Symbols: The Meaning of an

Initiation Ritual," *American Anthropologist* 70:1117–1131.

Spindler, George D., and Louise S. Spindler, 1971, *Dreamers without Power: The Menomini Indians of Wisconsin.* CSCA. New York: Holt, Rinehart and Winston, Inc.

Spiro, Melford, 1958, *Children of the Kibbutz.* Cambridge, Mass.: Harvard University Press.

Van Gennep, Arnold, 1960, *The Rites of Passage.* Chicago: University of Chicago Press.

Whiting, Beatrice B., ed., 1963, *Child Rearing in Six Cultures.* New York: John Wiley & Sons, Inc.

Whiting, John F., R. Kluckhohn, and A. Albert, 1958, "The Function of Male Initiation Ceremonies at Puberty." In E. Maccoby, T. Newcomb, and E. Hartley, eds., *Readings in Social Psychology.* New York: Holt, Rinehart and Winston, Inc.

Williams, Thomas R., 1965, *The Dusun: A North Borneo Society.* CSCA. New York: Holt, Rinehart and Winston, Inc.

Young, Frank, 1965, *Initiation Ceremonies.* Indianapolis: The Bobbs-Merrill Company.

American Cultural Values

CONRAD ARENSBERG AND ARTHUR NIEHOFF

There are few truly isolated peoples in the world. Everywhere people with particular cultures and societies are in contact with people who are different from them. If
they learn each other's languages and understand each other's customs they are on
the road to useful communication. However, when those in one culture believe that
by introducing change they will help those in another to improve their life style,
they face another difficulty. People do not want the same things; they do not go
about getting what they do want in the same ways. In this article Conrad Arensberg
and Arthur Niehoff show how American values have often frustrated those who
would help change "underdeveloped" countries.

MISINTERPRETATION

In order to understand how ideas are transferred
from one culture to another it is very important
to know the role and characteristics of the
change agents involved. Several of the cases in
this manual indicate that a failure was due to the
change agent's misinterpretation of the motives
and needs of the hoped-for borrowers of the
innovations. Such misinterpretations may result
from the change agent's failure to learn enough
about the receiving culture; but they may also
rest on false suppositions, derived from assuming
that conditions taken for granted in the home
culture also exist in the other culture.

All men, in agrarian or industrial societies, have
much in common in the solution of their problems. A peasant farmer in India and a commercial
farmer in Texas are both pragmatic and must be
shown that an improvement is genuine before they
will adopt it, and a Lao farmer tries to get help

from the supernatural in producing rain just as the
American turns to prayer when a close family
member is seriously ill. Nevertheless, it still does
not follow that all the basic assumptions of people
with different cultures are the same. Despite similarities, the unlikenesses are significant enough to
block communication and thus impede change. If
the change agent expects the people of the recipient culture to have precisely the same motivations
or behaviors as are common in his culture, he is
seriously risking failure of understanding.

The worst part of most such misapprehension
of cultural realities is that it is unintentional. The
individual does what is "natural" or what makes
"common sense." He may not realize that his

Source: "American Cultural Values" from *Introducing
Social Change*, copyright 1971 by Conrad Arensberg and
Arthur Niehoff, eds. Reprinted by permission of authors.

"natural" tendencies to action are inevitably limited by his own cultural experience, including his unconscious assumptions. To examine the cultural as well as individual premises of one's own actions is a difficult process. If one always stayed with people of the same background, this examination would never be necessary and most people would probably be better off without doing it. However, if one is to deal with people of another culture, or simply to understand them at a distance, knowing one's own cultural assumptions is of the first importance. Thus, hybrid corn grown by Spanish-American farmers in Arizona was superior in terms of the Anglo-American economy and the change agent assumed the value of corn was the same. However, these Spanish-Americans valued it primarily for its taste and texture as a human food rather than as feed for animals. The United States administrators of Palau assumed that if individuals participated in an American system of electing public officials, democracy would be absorbed into the culture. However, the islanders interpreted leadership and social control differently, and manipulated their way around the "democratic" idea. In both cases the problems arose principally because of the cultural misperception of the planners who were putting mistaken reliance on "natural" and "common sense" assumptions which were relevant to the American scene but inadequate in contacts with people of another culture.

Culture creates unconscious blinders for all mankind. Other people do not act "naturally," that is, in accordance with a universal value system. Thus the American or other change agent must be given some opportunity of knowing himself as a product of American and Western culture. This means principally that he look analytically at his own assumptions and values. He should have some idea what influences his decisions and actions in introducing new ideas and what his reactions will be to difficulties among the people with whom he will be working. In short, he needs to know how being an American and a Westerner may help or hinder him in his mission.

In the age of cultural pluralism, what is meant by "American culture"? Is not the United States several streams of culture flowing side by side? There is probably more acceptance of this idea today than at any time since the founding of the country. And yet, there is still a national core, usually characterized as that of the middle class, having its origins in Western European culture. The language is English, the legal system derives from English common law, the political system of democratic elections comes from France and England, the technology is solidly from Europe, and even more subtle social values, such as egalitarianism (though modified), seem to be European derived. Thus, it seems justifiable to characterize the middle class value system of the United States, as derived originally from Europe but modified to suit local conditions, as the core of American culture.

All people born and raised in this country will have been conditioned by this national culture, although obviously the middle class will be most strongly marked. And though it is not implied here that there are no differences in other subcultural streams, it does mean that irrespective of region, national origin, race, class, and sex, there are points of likeness that will occur more frequently than among groups of people in other countries.

Where does this American character come from? As mentioned above, it seems to come from a European base that has been subsequently modified to meet local conditions. The values derived from life on the frontier, the great open spaces, the virgin wealth, and the once seemingly limitless resources of a "new world" appear to have affected ideas of freedom. Individualism seems to have been fostered by a commitment to "progress" which in turn was derived from expansion over three hundred years. Much of the religious and ethical tradition is believed to have come from Calvinist (Puritan) doctrine, particularly an emphasis on individual responsibility and the positive work ethic. Anglo-Saxon civil rights, the rule of law, and representative institutions were inherited from the English background;

ideas of egalitarian democracy and a secular spirit spring from the French and American Revolutions. The period of slavery and its aftermath, and the European immigration of three centuries, have affected the American character strongly.

AMERICAN CULTURE

Is it possible to provide a thumbnail sketch of the most obvious characteristics of this system? Most social scientists would probably agree to the following:

The number of people in America is considerable, compared to other countries, and they are located primarily in the cities and towns of a large area of diverse natural environments, still with considerable mineral and soil wealth and still not intensively exploited. There is an exceedingly elaborate technology and a wealth of manufactured goods that is now the greatest in the world.

Although the country has a strong agrarian tradition in which farming is still regarded as a family occupation, and although farming produces an extraordinary yield of foodstuffs and fibers, the nation has become urbanized and dominated by the cities. The farming population consists of less than 10 percent of the total, and agriculture has become so mechanized it can now be considered as merely another form of industry. Daily living is characteristically urban, regulated by the clock and calendar rather than by the seasons or degree of daylight. The great majority of individuals are employees, living on salaries paid by large, complex, impersonal institutions. Money is the denominator of exchange, even property having a value only in terms of its monetary worth. The necessities of life are purchased rather than produced for subsistence.

Because of the high standard of living and high level of technology, people have long lives. The birth rate is low but the death rate is among the lowest in the world. Thus, although there is a continuing expansion of population, it is much less rapid than in most of the agrarian nations.

Americans exhibit a wide range of wealth, property, education, manners, and tastes. However, despite diversities of origin, tradition, and economic level, there is a surprising conformity in language, diet, hygiene, dress, basic skills, land use, community settlement, recreation, and other activities. The people share a rather small range of moral, political, economic, and social attitudes, being divided in opinion chiefly by their denominational and occupational interests. Within the past decade there seems also to have been a separation of opinion based on age. There are some regional variations but these are far less than the tribal or ethnic pluralisms found in the new nations of South Asia and Africa. The narrow opinion range throughout the country seems to be primarily a product of the relatively efficient mass education system which blankets the country and the wide spread of mass communication, from which all people get the same message.

There are status differences, based mainly on occupation, education, and financial worth. Achievement is valued more than inheritance in determining an individual's position. Although in theory all persons have equal opportunities, certain limitations exist, particularly those based on ethnic background and sex. A Negro may be appointed as a member of the Cabinet, but it is improbable and he would not be elected as President at the present time. There are now Negro mayors, but there are still no Negro governors. Women also are prevented from serving in certain positions or occupations. Despite these limitations, most people move about freely; they change jobs and move up and down in status with considerable frequency.

The basic American kinship unit, though evidently weakening, is still the nuclear family of husband, wife, and children. Newly married couples set up their own small households and move several times in a lifespan. The family rarely has continuing geographical roots. Most couples have few children. Marital relationships are fluid and not particularly stable, with divorce quite common. Old people and unmarried adults usually live apart from their kin. Instead of strong kinship ties, people tend to rely on an enormous number of voluntary associations of common interest—parent-teachers' association, women's clubs, social fraternities, church clubs, recreational teams, political clubs, and many others.

The general level of education is high, with literacy normal but not universal. From the age of five to eighteen the child usually is in an academic institution, learning the culturally approved goals of good health, character, and citizenship. Also, he learns basic and standard skills rather than any hereditary specialization—reading, writing, arithmetic, typing, liberal arts, driving cars, basic mechanics, housekeeping. Specialization comes later in the professional training that ordinarily takes place in college. More and more young people are extending their education through four years in college, although this is not yet legally required.

The moral tone of the country is heavily Calvinist Protestant but there are many other sects of Christianity, besides other religions and cults. Religious beliefs and practices are concerned almost as much with general morality as with man's search for the afterlife or his worship of deities. Family relations, sexual customs, man's relationship to other men, and civic responsibility are all concerns of religion. A puritanic morality has become generalized and secularized, part of the total culture rather than that of any single religious sect. Formal religion is compartmentalized, as are many other aspects of American life. A high percentage of the Protestants who form the bulk of the population attend church infrequently, and religious ideas are seldom consciously mixed with secular ones. The church serves a strong social function, being the center of many clubs and groups. Religion can hardly be considered a particularly unifying institution of American life. The spirit of the country is secular and rationalistic. Most people are not antireligious but merely indifferent.

MATERIAL WELL-BEING

The rich resources of America, along with the extraordinary growth of its industrial economy, have brought a widespread wealth of material goods such as the world has not seen before. There has been a wholesale development and diffusion of the marvels of modern comfort— swift and pleasant transportation, central heating, air conditioning, instant hot and cold water, electricity, and laborsaving devices of endless variety. The high value placed on such comforts has caused industries to be geared to produce ever greater quantities and improved versions. Americans seem to feel that they have a "right" to such amenities.

Associated with this attitude toward comfort (which has itself resulted in elaborate waste disposal facilities), and an advanced state of medical knowledge, Americans have come to regard cleanliness as an absolute virtue. A most familiar slogan is, "Cleanliness is next to godliness," and although this is not heard as often as it once was, the word "dirty" is still one of the chief epithets in the language, as in "dirty old man," "dirty hippie," "dirty business," "dirty deal," etc.

Achievement and success are measured primarily by the quantity of material goods one possesses, both because these are abundant and because they indicate how much money an individual earns. This material evidence of personal worth is modified by the credit system; but still, credit purchases will carry an individual only so far, after which credit agencies will refuse to advance more without evidence of fundamental wealth.

Since there is little display value in the size of one's paycheck or bank account, the average individual buys prestige articles that others can see: expensive clothing or furniture, a fine car, a swimming pool, an expensive home, or one of the endless variety of devices that may have other functions but can also readily be seen by visitors—power mowers, barbecue paraphernalia, television, and stereophonic systems. A person's status is affected to a secondary degree by his level of education, type of occupation, and social behavior; but even these qualities seem to be significant only in terms of how much income they help him to obtain. Thus, a college professor who has earned his Ph.D. will have less status in the general community than a business executive or film actor who has no college education but commands a much larger salary.

People other than middle class Americans also value comfort and the saving of human labor, and one of the motivations to change everywhere is to perform traditional tasks more easily. However, many people of the world have found themselves unable to acquire so many laborsaving devices and have thus concentrated on the satisfaction of other needs; and it should be recognized that many of the spiritual or esthetic goals they pursue will outlast most of the machine-made devices treasured in America. But, their choices have been limited by their comparative poverty. Comfort in such circumstances has not been so highly valued; and in fact, Americans have been accused by this token of being excessively materialistic.

TWOFOLD JUDGMENTS

A special characteristic of Western thinking, fully reflected in American ways, is that of making twofold judgments based on principle. The structure of the Indo-European languages seems to foster this kind of thinking and the action that follows. A situation or action is assigned to a category held high, thus providing a justification for positive effort, or to one held low, with justification for rejection, avoidance, or other negative action. Twofold judgments seem to be the rule in Western and American life: moral-immoral, legal-illegal, right-wrong, sin-virtue, success-failure, clean-dirty, civilized-primitive, practical-impractical, introvert-extrovert, secular-religious, Christian-pagan. This kind of polarized thinking tends to put the world of values into absolutes, and its arbitrary nature is indicated by the fact that modern science no longer uses opposite categories, in almost all instances preferring to use the concept of a range with degrees of difference separating the poles.

Judgment in terms of principle is very old and pervasive as a means of organizing thought in Western and American life. It may derive from Judeo-Christian ideas. In any event, it is deeply rooted in the religions that have come from this base as well as in the philosophy of the West. Its special quality should be recognized. More is involved than merely thinking in opposites. Other peoples have invented dual ways of thinking: the Chinese Yin-and-Yang, the Zoroastrian dual (though equal) forces of good and evil, male and female principles, and the Hindu concept of the forces of destruction and regeneration as different aspects of the same power. However, other peoples do not usually rank one as superior and thus to be embraced on principle as a guide to conduct.

This kind of thinking seems to force Americans into positions of exclusiveness. If one position is accepted, the other must be rejected. There is little possibility of keeping opposite or even parallel ideas in one's thinking pattern. This is not the case in other cultures. In Buddhism and Hinduism disparate local beliefs exist alongside beliefs that are derived from the main theology. No one questions the fact that in Japan people may worship in a Buddhist temple as well as in a Shinto shrine; or that in the southern form of Buddhism, in Laos and Thailand, people propitiate the local spirits ("phi") as well as observe the ritual forms of Buddhism. This is quite different from the Christian attitude in which all that is believed to be supernatural but is not Christian is classified as superstition or paganism.

The average Westerner, and especially the American, bases his personal life and community affairs on principles of right and wrong rather than on sanctions of shame, dishonor, ridicule, or horror of impropriety. The whole legal system is established on the assumption that rational people can decide if things have been "wrong." The American is forced by his culture to categorize his conduct in universal, impersonal terms. "The law is the law" and "right is right," regardless of other considerations.

MORALIZING

One of the most basic of the twofold decisions Americans make is to classify actions as good or bad. Whether in the conduct of foreign affairs or bringing up children or dealing in the marketplace, Americans tend to moralize. Judging people and actions as absolutely right or wrong may have been a source of considerable strength in American history but it has also created pitfalls, particularly in the way it has influenced Americans in their relationship with other peoples. The attitude has frequently led Americans to indignation and even to warfare about the behavior of other peoples, Vietnam providing the most obvious recent example.

Every people has its own code of proper conduct. This is such an important part of any culture that some effort to understand it must be made. But this aspect of a cultural system is probably the most difficult to learn. And the greatest difficulties will occur if the outsider assumes that other people's basis of judgment is the same as his, or even that proper conduct will be based on moral rather than other kinds of principles.

In many other cultures, rank or esteem, the dignity of a person, the honor of an individual, compassion for an unfortunate, or loyalty to a kinsman or co-religionist may be the basis for judgment as to proper conduct. Most forms of sexual behavior may not be considered subject to moral considerations. The American, as an heir to the Western tradition, is familiar and comfortable with a code of conduct derived from absolute principles (mostly religious) and supported by a code of law enforced by central authorities. This entire code is supposed to be impersonal, and to a considerable extent it is. The morality tale of the honest, law-abiding policeman or judge who punishes his own law-breaking son probably does occur more frequently in America than in societies where kinship considerations are given more weight.

One other feature of this kind of thinking that can lead to considerable personal and public problems is that the American tends to overreact to the discovery that the ideal behavior he was taught to expect from parent, public servants, spouses, and other adults is not always present in real life. Some individuals react by becoming "tough" and "cynical" and "wise" to the corruption of the world. Others, particularly exemplified by the youth of the past decade, organize to eliminate by whatever means are available the "failures" of the older generation. This kind of thinking encourages the individual to believe that, whatever differs from the ideal version of high moral excellence is of the utmost depravity. It tends to direct the individual to see corruption and evil everywhere. And while such moralistic indignation may serve the culture well in some instances (as in the fight against pollution), it can also have negative consequences, particularly when the moralizer is trying to work with people of another culture.

WORK AND PLAY

Another kind of twofold judgment that Americans tend to maintain is based on a qualitative distinction between work and play. To most persons brought up in the present-day American environment of farming, business, or industry, work is what they do regularly, purposefully, and even grimly, whether they enjoy it or not. It is a necessity, and for the middle aged, a duty. A man is judged by his work. When strangers meet and attempt to establish cordial relationships, one of the first topics of discussion is the kind of work each does. It is a primary role classifier. Work is a serious, adult business, and a man is supposed to "get ahead" or "make a contribution" to community or mankind through his work.

Play is different. It is fun, an outlet from work, without serious purpose except possibly to make subsequent work more efficient. It is a lesser category, a later topic of conversation after one's occupation is identified. And although some persons may "enjoy their work," this is a matter of luck and by no means something that everyone can count on since all jobs contain some "dirty work," tedium, and tasks that one completes just by pushing on. Work and play are considered to be different worlds; there is a time and place for each, but when it is time for work, then lighter pursuits should be put aside. There is a newer emphasis in contemporary America on pleasure-seeking as a primary goal of life, but so far this seems to be an attitude espoused by a minority only, the young who have rejected the former goals of society and the retired old who have already completed their years of work.

The American habit of associating work with high or necessary purpose and grim effort and play with frivolity or pleasure seems to have a positive function in the American cultural context, but it may be quite out of place in another culture. For many peoples the times of most important work may also be times of festivity or ceremony. Work and play may be interwoven. A threshing floor may be a dancing arena, and building a new house or netting a school of fish may provide the occasion for a whole community to sing and joke together. Preparing the proper songs or dishes will be as "practical" an activity as cutting thatch or caring for nets.

The combination of work and play is not completely foreign to Americans, although urban industrial society does not seem favorable for it. The American frontier, and even Midwest farming communities until thirty or forty years ago, combined the two in their husking bees, house-raising and threshing parties. In the early decades of this century, before wheat combines and farms of large acreage dominated agriculture in the Midwest, farmers made the social and work rounds for several weeks in midsummer. Not only did they work together, but they also feasted, socialized, and even managed a considerable amount of courting. It was a point of pride for each farmer's wife to have the largest quantities of elaborate food available for the men when they came in from the fields. The unmarried girls made a particular effort to be there to search out the bachelors. It was a gay time as well as a time of hard work. It should also be pointed out that song and work has been well represented in the American past in the vast repertory of work songs that were once sung by occupational groups.

Basically, the nonindustrial societies have patterns of work and play that are closer to those known to preindustrial Americans; work and play are intermixed rather than distinct forms of activity.

TIME IS MONEY

Closely related to the American distinction between work and play is a special attitude toward time. Whenever Americans interact with people in nonindustrial countries, both quickly become aware that their outlook in regard to time is different. In many such countries the local people actually make a distinction in the spoken language, referring to *hora Americana* versus *hora Mexicana* or *mong Amelikan* versus *mong Lao*. When referring to the American version, they mean that it is exact, that people are punctual, activities are scheduled, time is apportioned for separate activities, and the measure is the mechanical clock; their own time lacks this precision.

Probably misunderstandings with people of other cultures occur most frequently in relation to work. For Americans, "time is money." Work is paid for in money and one should balance his work against time or through regular periods for a fixed salary. A person works for a stated number of dollars per hour and eight or ten hours per day for 40 or 48 hours a week. Work beyond the normal is "overtime." Play or leisure time is before or after work time. An employer literally buys the time of his workers along with their skills, and schedules and assigns work to be balanced against the gain he will obtain. In this way of thinking, time can be turned into money, both for the employer and employee, and work turned out faster than planned can release extra time for more work and more gain.

Equating work with time, using the least amount of time to produce the largest amount of work, expecting that time paid for will be marked by sustained effort, budgeting of man hours in relation to the cost of the end product—these are central features of the American industrial economy that have contributed a great deal to its productiveness. And although Americans may complain about the necessity of routine and the tyranny of the clock during working hours, they are thoroughly accustomed to such strictures. The activities of leisure—eating, sleeping, playing, courting—must take place during "time off." No wonder time to them is scarce and worth saving.

Such a precise concept of time is usually foreign to peoples of nonindustrial cultures. In most agrarian societies, especially in the villages, time is geared to seasonal requirements and the amount of daylight available. Many routines reflect, not hourly or daily repetitions based on wage labor, but the needs of individual and social life, the cycles of crops, fluctuations in daily temperature, and the round of ceremonial observances. The cities of these countries have all adopted the Western concept of time to some degree, although it is frequently noted that the rural pattern is still maintained in modified form in the urban context. Individuals simply do not keep hours or appointments precisely and are surprised when they learn that an American is irritated by a missed appointment.

EFFORT AND OPTIMISM

Americans are an active people. They believe that problems should be identified and effort should be expended to solve them. Effort is good in itself, and with proper effort one can be optimistic about success. The fact that some problems may be insoluble is very difficult for an American to accept. The high value connected with effort often causes Americans to cite the principle that "It is better to do something than to just stand around." This thinking is based on the concept that the universe is mechanistic (it can be understood in terms of causes and effects), man is his own master, and he is perfectible almost without limit (DuBois, 1955: 1233–1234). Thus, with enough effort, man can improve himself and manipulate the part of the universe that is around him.

This national confidence in effort and activity, with an optimism that trying to do something about a problem will almost invariably bring success in solving it, seems to be specifically American. Such an attitude is probably a product of the continual expansion of American culture during the past three hundred years, first along America's frontiers and later in its industrial growth. Obstacles existed only to be overcome, and bad conditions needed only be recognized to be rectified.

Effort and optimism permeate the life of the individual because of his cultural upbringing. Coming from an "open class system," where status is usually achieved rather than inherited, both privilege and authority should be deserved and won.

Effort, achievement, and success are woven through the fabric of American life and culture. Activist, pragmatic values rather than contemplative or mystical ones are the basis of the American character. Serious effort to achieve success is both a personal goal and an ethical imperative. The worthwhile man is the one who "gets results" and "gets ahead." A failure "gets nowhere" or "gets no results," for success is measured by results (although there is a little "credit for trying"). The successful man "tackles a problem," "does something about it," and "succeeds" in the process. A failure is unsuccessful through his own fault. Even if he had "bad breaks" he should have tried again. A failure in life "didn't have the guts" to "make a go of it" and "put himself ahead."

This is a very severe code. No one is certain how widespread it is among Americans but it is probably recognizable to most. It indicates a culture in which effort is rewarded, competition is enforced, and individual achievement is paramount. Unfortunately, the code raises serious problems. One of the most important is that it calls all those in high positions successes and all those in low ones "failures" even though everyone knows the majority must be in lower positions. A code of this sort by its very nature creates much frustration in all those who have not been able to achieve high positions.

This traditional optimism of the American personality has been tempered to a certain degree in recent years, though primarily in the kind of goals sought rather than whether they can be achieved. Concentration on pragmatic effort seems unchanged, and even those Americans who are most disillusioned with the current state of affairs seem convinced that enough effort will produce success—for their new goals, however, rather than the old ones.

But it has become clear to everyone that whatever effort is expended, some situations are beyond the American's ability to control. Problems once thought to be simple are now seen to have a complexity not previously recognized. A weaker enemy cannot simply be bombed into submission with more and more explosives. Industrial production cannot be guided by the profit motive alone if one wants to breathe clean air and to swim in clean water. The inner city of an industrial nation cannot survive if it is abandoned by the well-to-do who move to the suburbs. These are some of the problems that have arisen because of a simplistic view of manipulation of the environment, both human and natural. Some pundits now feel they are beyond human correction, but although the optimism of the average man has probably been tempered in recent decades, his method of overcoming these obstacles is unchanged—simply put in greater effort.

The American overseas is prone to evaluate people and situations according to this code. When he observes that those in authority have achieved their position by means other than their own effort, he may become bewildered, angered, or cynical. He may quickly make an activist judgment and try to remedy the situation, using his own code. Or he may shift (usually unconsciously) from the notion of work as task-oriented, which many peoples share in their own fashion, to an emphasis on busy work, on hurrying and pressuring, on encouraging activity for its own sake.

To peoples in other parts of the world, a history of failure in recent times has been as compelling as the technological and economic achievements of America. Their experiences may have taught them to value passivity, acceptance, and evasion rather than effort and optimism. This will not be because they have no interest in getting things done but because of their history of reversals. They lack the confidence of the American.

Before taking action, other peoples may therefore make many preparations which the American, so concerned with technical efficiency, will consider unnecessary. These may consist in extensive consultation with others to build up a consensus, giving favors to win personal loyalties, trying to adjust proposed plans to religious and other traditional beliefs, and considering all alternatives, including the real possibility of not risking action at all. American demands for bustle and effort, for getting down to business, may not only be interpreted as nagging, pushing, and ill-mannered, but sometimes as downright frightening, especially when a wrong judgment could lead to personal disaster. After an initial failure, the American determination to "try again" or "try harder the next time" may seem particularly foolhardy. Merely to intensify one's effort and to try again on a bigger scale when resources are limited may appear as the most reckless compounding of original folly.

And as is not unusual, other peoples frequently do judge American behavior correctly. The American passion to exert greater effort in the face of continuing difficulties has not always produced the hoped-for success. In Vietnam, for example, although an admittedly much weaker enemy clearly and early indicated that they would fight differently than in previous wars, the military heads of the United States went ahead with conventional bombing and ground maneuvers for almost ten years without ever altering their procedures significantly except to intensify them. At the end of this decade, the enemy seemed hardly any weaker than at the beginning. And it must be admitted that such a procedure is only possible for America because it has unprecedented wealth and industrial production.

The effort to which Americans normally commit themselves is expected to be direct and efficient. Americans want to "get down to business" and confine themselves to the problem or proposal specified. Misunderstandings have consequently occurred because other peoples, particularly Latins, have tended to be less direct. They indulge more in theoretical speech during conferences and discussions, refusing to confine themselves rigidly to the agenda at hand. All this indicates more concern with social values than is usual in the American manner of conducting affairs. Perhaps the impersonal, technological approach leads to more production but the social verities have their place also, and they are still significant in many parts of the world.

American assumptions about effort and optimism include a faith in progress and a constant view toward the future. Practically all life is arranged to fulfill the needs of children and of the generations to follow. There is a pervasive accent on youthfulness; the values exemplified in commercial advertising and entertainment almost always emphasize the young, and the old are not commonly sought out for their experience. Adults attempt to hold back middle and old age. In general, elderly people are bypassed, either left in old folks' homes or in isolated retirement, in both cases removed from practical affairs. An ironic aspect of the situation in the 1960s was the rejection by a considerable part of American youth of this idealized "youth culture." "You can't trust anyone over thirty," they say.

An accent on youthfulness is particularly American, although it seems to be shared to a lesser degree by other achievement-oriented industrial societies. In the agrarian nations or wherever tradition is important, people tend to equate age with experience. The old are treated with deference and the oldest male is usually the chief decision-maker of the basic kin unit.

Other cultures have had their periods of success, but it appears rare for progress to be a central value throughout the entire existence of a culture. It is only since World War II that American faith in the future has been modified significantly, with the realization that there are many undesirable consequences if technological progress is allowed to take place with few controls. But despite recent reversals, the general American attitude is still that the future should contain bigger and better successes, if not on this planet, then on others. This attitude also implies that the new and modern are better than the old and traditional. Technological and economic life must progress. No one—not even the strongest dissidents of the left or the right—expects to keep America as it is today or to return it to what it was yesterday.

MAN AND NATURE

The greater effort that normally marks the American's response to obstacles may sometimes seem shallow, irreverent, or premature to people in other cultures. Some obstacles deserve respect and there are limitations to what man can do, even if he is the cleverest manipulator of the environment to have appeared so far. The new ecological approach is an indication that the American is becoming aware of some limitations on his capacities, but whether this will deflect his value system in a basic way remains to be seen. Up to now, American man has attempted to conquer nature. It has been something to overcome, to improve, to tear down and rebuild in a better way. He has tried to "break the soil," to "harness" the natural resources, to treat the natural environment like a domestic animal. He has divided the plants and animals into categories of useful and harmful. Harmful plants are weeds and harmful animals are "varmints"—the first to be uprooted or poisoned and the second to be trapped, shot, or poisoned. American farmers and ranchers have been notorious for killing predators. The only kind of hawks they knew until recently were "chicken hawks" which were shot any time they appeared and their carcasses hung in long festoons on wire fences. Coyotes and bobcats are still trapped and hunted without compunction by Westerners, who can get bounties of a few dollars for the feet and ears of one of these animals. And although on occasion hawks and coyotes may kill a few chickens or sheep, they primarily live on mice, rats, rabbits and other small animals whose populations must be kept in balance by such predators. Even a weed is merely a "plant growing out of place" from man's point of view.

It must be admitted that many of the achievements of Americans are due to this conquering attitude toward nature. The enormous agricultural productivity is one such achievement, although credit must also go to the fact that there were large expanses of very fertile land available. But it must also be admitted that the American has paid and is continuing to pay high prices for these agricultural successes. Natural resources, particularly forests, water, and the air, have been squandered and despoiled over large areas. Nature's balance has often been upset. Such "wonder" insecticides as DDT are now under strong attack by conservationists as destroying many "useful" insects and birds, as well as for their effect on human health.

This conquering attitude toward nature appears to rest on at least three assumptions; that the universe is mechanistic, that man is its master, and that man is qualitatively different from all other forms of life. Specifically, American and Western man credits himself with a special inner consciousness, a soul, for which he does not give other creatures credit. In most of the non-Western world man is merely considered as one form of life, different only in degree from the others. The Western biologist also shares this view, which is the primary reason that traditional Western culture came into conflict with biological views in the nineteenth and twentieth centuries. In the so-called animistic religions, all living creatures are believed to have something corresponding to a soul, with no sharp dividing line between man and the other animals. Spirits are even attributed to plants and inanimate objects, such as soil, rocks, mountains, and rivers. In the Hindu and Buddhist world the belief in a cycle of rebirths strongly affirms man's kinship to nonhuman

forms. In the cycle of existences man can become an insect, a mammal, another type of man, or even a form of deity. The validity of such beliefs is far less important than the fact that man's attitude toward nature is influenced by them (and after all, there is no more empirical basis for Christian beliefs than for Buddhism or Hinduism). Basically, most people, (except Westerners) consider man and nature as one, and they more often work with nature than simply attempting to conquer it.

During long periods of trial and error, peoples of all cultures have worked out adaptations to their natural environment. These adaptations may lack much by Western standards but they do enable the inhabitants to survive, sometimes in quite difficult circumstances. Such people through experience have evolved systems of conservation, methods of stretching and restoring their slim resources, and elaborate accommodations to climate, vegetation, and terrain. Some such adaptations now embedded in tradition and religion are the Middle Eastern desert-derived pattern of Islamic ritual hygiene, austerity, and almsgiving; preindustrial Japanese frugalities in house structure, farming, and woodworking; and Southeast Asian village economies in the measured use of rice, bamboo, and fish. These and similar adaptations to natural environments are high developments in the balanced utilization of limited resources.

When, with a facile confidence that nature can be tamed by ever costlier mechanical devices, Americans and other Westerners attempt to brush aside the experience of centuries, it is perhaps temporarily exciting to the local people. However, they are not apt to be reassured if they have information about the realities of the environment that is ignored by the rushing, pushing, self-assured newcomers, particularly since the local solutions sometimes outlast the glamorous innovations of the specialists. For example, a well-drilling project in Laos was based on a system that had been worked out in Florida where the water table is high the year around. The specialist drilled wells in one large area of Laos during the rainy season and found water almost every time, at a relatively high level. However, all these wells went dry during the dry season, since in Southeast Asia the water level drops markedly during this period. Most Lao probably knew this and would have revealed it if asked.

In environments that seem adverse (such as the rainy tropics, the arctic, or the desert), experience has shown that Western man's goods and machines rot, rust, freeze, or grit up all too quickly, requiring huge and costly effort merely to keep them going. This is not surprising since this machinery was developed primarily for use in a temperate zone where precipitation is spread more or less evenly throughout the year.

A graphic example of the lack of adaptability of Western machines has been observed during the military struggles in Southeast Asia in recent years. Tanks and other mechanized equipment were developed with the solid land forms of America and Europe in mind. However, their use has been drastically curtailed in the rice paddies of Vietnam and Laos. The mobile foot soldier, unencumbered with heavy gear, can slip through the soggy fields and marshes in constant readiness to fight while the tank or halftrack is bogged down in mud. The insurgent forces in Laos and Vietnam have made their greatest drives just before the heavy rains set in, knowing that the mechanized forces with American equipment will be mostly immobilized until the land dries again.

EQUALITY OF MEN

The tendency to moralize has been operative in supporting another important trait of American culture, egalitarianism. Americans believe all people should have equal opportunities for achievement. This is more of moral imperative than an actual fact of American life and has always been so. From the earliest times there have been some groups of people who were treated as inferior, and great differences of wealth, education, influence, opportunity, and

privilege exist in the United States. Nevertheless, the experiences that Americans underwent along the frontiers and through the process of immigration did represent a huge historical experiment in social leveling. The legal and institutional heritage prescribes equal rights, condemns special privileges, and demands fair representation for every citizen. The latest efforts to obtain equal treatment for minority groups have been spearheaded by legal resolutions (Supreme Court decisions) and other re-emphases of the egalitarian nature of the society. Inequality, unless a product of achievement or lack of it, is considered to be wrong, bad, or "unfair."

There are, of course, ethnic minorities which have not been assimilated into the major society and which are treated unequally. The main disadvantaged groups now are of African, Mexican, and Amerindian ancestry. Although it is currently fashionable to regard this difference of treatment as based on race, other explanations are just as plausible. None of these groups really constitute a race and people with basically very similar appearances and genetic background (such as those of Italian, Spanish, Chinese, or Japanese ancestry) face much less discrimination. But these latter groups have attempted to adopt the Euro-American cultural pattern while Mexican-American and Amerindians have tended to maintain certain distinctive cultural patterns. The case of the Afro-American is probably unique, in that these people constitute the only group whose ancestors were held in slavery by the majority.

It is probable that the American attitude toward equality of treatment really means "within the major value system"; that is, people are, or should be, treated equally if they accept the basic beliefs and behavior of the social majority. In this sense, the American idea is similar to that of the Muslims, who have always taught that all men are equal under Allah; discrimination by race or any other criterion has been rare so long as one was dealing with acceptors of the faith, and within the ranks of believers the only significant feelings of superiority have been based on supposed relationships with the Prophet. People on a direct line of descent from Mohammed are considered higher than those on a more remote line.

There has been one other form of unequal treatment in American society, that between males and females. Although female liberation movements are fashionable now, the fact is that the American female is already in a position of more nearly equal treatment than in most other nations, and certainly those outside the West. In practice, women are barred from the highest positions and are discriminated against in certain professions. But there are few educational limitations and they can enter freely into economic affairs. Even marriage is considered to be a kind of partnership, an unusual arrangement among the vast range of cultures of the world.

Despite the remaining evidences of unequal treatment toward the unassimilated ethnic minorities and women, the basic American value judgment of equality among men (and women) has not changed. Open patterns of subordination, deference, and acceptance of underprivilege call forth sympathies for the "underdog" and American activist values call for efforts to do something about such matters. This impulse tempts Americans overseas to interfere directly in the life ways of other peoples. The American does not have the patience to deal with persons whose authority seems neither justified nor deserved, or to wait for the ordinary man who will act only when he has received the go-ahead from the figures of prestige or respect in his culture.

Another consequence of American egalitarianism is a preference for simple manners and direct, informal treatment of other persons. This can work to the American's advantage if kept within limits; but where people differ in rank and prestige, offense can be given if all are treated in a breezy, "kidding," impersonal manner. It is much better to try to acquire some of the local usages of long titles, elaborate forms of address and language, and manners of courtesy and deference, than to try to accustom other peoples to American ways. American "kidding" and humor are very special products of an egalitarian culture and generally work best at home.

Since all Americans are supposed to be equal in rights, and since "success" is a primary goal that can only be measured by achievement, a high value must be assigned to individuality. This accent on individual worth seems to be largely a heritage of frontier days and later economic expansion when there were plenty of opportunities for the individual to achieve according to his abilities. However, with population expansion and the filling up of the country, individuality has had to be limited to some extent. It is now known that the ravages of the natural environment are largely due to unchecked drives by industrialists toward individual achievement.

Although individual equality has been stressed throughout American history, the goals and ways of achieving success have been limited. The successful man was one who was better than everyone else but in a way similar to theirs; one might have more and better things than another, but they should be the same kinds of things. And with the full development of urban, corporate life, this similarity of goals seems to have evolved into personal conformity. The organization man has superseded the rugged individualist. Thus, individual self-sufficiency has steadily decreased. One indication of this development is a growing demand for security. And since Americans have abandoned the kinship system for this purpose, they now try to protect themselves with impersonal group insurance which they hope will cover all contingencies. In their efforts to attract new employees, corporations now advertise insurance benefits as much as the challenge of the work and the salary, and these "fringe benefits" are just as often the main concern of prospective employees. Americans buy insurance for the smallest items in their lives, even insuring household appliances against breakdown. Government too becomes more and more a giant insurance corporation, to its direct employees and to the citizenry in general.

HUMANITARIANISM

The American trait of coming to the aid of unfortunates is widespread and well known. It expresses itself in impersonal generosity which is activated by calls for help when unpredicted events of unfortunate or disastrous effect occur. Earthquakes, floods, famines, and epidemics are only a few of the kinds of events that strike a responsive chord in American society. At the end of both world wars American generosity was primarily responsible for getting European nations back on their feet. Not only are they generous, but Americans also show a tremendous amount of efficiency at such times, often more than in "normal" times.

A dramatic illustration of this competence was witnessed in the aftermath of a battle in Vientiane, Laos, at which time the capitol was badly damaged. American diplomatic and assistance efforts in the preceding years had not been particularly impressive. In fact, the battle occurred principally because American diplomatic and military bureaus had come to the point of backing two opposing ideological factions of Laotians, supplying both groups with weapons. U.S. assistance efforts had been bogged down by a lack of cultural understanding of the Lao and by administrative problems in the aid mission itself. But after the capitol had been heavily damaged by shelling, the American International Cooperation Administration, as well as other American groups in the city, went into action in a manner that was truly impressive. Although many areas had been flattened and an unknown number of people killed, within two to three weeks the city was on its feet again. Besides providing needed goods, the American officials thought nothing of working day and night, and their organizational ability was much more clearly demonstrated than in their inept efforts at military diplomacy which led to the battle. In three to four months, there was hardly a sign that the battle had taken place.

American humanitarianism is a characteristic that can hardly be criticized. It is of a special type, however, and contains one possible basis of misunderstanding in that it is usually highly organized and impersonal. For many other peoples humanitarianism is personal. They consequently do not share with everyone; they cannot. But through personal and kinship obligations, by religious almsgiving, and in other traditional ways, they give what they can. The American must not blind himself to the existence of these other patterns and also must perceive that other peoples are just not as rich as he is. The American tendency can hardly be praised if it is merely converted into a standard of negative judgment against other peoples' ways.

An American tends to condemn begging and the systems that support it, presumably because it involves personalized asking and giving. But it is worth while to look into the realities of such a system, as for instance that of *baksheesh*, the Middle Eastern begging tradition. The halt, lame, and blind line up with outstretched palm at the mosque or church door. The American is likely to condemn the cruelty of such a system, but in fact these people are being taken care of by their community according to traditional rules. Every member of the Islamic faithful is expected to give 10 percent of his income *(zaka)* in direct alms to the unfortunates who personally ask for it. This particular pattern of generosity is one that has been worked into the communal life of the society, in keeping with its meager resources. The difference between this system and the Community Chest is mainly one of organization and personalization.

STUDY QUESTIONS FOR PART 1

1. Spindler gives examples of cultural transmission from small, developing, homogeneous societies. Do such events of cultural transmission take place today within our contemporary American society? What are some examples of recruitment, discontinuity, and cultural compression in contemporary America?

2. Formal education is often encouraged in developing countries as a way to increase the standard of living and economic development in general. Does that work? What are your views of the pros, cons and alternatives to such policies?

3. Arnesberg and Niehoff wrote about U.S. cultural values in the 1970s. In what ways are their assessments still accurate today? What would you add to their list? What would you delete?

4. How do you feel about those values? What values on the list are personally meaningful for you? Why? Are there values on the list that you personally find objectionable? Why?

5. In contemporary schools there tends to be little deliberate discussion of values embedded in the curriculum and in how the roles of teachers and students are defined. Why do you think this is so? What are the effects of this on teachers and students? What are some positive and negative consequences you would expect to be associated with a deliberate and on-going discussion of these values?

6. To whose values should our public schools be responsive? Why? Who gets to decide this? Why?

7. Should we have a national school curriculum? Why?

Social Structure and Education

The previous readings offered a perspective on education as the transmission of culture and provided a framework for thinking about and understanding U.S. cultural values. The selections in Part 2 build on these themes and focus more directly on three broad, but related, questions:

- What is education?
- What societal needs does education serve?
- How are these needs met? Both reading selections reflect what is called a *functionalist* perspective of education.

Functionalism is a school of thought that seeks to explain social phenomena in terms of how the survival needs of society are served; in other words, how they help society adjust and adapt to changing social conditions. In the next two selections, both Durkheim (translated from French nearly 100 years ago—hence some of the awkward dated usage of language) and Feinberg and Soltis argue that the basic function of education is to ensure that children grow up to become citizens and workers who function in ways that allow the continued survival of a particular society.

Two key ideas are associated with this theory: role differentiation and social solidarity. As Feinberg and Soltis explain, they are "the two primary requirements of social life" from the functionalist perspective.

According to role differentiation, in modern societies there are many different roles that have to be filled. They are not all equally attractive or valued, nor do they all require similar knowledge, skills, or attitudes. Thus, one of the functions of the educational system is to be sure that people are able and trained to fill these different roles. Social solidarity ensures that there is a reasonable level of social stability among all the different people filling those different roles. The challenge here is that some roles have high prestige, status, and rewards, while others are relatively low in prestige, status, and rewards. To see a specific example of the potential threat to social solidarity posed by society's need for differentiated roles, read the explanation provided by Feinberg and Soltis for the differences in the selection, training, and rewards for physicians and teachers. After you read that, extend the example to include others, such as migrant laborers, bank clerks, food service workers, stockbrokers, custodians, nurses, postal workers, and so forth.

Functionalists believe that for society to survive, it requires both a sufficient degree of role differentiation to provide workers for all of the things that need to be done in a modern industrial society, and a sufficient level of social solidarity among those individuals for them to get along well enough to want to remain a member of the system. As Feinberg and Soltis explain, the way modern societies such as ours respond to this challenge is to have a system of universal, compulsory public education (p. 16). Public education provides a trained, ready work force.

What do we mean by education? The reading by Durkheim provides a thoughtful analysis of the complexities of this question and helps us understand the different ways in which this question has been answered over the centuries. As you will see from discussions in class, this is not a resolved issue. Indeed, many of the reforms witnessed in recent years can be interpreted as different perspectives on the meaning of education. You need to think about how you would answer this question, because the way you answer it will have a large influence on your approach to teaching.

Durkheim makes a number of very important observations about education. Among them are the ideas that education varies by social class and locality; given the adult role to be filled by a child, beyond a certain age, education needs to be more differentiated; for education to occur, children and adults must interact, with the adults influencing the children; a major objective of all education is to ensure that all children gain a basic understanding of what we know about human nature. This selection contains many other ideas.

For Durkheim, the focus and primary function of education is to prepare children for their roles as workers and members of the larger society. Durkheim makes an important distinction between what he refers to as the "individual being" and the "social being." In his view, the purpose of education is to shape the social being: "a system of ideas, sentiments and practices which express in us, not our personality, but the group or different groups of which we are a part; these are the religious beliefs, moral beliefs and practices, national or professional traditions, collective opinions of every kind. Their totality forms the social being" (p. 72). While Durkheim believes the development of the individual being is important, it is the socialization of children to membership in the larger group, outside the family, that is the critical function of education. What, then, is education? For Durkheim, "Education is, then, only the means by which society prepares within the children, the essential conditions of its very existence" (p. 71). Notice the functionalist point of view reflected in this observation.

What societal needs does education serve? Both articles tell us that education serves two basic needs of society: (1) to be sure that children are prepared in adequate numbers to fill a wide variety of social roles needed for a complex modern society such as ours to adapt and survive as the world's and our society's conditions change; and (2) to be sure that children acquire the attitudes, skills, and values needed to ensure that society can both achieve and maintain enough social solidarity to survive, and that workers and citizens believe in the system and want to remain a part of it.

How are these needs achieved? This question is answered in somewhat different ways by Durkheim and by Feinberg and Soltis. For Durkheim, there are two major ideas. One is that the major quality of the teacher is his/her moral authority. This, in combination with the teacher's belief in the importance of education and the relatively passive and vulnerable state of the child, gives the teacher an extraordinary amount of power to influence the child. The second critical way society's needs are achieved is through the role the State plays in education. Durkheim points out that the State has a vested interest in education and that it must intrude on a regular basis to remind the teacher of the values, attitudes, and sentiments the child is to be taught, in the interests of the State. "The role of the State is to outline these essential principles, to have them taught in its schools, to see to it that nowhere are children left ignorant of them, that everywhere they should be spoken of with the respect that is due them" (p. 81).

Feinberg and Soltis, while agreeing with the ideas expressed by Durkheim, answer the question somewhat differently. The needs of society for role differentiation and social solidarity, the requisites of society's survival from the functionalist's perspective, are achieved through a system of universal and compulsory public education. In this respect, their view is quite similar to Durkheim's. Going further, however, Feinberg and Soltis suggest that there are four key social norms that children learn by going to public school, and that these norms are instrumental to society's survival. These norms, originally posited by Robert Dreeben (1968), are independence, achievement, universalism, and specificity. For Dreeben, and for Feinberg and Soltis, these four norms are essential if one is to effectively function in a society such as ours.

These norms are theoretically best taught in the school, and they are reenforced and developed as children move from the lower grades through high school. Briefly, independence entails children learning that they must take responsibility for their actions, and that it is legitimate for others to hold them accountable for their actions. The norm of achievement is associated with learning that one will be judged by one's performance (an achievement), and not by some ascribed quality of the individual like race, religion, gender, class, or family background. The norm of universalism is concerned with learning that, with some specific exceptions, one must be prepared to set aside one's individuality and be ready to be treated as a member of a group (of similarly categorized persons); everyone gets treated the same. The norm of specificity addresses the occasion of exceptions to the norm of universality. That is, exceptions can be and are made, but they must be perceived as legitimate and fair. For example, being excused from attending the school assembly because of a previously scheduled doctor's appointment would be viewed as legitimate. However, being given permission to not attend the assembly because one is tired or wants to make after school plans with a friend would not be legitimate, because these are not specific categories of behavior relevant to being excused from a school event required of all students (except those with reasons that fit within specific and prescribed categories—like needing to see the nurse or going to a doctor's appointment).

As you read the next two selections, give special thought to what education is, the connections between education and society, and the ways in which education meets society's needs. Also remember that this is one view of education, and there are others. Think about why you agree or disagree with the functionalist perspective. If you disagree, what are some of the alternatives you might consider? Finally, why is it so important for a teacher to have a good understanding of education and its purposes?

Education: Its Nature and Its Role

Emile Durkheim

1. DEFINITIONS OF EDUCATION. CRITICAL EXAMINATION.

The word "education" has sometimes been used in a very broad sense to designate the totality of influences that nature or other men are able to exercise either on our intelligence or on our will. It includes, says John Stuart Mill, "all that we ourselves do and all that others do for us to the end of bringing us closer to the perfection of our nature. In its most widely accepted sense, it includes even indirect effects on the character and faculties of men produced by things having quite a different objective: by laws, by forms of government, the industrial arts, and even by physical phenomena, independent of human will, such as climate, soil, and locality." But this definition includes elements that are quite disparate, and that one cannot combine under a single heading without confusion. The influence of things on men is very different, in their processes and effects, from that which comes from men themselves; and the influence of peers on peers differs from that which adults exercise on youth. It is only the latter that concerns us here, and, therefore, it is this meaning that it is convenient to reserve for the word "education."

But what is the specific nature of this influence? Various answers have been given to this question; they can be divided into two main types.

Following Kant, "the end of education is to develop, in each individual, all the perfection of which he is capable." But what is meant by perfection? It is, as has often been said, the harmo-

nious development of all the human faculties. To carry to the highest point that can be reached all the capacities that are in us, to realize them as completely as possible, without their interfering with one another, is not this an ideal beyond which there can be no other?

But if, to a degree, this harmonious development is indeed necessary and desirable, it is not wholly attainable; for it is in contradiction to another rule of human behavior which is no less cogent; that which has us concentrate on a specific, limited task. We cannot and we must not all be devoted to the same kind of life; we have, according to our aptitudes, different functions to fulfill, and we must adapt ourselves to what we must do. We are not all made for reflection; there is need for men of feeling and of action. Conversely, there is need of those whose job is thinking. Now, thought can develop only in detachment from action, only by turning in upon itself, only by turning its object entirely away from overt action. From this comes a first differentiation which is accompanied by a break of equilibrium. And behavior, in turn, as thought, can take a variety of different and specialized forms. Doubtless this specialization does not exclude a certain common base and, consequently, a certain balance of functions, organic and psychic alike, without which the health of the individual would be endangered, as well as social cohesion. We see, thus, that perfect harmony cannot be presented as the final end of conduct and of education.

Still less satisfactory is the utilitarian definition, according to which the objective of education would be to "make the individual an instrument of happiness for himself and for his fellows" (James Mill); for happiness is an essentially subjective thing that each person appreciates in his own way. Such a formula, then, leaves the end of education undetermined and, therefore, education itself, since it is left to individual fancy. Spencer, to be sure, tried to define happiness objectively. For him, the conditions of happiness are those of life. Complete happiness is the complete life. But what is meant by life? If it is a matter of physical existence alone, one may well say: that without which it would be impossible; it implies, in effect, a certain equilibrium between the organism and its environment, and, since the two terms in relation are definable data, it must be the same with their relation. But one can express, in this way, only the most immediate vital necessities. Now, for man, and above all for the man of today, such a life is not life. We ask more of life than normal enough functioning of our organs. A cultivated mind prefers not to live rather than give up the joys of the intellect. Even from the material point of view alone, everything over and above what is strictly necessary cannot be exactly determined. The "standard of life," as the English say, the minimum below which it does not seem to us that we can consent to descend, varies infinitely according to conditions, milieux, and the times. What we found sufficient yesterday, today seems to us to be beneath the dignity of man, as we define it now, and everything leads us to believe that our needs in this connection grow increasingly.

We come here to the general criticism that all these definitions face. They assume that there is an ideal, perfect education, which applies to all men indiscriminately; and it is this education, universal and unique, that the theorist tries to define. But first, if history is taken into consideration, one finds in it nothing to confirm such an hypothesis. Education has varied infinitely in time and place. In the cities of Greece and Rome, education trained the individual to subordinate himself blindly to the collectivity, to become the creature of society. Today, it tries to make of the individual an autonomous personality. In Athens, they sought to form cultivated souls, informed, subtle, full of measure and harmony, capable of enjoying beauty and the joys of pure speculation; in Rome, they wanted above all for children to become men of action, devoted to military glory, indifferent to letters and the arts. In the Middle Ages, education was above all Christian; in the Renaissance, it assumes a more lay and literary character; today science tends to assume the place in education formerly occupied by the arts. Can it be said, then, that the fact is not the ideal; that if education has varied, it is because men have mistaken what it should be? But if Roman education had been infused with an individualism comparable to ours, the Roman city would not have been able to maintain itself; Latin civilization would not have developed, nor, furthermore, our modern civilization, which is in part descended from it. The Christian societies of the Middle Ages would not have been able to survive if they had given to free inquiry the place that we give it today. There are, then, ineluctable necessities which it is impossible to disregard. Of what use is it to imagine a kind of education that would be fatal for the society that put it into practice?

This assumption, so doubtful, in itself rests on a more general mistake. If one begins by asking, thus, what an ideal education must be, abstracted from conditions of time and place, it is to admit implicitly that a system of education has no reality in itself. One does not see in education a collection of practices and institutions that have been organized slowly in the course of time, which are comparable with all the other social institutions and which express them, and which, therefore, can no more be changed at will than the structure of the society itself. But it seems that this would be a pure system of *a priori* concepts; under this heading it appears to be a logical construct. One imagines that men of each age organize it voluntarily to realize a determined end; that, if this organization is not everywhere the same, it is because mistakes have been made concerning either the end that it is to pursue or the means of attaining it. From this point of view, educational systems of the past appear as so many errors, total or partial. No attention need be paid to them, therefore; we do not have to associate ourselves with the faulty observation or logic of our predecessors; but we can and must pose the question without concerning ourselves with solutions that have been given, that is to say, leaving aside everything that has been, we have only to ask ourselves what should be. The lessons of history can, moreover, serve to prevent us from repeating the errors that have been committed.

In fact, however, each society, considered at a given stage of development, has a system of education which exercises an irresistible influence on individuals. It is idle to think that we can rear our children as we wish. There are customs to which we are bound to conform; if we flout them too severely, they take their vengeance on our children. The children, when they are adults, are unable to live with their peers, with whom they are not in accord. Whether they had been raised in accordance with ideas that were either obsolete or premature does not matter; in the one case as in the other, they are not of their time and, therefore, they are outside the conditions of normal life. There is, then, in each period, a prevailing type of education from which we cannot deviate without encountering that lively resistance which restrains the fancies of dissent.

Now, it is not we as individuals who have created the customs and ideas that determine this type. They are the product of a common life, and they express its needs. They are, moreover, in large part the work of preceding generations. The entire human past has contributed to the formation of this totality of maxims that guide education today; our entire history has left its traces in it, and even the history of the peoples who have come before. It is thus that the higher organisms carry in themselves the reflection of the whole biological evolution of which they are the end product. Historical investigation of the formation and development of systems of education reveals that they depend upon religion, political organization, the degree of development of science, the state of industry, etc. If they are considered apart from all these historic causes, they become incomprehensible. Thus, how can the individual pretend to reconstruct, through his own private reflection, what is not a work of individual thought? He is not confronted with a *tabula rasa* on which he can write what he wants, but with existing realities which he cannot create, or destroy, or transform, at will. He can act on them only to the extent that he has learned to understand them, to know their nature and the conditions on which they depend; and he can understand them only if he studies them, only if he starts by observing them, as the physicist observes inanimate matter and the biologist, living bodies.

Besides, how else to proceed? When one wants to determine by dialectics alone what education should be, it is necessary to begin by asking what objectives it must have. But what is it that allows us to say that education has certain ends rather than others? We do not know *a priori* what is the function of respiration or of circulation in a living being. By what right would we be more well informed concerning the educational function? It will be said in reply that from all the evidence, its object is the training of children. But this is posing the problem in slightly different terms; it does not resolve it. It would be necessary to say of what this training consists, what its direction is, what human needs it satisfies. Now, one can answer these questions only by beginning with observation of what it has consisted of, what needs it has satisfied in the past. Thus, it appears that to establish the preliminary notion of education, to determine what is so called, historical observation is indispensable.

2. DEFINITION OF EDUCATION.

To define education we must, then, consider, educational systems, present and past, put them together, and abstract the characteristics which are common to them. These characteristics will constitute the definition that we seek.

We have already determined, along the way, two elements. In order that there be education, there must be a generation of adults and one of youth, in interaction, and an influence exercised by the first on the second. It remains for us to define the nature of this influence.

There is, so to speak, no society in which the system of education does not present a twofold aspect; it is at the same time one and manifold.

It is manifold. Indeed, in one sense, it can be said that there are as many different kinds of education as there are different milieux in a given society. Is such a society formed of castes? Education varies from one caste to another; that of the patricians was not that of the plebeians; that of the Brahman was not that of the Sudra. Similarly, in the Middle Ages, what a difference between the culture that the young page received, instructed in all the arts of chivalry, and that of the villein, who learned in his parish school a smattering of arithmetic, song and grammar! Even today, do we not see education vary with social class, or even with locality? That of the city is not that of the country, that of the middle class is not that of the worker. Would one say that this organization is not morally justifiable, that one can see in it only a survival destined to disappear? This proposition is easy to defend. It is evident that the education of our children should not depend upon the chance of their having been born here or there, of some parents rather than others. But even though the moral conscience of our time would have received, on this point, the satisfaction that it expects, education would not, for all that,

become more uniform. Even though the career of each child would, in large part, no longer be predetermined by a blind heredity, occupational specialization would not fail to result in a great pedagogical diversity. Each occupation, indeed, constitutes a milieu *sui generis* which requires particular aptitudes and specialized knowledge, in which certain ideas, certain practices, certain modes of viewing things, prevail; and as the child must be prepared for the function that he will be called upon to fulfill, education, beyond a certain age, can no longer remain the same for all those to whom it applies. That is why we see it, in all civilized countries, tending more and more to become diversified and specialized; and the specialization becomes more advanced daily. The heterogeneity which is thus created does not rest, as does that which we were just discussing, on unjust inequalities; but it is not less. To find an absolutely homogeneous and egalitarian education, it would be necessary to go back to prehistoric societies, in the structure of which there is no differentiation; and yet these kinds of societies represent hardly more than one logical stage in the history of humanity.

But, whatever may be the importance of these special educations, they are not all of education. It may even be said that they are not sufficient unto themselves; everywhere that one observes them, they vary from one another only beyond a certain point, up to which they are not differentiated. They all rest upon a common base. There is no people among whom there is not a certain number of ideas, sentiments and practices which education must inculcate in all children indiscriminately, to whatever social category they belong. Even in a society which is divided into closed castes, there is always a religion common to all, and, consequently, the principles of the religious culture, which is, then, fundamental, are the same throughout the population. If each caste, each family, has its special gods, there are general divinities that are recognized by everyone and which all children learn to worship. And as these divinities symbolize and personify certain sentiments, certain ways of conceiving the world and life, one cannot be initiated into their cult without acquiring, at the same time, all sorts of thought patterns which go beyond the sphere of the purely religious life. Similarly, in the Middle Ages, serfs, villeins, burgers and nobles received, equally, a common Christian education. If it is thus in societies where intellectual and moral diversity reach this degree of contrast, with how much more reason is it so among more advanced peoples where classes, while remaining distinct, are, however, separated by a less profound cleavage! Where these common elements of all education are not expressed in the form of religious symbols, they do not, however, cease to exist. In the course of our history, there has been established a whole set of ideas on human nature, on the respective importance of our different faculties, on right and duty, on society, on the individual, on progress, on science, on art, etc., which are the very basis of our national spirit; all education, that of the rich as well as that of the poor, that which leads to professional careers as well as that which prepares for industrial functions, has as its object to fix them in our minds.

From these facts it follows that each society sets up a certain ideal of man, of what he should be, as much from the intellectual point of view as the physical and moral; that this ideal is, to a degree, the same for all the citizens; that beyond a certain point it becomes differentiated according to the particular milieux that every society contains in its structure. It is this ideal, at the same time one and various, that is the focus of education. Its function, then, is to arouse in the child: (1) a certain number of physical and mental states that the society to which he belongs considers should not be lacking in any of its members; (2) certain physical and mental states that the particular social group (caste, class, family, profession) considers, equally, ought to be found among all those who make it up. Thus, it is society as a whole and each particular social milieu that determine the ideal that education realizes. Society can survive only if there exists

among its members a sufficient degree of homogeneity; education perpetuates and reinforces this homogeneity by fixing in the child, from the beginning, the essential similarities that collective life demands. But on the other hand, without a certain diversity all co-operation would be impossible; education assures the persistence of this necessary diversity by being itself diversified and specialized. If the society has reached a degree of development such that the old divisions into castes and classes can no longer be maintained, it will prescribe an education more uniform at its base. If at the same time there is more division of labor, it will arouse among children, on the underlying basic set of common ideas and sentiments, a richer diversity of occupational aptitudes. If it lives in a state of war with the surrounding societies, it tries to shape people according to a strongly nationalistic model; if international competition takes a more peaceful form, the type that it tries to realize is more general and more humanistic. Education is, then, only the means by which society prepares, within the children, the essential conditions of its very existence. We shall see later how the individual himself has an interest in submitting to these requirements.

We come, then, to the following formula: *Education is the influence exercised by adult generations on those that are not yet ready for social life. Its object is to arouse and to develop in the child a certain number of physical, intellectual and moral states which are demanded of him by both the political society as a whole and the special milieu for which he is specifically destined.*

3. CONSEQUENCES OF THE PRECEDING DEFINITION: THE SOCIAL CHARACTER OF EDUCATION.

It follows from the definition that precedes, that education consists of a methodical socialization of the young generation. In each of us, it may be said, there exist two beings which, while inseparable except by abstraction, remain distinct. One is made up of all the mental states that apply only to ourselves and to the events of our personal lives: this is what might be called the individual being. The other is a system of ideas, sentiments and practices which express in us, not our personality, but the group or different groups of which we are part; these are religious beliefs, moral beliefs and practices, national or professional traditions, collective opinions of every kind. Their totality forms the social being. To constitute this being in each of us is the end of education.

It is here, moreover, that are best shown the importance of its role and the fruitfulness of its influence. Indeed, not only is this social being not given, fully formed, in the primitive constitution of man; but it has not resulted from it through a spontaneous development. Spontaneously, man was not inclined to submit to a political authority, to respect a moral discipline, to dedicate himself, to be self-sacrificing. There was nothing in our congenital nature that predisposed us necessarily to become servants of divinities, symbolic emblems of society, to render them worship, to deprive ourselves in order to do them honor. It is society itself which, to the degree that it is firmly established, has drawn from within itself those great moral forces in the face of which man has felt his inferiority. Now, if one leaves aside the vague and indefinite tendencies which can be attributed to heredity, the child, on entering life, brings to it only his nature as an individual. Society finds itself, with each new generation, faced with a *tabula rasa*, very nearly, on which it must build anew. To the egoistic and asocial being that has just been born it must, as rapidly as possible, add another, capable of leading a moral and social life. Such is the work of education, and you can readily see its great importance. It is not limited to developing the individual organism in the direction indicated by its nature, to elicit the hidden potentialities that need only be manifested. It creates in man a new being.

This creative quality is, moreover, a special prerogative of human education. Anything else is what animals receive, if one can apply this name to the progressive training to which they are subjected by their parents. It can, indeed, foster the development of certain instincts that lie dormant in the animal, but such training does not initiate it into a new life. It facilitates the play of natural functions, but it creates nothing. Taught by its mother, the young animal learns more quickly how to fly or build its nest; but it learns almost nothing that it could not have been able to discover through its own individual experience. This is because animals either do not live under social conditions or form rather simple societies, which function through instinctive mechanisms that each individual carries within himself, fully formed, from birth. Education, then, can add nothing essential to nature, since the latter is adequate for everything, for the life of the group as well as that of the individual. By contrast, among men the aptitudes of every kind that social life presupposes are much too complex to be able to be contained, somehow, in our tissues, and to take the form of organic predispositions. It follows that they cannot be transmitted from one generation to another by way of heredity. It is through education that the transmission is effected.

However, it will be said, if one can indeed conceive that the distinctively moral qualities, because they impose privations on the individual, because they inhibit his natural impulses, can be developed in us only under an outside influence, are there not others which every man wishes to acquire and seeks spontaneously? Such are the diverse qualities of the intelligence which allow him better to adapt his behavior to the nature of things. Such, too, are the physical qualities, and everything that contributes to the vigor and health of the organism. For the former, at least, it seems that education, in developing them, may only assist the development of nature itself, may only lead the individual to a state of relative perfection toward which he tends by himself, although he may be able to achieve it more rapidly thanks to the co-operation of society.

But what demonstrates, despite appearances, that here as elsewhere education answers social necessities above all, is that there are societies in which these qualities have not been cultivated at all, and that in every case they have been understood very differently in different societies. The advantages of a solid intellectual culture have been far from recognized by all peoples. Science and the critical mind, that we rank so high today, were for a long time held in suspicion. Do we not know a great doctrine that proclaims happy the poor in spirit? We must guard against believing that this indifference to knowledge had been artificially imposed on men in violation of their nature. They do not have, by themselves, the instinctive appetite for science that has often and arbitrarily been attributed to them. They desire science only to the extent that experience has taught them that they cannot do without it. Now, in connection with the ordering of their individual lives they had no use for it. As Rousseau has already said, to satisfy the vital necessities, sensation, experience and instinct would suffice as they suffice for the animal. If man had not known other needs than these, very simple ones, which have their roots in his individual constitution, he would not have undertaken the pursuit of science, all the more because it has not been acquired without laborious and painful efforts. He has known the thirst for knowledge only when society has awakened it in him, and society has done this only when it has felt the need of it. This moment came when social life, in all its forms, had become too complex to be able to function otherwise than through the co-operation of reflective thought, that is to say, thought enlightened by science. Then scientific culture became indispensable, and that is why society requires it of its members and imposes it upon them as a duty. But in the beginning, as long as social organization is very simple and undifferentiated, always self-sufficient, blind tradition suffices, as does instinct in the animal. Therefore thought and free inquiry are useless and even dangerous, since they can only threaten tradition. That is why they are proscribed.

It is not otherwise with physical qualities. Where the state of the social milieu inclines pub-lic sentiment toward asceticism, physical education will be relegated to a secondary place. Something of this sort took place in the schools of the Middle Ages; and this asceticism was necessary, for the only manner of adapting to the harshness of those difficult times was to like it. Similarly, following the current of opinion, this same education will be understood very differently. In Sparta its object above all was to harden the limbs to fatigue; in Athens, it was a means of making bodies beautiful to the sight; in the time of chivalry it was required to form agile and supple warriors; today it no longer has any but a hygienic end, and is concerned, above all, with limiting the dangerous effects of a too intense intellectual culture. Thus, even the qualities which appear at first glance so spontaneously desirable, the individual seeks only when society invites him to, and he seeks them in the fashion that it prescribes for him.

We are not in a position to answer a question raised by all that precedes. Whereas we showed society fashioning individuals according to its needs, it could seem, from this fact, that the individuals were submitting to an insupportable tyranny. But in reality they are themselves interested in this submission; for the new being that collective influence, through education, thus builds up in each of us, represents what is best in us. Man is man, in fact, only because he lives in society. It is difficult, in the course of an article, to demonstrate rigorously a proposition so general and so important, and one which sums up the works of contemporary sociology. But first, one can say that it is less and less disputed. And more, it is not impossible to call to mind, summarily, the most essential facts that justify it.

First, if there is today an historically established fact, it is that morality stands in close relationship to the nature of societies, since, as we have shown along the way, it changes when societies change. This is because it results from life in common. It is society, indeed, that draws us out of ourselves, that obliges us to reckon with other interests than our own, it is society that has taught us to control our passions, our instincts, to prescribe law for them, to restrain ourselves, to deprive ourselves, to sacrifice ourselves, to subordinate our personal ends to higher ends. As for the whole system of representation which maintains in us the idea and the sentiment of rule, of discipline, internal as well as external—it is society that has established it in our consciences. It is thus that we have acquired this power to control ourselves, this control over our inclinations which is one of the distinctive traits of the human being and which is the more developed to the extent that we are more fully human.

We do not owe society less from the intellectual point of view. It is science that elaborates the cardinal notions that govern our thought: notions of cause, of laws, of space, of number, notions of bodies, of life, of conscience, of society, and so on. All these fundamental ideas are perpetually evolving, because they are the recapitulation, the resultant of all scientific work, far from being its point of departure as Pestalozzi believed. We do not conceive of man, nature, cause, even space, as they were conceived in the Middle Ages; this is because our knowledge and our scientific methods are no longer the same. Now, science is a collective work, since it presupposes a vast co-operation of all scientists, not only of the same time, but of all the successive epochs of history. Before the sciences were established, religion filled the same office; for every mythology consists of a conception, already well elaborated, of man and of the universe. Science, moreover, was the heir of religion. Now, a religion is a social institution.

In learning a language, we learn a whole system of ideas, distinguished and classified, and we inherit from all the work from which have come these classifications that sum up centuries of experiences. There is more: without language, we would not have, so to speak, general ideas; for it is the word which, in fixing them, gives to concepts a consistency sufficient for them to be able to be handled conveniently by the mind. It is language, then, that has allowed us to raise ourselves above pure sensation; and it is not necessary to demonstrate that language is, in the first degree, a social thing.

One sees, through these few examples, to what man would be reduced if there were withdrawn from him all that he has derived from society: he would fall to the level of an animal. If he has been able to surpass the stage at which animals have stopped, it is primarily because he is not reduced to the fruit only of his personal efforts, but cooperates regularly with his fellow-creatures; and this makes the activity of each more productive. It is chiefly as a result of this that the products of the work of one generation are not lost for that which follows. Of what an animal has been able to learn in the course of his individual existence, almost nothing can survive him. By contrast, the results of human experience are preserved almost entirely and in detail, thanks to books, sculptures, tools, instruments of every kind that are transmitted from generation to generation, oral tradition, etc. The soil of nature is thus covered with a rich deposit that continues to grow constantly. Instead of dissipating each time that a generation dies out and is replaced by another, human wisdom accumulates without limit, and it is this unlimited accumulation that raises man above the beast and above himself. But, just as in the case of the cooperation which was discussed first, this accumulation is possible only in and through society. For in order that the legacy of each generation may be able to be preserved and added to others, it is necessary that there be a moral personality which lasts beyond the generations that pass, which binds them to one another: it is society. Thus the antagonism that has too often been admitted between society and individual corresponds to nothing in the facts. Indeed, far from these two terms being in opposition and being able to develop only each at the expense of the other, they imply each other. The individual, in willing society, wills himself. The influence that it exerts on him, notable through education, does not at all have as its object and its effect to repress him, to diminish him, to denature him, but, on the contrary, to make him grow and to make of him a truly human being. No doubt, he can grow thus only by making an effort. But this is precisely because this power to put forth voluntary effort is one of the most essential characteristics of man.

4. THE ROLE OF THE STATE IN EDUCATION

This definition of education provides for a ready solution of the controversial question of the duties and the rights of the State with respect to education.

The rights of the family are opposed to them. The child, it is said, belongs first to his parents; it is, then, their responsibility to direct, as they understand it, his intellectual and moral development. Education is then conceived as an essentially private and domestic affair. When one takes this point of view, one tends naturally to reduce to a minimum the intervention of the State in the matter. The State should, it is said, be limited to serving as an auxiliary to, and as a substitute for, families. When they are unable to discharge their duties, it is natural that the State should take charge. It is natural, too, that it make their task as easy as possible, by placing at their disposal schools to which they can, if they wish, send their children. But it must be kept strictly within these limits, and forbidden any positive action designed to impress a given orientation on the mind of the youth.

But its role need hardly remain so negative. If, as we have tried to establish, education has a collective function above all, if its object is to adapt the child to the social milieu in which he is destined to live, it is impossible that society should be uninterested in such a procedure. How could society not have a part in it, since it is the reference point by which education must direct its action? It is, then, up to the State to remind the teacher constantly of the ideas, the sentiments that must be impressed upon the child to adjust him to the milieu in which he must live. If it were not always there to guarantee that pedagogical influence be exercised in a social way, the latter would necessarily be put to the service of private beliefs, and the whole nation would be divided and would break down into an incoherent multitude of little fragments in conflict with one another. One could not contradict more completely the fundamental end of all education. Choice is necessary: if one attaches some value to the existence of society—and we have just seen what it means to us—education must assure, among the citizens, a sufficient community of ideas and of sentiments, without which any society is impossible; and in order that it may be able to produce this result, it is also necessary that education not be completely abandoned to the arbitrariness of private individuals.

Since education is an essentially social function, the State cannot be indifferent to it. On the contrary, everything that pertains to education must in some degree be submitted to its influence. This is not to say, therefore, that it must necessarily monopolize instruction. The question is too complex to be able to be treated thus in passing; we shall discuss it later. One can believe that scholastic progress is easier and quicker where a certain margin is left for individual initiative; for the individual makes innovations more readily than the State. But from the fact that the State, in the public interest, must allow other schools to be opened than those for which it has a more direct responsibility, it does not follow that it must remain aloof from what is going on in them. On the contrary, the education given in them must remain under its control. It is not even admissible that the function of the educator can be fulfilled by anyone who does not offer special guarantees of which the State alone can be the judge. No doubt, the limits within which its intervention should be kept may be rather difficult to determine once and for all, but the principle of intervention could not be disputed. There is no school which can claim the right to give, with full freedom, an antisocial education.

It is nevertheless necessary to recognize that the state of division in which we now find ourselves, in our country, makes this duty of the State particularly delicate and at the same time more important. It is not, indeed, up to the State to create this community of ideas and sentiments without which there is no society; it must be established by itself, and the State can only consecrate it, maintain it, make individuals more aware of it. Now, it is unfortunately indisputable that among us, this moral unity is not at all points what it should be. We are divided by divergent and even sometimes contradictory conceptions. There is in these divergences a fact which it is impossible to deny, and which must be reckoned with. It is not a question of recognizing the right of the majority to impose its ideas on the children of the minority. The school should not be the thing of one party, and the teacher is remiss in his duties when he uses the authority at his disposal to influence his pupils in accordance with his own preconceived opinions, however justified they may appear to him. But in spite of all the differences of opinion, there are at present, at the basis of our civilization, a certain number of principles which, implicitly or explicitly, are common to all, that few indeed, in any case, dare to deny overtly and openly: respect for reason, for science, for ideas and sentiments which are at the base of democratic morality. The role of the State is to outline these essential principles, to have them taught in its schools, to see to it that nowhere are children left ignorant of them, that everywhere they should be spoken of with the respect which is due them. There is in this connection an influence to exert which will perhaps be all the more efficacious when it will be less aggressive and less violent, and will know better how to be contained within wise limits.

5.   THE POWER OF EDUCATION. THE MEANS OF INFLUENCE

After having determined the end of education, we must seek to determine how and to what extent it is possible to attain this end, that is to say, how and to what extent education can be efficacious.

This question has always been very controversial. For Fontenelle, "neither does good education make good character, nor does bad education destroy it." By contrast, for Locke, for Helvetius, education is all-powerful. According to the latter, "all men are born equal and with equal aptitudes; education alone makes for differences." The theory of Jacotot resembles the preceding.

The solution that one gives to the problem depends on the idea that one has of the importance and of the nature of the innate predispositions, on the one hand, and, on the other, of the means of influence at the disposal of the educator.

Education does not make a man out of nothing, as Locke and Helvetius believed; it is applied to predispositions that it finds already made. From another point of view, one can concede, in a general way, that these congenital tendencies are very strong, very difficult to destroy or to transform radically; for they depend upon organic conditions on which the educator has little influence. Consequently, to the degree that they have a definite object, that they incline the mind and the character toward narrowly determined ways of acting and thinking, the whole future of the individual finds itself fixed in advance, and there does not remain much for education to do.

But fortunately one of the characteristics of man is that the innate predispositions in him are very general and very vague. Indeed, the type of predisposition that is fixed, rigid, invariable, which hardly leaves room for the influence of external causes, is instinct. Now, one can ask if there is a single instinct, properly speaking, in man. One speaks, sometimes, of the instinct of preservation; but the word is inappropriate. For an instinct is a system of given actions, always the same, which, once they are set in motion by sensation, are automatically linked up with one another until they reach their natural limit, without reflection having to intervene anywhere; now, the movements that we make when our life is in danger do not all have any such fixity or automatic invariability. They change with the situation; we adapt them to circumstances: this is because they do not operate without a certain conscious choice, however rapid. What is called the instinct of preservation is, after all, only a general impulse to flee death, without the means by which we seek to avoid it being predetermined once and for all. One can say as much concerning what is sometimes called, not less inexactly, the maternal instinct, the paternal instinct, and even the sexual instinct. These are drives in a given direction; but the means by which these drives are expressed vary from one individual to another, from one occasion to another. A large area remains reserved, then, for trial and error, for personal accommodations, and, consequently, for the effect of causes which can make their influence felt only after birth. Now, education is one of these causes.

It has been claimed, to be sure, that the child sometimes inherits a very strong tendency toward a given act, such as suicide, theft, murder, fraud, etc. But these assertions are not at all in accord with the facts. Whatever may have been said about it, one is not born criminal; still less is one destined from birth for this or that type of crime; the paradox of the Italian criminologists no longer counts many defenders today. What is inherited is a certain lack of mental equilibrium, which makes the individual refractory to coherent and disciplined behavior. But such a temperament does not predestine a man to be a criminal any more than to be an explorer seeking adventure, a prophet, a political innovator, an inventor, etc. As much can be said of any occupational aptitudes. As Bain remarked, "the son of a great philologist does not inherit a single word; the son of a great traveler can, at school, be surpassed in geography by the son of a miner." What the child receives from his parents are very general faculties; some force of attention, a certain amount of perseverance, a sound judgment, imagination, etc. But each of these faculties can serve all sorts of different ends. A child endowed

with a rather lively imagination will be able, depending on circumstances, on the influences that will be brought to bear upon him, to become a painter or a poet, or an engineer with an inventive mind, or a daring financier. There is, then, a considerable difference between natural qualities and the special forms that they must take to be utilized in life. This means that the future is not strictly predetermined by our congenital constitution. The reason for this is easy to understand. The only forms of activity that can be transmitted by heredity are those which are always repeated in a sufficiently identical manner to be able to be fixed, in a rigid form, in the tissues of the organism. Now, human life depends on conditions that are manifold, complex, and, consequently, changing; it must itself, then, change and be modified continuously. Thus it is impossible for it to become crystallized in a definite and positive form. But only very general, very vague dispositions, expressing the characteristics common to all individual experiences, can survive and pass from one generation to another.

To say that innate characteristics are for the most part very general, is to say that they are very malleable, very flexible, since they can assume very different forms. Between the vague potentialities which constitute man at the moment of birth and the well-defined character that he must become in order to play a useful role in society, the distance is, then, considerable. It is this distance that education has to make the child travel. One sees that a vast field is open to its influence.

But, to exert this influence, does it have adequate means?

In order to give an idea of what constitutes the educational influence, and to show its power, a contemporary psychologist, Guyau, has compared it to hypnotic suggestion; and the comparison is not without foundation.

Hypnotic suggestion presupposes, indeed, the following two conditions: (1) The state in which the hypnotized subject is found is characterized by its exceptional passivity. The mind is almost reduced to the state of a *tabula rasa;* a sort of void has been achieved in his consciousness; the will is as though paralyzed. Thus, the idea suggested, meeting no contrary idea at all, can be established with a minimum of resistance; (2) however, as the void is never complete, it is necessary, further, that the idea take from the suggestion itself some power of specific action. For that, it is necessary that the hypnotizer speak in a commanding tone, with authority. He must say: *I wish;* he must indicate that refusal to obey is not even conceivable, that the act must be accomplished, that the thing must be seen as he shows it, that it cannot be otherwise. If he weakens, one sees the subject hesitate, resist, sometimes even refuse to obey. If he so much as enters into discussion, that is the end of his power. The more suggestion goes against the natural temperament of the subject, the more will the imperative tone be indispensable.

Now, these two conditions are present in the relationship that the educator has with the child subjected to his influence: (1) The child is naturally in a state of passivity quite comparable to that in which the hypnotic subject is found artificially placed. His mind yet contains only a small number of conceptions able to fight against those which are suggested to him; his will is still rudimentary. Therefore he is very suggestible. For the same reason he is very susceptible to the force of example, very much inclined to imitation. (2) The ascendancy that the teacher naturally has over his pupil, because of the superiority of his experience and of this culture, will naturally give to his influence the efficacious force that he needs.

This comparison shows how far from helpless the educator is; for the great power of hypnotic suggestion is known. If, then, educational influence has, even in a lesser degree, an analogous efficacy, much may be expected of it, provided that one knows how to use it. Far from being discouraged by our impotence, we might well, rather, be frightened by the scope of our power. If teacher and parents were more consistently

aware that nothing can happen in the child's presence which does not leave some trace in him, that the form of his mind and of his character depends on these thousands of little unconscious influences that take place at every moment and to which we pay no attention because of their apparent insignificance, how much more would they watch their language and their behavior! Surely, education cannot be very effective when it functions inconsistently. As Herbart says, it is not by reprimanding the child violently from time to time that one can influence him very much. But when education is patient and continuous, when it does not look for immediate and obvious successes, but proceeds slowly in a well-defined direction, without letting itself be diverted by external incidents and adventitious circumstances, it has at its disposal all the means necessary to affect minds profoundly.

At the same time, one sees what is the essential means of educational influence. What makes for the influence of the hypnotist is the authority which he holds under the circumstances. By analogy, then, one can say that education must be essentially a matter of authority. This important proposition can, moreover, be established directly. Indeed, we have seen that the object of education is to superimpose, on the individual and asocial being that we are at birth, an entirely new being. It must bring us to overcome our initial nature; it is on this condition that the child will become a man. Now, we can raise ourselves above ourselves only by a more or less difficult effort. Nothing is so false and deceptive as the Epicurean conception of education, the conception of a Montaigne, for example, according to which man can be formed while enjoying himself and without any other spur than the attraction of pleasure. If there is nothing somber in life and if it is criminal artificially to make it so in the eyes of the child, it is, however, serious and important; and education, which prepares for life, should share this seriousness. To learn to contain his natural egoism, to subordinate himself to higher ends, to submit his desires to the control of his will, to confine them within proper limits, the child must exercise strong self-control. Now, we restrain ourselves, we limit ourselves, only for one or the other of the following two reasons: because it is necessary through some physical necessity, or because we must do it on moral grounds. But the child cannot feel the necessity that imposes these efforts on us physically, for he is not faced directly with the hard realities of life which make this attitude indispensable. He is not yet engaged in the struggle; whatever Spencer may have said about it, we cannot leave him exposed to these too harsh realities. It is necessary, then, that he be already formed, in large part, when he really encounters them. One cannot, then, depend on their influence to make him bow his will and acquire the necessary mastery over himself.

Duty remains. The sense of duty is, indeed, for the child and even for the adult, the stimulus *par excellence* of effort. Self-respect itself pre-supposes it. For, to be properly affected by reward and punishment, one must already have a sense of his dignity and, consequently, of his duty. But the child can know his duty only through his teachers or his parents; he can know what it is only through the manner in which they reveal it to him through their language and through their conduct. They must be, then, for him, duty incarnate and personified. Thus moral authority is the dominant quality of the educator. For it is through the authority that is in him that duty is duty. What is his own special quality is the imperative tone with which he addresses consciences, the respect that he inspires in wills and which makes them yield to his judgment. Thus it is indispensable that such an impression emanate from the person of the teacher.

It is not necessary to show that authority, thus understood, is neither violent nor repressive; it consists entirely of a certain moral ascendancy. It presupposes the presence in the teacher of two principal conditions. First, he must have will. For authority implies confidence, and the child can-not have confidence in anyone whom he sees hesitating, shifting, going back on his decision. But this first condition is not the most essential. What is important above all is that the teacher really feels in himself the authority, the feeling for which he is to transmit. It constitutes a force which he can manifest only if he possesses it effectively. Now, where does he get it from? Would it be from the power which he does have, from his right to reward and punish? But fear of chastisement is quite different from respect for authority. It has moral value only if chastisement is recognized as just even by him who suffers it, which implies that the authority which punishes is already recognized as legitimate. And this is the question. It is not from the outside that the teacher can hold his authority, it is from himself; it can come to him only from an inner faith. He must believe, not in himself, no doubt, not in the superior qualities of his intelligence or of his soul, but in his task and in the importance of his task. What makes for the authority which is so readily attached to the word of the priest, is the high idea that he has of his calling; for he speaks in the name of a god in whom he believes, to whom he feels himself closer than the crowd of the uninitiated. The lay teacher can and should have something of this feeling. He too is the agent of a great moral person who surpasses him: it is society. Just as the priest is the interpreter of his god, the teacher is the interpreter of the great moral ideas of his time and of his country. Let him be attached to these ideas, let him feel all their grandeur, and the authority which is in them, and of which he is aware, cannot fail to be communicated to his person and to everything that emanates from him. Into an authority which flows from such an impersonal source there could enter no pride, no vanity, no pedantry. It is made up entirely of the respect which he has for his functions and, if one may say so, for his office. It is this respect which, through word and gesture, passes from him to the child.

Liberty and authority have sometimes been opposed, as if these two factors of education contradicted and limited each other. But this opposition is factitious. In reality these two terms imply, rather than exclude, each other. Liberty is the daughter of authority properly understood. For to be free is not to do what one pleases; it is to be master of oneself, it is to know how to act with reason and to do one's duty. Now, it is precisely to endow the child with this self-mastery that the authority of the teacher should be employed. The authority of the teacher is only one aspect of the authority of duty and of reason. The child should, then, be trained to recognize it in the speech of the educator and to submit to its ascendancy; it is on this condition that he will know later how to find it again in his own conscience and to defer to it.

The Functionalist Perspective on Schooling

WALTER FEINBERG AND JONAS SOLTIS

FUNCTIONALISM

Functionalism is a general theoretical orientation about how social events and institutions are to be viewed. It is an orientation that has been especially prominent in the fields of anthropology (the study of culture) and sociology (the study of society). Its basic insight, however, is drawn from the field of biology. Functionalists note that the various systems of a biological organism serve different survival functions. In mammals, for example, the stomach, small intestine, and other organs digest food, while the heart pumps blood, thereby bringing oxygen from the lungs to different parts of the body. There are other organs that remove waste and still others that function in the reproduction process. Other species, such as fish, may have organs that are structured quite differently but serve the same survival needs. Carrying this insight from the biological to the social sphere, functionalists argue that if we want to understand a certain social practice or institution, we must consider the way in which it serves to further the survival of the social system as a whole. For example, if we want to understand the role that mass, compulsory schooling serves in contemporary society, we would be advised to explore the social needs it serves and the ways it works to meet those needs. For the functionalist, there is a similar kind of explanation for such seemingly different questions as why certain animal species kill some of their newborn, why different species of fireflies display different coded lights, why physicians have high incomes, and

why schools use standardized IQ tests. The point is that each question is answered in terms of some basic survival need that is being served.

Just as the different parts and behaviors of an organism can be understood in terms of the function they serve in meeting the needs of survival, so, too, the functionalist argues, can the practices and the institutions of a society be explained in terms of meeting certain social survival needs. Because different environments require different responses, the way in which such needs are met may differ. However, an adequate understanding of a social institution or a practice must be grounded in an understanding of the need that it functions to serve and the way that it does so. Thus, functionalists tend to look at social institutions and practices in terms of their contribution to the adaptation and adjustment of the total social system.

Consider the selection, training, and rewarding of physicians and teachers in our society. From a functionalist point of view we would seem to need both to survive, but how might we explain the large differences in income, status, and prestige that exist between doctors and teachers? A functionalist explanation would go something like this: There are many tasks in a society that a large number of people can perform, and so a large wage is not required to

Source: "The Functionalist Perspective on Schooling" from *School and Society*, by Walter Feinberg and Jonas Soltis, copyright 1985. Reprinted by permission of Teachers College Press.

encourage people to undertake these tasks. However, there are some needs in modern society that can be served only by the special talents of a relatively few people. The practice of medicine is one of these, and the development of this talent requires many years of training and education. Therefore, as encouragement for talented people to undertake this special sacrifice, society provides extra incentives. Higher income and enhanced status are society's ways of providing such incentives and of ensuring that these specialized needs are met. As long as many more people have the talent to become teachers than to become doctors, then the difference in status and income will remain.

In a similar way, functionalists argue that all societies require that their members perform different tasks. Selection, socialization, and training processes are needed to assure that jobs, even unpleasant or demanding ones, get done. Even in primitive societies, role differentiation will be found as some members hunt, others gather, and still others prepare food. In primitive societies, however, role differentiation is not intense, and one member's contribution to the society can often be seen by all other members. Because contributions made by different people performing different roles are visible to all and everyone participates in the tribal rituals, the group develops a shared value system and cognitive orientation; thus their sense of group solidarity is maintained.

For the functionalists, *role differentiation* and *social solidarity* are the two primary requirements of social life. They must be present in primitive and modern societies alike. In primitive societies these requirements can be met through the informal education that occurs within the family and the community. In highly complex, modern societies, however, where roles change from one generation to the next, a more formal structure is required to assure that the education of the young takes place and that role differentiation and group solidarity are achieved. A system of universal, compulsory, public education is established to accomplish this. Compulsory edu-

cation is also able to assure that older, dysfunctional habits, attitudes, and loyalties are replaced by newer, more functional ones. Compulsory education facilitates the development of new skills that the continuous expansion of technology requires. Just think, for example, of the changes being wrought in our society and our schools today by the advent of computers.

From the functionalist point of view, universal compulsory education is closely related to the requirements of industrial society. Schools perform in a formal way those basic tasks that simpler societies are able to perform informally through the ongoing activity of the family, the community, or the tribe. For example, in most traditional societies, children learn to work by watching their parents and other adults working and by participating in that work at increasing levels of responsibility. In modern societies, children have little opportunity to watch their parents work, and schools must now teach many of the requisite skills and attitudes.

This brings us to another feature that is often associated with functionalism. This feature is a stage theory that is used to explain the "development" from simple, traditional social structures to more complex, modern ones. Functionalists who accept a stage theory believe that the movement from traditional to modern society can be explained in terms of different kinds of functional integration. Wilber Moore, in his summary of functionalism, describes one widely accepted model as follows:

> Stage one is the functionally integrated and therefore relatively static traditional society; stage two comprises the transitional process of structural alteration in the direction of modernity; stage three is the functionally integrated fully . . . modernized society.

This extension of functionalism has sparked considerable debate both inside and outside of the functionalist camp. Some argue that a stage theory is too ambitious. There is not just one pattern of development that holds for all societies, nor possibly should all societies become "modernized." Others note that the image presented of modern society as essentially democratic and free justifies morally questionable attempts to change the nature of traditional societies. Nevertheless, while stage theory has not been fully accepted by all functionalists, it has been an important feature of the work of some of its major advocates. Moreover, it has had significant influence on matters of educational policy in Third World countries.

Those who accept a stage theory of development are often quite explicit in proclaiming the benefits of modern societies over traditional ones. In their view modern societies are able to satisfy more needs for more people, and compulsory schooling is seen as an essential part of this process. School provides the role differentiation and solidarity that in most traditional societies are developed through other means. In traditional societies individuals have little chance to advance beyond the station into which they were born. Training for positions of leadership is only available to those with the appropriate birthright. In contemporary industrial society schools replace parental status as the principal selection mechanism. Moreover, they provide the training appropriate for participation in the social order at a certain level. Many functionalists argue that modern schools perform these tasks in a much more efficient, fair, and humane way than they have been performed in societies without a system of universal, compulsory education.

Many functionalists believe that schools are the essential transformation mechanism between life in the family and life as an adult in a modern, urban, industrial society. One of the most succinct descriptions of this functionalist view of schooling is provided by Robert Dreeben in *On What Is Learned in School*. Dreeben argues that schoolchildren learn to function according to the norms that are appropriate to economic and political life in the modern world. Norms are standards used to govern one's conduct in appropriate situations. Dreeben observes that such

learning not only derives from the subject matter that is explicitly taught in the school but also happens as children begin to function according to the organizational patterns that are a fundamental part of school life. In this latter case, it is the *ways* things are taught, rather than *what* is taught, that enable such norms to be learned. According to Dreeben, four key norms are learned in school as a youngster passes from the lower to the higher grades and from membership in the family to membership in the society. He calls these norms "independence," "achievement," "universalism," and "specificity." He believes that they can only be taught effectively and on a large scale in schools.

The norm of *independence* refers to the learning that occurs when children come to take responsibility for their own action and to acknowledge that others have a right to hold them accountable for such action. Schoolchildren learn this norm through such things as sanctions against cheating and plagiarism. These sanctions prepare students for adult life and for the kind of occupations that will require them to take on individual responsibility. The adoption of this norm teaches children to be personally accountable for their own performance. Learning the norm of *achievement* is learning that one will be judged by one's performance and not, for example, by one's effort or good intentions. Students also learn to judge their own performance against that of others. Here some students must learn to cope with failure and to acknowledge the greater skills of others in certain areas of performance.

The norms of *universalism* and *specificity* refer to the treatment of a person in terms of some standardized basis of comparison. For example, for certain purposes, all first graders (specificity) are considered appropriate to compare with one another (a universal group). These norms are reflected in the schools in many different ways. For example, when a child's request for an excuse for a late assignment is met with the response, "If I make an exception for you, I will have to make one for everyone else," the norm of universalism is being expressed. If the teacher says, "John is a member of the basketball team and so is excused from tonight's assignment because of the game," the norm of specificity is being invoked.

Universalism, according to Dreeben, refers to the uniform treatment of individuals as members of one or more specific categories, for example, team members, bus students, or graduating seniors. The important point about learning to accept the norm of universalism is that, in doing so, one becomes willing in certain circumstances to put aside one's individuality and be treated as a member of a group. Universalism requires the same treatment for all. For instance, all team members may be required to attend all practice sessions. *Specificity* allows for exceptions to be made. The coach may excuse a team member from practice because the player observes a religious holiday not observed by others on the team. *Particularism* makes illegitimate exceptions. If the coach gives special advantage to one youngster because he happens to be the child of a fellow teacher, we have an instance of particularism. The norm of specificity is related to that of universalism. It speaks to our obligation to treat people similarly only on the basis of the specific categories that are relevant to the task at hand. Students learn that exceptions can be made only if they are made on legitimate grounds. For some activities the number of relevant categories for specificity may be quite large. For example, the elementary school teacher may find age, ability, maturity, and family stability to be relevant. The high school teacher may only consider performance in one subject to be relevant.

The four norms may or may not be taught in the family as well as in the school. When such norms are taught in the family, however, there is a difference. Unlike the family, Dreeben observes, the school provides youngsters with a group of peers against whose performances their own individual performance can be judged. In school youngsters are grouped together according to age, and this provides them with a visible point against which to compare their own independence and achievement. Comparison with others as peers is also basic to learning the norms of universalism and specificity, and many such opportunities present themselves in school.

As a functionalist, Dreeben believes that the four norms of independence, achievement, universalism, and specificity are precisely those that are required to act as a worker and a citizen in contemporary industrial society. By learning to accept the four norms that are transmitted through participation in school life, students develop the "psychological capacities that enable them to participate in the major institutional areas of society, to occupy the component social positions of these areas, and to cope with the demands and exploit the opportunities that these positions characteristically present."

EQUALITY OF EDUCATIONAL OPPORTUNITY

You can see the influence of these norms, which you may have learned in school, by observing your own reaction to the following fictional advertisement: "Wanted, white Christian male, Ivy League graduate, for managerial work in a major marketing firm. Excellent opportunities for advancement."

There was a time when advertisements similar to this were not unusual, and many ethnic groups have stories about such overt discrimination. Today such an advertisement would clearly demand attention. It violates many people's sense of fairness (as well as the laws against discrimination) because it stipulates qualifications that seem to be irrelevant for successful performance in the position. Dreeben and other functionalists believe that the unfavorable reaction that would likely greet an advertisement of this kind can be attributed to the role that schools have played in developing the psychological attitudes that a commitment to the norms of universalism and achievement entails. We have become used to expecting that rewards will be granted on the basis of achievement and merit. Thus, the norms developed in school are related to an important ethical principle that is associated with contemporary industrial societies—the principle of equal opportunity.

The idea of equal opportunity means that individuals are to be chosen for certain roles and rewarded on the basis of *achieved*, rather than *ascribed*, characteristics. An ascribed characteristic is one that belongs to a person by virtue of his or her birth and background. Wherever political office, income, or rights are determined on the basis of family background alone, then we have a situation in which rewards are distributed according to ascribed qualities. When factors that are irrelevant to the task at hand are discounted, and a person is rewarded according to performance or to qualities that signal a promise for high-level performance, then we have a situation in which rewards are distributed according to achieved qualities. In most instances people will identify social-class background, race, religion, and sex as irrelevant, ascribed characteristics, and they will identify talent, ability, and motivation as relevant, achieved ones.

Functionalists give three reasons for the movement from ascribed to achieved rewards in modern societies. First, it is thought that the ever-expanding skills required by industrial society often render obsolete the skills passed on by the family or the local community. Thus, to reward qualities that have been passed on from one generation to the next may well be to retard the development of the new knowledge and skills required to meet modern needs. Second, the expanding need for new skills requires that opportunities be opened to talented people from groups that have traditionally been denied them. Third, political stability requires that those who have not been rewarded, as well as those who have, believe that they competed under a fair system of rules. Thus, the ideal of equal opportunity is thought to be not only ethically sound but also consistent with the requirements of stability in modern society.

It should be recalled that the transition from the personal life of the family to modern bureaucratic life described by the functionalists does not necessarily take place on the conscious level. If we ask teachers what they are doing at any particular moment, they are likely to answer in very specific ways, with such typical responses as "I am teaching spelling" or "I am working with the children on fractions." Seldom will teachers respond with comments like "I am teaching my students to judge themselves and others according to relevant categories" or "I am teaching them how to function in bureaucracies." Yet, according to the functionalists, this is precisely what is being accomplished. The interesting question to ask and answer is "How?"

The idea of the "hidden curriculum" has been one of the concepts that has been used to explain the school's role in making possible the transition from life in the family to a life of work and citizenship. The hidden curriculum refers to the organizational features and routines of school life that provide the structure needed to develop the psychological dispositions appropriate for work and citizenship in industrial society. The waiting in line, the vying for the teacher's attention, the sanctions against "cheating," the scheduling of activities according to the demands of the clock, all contribute to the development of behavior required by modern institutions. The student learns to channel and control impulses according to the institutionally approved patterns of behavior.

EDUCATIONAL REFORM: THREE CASES

Functionalism has served as more than just a scientific theory used to understand the role that schools and other institutions play in society. It has also served as a theoretical guide for people interested in the reform and improvement of modern society. In other words, it has served as both the scientific foundation and the justification for many different kinds of educational reform in the twentieth century. The use of functionalism by educational reformers is quite understandable. Once it is recognized that modern schooling is required to meet the needs of contemporary society, then it is quite a natural step to try to identify the precise nature of those needs and to mold educational policy to try to meet them more effectively. Much of educational reform has been built on the functionalist view that schools serve to help people adapt to the changing life of modern society. When adaptation becomes a problem and dysfunction results, it is quite reasonable for some people to think of schooling as a way to correct it. We can illustrate the connection between functionalism and educational reform by considering some imaginary cases.

First, imagine that you are not only a functionalist but also the head of state of a nation that just gained independence from a colonial power. The state you govern contains two tribes that are relatively equal in size and power. However, these major tribal groups have had a history of antagonism toward one another, and it was only resistance to the external colonial power that brought them together as a unified force. As leader of the new country, you are aware that within twenty years the northern tribal group will suffer a drought because the neighboring country is damming and diverting the river that flows first through its territory. You also know that only the food resources of the southern tribe will enable the north to avoid catastrophe. If the catastrophe is avoided, the northern tribal province should flourish and contribute much to the wealth of the entire nation. The difficulty that must be faced, however, is that present tribal loyalties would never allow the needed transfer of resources to take place. Without this transfer, the catastrophe cannot be avoided. Given this situation, it is decided that the only hope is to begin to shift personal loyalty from the tribal group to the nation. In order to do this, you begin to develop a public system of education and to offer special incentives for attendance. You mandate that the curriculum of the school will stress national purposes rather than tribal ones, and the most successful students will be offered the opportunity to attend the national, multitribal university and to take up leadership positions in the government. What else might you do?

Here is a second situation. Again imagine that you are a governmental leader in a society where the largest part of the population is in the agricultural sector. For the last three decades, however, there has been a decided movement toward urban areas. At the same time that factory production is becoming mechanized, so, too, is agricultural production. Because factory work is expanding rapidly, there is a need for more urban workers. On the farm, because of mechanization, fewer people are needed to produce more and more basic food products and fiber. However, as this urban migration is occurring, it is noticed that many of the basic work and sanitation habits that were appropriate for the farm are continuing in the city, even though they are no longer functional. For many of the new city dwellers, for example, money management is a problem. On the farm, basic needs could be more or less met without depending upon a long train of suppliers. In the city, this is not the case. There it is necessary to have the cash required to buy essential goods, and this means that the newcomer has to find a way both to make a wage and to manage it once it is made. In addition, the entire family structure is changing, and machines are reducing the need for child labor. Nevertheless, many children still work in factories. For those who do not, there are no relatives available to provide the attention and care they require while their parents work in factories. Many people have begun to feel that, without proper guidance, life in the city is becoming unhealthy for many children and that some new structure is needed for them. Yet as long as child labor is available, it provides a source of cheap workers for many businesses. Not to hire children is to operate at a competitive disadvantage. Schools are available, but many children do not attend them for a variety of reasons. The solution that you propose is to make school attendance compulsory into adolescence and to prohibit child labor. In this way no single business will be placed at an unfair advantage, and a substitute institution will take the place of the dwindling extended family. What other educational reforms might you propose to deal with the social problems that now exist in this society?

Imagine a third situation: A compulsory system of education has been operating in your country for a number of years, a reasonably high rate of literacy has been achieved, and for most groups the transition from rural to urban life has been accomplished. However, new technological advances have been developing that will require more scientists, engineers, and managers than are being produced by the present system. Over the years universities have remained the domain of the well-to-do, providing the children of this group with the polish needed to maintain their family position. However, if the new needs are not met, foreign competition threatens to overtake your nation's external markets and even to penetrate the home market. Your educational advisers have assured you that ample talent to fill the required need can be found among the general population. Unfortunately, few means exist to identify such talent, and the resources of higher education are not sufficient to train it. You respond by calling a meeting of leading educators, in which it is resolved to develop a fair national system of testing that will be used to identify talented members from all classes in the society who will be able to benefit from a university education. In addition, university educators promise to reform their curriculum by placing a new emphasis on science, mathematics, engineering, and business and by introducing graduate research programs that will assure a steady growth of knowledge in these areas. You agree to fund these proposals.

The three situations presented above are hypothetical; they do not attempt to describe the experience of any single country. They do,

however, represent a functionalist approach to thinking about the establishment, maintenance, and change of a national system of compulsory education. In the situations above, at least three functions are represented. In the first instance, the school system will serve to establish a single, national identity and will thereby be used to overcome the strife created by conflicting tribal loyalties. In other words, it is serving the function of social integration. In the second instance, schooling is made compulsory in order to develop new habits and attitudes that changing times require. Here it is serving what may be called the function of social re-integration. In the third situation, the educational system will be fine tuned, or rationalized, to provide the higher-level skills demanded by international competition. In other words, it will be used to identify talent from all segments of society and to provide the training that higher-level skills demand. In this case, the school is serving the function of role differentiation. . . .

ASSIMILATION, POLITICAL SOCIALIZATION, AND MODERNIZATION

Many reformers, arguing along functionalist lines, view the school as society's primary instrument for meeting the demands of our modern political, social, and economic life. Specifically, they argue that schools must teach students to act according to democratic principles, to tolerate diversity, and to work in a specialized, highly technical economy. Add to these three political, social, and economic goals that a person should expect to be rewarded according to merit, and you have the basic elements required for developing and maintaining a modern, functional, meritocratic society. Three basic processes are related to this perception of the social function of the school. These are the school's role in cultural assimilation, political socialization, and modernization. The first two processes, assimilation and political socialization, are closely aligned to the functionalists' view on social integration and solidarity; the third process, modernization, is aligned to their view on role differentiation and development theory.

Assimilation is a cultural concept. It refers to the process whereby one group, usually a subordinate one, becomes indistinguishable from another group, usually a dominant one. As one group takes on the dress, speech patterns, tastes, attitudes, and economic status of the dominant group, the process of assimilation occurs. *Political socialization* is primarily a political concept. It is also, secondarily, a psychological one. In the context of modern society it refers to the widening of a person's political loyalty beyond the local group to the nation as a whole. It also refers to the process whereby a person comes to accept the decision-making process of modern democratic forms of government. *Modernization* is both an economic and a social concept. It refers to the development of the meritocratic, bureaucratic, and individualistic form of life that is associated with modern society and is viewed as a prerequisite for technological and economic development.

These three processes overlap. For example, assimilation involves, among other things, a change in the wants of the members of the newer groups. Modernization presupposes just such a change. After all, a meritocracy depends upon people wanting what it offers as rewards. Similarly, political socialization may be seen as a more specific case of assimilation. Nevertheless, while these processes overlap, they can be treated separately. In this section we examine the relationship between educational reform and the twin processes of assimilation and political socialization first and then look at educational reform and modernization.

As immigration from non-English-speaking areas increased during the early part of this century, reformers in the United States looked to the schools as a major instrument for assimilating new groups into what was called "the American way of life." People differed about the form that assimilation should take, however. Some believed that immigration should be restricted to those groups from Northern and Western Europe whose values were felt to be already in accord with the ideas of American culture. Others believed that immigration could be opened to groups from other countries if the schools proved able to "wash out" native cultural patterns and impose standards on the newcomers that were in keeping with "the American way of life." Still other reformers argued that each new culture had its own unique contribution to make to American society and that cultural identity should be nurtured in the schools. These people argued that the schools' responsibility should be to develop in each student a commitment to the ideal of a pluralistic society. Even though there were such different opinions about the form that social integration should take, there was agreement that political and technological concerns required a new pattern of assimilation.

Many educational reformers have looked to the schools to help assimilate new groups into the ongoing culture and to develop a common allegiance to democratic principles. There continue to be many differences among educators, as well as among political figures and within the general public, as to the best way to carry out this task. Some believe that schools should carry on a direct assault against political doctrines that are seen as alien to the values they associate with American democracy. Thus some state governments have passed laws mandating that schools teach courses about "the evils of communism." Others have argued that the schools should reflect in their own structures and curricula the decision-making process they associate with democratic forms of life. The encouragement of student government has been one response to this view. Others have proposed that students should be able to participate more fully in the planning and development of their own educational programs. Despite these differences, there has been agreement among many, both within education and outside it, that schools have an important role to play in the political socialization of the young.

Political socialization has a special importance in schooling in larger industrial societies, where much of the information that goes into the making of a political decision is not available to the public. When a government decides to raise taxes, go to war, or integrate a school, for instance, it requires a general acceptance by its citizenry of a number of things. First, it requires that the public believes that the government is acting as a representative of the general population. Second, it requires that the public believes that the government is acting in good faith. And third, it requires that each individual believes that the government has the support and the power to enforce its will. The first of these requirements means that students who will become citizens must develop faith in the process through which political representatives are chosen and their laws are made. The second requires that they have at least minimal faith in government officials and agencies. The third requires that students believe that most of the other people in the society have the kind of faith mentioned in the first two points above and therefore are in fact willing to act upon their government's orders. . . .

The role of the school in modernization is closely tied to both the cultural and the political functions of schooling. It refers to the development of a bureaucratic, individualized form of life in which the production (and to some extent the consumption) process is rationalized to meet the requirements of efficiency. When the term *modernization* is used by contemporary scholars and reformers, it is usually meant to indicate the process whereby a preindustrial society develops its agriculture, industry, and technology in a way that parallels the development that took place in Western Europe and the United States during and after the Industrial Revolution. Modernization theorists believe that economic growth in both agriculture and manufacturing depends upon the development of a market economy with a certain degree of centralized planning, the introduction of a meritocratic reward structure, and the development of a national bureaucracy.

Modernization theory has also emphasized the importance of the development of "human capital." This emphasis is of special significance to educators. The idea is that if the movement toward industrialization is to be effective, then there must be not only investment in machinery and capital equipment, there must also be a similar investment in the development of human skills. In other words, education has an *economic* value for the society at large, and a large part of the process of modernization involves identifying and training new talent so that it is able to make effective use of innovative technologies.

The development of human capital is perceived as important in both technologically developed societies and in technologically developing ones. In developed societies it is perceived as a way to maintain the social wealth that past generations have established, while accelerating economic growth by bringing talented members from minority populations into the production process. Indeed, in some instances human capital theorists have argued that the greatest value may be reaped by investing more educational resources in groups that have previously been left behind in the educational process. In some circumstances the value added to the total wealth of a society may be increased more by investing additional resources in the education of an underachieving minority than in the already well-educated majority. In these circumstances human capital theory has provided strong arguments for opening educational opportunities to underrepresented minorities.

For technologically developing countries, the development of human capital is seen as essential in meeting the various "manpower" needs of the society at different occupational levels. Depending on the circumstances, there are a number of different kinds of choices that might be rational. For example, given a limited amount of resources, "manpower" planners might decide to allocate training funds for only a few positions requiring university-level education and concentrate the largest amount of educational resources for developing primary school education on a wider scale. In some situations it might be most cost-effective to train the nation's professional and technical elite in university facilities outside of the country, while using most of the educational resources within the country to build primary and secondary schools. Whatever the specific arrangement may be, the basic idea here is that the development of the educational system should be guided by and be functionally related to the overall requirements of the workforce.

. . . We have described a functionalist approach to understanding and dealing with the relation of school to society. Functionalists view society as analogous to a biological organism whose various parts have evolved in an integrated way to meet needs and enhance the capacity for survival. From this analogy, the functionalist argues that schools serve to meet some of the essential needs of modern society. There is an important difference between social and biological functionalism, however. Organisms cannot readily change their organs nor alter their imprinted behaviors. Societies and schools can and do change, sometimes rapidly and radically. Some changes are brought about by the force of events, but others are consciously intended. Functionalism offers a way of thinking about the structuring, organizing, and reforming of schools in order to serve the perceived needs and purposes of society. But when this is done, some people get uncomfortable with the idea of manipulating people to achieve social ends. . . .

STUDY QUESTIONS FOR PART 2

1. Durkheim, a Frenchman, wrote nearly a century ago about the need for education to create homogeneity among students and prescribed methodical socialization as the duty of educators. Is this perspective valid today? Why? Why not?

2. What is the role of the state and nation in education? As we move toward a more global society and an electronically shrinking world, is it important that the United States develop a *national* curriculum for our schools? What would you see as the advantages and disadvantages of such a system? Who would benefit; why?

3. Functionalists believe that formal education has the ability to equalize and level-out other life-conditions (poverty, ethnicity, gender, class, etc.) and, that by educating all citizens and giving everyone an opportunity to go to school, everyone will get a fair chance to achieve that of which they are capable. Do you believe that this is a reasonable premise and that it is working for the majority of children? Why? Why not?

4. What is the difference between achieved and ascribed status? Give three examples. What counts in schools? Why do you feel this way? What is the evidence to which you can point to support your view?

5. Should education be the act of giving out information and facts or should it try to influence what and how students think? Many argue for clear content/subject standards. Do you agree with this stance? What is the reasoning behind your view?

Socialization
and Progress

The following selections address several basic questions of the role of school in society and the connections between schooling and social progress:

- Should schools strive to change society or should they mirror society?
- What connections should there be between what is learned in school and the knowledge, skills, values, and attitudes needed to enable the U.S. work force to remain competitive in a global marketplace?
- Given our postindustrial era and the emergence of global and instantaneous electronic communication, what adaptations do you foresee for the work of teachers and the role of educators in our society?

Writing in 1899, John Dewey reflected on the connections between the changes he observed in the methods and curricula of schooling and broader changes in the larger society. His basic strategy was to see if he could find examples of changes in the school that mirrored changes in society. The industrial revolution had been under way for some time at this point, and many changes were to be observed in society: the shift from an agrarian, rural life to industrial, urban living; an orientation to mass production, rapid global communication, and world markets in contrast to the former family-based model with service to the immediate community being the norm. Dewey concluded that these, and a multitude of lifestyle changes, had a major impact on the nature of school curricula and methods. The example he chose for illustrative purposes was the emergence within schools of attention to what he referred to as "manual training."

What Dewey draws attention to here are the close connections between school and society. As the two previous readings observed, society's system of education plays a vital role in society's survival, helping it make the adjustments and adaptations required of the times. Dewey and Dreeben both observe the important role played by schools in facilitating the shift from a household and neighborhood economy rooted in agriculture and small family enterprises to a factory-based economy rooted in mass production and urban living where most of the work occurred outside the home.

Dewey believed that the shift he observed regarding the new emphasis on manual training was a great innovation for the times, as schools had until very recently been dominated by what Dewey referred to as a medieval conception of learning (p. 102). What he meant by this is that the curriculum was almost entirely intellectual in orientation and quite removed from the reality of daily living. He heralded this shift to a curriculum that was more responsive to children's natural inclination to "make and do" (p. 103) as a way to make learning more meaningful: "The occupation supplies the child with a genuine motive; it gives him experience at first hand; it brings him into contact with realities" (p.101).

Dewey believed that children learn best from experience and that the school had historically been too removed from real life—and thus difficult for most children.

"The simple facts of the case are that in the great majority of human beings the distinctively intellectual interest is not dominant. They have the so-called practical impulse and disposition. In many of those in whom by nature intellectual interest is strong, social conditions prevent its adequate realization" (p. 103). For Dewey, the way to guarantee a good society would be to " . . . make each one of our schools an embryonic community life, active with types of occupations that reflect the life of the larger society, and permeated throughout with the spirit of art, history, and science" (p. 104).

The questions embedded in Dewey's propositions are still argued and examined to this day. What are your thoughts on these matters? Are schools today too removed from needed life skills? Do you believe that most people don't have a dominant interest in matters of the mind? Would children learn more if schools were more like natural communities, organized around the types of activities and problems found in the surrounding community? What did Dewey mean when he referred to social conditions preventing some children with the ability and motivation from pursuing the intellectual development afforded by schools?

Dewey's selection reminds us of the important connection functionalists draw between schooling and certain needs society has for its survival. Was Dewey arguing merely that schools should teach children more utilitarian skills, appropriate to the world of work? Perhaps Dewey is suggesting that by providing children with the opportunity to work as members of a community they will learn many of the attitudes and values required for success as workers and adult citizens. Perhaps Dewey, as Durkheim, was concerned with the importance of developing the child's "social being," and not just his/her individual intellectual capabilities. As Dewey states at the beginning of his essay, it is critical to look at the broader social dimension of school and not be restricted only to a focus on individual accomplishment. While important, individual achievement in the traditional school subjects is perhaps not the most important dimension of schooling. Or is it?

How does this "social being" get developed? Typically it is not addressed in the curriculum as an explicit school subject like math or Spanish. The closest a school might come today would probably be a vocational class that teaches students to be medical assistants or clerical workers, for example. Some schools have group agricultural or home building projects. The fact is, the development of the "social" being is not a manifest part of the school curriculum. It is, rather, a product of what others have termed the "hidden curriculum"; learning that is a latent function of participating in the regular academic curriculum as well as in the many extracurricular activities in most secondary schools.

Dreeben discusses four norms learned as a result of schooling. These include the norms of independence, achievement, universalism, and specificity. One answer to the question "What is learned in school?" is learning associated with the manifest curriculum—geography, writing, arithmetic, and assorted other facts and skills. While functional to some degree in terms of preparation for adulthood and entry into the work force, such learning is almost exclusively what Durkheim would refer to as learning related to development of the individual being. Dewey would call this learning "accomplishments of the individual." Another answer to the question "What is learned in school?" is learning associated with the latent curriculum—the four norms observed by Dreeben. These norms are concerned primarily with the development of the "social being." To paraphrase Dreeben, these four norms are an outcome of *how* things are done in schools. They are not an explicit aspect of the curriculum. Nevertheless, the learning that occurs around these four norms is *functional* in helping children and adolescents develop the social and psychological orientations to succeed as workers and as adult citizens.

Dreeben provides numerous examples of how these four norms are learned as a result of student participation in both the academic curriculum and in extracurricular activities. While not an explicit aspect of the goals and objectives of schooling, what students do in school—how schooling gets accomplished—has the effect of fostering the development of these norms. While this is generally a positive effect for most students, Dreeben points out that this may not be the case for all. That is, "the conditions conducive to their development are also conducive to the creation of results widely regarded as undesirable" (p. 86). Dreeben offers these examples:

> . . . . a sense of accomplishment and mastery, on the one hand, and a sense of incompetence and ineffectualness, on the other, both represent psychological consequences of continuously coping with tasks on an achievement basis. Similarly with independence: self-confidence and helplessness can each derive from a person's self-imposed obligation to work unaided and accept individual responsibility for his actions. Finally, willingness to acknowledge the rightness of categorical and specific treatment may indicate the capacity to adapt to a variety of social situations in which only a part of one's self is invested, or it may indicate a sense of personal alienation and isolation from human relationships. (p. 86)

So what is desirable? Dreeben makes a very strong case that these four norms are learned as a result of how schooling gets accomplished. For example, school bells ring to get students used to being on time and ready to work. That, in turn, prepares them to punch a time clock once they enter the world of work. Given the possibility that not just the more desirable consequences will result, should schools strive to avoid these norms and teach others? Could they? How? Why? What would replace them? These questions bring us to the third selected reading. In their examination of the importance of the idea of becoming and being a reflective teacher, Grant and Zeichner suggest that one of the most important things for a teacher to do is to think about one's teaching, the effects of schooling, and who is and isn't being served well by the school.

Grant and Zeichner urge teachers to be deliberate in choosing what kind of teacher they want to be. They argue for a model or image called the "reflective teacher." The main idea here is that as a teacher one develops the habit of reflection and engages in a critical examination of one's teaching, the school's curriculum, who is served and who isn't, and so forth. That is, teachers assume a moral obligation to think about their activities and effects as teachers and to consider the ramifications of the political, educational, and social contexts within which their teaching is embedded (p. 50)

They discuss three attitudes defined by Dewey that can help one be a reflective teacher. These include being open-minded, taking responsibility, and approaching the teaching task wholeheartedly. Being open-minded refers to the ability to genuinely consider that alternatives to existing school practices always exist, and that the current practice may or may not be the best practice given changing conditions. Responsibility refers to being aware of your actions as a teacher and being tuned-in to the effects of your actions on others. Are ditto sheets really the best instructional vehicle for a given lesson? If programs for gifted students are so effective, why not stimulate all children with appropriately challenging curricula? Is the gain for students of supplementing the regular text worth the time and energy required to locate other sources? Wholeheartedness refers to one's being dedicated and highly committed to serving all students and to giving each pupil your very best as a teacher. Some students are a delight, others are incorrigible, and some may have very severe learning disabilities. Do you give as much to each? Perhaps you give a little extra to some because you know that without the extra attention they just aren't going to make it! This is being wholehearted, and the sign of a reflective teacher.

Becoming a reflective teacher is not easy, but Grant and Zeichner include in their discussion a number of good ideas to help you develop your capacity to be reflective. Maybe you want to adopt another image besides being a reflective teacher. What would it look like? How would you defend your viewpoint? Remember the choice is yours, and the important thing is to think deliberately about what kind of teacher you want to be, and then to set a course of action for achieving your goal. As you move toward your ideal, keep in mind the critical importance of what happens in school to the continuing development and survival of the society. Given the emerging advances in technology and the increasing speed and globalization of communication, what should students learn in school? How will the school accomplish this? How will it help students become good citizens and workers? How will it help our society continue to adapt and survive as conditions in the world change?

The School and Social Progress

John Dewey

We are apt to look at the school from an individualistic standpoint, as something between teacher and pupil, or between teacher and parent. That which interests us most is naturally the progress made by the individual child of our acquaintance, his normal physical development, his advance in ability to read, write, and figure, his growth in the knowledge of geography and history, improvement in manners, habits of promptness, order, and industry—it is from such standards as these that we judge the work of the school. And rightly so. Yet the range of the outlook needs to be enlarged. What the best and wisest parent wants for his own child, that must the community want for all of its children. Any other ideal for our schools is narrow and unlovely; acted upon, it destroys our democracy. All that society has accomplished for itself is put, through the agency of the school, at the disposal of its future members. All its better thoughts of itself it hopes to realize through the new possibilities thus opened to its future self. Here individualism and socialism are at one. Only by being true to the full growth of all the individuals who make it up, can society by any chance be true to itself. And in the self-direction thus given, nothing counts as much as the school, for, as Horace Mann said, "Where anything is growing, one former is worth a thousand re-formers."

Whenever we have in mind the discussion of a new movement in education, it is especially necessary to take the broader, or social view. Otherwise, changes in the school institution and tradition will be looked at as the arbitrary inventions of particular teachers; at the worst transitory fads, and at the best merely improvements in certain details—and this is the plane upon which it is too customary to consider school changes. It is as rational to conceive of the locomotive or the telegraph as personal devices. The modification going on in the method and curriculum of education is as much a product of the changed social situation, and as much an effort to meet the needs of the new society that is forming, as are changes in modes of industry and commerce.

It is to this, then, that I especially ask your attention: the effort to conceive what roughly may be termed the "New Education" in the light of larger changes in society. Can we connect this "New Education" with the general march of events? If we can, it will lose its isolated character, and will cease to be an affair which proceeds only from the over-ingenious minds of pedagogues dealing with particular pupils. It will appear as part and parcel of the whole social evolution, and, in its more general features at least, as inevitable. Let us then ask after the main aspects of the social movement; and afterwards turn to the school to find what witness it gives of effort to put itself in line. And since it is quite impossible to cover the whole ground, I shall for the most part confine myself to one typical thing

---

Source: "The School and Social Progress" by John Dewey was originally published as a pamphlet in 1899 by the University of Chicago Press. Material is in the public domain.

in the modern school movement—that which passes under the name of manual training, hoping if the relation of that to changed social conditions appears, we shall be ready to concede the point as well regarding other educational innovations.

I make no apology for not dwelling at length upon the social changes in question. Those I shall mention are writ so large that he who runs may read. The change that comes first to mind, the one that overshadows and even controls all others, is the industrial one—the application of science resulting in the great inventions that have utilized the forces of nature on a vast and inexpensive scale: the growth of a world-wide market as the object of production, of vast manufacturing centers to supply this market, of cheap and rapid means of communication and distribution between all its parts. Even as to its feebler beginnings, this change is not much more than a century old; in many of its most important aspects it falls within the short span of those now living. One can hardly believe there has been a revolution in all history so rapid, so extensive, so complete. Through it the face of the earth is making over, even as to its physical forms; political boundaries are wiped out and moved about, as if they were indeed only lines on a paper map; population is hurriedly gathered into cities from the ends of the earth; habits of living are altered with startling abruptness and thoroughness; the search for the truths of nature is infinitely stimulated and facilitated and their application to life made not only practicable, but commercially necessary. Even our moral and religious ideas and interests, the most conservative because the deepest-lying things in our nature, are profoundly affected. That this revolution should not affect education in other than formal and superficial fashion is inconceivable.

Back of the factory system lies the household and neighborhood system. Those of us who are here today need go back only one, two, or at most three generations, to find a time when the household was practically the center in which were carried on, or about which were clustered, all the typical forms of industrial occupation. The clothing worn was for the most part not only made in the house, but the members of the household were usually familiar with the shearing of the sheep, the carding and spinning of the wool, and the plying of the loom. Instead of pressing a button and flooding the house with electric light, the whole process of getting illumination was followed in its toilsome length, from the killing of the animal and the trying of fat, to the making of wicks and dipping of candles. The supply of flour, of lumber, of foods, of building materials, of household furniture, even of metal ware, of nails, hinges, hammers, etc., was in the immediate neighborhood, in shops which were constantly open to inspection and often centers of neighborhood congregation. The entire industrial process stood revealed, from the production on the farm of the raw materials, till the finished article was actually put to use. Not only this, but practically every member of the household had his own share in the work. The children, as they gained in strength and capacity, were gradually initiated into the mysteries of the several processes. It was a matter of immediate and personal concern, even to the point of actual participation.

We cannot overlook the factors of discipline and of character-building involved in this: training in habits of order and of industry, and in the idea of responsibility, of obligation to do something, to produce something, in the world. There was always something which really needed to be done, and a real necessity that each member of the household should do his own part faithfully and in coöperation with others. Personalities which became effective in action were bred and tested in the medium of action. Again, we cannot overlook the importance for educational purposes of the close and intimate acquaintance got with nature at first hand, with real things and materials, with the actual processes of their manipulation, and the knowledge of their social necessities and uses. In all this there was continual training of observation, of ingenuity, constructive imagination, of logical thought, and of the sense of reality acquired through first-hand contact with actualities. The educative forces of the domestic spinning and weaving, of the saw-mill, the grist-mill, the copper shop, and the blacksmith forge, were continuously operative.

No number of object-lessons, got up *as* object-lessons for the sake of giving information, can afford even the shadow of a substitute for acquaintance with the plants and animals of the farm and garden, acquired through actual living among them and caring for them. No training of sense-organs in school, introduced for the sake of training, can begin to compete with the alertness and fullness of sense-life that comes through daily intimacy and interest in familiar occupations. Verbal memory can be trained in committing tasks, a certain discipline of the reasoning powers can be acquired through lessons in science and mathematics; but, after all, this is somewhat remote and shadowy compared with the training of attention and of judgment that is acquired in having to do things with a real motive behind and a real outcome ahead. At present, concentration of industry and division of labor have practically eliminated household and neighborhood occupations—at least for educational purposes. But it is useless to bemoan the departure of the good old days of children's modesty, reverence, and implicit obedience, if we expect merely by bemoaning and by exhortation to bring them back. It is radical conditions which have changed, and only an equally radical change in education suffices. We must recognize our compensations—the increase in toleration, in breadth of social judgment, the larger acquaintance with human nature, the sharpened alertness in reading signs of character and interpreting social situations, greater accuracy, of adaptation to differing personalities, contact with greater commercial activities. These considerations mean much to the city-bred child of today. Yet there is a real problem: how shall we retain these advantages, and yet introduce into the school something representing the other side of life—occupations which exact personal responsibilities and

which train the child with relation to the physical realities of life?

When we turn to the school, we find that one of the most striking tendencies at present is toward the introduction of so-called manual training, shop-work, and the household arts—sewing and cooking.

This has not been done "on purpose," with a full consciousness that the school must now supply that factor of training formerly taken care of in the home, but rather by instinct, by experimenting and finding that such work takes a vital hold of pupils and gives them something which was not to be got in any other way. Consciousness of its real import is still so weak that the work is often done in a half-hearted, confused, and unrelated way. The reasons assigned to justify it are painfully inadequate or sometimes even positively wrong.

If we were to cross-examine even those who are most favorably disposed to the introduction of this work into our school system, we should, I imagine, generally find the main reasons to be that such work engages the full spontaneous interest and attention of the children. It keeps them alert and active, instead of passive and receptive; it makes them more useful, more capable, and hence more inclined to be helpful at home; it prepares them to some extent for the practical duties of later life—the girls to be more efficient house managers, if not actually cooks and sempstresses; the boys (were our educational system only adequately rounded out into trade schools) for their future vocations. I do not underestimate the worth of these reasons. Of those indicated by the changed attitude of the children I shall indeed have something to say in my next talk, when speaking directly of the relationship of the school to the child. But the point of view is, upon the whole, unnecessarily narrow. We must conceive of work in wood and metal, of weaving, sewing, and cooking, as methods of life not as distinct studies.

We must conceive of them in their social significance, as types of the processes by which society keeps itself going, as agencies for bringing home to the child some of the primal necessities of community life, and as ways in which these needs have been met by the growing insight and ingenuity of man; in short, as instrumentalities through which the school itself shall be made a genuine form of active community life, instead of a place set apart in which to learn lessons.

A society is a number of people held together because they are working along common lines, in a common spirit, and with reference to common aims. The common needs and aims demand a growing interchange of thought and growing unity of sympathetic feeling. The radical reason that the present school cannot organize itself as a natural social unit is because just this element of common and productive activity is absent. Upon the playground, in game and sport, social organization takes place spontaneously and inevitably. There is something to do, some activity to be carried on, requiring natural divisions of labor, selection of leaders and followers, mutual coöperation and emulation. In the schoolroom the motive and the cement of social organization are alike wanting. Upon the ethical side, the tragic weakness of the present school is that it endeavors to prepare future members of the social order in a medium in which the conditions of the social spirit are eminently wanting.

The difference that appears when occupations are made the articulating centers of school life is not easy to describe in words; it is a difference in motive, of spirit and atmosphere. As one enters a busy kitchen in which a group of children are actively engaged in the preparation of food, the psychological difference, the change from more or less passive and inert recipiency and restraint to one of buoyant outgoing energy, is so obvious as fairly to strike one in the face. Indeed, to those whose image of the school is rigidly set the change is sure to give a shock. But the change in the social attitude is equally marked. The mere absorption of facts and truths is so exclusively individual an affair that it tends very naturally to pass into selfishness. There is no obvious social

motive for the acquirement of mere learning, there is no clear social gain in success thereat. Indeed, almost the only measure for success is a competitive one, in the bad sense of that term—a comparison of results in the recitation or in the examination to see which child has succeeded in getting ahead of others in storing up, in accumulating the maximum of information. So thoroughly is this the prevalent atmosphere that for one child to help another in his task has become a school crime. Where the school work consists in simply learning lessons, mutual assistance, instead of being the most natural form of coöperation and association, becomes a clandestine effort to relieve one's neighbor of his proper duties. Where active work is going on all this is changed. Helping others, instead of being a form of charity which impoverishes the recipient, is simply an aid in setting free the powers and furthering the impulse of the one helped. A spirit of free communication, of interchange of ideas, suggestions, results, both successes and failures of previous experiences, becomes the dominating note of the recitation. So far as emulation enters in, it is in the comparison of individuals, not with regard to the quantity of information personally absorbed, but with reference to the quality of work done— the genuine community standard of value. In an informal but all the more pervasive way, the school life organizes itself on a social basis.

Within this organization is found the principle of school discipline or order. Of course, order is simply a thing which is relative to an end. If you have the end in view of forty or fifty children learning certain set lessons, to be recited to a teacher, your discipline must be devoted to securing that result. But if the end in view is the development of a spirit of social coöperation and community life, discipline must grow out of and be relative to this. There is little order of one sort where things are in process of construction; there is a certain disorder in any busy workshop; there is not silence; persons are not engaged in maintaining certain fixed physical postures; their arms are not folded; they are not holding their books thus and so. They are doing a variety of things, and there is the confusion, the bustle, that results from activity. But out of occupation, out of doing things that are to produce results, and out of doing these in a social and coöperative way, there is born a discipline of its own kind and type. Our whole conception of school discipline changes when we get this point of view. In critical moments we all realize that the only discipline that stands by us, the only training that becomes intuition, is that got through life itself. That we learn from experience, and from books or the sayings of others *only* as they are related to experience, are not mere phrases. But the school has been so set apart, so isolated from the ordinary conditions and motives of life, that the place where children are sent for discipline is the one place in the world where it is most difficult to get experience—the mother of all discipline worth the name. It is only where a narrow and fixed image of traditional school discipline dominates, that one is in any danger of overlooking that deeper and infinitely wider discipline that comes from having a part to do in constructive work, in contributing to a result which, social in spirit, is none the less obvious and tangible in form—and hence in a form with reference to which responsibility may be exacted and accurate judgment passed.

The great thing to keep in mind, then, regarding the introduction into the school of various forms of active occupation, is that through them the entire spirit of the school is renewed. It has a chance to affiliate itself with life, to become the child's habitat, where he learns through directed living; instead of being only a place to learn lessons having an abstract and remote reference to some possible living to be done in the future. It gets a chance to be a miniature community, an embryonic society. This is the fundamental fact, and from this arise continuous and orderly sources of instruction. Under the industrial *regime* described, the child, after all, shared in the work, not for the sake of the sharing, but for the sake of the product. The educational results secured were real, yet incidental and dependent. But in the school the typical occupations followed are freed from all economic stress. The aim is not the economic value of the products, but the development of social power and insight. It is this liberation from narrow utilities, this openness to the possibilities of the human spirit that makes these practical activities in the school allies of art and centers of science and history.

The unity of all the sciences is found in geography. The significance of geography is that it presents the earth as the enduring home of the occupations of man. The world without its relationship to human activity is less than a world. Human industry and achievement, apart from their roots in the earth, are not even a sentiment, hardly a name. The earth is the final source of all man's food. It is his continual shelter and protection, the raw material of all his activities, and the home to whose humanizing and idealizing all his achievement returns. It is the great field, the great mine, the great source of the energies of heat, light, and electricity; the great scene of ocean, stream, mountain, and plain, of which all our agriculture and mining and lumbering, all our manufacturing and distributing agencies, are but the partial elements and factors. It is through occupations determined by this environment that mankind has made its historical and political progress. It is through these occupations that the intellectual and emotional interpretation of nature has been developed. It is through what we do in and with the world that we read its meaning and measure its value.

In educational terms, this means that these occupations in the school shall not be mere practical devices or modes of routine employment, the gaining of better technical skill as cooks, seamstresses, or carpenters, but active centers of scientific insight into natural materials and processes, points of departure whence children shall be led out into a realization of the historic development of man. The actual significance of this can be told better through one illustration taken from actual school work than by general discourse.

There is nothing which strikes more oddly upon the average intelligent visitor than to see boys as well as girls of ten, twelve, and thirteen years of age engaged in sewing and weaving. If we look at this from the standpoint of preparation of the boys for sewing on buttons and making patches, we get a narrow and utilitarian conception—a basis that hardly justifies giving prominence to this sort of work in the school. But if we look at it from another side, we find that this work gives the point of departure from which the child can trace and follow the progress of mankind in history, getting an insight also into the materials used and the mechanical principles involved. In connection with these occupations, the historic development of man is recapitulated. For example, the children are first given the raw material—the flax, the cotton plant, the wool as it comes from the back of the sheep (if we could take them to the place where the sheep are sheared, so much the better). Then a study is made of these materials from the standpoint of their adaptation to the uses to which they may be put. For instance, a comparison of the cotton fiber with wool fiber is made. I did not know until the children told me, that the reason for the later development of the cotton industry as compared with the woolen is, that the cotton fiber is so very difficult to free by hand from the seeds. The children in one group worked thirty minutes freeing cotton fibers from the boll and seeds, and succeeded in getting out less than one ounce. They could easily believe that one person could only gin one pound a day by hand, and could understand why their ancestors wore woolen instead of cotton clothing. Among other things discovered as affecting their relative utilities, was the shortness of the cotton fiber as compared with that of wool, the former being one-tenth of an inch in length, while that of the latter is an inch in length; also that, the fibers of cotton are smooth and do not cling together, while the wool has a certain roughness which makes the fibers stick, thus assisting the spinning. The children worked this out for them-

selves with the actual material, aided by questions and suggestions from the teacher.

Then they followed the processes necessary for working the fibers up into cloth. They re-invented the first frame for carding the wool—a couple of boards with sharp pins in them for scratching it out. They re-devised the simplest process for spinning the wool—a pierced stone or some other weight through which the wool is passed, and which as it is twirled draws out the fiber; next the top, which was spun on the floor, while the children kept the wool in their hands until it was gradually drawn out and wound upon it. Then the children are introduced to the invention next in historic order, working it out experimentally, thus seeing its necessity, and tracing its effects, not only upon that particular industry, but upon modes of social life—in this way passing in review the entire process up to the present complete loom, and all that goes with the application of science in the use of our present available powers. I need not speak of the science involved in this—the study of the fibers, of geographical features, the conditions under which raw materials are grown, the great centers of manufacture and distribution, the physics involved in the machinery of production; nor, again, of the historical side—the influence which these inventions have had upon humanity. You can concentrate the history of all mankind into the evolution of the flax, cotton, and wool fibers into clothing. I do not mean that this is the only, or the best, center. But it is true that certain very real and important avenues to the consideration of the history of the race are thus opened—that the mind is introduced to much more fundamental and controlling influences than usually appear in the political and chronological records that pass for history.

Now, what is true of this one instance of fibers used in fabrics (and, of course, I have only spoken of one or two elementary phases of that) is true in its measure of every material used in every occupation, and of the processes employed. The occupation supplies the child with a genuine motive; it gives him experience at first hand; it brings him into contact with realities. It does all this, but in addition it is liberalized throughout by translation into its historic values and scientific equivalencies. With the growth of the child's mind in power and knowledge it ceases to be a pleasant occupation merely, and becomes more and more a medium, an instrument, an organ—and is thereby transformed.

This, in turn, has its bearing upon the teaching of science. Under present conditions, all activity, to be successful, has to be directed somewhere and somehow by the scientific expert—it is a case of applied science. This connection should determine its place in education. It is not only that the occupations, the so-called manual or industrial work in the school, give the opportunity for the introduction of science which illuminates them, which makes them material, freighted with meaning, instead of being mere devices of hand and eye; but that the scientific insight thus gained becomes an indispensable instrument of free and active participation in modern social life. Plato somewhere speaks of the slave as one who in his actions does not express his own ideas, but those of some other man. It is our social problem now, even more urgent than in the time of Plato, that method, purpose, understanding, shall exist in the consciousness of the one who does the work, that his activity shall have meaning to himself.

When occupations in the school are conceived in this broad and generous way, I can only stand lost in wonder at the objections so often heard, that such occupations are out of place in the school because they are materialistic, utilitarian, or even menial in their tendency. It sometimes seems to me that those who make these objections must live in quite another world. The world in which most of us live is a world in which everyone has a calling and occupation, something to do. Some are managers and others are subordinates. But the great thing for one as for the other is that each shall have had the education which enables him to see within his daily

work all there is in it of large and human significance. How many of the employed are today mere appendages to the machines which they operate! This may be due in part to the machine itself, or to the *régime* which lays so much stress upon the products of the machine; but it is certainly due in large part to the fact that the worker has had no opportunity to develop his imagination and his sympathetic insight as to the social and scientific values found in his work. At present, the impulses which lie at the basis of the industrial system are either practically neglected or positively distorted during the school period. Until the instincts of construction and production are systematically laid hold of in the years of childhood and youth, until they are trained in social directions, enriched by historical interpretation, controlled and illuminated by scientific methods, we certainly are in no position even to locate the source of our economic evils, much less to deal with them effectively.

If we go back a few centuries, we find a practical monopoly of learning. The term *possession* of learning was, indeed, a happy one. Learning was a class matter. This was a necessary result of social conditions. There were not in existence any means by which the multitude could possibly have access to intellectual resources. These were stored up and hidden away in manuscripts. Of these there were at best only a few, and it required long and toilsome preparation to be able to do anything with them. A high-priesthood of learning, which guarded the treasury of truth and which doled it out to the masses under severe restrictions, was the inevitable expression of these conditions. But, as a direct result of the industrial revolution of which we have been speaking, this has been changed. Printing was invented; it was made commercial. Books, magazines, papers were multiplied and cheapened. As a result of the locomotive and telegraph, frequent, rapid, and cheap intercommunication by mails and electricity was called into being. Travel has been rendered easy; freedom of movement, with its accompanying exchange of ideas, indefinitely facilitated. The result has been an intellectual revolution. Learning has been put into circulation. While there still is, and probably always will be, a particular class having the special business of inquiry in hand, a distinctively learned class is henceforth out of the question. It is an anachronism. Knowledge is no longer an immobile solid; it has been liquified. It is actively moving in all the currents of society itself.

It is easy to see that this revolution, as regards the materials of knowledge, carries with it a marked change in the attitude of the individual. Stimuli of an intellectual sort pour in upon us in all kinds of ways. The merely intellectual life, the life of scholarship and of learning, thus gets a very altered value. Academic and scholastic, instead of being titles of honor, are becoming terms of reproach.

But all this means a necessary change in the attitude of the school, one of which we are as yet far from realizing the full force. Our school methods, and to a very considerable extent our curriculum, are inherited from the period when learning and command of certain symbols, affording as they did the only access to learning, were all-important. The ideas of this period are still largely in control, even where the outward methods and studies have been changed. We sometimes hear the introduction of manual training, art and science into the elementary, and even the secondary schools, deprecated on the ground that they tend toward the production of specialists—that they detract from our present scheme of generous, liberal culture. The point of this objection would be ludicrous if it were not often so effective as to make it tragic. It is our present education which is highly specialized, one-sided and narrow. It is an education dominated almost entirely by the medieval conception of learning. It is something which appeals for the most part simply to the intellectual aspect of our natures, our desire to learn, to accumulate information, and to get control of the symbols of learning; not to our impulses and tendencies to make, to do, to create, to produce, whether in the form of

utility or of art. The very fact that manual training, art and science are objected to as technical, as tending toward mere specialism, is of itself as good testimony as could be offered to the specialized aim which controls current education. Unless education had been virtually identified with the exclusively intellectual pursuits, with learning as such, all these materials and methods would be welcome, would be greeted with the utmost hospitality.

While training for the profession of learning is regarded as the type of culture, as a liberal education, that of a mechanic, a musician, a lawyer, a doctor, a farmer, a merchant, or a railroad manager is regarded as purely technical and professional. The result is that which we see about us everywhere—the division into "cultured" people and "workers," the separation of theory and practice. Hardly one per cent of the entire school population ever attains to what we call higher education; only five per cent to the grade of our high school; while much more than half leave on or before the completion of the fifth year of the elementary grade. The simple facts of the case are that in the great majority of human beings the distinctively intellectual interest is not dominant. They have the so-called practical impulse and disposition. In many of those in whom by nature intellectual interest is strong, social conditions prevent its adequate realization. Consequently by far the larger number of pupils leave school as soon as they have acquired the rudiments of learning, as soon as they have enough of the symbols of reading, writing, and calculating to be of practical use to them in getting a living. While our educational leaders are talking of culture, the development of personality, etc., as the end and aim of education, the great majority of those who pass under the tuition of the school regard it only as a narrowly practical tool with which to get bread and butter enough to eke out a restricted life. If we were to conceive our educational end and aim in a less exclusive way, if we were to introduce into educational processes the activities which appeal to those whose dominant interest is to do and to make, we should find the hold of the school upon its members to be more vital, more prolonged, containing more of culture.

But why should I make this labored presentation? The obvious fact is that our social life has undergone a thorough and radical change. If our education is to have any meaning for life, it must pass through an equally complete transformation. This transformation is not something to appear suddenly, to be executed in a day by conscious purpose. It is already in progress. Those modifications of our school system which often appear (even to those most actively concerned with them, to say nothing of their spectators) to be mere changes of detail, mere improvement within the school mechanism, are in reality signs and evidences of evolution. The introduction of active occupations, of nature study, of elementary science, of art, of history; the relegation of the merely symbolic and formal to a secondary position, the change in the moral school atmosphere, in the relation of pupils and teachers—of discipline; the introduction of more active, expressive, and self-directing factors—all these are not mere accidents, they are necessities of the larger social evolution. It remains but to organize all these factors, to appreciate them in their fullness of meaning, and to put the ideas and ideals involved into complete, uncompromising possession of our school system. To do this means to make each one of our schools an embryonic community life, active with types of occupations that reflect the life of the larger society, and permeated throughout with the spirit of art, history, and science. When the school introduces and trains each child of society into membership within such a little community, saturating him with the spirit of service, and providing him with the instruments of effective self-direction, we shall have the deepest and best guarantee of a larger society which is worthy, lovely, and harmonious.

On Becoming a Reflective Teacher

CARL A. GRANT AND KENNETH M. ZEICHNER

If teachers today are to initiate young people into an ethical existence, they themselves must attend more fully than they normally have to their own lives and its requirements; they have to break with the mechanical life, to overcome their own submergence in the habitual, even in what they conceive to be virtuous, and to ask the "why" with which all moral reasoning begins.[1]

Maxine Greene, *Teacher as Stranger*

As you proceed with your professional education, you will continually be confronted with numerous choices about the kind of teacher to become. Recent literature in education has clearly shown that teachers differ substantially according to their goals and priorities and to the instructional and classroom management strategies that they employ. These differences among teachers have usually been portrayed as contrasting "types." For example, much has been written in recent years about the differences between teachers who are "open or traditional," "child-centered or subject-centered," "direct or indirect," and "humanistic or custodial." These dichotomies attempt to differentiate teachers who hold different views about what is important for children to learn, preferred instructional and management strategies, and types of curricular materials, and about the kinds of school and classroom organizational structures within which they want to work. The kind of teacher you wish to become, the stands you take on educational issues, and the knowledge and skills you need for putting your beliefs into action all represent decisions you as a prospective teacher need to make.

Over a hundred years of educational research has yet to discover the most effective instructional methods and school and classroom organizational structures for all students. This, together with the fact that "rules for practice" cannot now and probably never will be easily derived from either college coursework or practical school experience, makes your choices regarding these issues and the manner in which you determine them of great importance.

With regard to instructional strategies and methods, you will literally be bombarded in your courses and practicums with suggestions and advice regarding the numerous techniques and strategies that are now available for the instruction of children in the various content areas. For example, you will be taught various strategies for leading discussions, managing small groups, designing learning centers, administering diagnos-

Source: "On Becoming a Reflective Teacher" from *Preparing for Reflective Teaching,* copyright 1984 by Carl Grant and Ken Zeichner. Reprinted by permission of the authors.

tic and evaluative procedures, and teaching concepts and skills.

Furthermore, in each of the content areas there are choices to be made about a general approach or orientation to instruction over and above the choice of specific instructional techniques and procedures. You, ultimately, must make decisions about which approach or combination of approaches to employ amid competing claims by advocates that their approach offers the best solution to problems of instruction.

Undoubtedly, there is a great deal of debate in education today over how to go about teaching agreed upon content and skills and about the ways to manage classrooms and children. However, the question of *what* to teach, and to whom, precedes the question of *how* to teach. The selection of content to be taught to a particular group of children and of the types of instructional materials and resources to support this process are issues of great importance despite the fact that any school in which you are likely to work will have some set of policies. Although there are limits placed upon teachers regarding curricular content and materials, teachers usually have some latitude in the selection of specific content and materials within broad curricular guidelines.

For example, in the state of Wisconsin it is required that teachers teach the history of their state as part of the 4th grade social studies curriculum. Within these guidelines, individual teachers usually have some degree of choice about what to teach or emphasize about Wisconsin history and about what materials to use. This holds true in many curricular areas; even where schools have adopted particular instructional approaches and programs, such as in reading and math, teachers are still permitted some degree of personal discretion in the selection of content and materials.

You will also face a set of options about the kinds of school organizational structures in which you will work, and you will need to be aware that not all structures are compatible with all positions on issues of curriculum and instruction. At the elementary school level, for example, do you prefer to work in a self-contained classroom with one group of children or do you prefer to work closely with colleagues in a departmentalized context, such as is found in many individually guided education schools? Furthermore, you must begin to form positions about the kinds of school and classroom structures that will support the kind of teaching you want to do.

In addition to these numerous choices and issues, there is another and more basic choice facing you. This choice concerns the way in which you go about formulating positions with regard to the issues mentioned above. To what degree will you consciously direct this process of decision making in pursuit of desired ends and in light of educational and ethical principles? On the other hand, to what degree will your decisions be mechanically directed by others; by impulse, tradition, and authority? An important distinction is made between being a reflective or an unreflective teacher, and it necessarily involves every prospective teacher no matter what your orientation and regardless of the specific position that you eventually adopt on the issues of curriculum and instruction.

You may be wondering what we mean by being a reflective teacher. In the early part of this century, John Dewey made an important distinction between human action that is reflective and that which is routine. Much of what Dewey had to say on this matter was directed specifically to teachers and prospective teachers, and his remarks remain very relevant for those in the process of becoming teachers in the 1980s. According to Dewey,[2] *routine action* is behavior that is guided by impulse, tradition, and authority. In any social setting, and the school is no exception, there exists a taken-for-granted definition of everyday reality in which problems, goals, and the means for their solution become defined in particular ways. As long as everyday life continues without major interruption, this reality is perceived to be unproblematic. Furthermore, this dominant world view is only one of the many views of reality that would theoretically be possible, and it serves as a barrier to recognizing and experimenting with alternative viewpoints.

Teachers who are unreflective about their work uncritically accept this everyday reality in schools and concentrate their efforts on finding the most effective and efficient means to achieve ends and to solve problems that have largely been defined for them by others. These teachers lose sight of the fact that their everyday reality is only one of many possible alternatives. They tend to forget the purposes and ends toward which they are working.

Dewey defines *reflective action*,[3] on the other hand, as behavior which involves active, persistent, and careful consideration of any belief or practice in light of the grounds that support it and the further consequences to which it leads. According to Dewey, reflection involves a way of meeting and responding to problems. Reflective teachers actively reflect upon their teaching and upon the educational, social and political contexts in which their teaching is embedded.

There are three attitudes that Dewey defines as prerequisites for reflective action.[4] First, *openmindedness* refers to an active desire to listen to more sides than one, to give full attention to alternate possibilities, and to recognize the possibility of error even in the beliefs that are dearest to us. Prospective teachers who are openminded are continually examining the rationales (educational or otherwise) that underlie what is taken to be natural and right and take pains to seek out conflicting evidence on issues of educational practice.

Second, an attitude of *responsibility* involves careful consideration of the consequences to which an action leads. Responsible student teachers ask themselves why they are doing what they are doing in the classroom in a way that transcends questions of immediate utility and in light of educational purposes of which they are aware. If all that is taught in schools were imparted through the formally sanctioned academic curriculum and if all of the consequences of teach-

ers' actions could be anticipated in advance, the problem here would be much simpler than it is in actuality. However, there is a great deal of agreement among educators of various ideological persuasions that much of what children learn in school is imparted through the covert processes of the so called "hidden curriculum" and that many consequences of the actions of educators are unanticipated outcomes that often contradict formally stated educational goals. Given the powerful impact of the hidden curriculum on the actual outcomes of schooling and the frequently unanticipated consequences of our actions, reflection about the potential impact of our actions in the classroom is extremely important.

The third and final attitude of the reflective teacher is one of *wholeheartedness*. This refers to the fact that openmindedness and responsibility must be central components in the life of the reflective teacher and implies that prospective teachers who are reflective must take active control over their education as teachers. A great deal of research demonstrates that prospective teachers very quickly adopt beliefs and practices of those university and school instructors with whom they work. Many prospective teachers seem to become primarily concerned with meeting the oftentimes conflicting expectations of university professors and cooperating teachers, and with presenting a favorable image to them in the hope of securing favorable evaluations. This impression management is understandable and is a natural consequence of existing power relationships in teacher education, but the divided interest that results tends to divert students' attention from a critical analysis of their work and the context in which it is performed. If reflectiveness is to be part of the lives of prospective teachers, students will have to seek actively to be openminded and responsible or else the pressure of the taken-for-granted institutional realities will force them back into routine behavior.

Possession of these attitudes of openmindedness, responsibility, and wholeheartedness, together with a command of technical skills of inquiry (for example observation) and problem solving define for Dewey a teacher who is reflective. Reflection, according to Dewey,

> emancipates us from merely impulsive and routine activity . . . enables us to direct our actions with foresight and to plan according to ends in view of purposes of which we are aware. It enables us to know what we are about when we act.[5]

On the other hand, according to Dewey, to cultivate unreflective activity is "to further enslavement for it leaves the person at the mercy of appetite, sense and circumstance."[6]

Choosing between becoming a reflective teacher or an unreflective teacher is one of the most important decisions that you will have to make. The quality of all of your decisions regarding curriculum and instruction rests upon this choice.

You are probably saying to yourself, "Of course I want to be a reflective teacher, who wouldn't. But, you need to tell me more." The following sections of the paper discuss the three characteristics of reflective thinking in relation to classroom teaching, analyze whether reflective teaching is a realistic and/or desirable goal, and offer suggestions for how you can begin to become a reflective teacher.

FURTHER INSIGHT

We have pointed out that openmindedness, responsibility, and wholeheartedness are the characteristics of reflective thinking. Let us now discuss each characteristic in relation to classroom teaching.

Openmindedness

When you begin to teach, both as a student teacher and as a licensed teacher, you will most likely be asked to accept teaching procedures and strategies that are already being used in that school or classroom. Will you accept these without question, or will you explore alternative ways of looking at existing teaching practices? For example, celebrating holidays like Thanksgiving and Columbus Day helps to affirm the prevailing historical accounts of these days as well as the customs and traditions associated with them. As a teacher, would you be willing to reevaluate what and how you teach about holidays if some of the students in your class hold a different point of view about them? Would you modify your teaching to take into account their views and beliefs? Being a reflective teacher means that you keep an open mind about the content, methods, and procedures used in your classroom. You constantly reevaluate their worth in relation to the students currently enrolled and to the circumstances. You not only ask why things are the way that they are, but also how they can be made better.

The reflective teacher understands that school practices are not accepted because they are clothed in tradition. If, for example, most of the boys but only a few of the girls are being assigned to Industrial Arts, you should inquire as to why this is happening. You could then begin to formulate teaching and counseling plans (for example, career opportunities, workshops) that would allow students regardless of gender to benefit from the training that is available in those courses.

Responsibility

Teaching involves moral and responsible action. Teachers make moral choices when they make voluntary decisions to have students attain one educational objective instead of another. These decisions are conscious actions that result in certain consequences. These actions can be observed when teachers develop curriculum and choose instructional materials. For example, until recently a textbook company had two basal readers in its reading series. One basal reader was somewhat racially integrated and the other had all white characters. When teachers consciously chose one basal reader over the other or did not modify the all white reader to correct the racial bias, they made a decision that affected not only their students' racial attitudes and understanding about different groups of people, but also their attitudes about themselves. In other words, teachers can encourage ethnocentric attitudes as well as teach an unrealistic view of the world community beyond the school community by failing to provide knowledge about other groups.

As a reflective teacher you are aware of your actions and their consequences. You are aware that your teaching behavior should not be conditioned merely by the immediate utility of an action. For example, it may be much easier to have your students answer questions or work problems on conveniently prepared ditto sheets than to have them do small group projects or hold classroom debates. It may also be much easier if you use one textbook to teach a unit on the Mexican American War than if you use multiple textbooks and other historical documents that would represent both governments' points of view. But immediate utility cannot become the sole justification for your actions and cannot excuse you from the consequences of your actions. Your actions must have a definite and responsibly selected purpose. You have an obligation to consider their consequences in relation to the lives of the students you have accepted the responsibility to teach.

Wholeheartedness

A reflective teacher is not openminded and responsible merely when it is convenient. Openmindedness and responsibility are integral, vital dimensions of your teaching philosophy and behavior. For example, we have seen teachers publicly advocate a belief in integrating handicapped students into the regular class; however, when observing in their classrooms, we saw the handicapped students treated in isolation because the curriculum and the instructional strategies had not been modified to capitalize upon the students' strengths or to acknowledge the students' individual differences. The teachers often left handicapped students to sit in the outer boundaries of the classroom instead of changing the physical environment of the classroom—desk arrangements—to allow them to move about freely as other students would. As a reflective teacher, you do not hesitate or forget to fight for your beliefs and for a quality education for all.

The reflective teacher is dedicated and committed to teaching *all students*, not just certain students. Many of your peers say they want to teach because they love and enjoy working with kids. Are they *really* saying *any* and *all* kids, or are they saying kids that are just like them? The story of Mary Smith will help to illustrate our point. During a job interview with a rural school system, Mary Smith, a graduate from a large urban university, was composed and fluent in discussing teaching methods and curriculum. She also stressed her genuine love for and enjoyment of children and her desire to help them. Her "performance" was so compelling that she was invited to accept a teaching position. Mary Smith, we must point out, believed what she said in the interview and eagerly looked forward to her teaching assignment. Her assignment was to a six room rural school, where the majority of the students spoke with a heavy regional dialect that she had never before heard. The students' reading and mathematics achievement according to standardized tests was three to four years below grade level. Their behavior and attitudes toward school were different from what she had been accustomed to. They regarded the schools as boring and irrelevant to their life style and their future, and they demonstrated their disregard for the school and the teacher by disobeying many instructional and behavioral "requests." Mary tried diligently for three months to get the students to cooperate and follow her instructions. At the beginning of the fourth month, however, she resigned her position. In her letter of resignation she stated that "these kids are not ready to accept what I have been trained to give them. Therefore, I will seek teaching employment where the students want to learn."

There are many teachers like Mary Smith, but the reflective teacher is not one of them. The reflective teacher is wholehearted in accepting *all* students and is willing to learn about and affirm the uniqueness of each student for whom he or she accepts responsibility. If you are a reflective teacher, your teaching behavior is a manifestation of your teaching philosophy and you are unswerving in your desire to make certain that the two become one and the same.

Is Reflective Teaching a Realistic and/or Desirable Goal?

Throughout this century many educators have argued that teachers need to be more reflective about their work. The argument is often made that schools and society are constantly changing and that teachers must be reflective in order to cope effectively with changing circumstances. By uncritically accepting what is customary and by engaging in fixed and patterned behaviors, teachers make it more unlikely that they will be able to change and grow as situations inevitably change. Furthermore, it is commonly accepted that no teacher education program, whatever its focus, can prepare teachers to work effectively in all kinds of classroom settings. Therefore, it becomes important for you to be reflective in order that you may intelligently apply the knowledge and skills gained in your formal preparation for teaching to situations that may be very different from those you experienced during your training.

At the same time many questions have been raised about whether reflective teaching is a realistic or even necessary goal to set before prospective teachers. The purpose of this section is to examine briefly three of the most common objections that have been raised about the goal of reflective teaching and to demonstrate how, despite these doubts, it is still possible and desirable for teachers to work toward a more reflective orientation to both their work and their workplace.

Is It Possible to Take the Time to Reflect?

Many have argued that the nature of teaching and the ecology of classrooms make reflective teaching unrealistic and even undesirable. For example, it is frequently pointed out that classrooms are fast-paced and unpredictable environments where teachers are often required to make spontaneous decisions in response to children's ongoing reactions to an instructional program. Phillip Jackson has estimated that teachers engage in approximately 1,000 interpersonal interactions on any given day and there is no way to describe life in the classroom as anything but extremely complex.[7]

Furthermore, institutional constraints such as high pupil-teacher ratios, the lack of released time for reflection, and pressures to cover a required curriculum with diverse groups of children who are compelled to come to school shape and limit the range of possible teacher actions. The point is made that teachers do not have the time to reflect given the necessity of quick action and the press of institutional demands. According to this view, intuitiveness (as opposed to reflectiveness) is an adaptive response and a natural consequence of the fast-paced unpredictable nature of classroom life and is necessary for teachers to be able to negotiate classroom demands.

Phillip Jackson expresses serious doubts about whether teachers could even function at all in classrooms if they spent more time reflecting about the purposes and consequences of their work.

> If teachers sought a more thorough understanding of their world, insisted on greater rationality in their actions, were completely openminded in their consideration of pedagogical choices and profound in their view of the human condition, they might well receive greater applause from intellectuals, but it is doubtful that they would perform with greater efficiency in the classroom. On the contrary, it is quite possible that such paragons of virtue, if they could be found to exist, would actually have a deuce of a time coping in any sustained way with a class of third graders or a play yard full of nursery school tots.[8]

While classrooms are indeed fast-paced and complex environments, it does not automatically follow that reflective teaching is incompatible with this reality and that teachers by necessity must rely primarily upon intuition and unreflective actions. Several studies[9] have convincingly shown that the quality of teacher deliberations *outside* of the classroom (for example, during planning periods or team meetings) affects the quality of their future actions *within* the classroom. As Dewey points out, "To reflect is to look back on what has been done to extract the meanings which are the capital stock for dealing with further experience."[10] Reflection which is directed toward the improvement of classroom practice does not necessarily need to take place within the classroom to have an impact on classroom practice. Despite the fact that reflection as has been defined in this paper does not occur in many schools even when there has been time set aside for that purpose,[11] the possibility still exists.

Furthermore, the fast pace of classroom life does not preclude a certain amount of reflection within its boundaries. Those who have written about reflective teaching have never argued for "complete openness of mind." On the contrary, reflective teaching involves a balance between thought and action; a balance between the arrogance that blindly rejects what is commonly accepted as truth and the servility that blindly receives this "truth." There is clearly such a thing as too much thinking, as when a person finds it difficult to reach any definite conclusion and wanders helplessly among the multitude of choices presented by a situation, but to imply that reflection necessarily paralyzes one from action is to distort the true meaning of reflective teaching.

Is It Possible to Act on the Results of Reflection?

Another objection that has frequently been raised is that even if teachers do reflect on the purposes and consequences of their actions, they are not able to act on the results of their inquiries if the desired course of action is in conflict with the dominant institutional norms of their school. According to this view, teachers are basically functionaries within a bureaucratic system; they have prescribed roles and responsibilities, and in order to survive in that system they must always give way to institutional demands. In other words, why bother with reflection if you always have to do what you are told to do anyway? Encouraging prospective teachers to reflect about their work is viewed as a hopeless endeavor, because whatever habits of reflectiveness are developed during preservice training will inevitably be "washed out" by inservice school experience as teachers are forced into standardized patterns of behavior and into conformity with bureaucratic norms of obedience and loyalty to those in authority. As Wayne Hoy and William Rees[12] point out, the forces of bureaucratic socialization in schools are strong and efficient.

As was mentioned earlier, there is little doubt that schools as institutions and the societal contexts in which they are embedded exert numerous pressures on teachers to conform to certain behavioral norms, to cover certain curricular content and to use particular methods of instruction and classroom management. However, while they are necessarily constrained by these institutional pressures and by their own individual biases and predispositions, teachers do to varying degrees play active roles in shaping their own occupational identities. If, for example, you were to survey the teachers within a given school, it would probably be fairly easy to identify a dominant "teacher culture" in that school, which defines a set of viewpoints about curriculum, instruction, classroom management and organization. Yet, at the same time, you will inevitably find differences and conflicts among teachers in that school in terms of their beliefs, their instructional methods, and the ways in which they have organized their classrooms. Not all teachers in a given school are alike, and the very existence of these differences within the same institutional conditions is evidence of the potential for teachers to act upon their beliefs even if they conflict with the dominant viewpoints in a given setting.

In reality, the habits of mind and pedagogical skills that you develop now in your formal education for teaching will not necessarily be "washed out" by school experience. The world of teaching necessarily involves a constant interplay between choice and constraint. No matter how prescribed the curriculum and whatever the degree of consensus over behavioral norms for teachers in the settings in which you will work, there will always be some degree of conflict over what is natural and right and some amount of space for you to act alone or with others to reshape the nature of the school in which you work. There are more than a few teachers who do not fit the bureaucratic mold that is frequently portrayed in educational literature, and there is potentially enough room for most teachers within their prescribed roles for some degree of reflection to take place.

Is It Necessary to Reflect?

A third objection that has been raised about reflective teaching is that it is not necessary to be reflective in order to be an effective teacher. Advocates of this position point to the many highly regarded teachers in our schools who succeed without apparently reflecting on the purposes and consequences of their work. For example, Phillip Jackson studied fifty teachers who were identified by their principals and by general reputation as being outstanding teachers, and he concluded that these exemplars of educational practice approached their work in classrooms largely through intuition rather than through any process of rational analysis.

This conclusion has been confirmed by much of the recent research on teacher thinking[13] by studies of teacher-pupil interactions[14] and by Dan Lortie's[15] study of the "ethos" of the teaching profession. According to many education researchers, teachers for the most part, including good teachers, do not seem to be especially reflective or analytic about their work. On the contrary, a substantial number of teachers seem to accept uncritically what is currently fashion-

able. As a result, the position is often taken that it is unnecessary to be reflective because one can be a good teacher without being so.

There are several responses that one could make to this objection. First, there are numerous problems with the conclusions that many researchers have drawn about the predominance of intuitive behavior. Specifically, while it may be true that many teachers rely primarily on instinct and feeling while in the classroom, there is no basis for concluding that good teachers do not put a lot of thought into their work both before and after instruction. Many of these researchers have failed to study what teachers actually do in their classes and how they construct and justify specific activities. What actually goes on in the minds of good teachers—when it is studied—is still not well understood. Furthermore, there are some real problems with the view that university scholars are as a group more reflective than teachers, especially when these conclusions are drawn by those who identify themselves as being most reflective. In our view there is no convincing evidence that those in universities are any more or less likely as a group to be reflective or analytic about their work than teachers are.

Our own experience in talking with teachers has convinced us that the really good ones do reflect upon their work and that educational researchers have failed to capture much of what goes on in the minds of teachers. In fact, studies of attempted school reform provide some evidence that teachers *do* reflect. For example, those who have studied the processes of change in schools have generally concluded that teachers are very selective about what they will incorporate into their classrooms, and in our view this selectivity refutes the position that there is little thought and judgment underlying teachers' work.[16]

There is one further reason for rejecting the view that reflective teaching is not necessary. Scheffler clearly summarizes this view:

Justification for reflection is not . . . simply a matter of minimal necessity. It is rather a matter of desirability, and a thing may be desirable, not because it is something that we could not do without, but because it transforms and enhances the quality of what we do and how we live.[17]

As Scheffler's statement points out, you may be able to get by, by putting little thought into your work, but if you want to strive to be the best teacher that you possibly can, then there is in reality no alternative to reflective teaching. Many teachers profess that they want their students to be thoughtful about the work that they do in school so that they will eventually develop an independence of mind that will enable them to be active participants in a democratic society. If we hold these goals for our children, the place to begin is with ourselves. If the schools of today were all that they could be, one could safely ignore our arguments. But if there is more that we can do to make our schools and our society more enriching, humane and just, then we need reflective teachers to play an integral role in this process.

HOW TO BEGIN

You may be asking, "How can I become reflective, especially given the fact that I haven't started teaching yet?" The suggestions that we will now offer will help you get started. Remember, becoming a reflective teacher is a continual process of growth.

Many educators have correctly pointed out that even before you enter a formal program of teacher preparation you have already been socialized to some extent by the twelve years or more you have spent as a student. You have spent literally thousands of hours assessing schools and classrooms and have by now internalized (largely unconsciously) conceptions of children, learning, the roles of teacher and student, curriculum, beliefs and assumptions concerning almost every issue related to schooling. From our point of view, a good place to begin the process of reflective teaching is to examine these numerous predispositions that you bring with you into formal preparation for teaching. Consciously or not, these will affect how you will perceive what will be presented to you in your teacher education program and how you will interpret your own and others' actions in the classroom.

It is important for you to begin to discriminate between beliefs and assumptions that rest upon tested evidence and those that do not, and to be cautious about putting confidence into beliefs that are not well justified. Some of our ideas have, in fact, been picked up from other people merely because they are widely accepted views, not because we have examined them carefully. Because of the nature of teaching, we may often be compelled to act without full confidence in a point of view or an approach to a problem. This is unavoidable. However, if we remain tentative about our beliefs, the possibility will remain that we may revise our thinking if future evidence warrants it. On the other hand, if we are dogmatic about our beliefs and refuse to entertain the possibility that we may be in error, the avenues for further growth are closed off. There are no greater errors that prospective teachers can make than those that stem from an unbending certainty in one's beliefs.

In *Dilemmas of Schooling*, Ann and Harold Berlak propose several specific steps for proceeding with a reflective analysis of the assumptions and beliefs regarding schooling that one brings into one's teacher preparation.[18] The first step is to begin to articulate your current beliefs regarding a host of specific issues and to examine the assumptions that underlie these beliefs. For example, what knowledge and skills should be taught to different groups of children? How much control should a teacher exert over children's learning and behavior? To what extent should teachers transmit a common core of values and beliefs to all children, and to what extent should the curriculum attend to the cultural knowledge and background experiences of children? The issues here are endless. The above examples are only intended as illustrations of the kinds of questions that can be considered.

The next step is to compare your own beliefs with the beliefs of others. It is important for you to seek actively to understand the beliefs of others (peers, instructors, friends) within your formal courses and, more generally, by reading, observing, and talking to others in both professional and nonprofessional settings. Prospective teachers who are sensitive to the tentative nature of their beliefs take pains to examine any issue from more than one perspective.

Once you have begun to identify the substance of your own beliefs and have become more conscious of alternatives that exist or could be created, it is important for you to do some thinking about the origins and consequences of these beliefs. For example, how has your own biographical history (for example, unique factors in your upbringing, your school experience as a pupil) affected the way in which you currently think about issues of schooling? Which of your current beliefs have you examined carefully through weighing and then rejecting alternative points of view, and which do you hold merely because they are widely accepted by those with whom you associate? Also, which of your current beliefs are the result of outside forces over which you have no control, and which beliefs are merely rationalizations masking an unwillingness to risk the difficulties and/or the possible displeasure of others that would result from their implementation?

Along with doing this analysis of the origin of your beliefs, you should begin to consider the possible consequences for yourself and others of holding particular beliefs. For example, what meanings (intended and unintended) are children likely to take from particular beliefs if they were actually implemented in the classroom? In considering the likely consequences of various courses of action it is important to consider more than the immediate utility of an action. The costs associated with what works in the short run to help you get through a lesson smoothly at times may outweigh the benefits to be gained.

Because of the intimate relationship that exists between the school and society, any con-

sideration of the consequences of an educational action must inevitably take one beyond the boundaries of the classroom and even the school itself. There is no such thing as a neutral educational activity. Any action that one takes in the classroom is necessarily linked to the external economic, political and social order in either a primarily integrative or a creative fashion. Either a teaching activity serves to integrate children into the current social order or it provides children with the knowledge, attitudes or skills to deal critically and creatively with that reality in order to improve it. In any case, all teaching is embedded in an ideological background, and one cannot fully understand the significance or consequences of an activity unless one also considers that activity in light of the more general issues of social continuity and change.

For example, what are the likely consequences for the life chances of various groups of children if you present school knowledge as certain and objective to some groups of children and stress the tentativeness of knowledge to others? In other words, if you teach some students to accept what they are told and others to question and make their own decisions, how will this affect the social roles they hold later, and which group of children will you be preparing for which social roles? This example is cited to make the point that one can at least begin to identify the connections between everyday classroom practices and issues of social continuity and change. Because of the numerous forces acting upon children over a period of many years, we can never be certain of the effect that any given course of action by one teacher has in the long run, but it is certain that, despite the complexity, linkages do exist. It is important at least to attempt to think about the consequences of our actions in a way that transcends questions of immediate utility.

Finally, once you have begun to think about the origins and consequences of the beliefs that you bring into your formal education, the issue of "craft" also needs to be considered. What knowledge and skills will you need to gain in order to implement successfully the kind of teaching that follows from your educational beliefs? If you as a prospective teacher are reflective, you do not passively absorb any and all of the skills and knowledge that others have decided are necessary for your education as a teacher. The craft knowledge and skills for teaching that you will gain during your formal preparation will originate from two major sources: your university instructors and supervisors, and the teachers and administrators with whom you will work during your practicum experiences in schools. If you are reflective about your own education for teaching, you will give some direction to the craft knowledge and skills that you learn in your training.

Within the university your socialization for teaching is much more than the learning of "appropriate" content and procedures for teaching. The knowledge and skills that will be communicated to you through your university courses are not neutral descriptions of how things are; in reality, they are *value governed selections* from a much larger universe of possibilities. Selections that reflect the educational ideologies of the instructors with whom you come into contact. Some things have been selected for your pursuance while other things have been deemphasized or even ignored. These selections reflect at least implicitly answers to normative questions about the nature of schooling, the appropriate roles for teachers and students, how to classify, arrange and evaluate educational knowledge, and how to think about educational problems and their solutions. But just as you will find diversity in the educational perspectives of a group of teachers in any given school, within any university program different university instructors will emphasize, deemphasize and ignore difficult points of view. As a result, it often becomes necessary for you to make decisions about the relevance of conflicting positions on an issue and to seek out information that supports views that may have been selected out by your instructors.

Therefore, if you want to give some direction to your education and to play an active role in shaping your own occupational identity, it becomes important for you to be constantly critical and reflective about that which is presented to you and that which has been omitted. That which is presented to you may or may not be the most appropriate craft knowledge and skill to help you get where you want to go. You need to filter all that is offered to you through your own set of priorities. At the same time, identify and use the instructors' stances about educational issues as alternatives that can help you develop your own beliefs. Generally, the same critical orientation that we have encouraged you to bring to bear upon your own prior experiences and beliefs should also be applied to that which is imparted to you by university instructors. Specifically, what are the origins and consequences of the viewpoints presented, and of the alternatives that are available or could be created?

Finally, one important part of your education for teaching will be the time you spend observing and working with teachers and administrators in school practicums. When you participate in a practicum you come into a setting (someone else's classroom) after certain patterns have been established and after certain ways of organizing time, space, instruction and so forth have become routine. Cooperating teachers, who make many of these decisions, will often not take the time to explain to you how and why these decisions have been made, partly because the routines are by then part of the taken-for-granted reality of their classrooms. Consequently, prospective teachers often fail to grasp how what they see came to be in the first place and are often incapable of creating certain structures on their own once they have their own classrooms. This is a serious lapse in an education student's learning because it is difficult to understand any setting adequately without understanding how it was produced. If you want to understand the settings in which you will work, you will need to question your teachers about the reasons underlying what exists and is presently taken for granted. The following questions illustrate the things you should seek to understand: Why is the school day organized as it is? Why is math taught every day but science taught only once per week? How and why was it decided to teach this particular unit on pollution? How are children placed into groups for reading and what opportunities exist for movement among groups? These regularities exist for particular reasons and it is up to you to seek an understanding of how what is, came to be.

You will also need to ask your cooperating teachers about the ways in which particular decisions are being made while you are there. Although many of the basic patterns of classrooms will be established before you arrive, others will still be developing. The basic problem here is for you to gain an understanding of the thought processes that underlie your cooperating teacher's current actions. Importantly, many researchers have discovered that unless education students initiate these kinds of discussions with their mentors, the logic behind classroom decisions is often missed by prospective teachers.[19] Experienced teachers may take many important factors for granted, and unless you actively probe for what underlies their behavior you will miss much of what is significant about the nature of teacher decision-making.

Seymour Sarason proposes that two basic questions be asked of any educational setting. One is what is the rationale underlying the setting? And the other is what is the universe of alternatives that could be considered?[20] We strongly feel that asking these questions is necessary in order for you to gain the maximum benefit from your practical experience in schools. If you choose not to follow our advice but to take a primarily passive role as a student teacher, your learning will be limited to that which you happen upon by chance. If you want to be a certain kind of teacher and to have a particular quality of impact on children, you will need to ensure that your education for teaching will help you get where you want to go

and that where you want to go is worth the effort. As you gain more experience you may frequently change your mind about the kind of teacher you want to become, but taking an active part in your own professional preparation will at least give you some control over determining the direction in which you are headed.

We have attempted to alert you to some of the numerous issues that you will have to confront during the next few years of your education for teaching. We have argued that there is a fundamental choice for you to make: whether you will give some direction to your training or let others direct it for you. In doing so, we have argued that reflective teaching is both possible and desirable. If the teachers of tomorrow are to contribute to the revitalization and renewal of our schools, there is no alternative. However, as in all decisions, the final choice is up to you.

NOTES

[1] Maxine Greene, *Teacher as Stranger* (Belmont, CA: Wadsworth Publishing Co., 1973), p. 46.

[2] John Dewey, *How We Think: A Restatement of the Relation of Reflective Thinking to the Educative Process* (Chicago: Henry Regnery and Co., 1933).

[3] *Ibid.*

[4] *Ibid.*

[5] *Ibid.*, p. 17.

[6] *Ibid.*, p. 89.

[7] Phillip Jackson, *Life in Classrooms* (New York: Holt, Rinehart and Winston, 1968).

[8] *Ibid.*, p. 151.

[9] For example, see John Eliott, "Developing Hypotheses about Classrooms From Teachers' Personal Constructs," *Interchange* 7:2 (1976–1977) 1–22.

[10] Dewey, *How We Think*, p. 87.

[11] Frequently, discussions that occur among teachers during planning sessions, team meetings, etc., focus almost entirely on procedural issues (for example, *How* will we teach what has already been decided to teach?) to the neglect of curricular questions, such as "What should we be teaching and why?" See Thomas Popkewitz, B. Robert Tabachnick, and Gary Wehlage, *The Myth of Educational Reform* (Madison: University of Wisconsin Press, 1982) for an example of how this

occurs in exemplary "individually guided education" schools.

[12] Wayne Hoy and William Rees, "The Bureaucratic Socialization of Student Teachers," *Journal of Teacher Education*, 28 (January-February, 1977) 23–26.

[13] Christopher Clark and Robert Yinger, "Research on Teacher Thinking," *Curriculum Inquiry*, 7 (Winter, 1977): 279–304.

[14] Jere Brophy and Thomas Good, *Teacher-Pupil Relationships: Causes and Consequences* (New York: Holt, Rinehart and Winston, 1974).

[15] Dan Lortie, *School Teacher* (Chicago: University of Chicago Press, 1975).

[16] John Goodlad and M. Frances Klein, *Behind the Classroom Door* (Washington, Ohio: Jones Publishers, 1970).

[17] Israel Scheffler, "University Scholarship and the Education of Teachers," *Teachers College Record* 70 (October, 1968) 1–12.

[18] Ann Berlak and Harold Berlak, *Dilemmas of Schooling* (London: Methuen, 1981).

[19] B. Robert Tabachnick, Thomas Popkewitz, and Kenneth Zeichner, "Teacher Education and the Professional Perspectives of Student Teachers," *Interchange* 10:4 (1979–80) 12–29.

[20] Seymour Sarason, *The Culture of the School and the Problem of Change* (Boston: Allyn and Bacon, 1971).

The Contribution of Schooling to the Learning of Norms: Independence, Achievement, Universalism, and Specificity

ROBERT DREEBEN

Generally speaking . . . a teacher must balance a concern with specific accomplishments with some concern for a state of well-being: he has to keep a relatively "happy" class which "learns." But a class is more than a collection of individuals. The teacher always has to manage children in groups. His acts towards individuals must somehow be interpreted either as expressions of general rules or of a particular circumstance. In the latter case he must draw the further line between legitimate special treatment and favoritism. He must teach the relegation of private needs as well as their occasional relevance.

Kaspar D. Naegele, "Clergymen, Teachers, and Psychiatrists: . . . "

In speaking of these four ideas as norms, I mean that individuals accept them as legitimate standards for governing their own conduct in the appropriate situations. Specifically, they accept the obligations to (1) act by themselves (unless collaborative effort is called for), and accept personal responsibility for their conduct and accountability for its consequences; (2) perform tasks actively and master the environment according to certain standards of excellence; and (3) acknowledge the rights of others to treat them as members of categories (4) on the basis of a few discrete characteristics rather than on the full constellation of them that represent the whole person. I treat these four norms because they are integral parts of public and occupational life in industrial societies, or institutional realms adjacent to the school.

In earlier parts of this book, I have discussed only the pre-adult phases of socialization, which occur in the family of orientation and in the school. In one sense, at least for men, full adult status requires occupational employment, and

one of the outcomes of schooling is employability. The capacity to hold a job involves not only adequate physical capacities (in part the outcome of biological maturation), but also the appropriate intellectual and psychological skills to cope with the demands of work. The requirements of job-holding are multifarious; however, most occupations require, among other things, that individuals take personal responsibility for the completion and quality of their work and individual accountability for its shortcomings, and that they perform their tasks to the best of their ability.

Public life extends beyond occupational employment. Even though people work as members of occupational categories, and in association with others as clients, patients, customers, parish-

---

Source: "The Contribution of Schooling to the Learning of Norms: Independence, Achievement, Universalism, and Specificity" from *On What is Learned in School,* by Robert Dreeben, copyright 1968. Reprinted by permission of the author.

ioners, students, and so on, they also have nonoccupational identities as voters, communicants, petitioners, depositors, applicants, and creditors (to name just a few), in which people are similarly classified according to one primary characteristic, irrespective of how they differ otherwise.

Goode observes:

> The prime social characteristic of modern industrial enterprise is that the individual is ideally given a job on the basis of his ability to fulfill its demands, and that this achievement is evaluated universalistically; the same standards apply to all who hold the same job.[1]

Industrially oriented societies tend to have occupational systems based on normative principles different from those of kinship units. Many observers, recognizing that individuals must undergo psychological changes of considerable magnitude in order to make the transition from family of orientation to economic employment,[2] have noted (but at the same time understated) the contribution of schooling. Eisenstadt, for example, in an otherwise penetrating analysis of age-grouping, restricts his treatment of the school's contribution to that of " . . . adapting the psychological (and to some extent also physiological) learning potential of the child to the various skills and knowledges which must be acquired by him."[3] Eisenstadt's emphasis is too narrowly limited to those cognitive outcomes of schooling related to instrumental knowledge.

Furthermore, while stressing the transition between family and occupation, most writers have largely ignored the contribution of schooling to the development of psychological capacities necessary for participating in other (noneconomic) segments of society. It is my contention that the social experiences available to pupils in schools, by virtue of the nature and sequence of their structural arrangements, provide opportunities for children to learn norms characteristic of several facets of adult public life, occupation being but one.

The social properties of schools are such that pupils, by coping with the sequence of classroom tasks and situations, are more likely to learn the principles (i.e., social norms) of independence, achievement, universalism, and specificity than if they had remained full-time members of the household. Although I have spoken thus far only of the similarities and differences between the family and the school, the nature of that comparison is largely determined by the character of public institutions, in particular the economy and the polity. Schools, that is to say, form one of several institutional linkages between the household and the public sphere of adult life, a linkage organized around stages of the life cycle in industrial societies. There is substantial evidence that conduct in the family and conduct on the job are governed by contrasting normative principles. From this we can imply that if the education of children were carried on primarily within the jurisdiction of the family, the nature of experiences available in that setting would not provide conditions appropriate for acquiring those capacities that enable people to participate competently in the public realm.

It is not inevitable that schools should provide such an institutional linkage, but the fact of the matter is that they do, even though there are other candidates for the job. Mass media, for example, might perform a comparable knowledge-dispensing function, and if their potentialities for effecting more profound psychological changes were plumbed, they might constitute an agency sufficiently potent to bring about changes in principles of conduct. The media have not yet proved up to the job, however, perhaps in part because children's early experiences in the family predispose them to be responsive to human agents, and the media do not provide such agents. In fact, much research on the impact of mass media points to the importance of human links in the chain from source to audience. Occupational apprenticeship might be an acceptable substitute for the schools; it has the human element and is directly related to occupational employment, one of the main locations of men's engagement in the public sphere of industrial society. Apprenticeship, however, like the media, has its own liabilities, one of which is that it continues relationships of dependency (not of child on parent, but of worker on employer), and those relationships are often found to be incompatible with many of the institutional demands of public life. Since the media and apprenticeship arrangements do not exhaust the possibilities, and since I am not trying to demonstrate the inevitability of schools, the impact of schooling remains to be explained, because schools are what we have. I turn, then, to a discussion of how the experiences of schooling contribute to the acquisition of the four norms in question.

INDEPENDENCE

One answer to the question, "What is learned in school?" is that pupils learn to acknowledge that there are tasks they must do alone, and to do them that way. Along with this self-imposed obligation goes the idea that others have a legitimate right to expect such independent behavior under certain circumstances.[4] Independence has a widely acknowledged though not unequivocal meaning. In using it here I refer to a cluster of meanings: doing things on one's own, being self-reliant, accepting personal responsibility for one's behavior, acting self-sufficiently,[5] and handling tasks with which, *under different circumstances*, one can rightfully expect the help of others. The pupil, when in school, is separated from family members who have customarily provided help, support, and sustenance, persons on whom he has long been dependent.

A constellation of classroom characteristics, teacher actions, and pupil actions shape experiences in which the norm of independence is learned. In addition to the fact that school children are removed from persons with whom they have already formed strong relationships of dependency, the sheer size of a classroom assemblage limits each pupil's claim to personal contact with the

teacher, and more so at the secondary levels than at the elementary. This numerical property of classrooms reduces pupils' opportunities for establishing new relationships of dependency with adults and for receiving help from them.

Parents expect their children to act independently in many situations, but teachers are more systematic in expecting pupils to adhere to standards of independence in performing academic tasks. There are at least two additional aspects of classroom operation that bear directly on learning the norm of independence: rules about cheating and formal testing. Let us consider cheating first. The word itself is condemnatory in its reference to illegal and immoral acts. Most commonly, attention turns to how much cheating occurs, who cheats, and why. But these questions, while of great importance elsewhere, are of no concern here. My interest is in a different problem: to what types of conduct is the pejorative "cheating" assigned?

In school, cheating pertains primarily to instructional activities and usually refers to acts in which two or more parties participate when the unaided action of only one is expected. Illegal or immoral acts such as stealing and vandalism, whether carried out by individuals or groups, are not considered cheating because they have no direct connection with the central academic core of school activities. Nor is joint participation categorically proscribed; joint effort is called cooperation or collusion depending on the teacher's prior definition of the task.

Cheating takes many forms, most of which involve collective effort. A parent and a child may collaborate to produce homework; two pupils can pool their wisdom (or ignorance, as the case may be) in the interest of passing an examination. In both cases the parties join deliberately, although deliberateness is not essential to the definition; one pupil can copy from another without the latter knowing. In the case of plagiarism, of course, the second party is not a person at all, but information compiled by another. The use of crib notes, perhaps a limiting case, involves no collusion; it consists, rather, of an illegitimate form of help. These are the main forms of school cheating, but there are many variations, routine to exotic. Thus actions called cheating are those closely tied to the instructional goals of the school and usually involve assisted performance when unaided performance is expected. As one observer put it: Pupils " . . . *must learn to distinguish between cooperating and cheating.*"[6]

The irony of cheating *in school* is that the same kinds of acts are considered morally acceptable and even commendable in other situations. It is praiseworthy for one friend to assist another in distress, or for a parent to help a child; and if one lacks the information to do a job, the resourceful thing is to look it up. In effect, many school activities called cheating are the customary forms of support and assistance in the family and among friends.

In one obvious sense, school rules against cheating are designed to establish the content of moral standards. In another sense, the school attaches the stigma of immorality to certain types of behavior for social as distinct from ethical reasons; namely, to change the character of prevailing social relationships in which children are involved. In the case of homework, the school, in effect, attempts to redefine the relationship between parents and children by proscribing one kind of parental support, which is not a problem in other circumstances. The teacher has no direct control over parents but tries to influence them at a distance by asking their adherence to a principle clothed in moral language whose violations are punishable. The line between legitimate parental support (encouraged when it takes the form of parents stressing the importance of school and urging their children to do well) and collusion is unclear, but by morally proscribing parental intervention beyond a certain point, the teacher attempts to limit the child's dependence on family members in doing his school work. In other words, he expects the pupil to work independently. The same argument applies to pupils and

their friends; the teacher attempts to eliminate those parts of friendship that make it difficult or impossible for him to discover what a pupil can do on his own. In relationships with kin and friends, the customary sources of support in times of adversity, the school intervenes by restricting solidarity and, in the process, determines what the pupil can accomplish unaided. The pupil, for his part, discovers which of his actions he is held accountable for individually within the confines of tasks set by the school.

This argument is indirectly supported by the comparison between schooling and the occupational employment for which school is intended as preparation. The question here is the sense in which school experience is preparatory. Usually workers are not restricted in seeking help on problems confronting them; on the contrary, many occupations provide resources specifically intended to be helpful: arrangements for consultation, libraries, access to more experienced colleagues, and so on. Only in rare situations are people expected not to enlist the aid of family and friends in matters pertaining to work where that aid is appropriate. In other words, activities on the job, directly analogous to school work, do not carry comparable restrictions. However, people in their occupational activities are required to accept individual responsibility and accountability for the performance of assigned and self-initiated tasks. To the extent that the school contributes to the development of independence, the preparation lies more in the development of a psychological disposition to act independently than to perform a certain range of tasks without help.

Second, as to testing, and particularly the use of achievement tests; most important for independence are the social conditions designed for the *administration* of tests, not their content or format. By and large, pupils are tested under more or less rigorously controlled conditions. At one end of the spectrum, formal standardized tests are administered most stringently; pupils are physically separated, and the testing room is patrolled by proctors whose job is to discover contraband and to guarantee that no communication occurs, these arrangements being designed so that each examination paper represents independent work. At the other end, some testing situations are more informal, less elaborately staged, although there is almost always some provision to ensure that each pupil's work represents the product of only his own efforts.

Testing represents an approach to establishing the norm of independence, which is different from the proscription against cheating even though both are designed to reduce the likelihood of joint effort. Whereas the rules against cheating are directed toward delineating the form of appropriate behavior, the restrictions built into the testing situation provide physical constraints intended to guarantee that teachers will receive samples of the work pupils do unassisted. Actually, unless they stipulate otherwise, teachers expect pupils to do most of their everyday work by themselves; daily assignments provide the opportunities for and practice in independent work. Tests, because they occur at less frequent intervals than ordinary assignments, cannot provide comparably frequent opportunities; by the elaborate trappings of their administration, particularly with college entrance exams, and the anxiety they provoke, they symbolize the magnitude of the stakes.

It may be objected that in emphasizing independence I have ignored cooperation, since an important item on the school agenda is the instruction of pupils in the skills of working with others. Teachers do assign work to groups and expect a collaborative product, and to this extent they require the subordination of individual to collective efforts, but judging the product according to collective standards is another question.

To evaluate the contribution of each member of a working team, the teacher must either judge the quality of each one's work, in effect relying on the standard of independence, or rate each contribution according to the quality of the total product. The latter procedure rests on the assumption that each member has contributed equally, an untenable assumption if one member has carried the rest or if a few members have carried a weak sister. That occurrences of this kind are usually considered "unfair" suggests the normative priority of independence and the simple fact of life in industrial societies; i.e., that institutions of higher learning and employers want to know how well each person can do and put constraints on the schools in order to find out. Thus, although the school provides opportunities for pupils to gain experience in cooperative situations, in the last analysis it is the individual assessment that counts.

ACHIEVEMENT

Pupils come to accept the premise that they should perform their tasks the best they can, and act accordingly. The concept of achievement, like independence, has several referents. It usually denotes activity and mastery, making an impact on the environment rather than fatalistically accepting it, and competing against some standard of excellence. Analytically, the concept should be distinguished from independence, since, among other differences, achievement criteria can apply to activities performed collectively.

Much of the recent literature treats achievement in the context of child-rearing within the family as if achievement motivation were primarily a product of parental behavior.[7] Even though there is reason to believe that early childhood experiences in the family do contribute to its development, classroom experiences also contribute through teachers' use of resources beyond those ordinarily at the command of family members.

Classrooms are organized around a set of core activities in which a teacher assigns tasks to pupils and evaluates and compares the quality of their work. In the course of time, pupils differentiate themselves according to how well they perform a variety of tasks, most of which require the use of symbolic skills. Achievement standards are not limited in applicability to the classroom nor is their content restricted to the cognitive areas.

Schools afford opportunities for participation in a variety of extra-curricular activities, most conspicuously athletics, but also music, dramatics, and a bewildering array of club and small group activities serving individual interests and talents.

The direct relevance of classroom work in providing task experience judged by achievement criteria is almost self-evident; the experience is built into the assignment-performance-evaluation sequence of the work. Less evident, however, is the fact that these activities force pupils to cope with various degrees of success and failure, both of which can be psychologically problematic. Consistently successful performance requires that pupils deal with the consequences of their own excellence in a context of peer equality in nonacademic areas. For example, they confront the dilemma inherent in having surpassed their age-mates in some respects while depending on their friendship and support in others, particularly in out-of-school social activities. The classroom provides not only the achievement experience itself but by-products of it, taking the form of dilemma just described.

Similarly, pupils whose work is consistently poor not only must participate in achievement activities leading to their failure, they must also experience living with that failure. They adopt various modes of coping with this, most of which center around maintaining personal self-respect in the face of continuing assaults upon it. Probably a minority succeed or fail consistently; a majority, most likely, do neither one consistently, but nonetheless worry about not doing well. Schooling, then, assures most pupils the experiences of both winning and losing, and to the extent that they gain some modicum of gratification from academic activities, it teaches them to approach their work in a frame of mind conducive to achievement. At the same time they learn how to cope, in a variety of ways and more or less well, with success and failure.

Failure is perhaps the more difficult condition with which to cope because it requires acknowledgement that the premise of achievement, to which failure itself can be attributed in part, is a

legitimate principle by which to govern one's actions. Yet situations that constrain people to live with personal failure are endemic to industrial societies in which many facets of public life are based on achievement principles; political defeat and occupational non-promotion being two cases in point.

As suggested earlier, the school provides a broad range of experiences other than those restricted to the classroom and academic in nature; these experiences are also based on achievement criteria but differ in several important respects. Alternatives to academic performance give the pupil a chance to succeed in achievement-oriented activities even though he may not be able to do well in the classroom.

How these alternative activities differ from those of the classroom is as important as the fact that they do so differ, as evidenced by the case of athletics. Competitive sports resemble classroom activities in that both provide participants with the chance to demonstrate individual excellence. However, the former—and this is more true of team than individual sports—permit collective responsibility for defeat, whereas the latter by and large allow only individual responsibility for failure. That is to say, the chances of receiving personal gratification for success are at least as great in sports as in the classroom, while the assault on personal self-respect for failure is potentially less intense. Athletics should not be written off as a manifestation of mere adolescent nonintellectualism, as recent writers have treated it.[8] I do not suggest that athletics has an as yet undiscovered intellectual richness; rather that its contribution should not be viewed simply in terms of intellectuality. Wilkinson, in talking about athletics in the British public schools, makes a similar argument, not so much in terms of mitigating the psychological consequences of achievement for individuals as in striking a balance between competition and social cooperation:

On the football field and on the river, the public school taught its boys to compete, not so much in personal contests, as in struggles between groups—between teams, houses, and schools. . . . They preserved middle-class morality and energy, but they adapted these to the needs of the public servant,[9]

so important, according to Wilkinson, in establishing the ethic that private privilege meant public duty.

A similar contention holds for music and dramatics; both provide the potentiality for individual accomplishment and recognition without the persistent, systematic, and potentially corrosive evaluation typical of the classroom. Finally, in various club activities based on interest and talent, a pupil can do the things he is good at in the company of others who share an appreciation for them. In all these situations, either the rigors of competition and judgment characteristic of the classroom are mitigated, or the activity in question has its own built-in source of support and personal protection, not to the same extent as in the family, but more than is available in the crucible of the classroom.

The school provides a wider variety of achievement experiences than does the family, but it also has fewer resources for supporting and protecting pupils' self-respect in the face of failure. As pupils proceed through successive school levels, the rigors of achievement increase, at least for those who continue along the main academic line. Moreover, at the secondary levels the number of activities governed according to achievement principles increases as does the variety of these activities. As preparation for adult public life in which the application of these principles is widespread, schooling contributes to personal development in assuring that the majority of pupils not only will have performed tasks according to the achievement standard, but that they will have had experience in an expanding number of situations in which activities are organized according to it.

Unlike independence and achievement, universalism and specificity are not commonly regarded as good things. Parents and teachers admonish children to act independently and do their work well; few of them support the idea that people should willingly acknowledge their similarity to one another in specifically categorical terms while ignoring their obvious differences; that is, in a sense, denying their own individuality.

Ideologically, social critics have deplored the impersonal, ostensibly dehumanizing, aspects of categorization, a principle widely believed to lie at the heart of the problem of human alienation; the attachment of man to machine, the detachment of man from man. Often ignored, however, is the connection between this principle and the idea of fairness, or equity. Seen from this vantage point, categorization is widely regarded as a good thing, especially when contrasted to nepotism, favoritism, and arbitrariness. People resent the principle when they think they have a legitimate reason to receive special consideration, and when their individuality appears to vanish by being "processed." Yet when a newcomer breaks into a long queue of patiently waiting people instead of proceeding to the end of the line, they usually condemn him for acting unfairly (for not following the standard rule for all newcomers to a line). They do *not* react by expressing any sense of their own alienation, since they accept the same categorical principle as binding on themselves. In other words, this is not the occasion to proclaim one's individuality, but to act like everybody else and be sure they do likewise. The contrasts between the two dualities (individuality and dehumanization, fairness and special privilege) are similarly predicated on the principles of universalism and specificity; people differ in their posture toward each duality according to ideological position, situation, and, more cynically, in their conception of self-interest.

The concepts of universalism and specificity have been formulated most comprehensively by Parsons, though only part of his formulation is directly germane to this discussion. As part of his concern with social systems, Parsons views universalism as one horn of a dilemma (the other being particularism) in role definition; under what circumstances does the occupant of one social position govern his actions by adopting one standard or another when dealing with the occupant of another social position? My concern, however, is not with a selection among alternative, conflicting standards, but with the conditions under which individuals learn to impose the standards of universalism and specificity on themselves and to act accordingly.

Defining the central theme of universalism raises problems because the term has been assigned a variety of meanings, not all of them clear.[10] The relevant distinction here is whether individuals are treated in terms of their membership in categories or as special cases. In one respect or another an individual can always be viewed as a member of one or more categories, universalistically; he is viewed particularistically if, considering his similarity to others in the same category, he still receives special treatment. As Blau puts it:

> An attribute is defined as a universalistic standard if persons, regardless of their own characteristics, direct a disproportionate number of their positive (or negative) evaluations to others with a certain characteristic. An attribute is defined as a particularistic standard if persons tend to direct their positive (or, in special cases, negative) evaluations to others whose characteristics are like their own.[11]

The treatment of others does not become more particularistic as an increasing number of categories is taken into account. If age, sex, religion, ethnicity, and the like are considered, all examples of general categories, treatment is still categorical in nature because it is oriented to categorical similarities and not to what is special about the person. Thus, *"A man's orientation toward his family,"* according to Blau, *"is considered particularistic because it* singles out for special attention *the members of an ingroup, rather than persons with a certain attribute regardless of whether it makes them part of his ingroup or not."*[12]

The norm of specificity is easily confused with universalism despite its distinctiveness. It refers to the scope of one person's interest in another; to the obligation to confine one's interest to a narrow range of characteristics and concerns, or to extend them to include a broad range.[13] The notion of relevance is implicit; the characteristics and concerns that should be included within the range, whether broad or narrow, are those considered relevant in terms of the activities in which the persons in question are involved. Doctors and storekeepers, for example, differ in the scope of the interest they have in the persons seeking their services, but the content of their interests also varies according to the nature of the needs and desires of those persons.

It is my contention that what the school contributes to the acceptance by children of those norms that penetrate many areas of public life is critical, because children's pre-school experience in the family is weighted heavily on the side of special treatment and parental consideration of the whole child. To say that children learn the norm of universalism means that they come to accept being treated by others as members of categories (in addition to being treated as special cases, as in the family).

Categorization

Schools provide a number of experiences that families cannot readily provide because of limitations in their social composition and structure. One such experience is the systematic establishment and demarcation of membership categories. First, by assigning all pupils in a classroom the same or similar tasks to perform, teachers in effect make them confront the same set of demands. Even if there are variations in task content, class members still confront the same teacher and the obligations he imposes. Second, parity of age creates a condition of homogeneity according to developmental stage, a rough equalization of pupil capacities making it possible for teachers to assign similar tasks. Third, through the process of yearly promotion from grade to grade, pupils cross the boundaries separating one age category from another. With successive boundary crossings comes the knowledge that each age-grade category is associated with a particular set of circumstances (e.g., teachers, difficulty of tasks, subject matter studied). Moreover, pupils learn the relationship between categories and how their present position relates to past and future positions by virtue of having experienced the transitions between them. In these three ways, the grade (more specifically the classroom within the grade) with its age-homogeneous membership and clearly demarcated boundaries provides a basis for categorical grouping that the family cannot readily duplicate. Most important, the experiences of membership in a group of age-equals and repeated boundary crossings makes it possible for pupils to acquire a relativity of perspective, a capacity to view their own circumstances from other vantage points that they themselves have occupied.[14]

Although each child holds membership in the category "children" at home, parents, in raising them, tend to take age differences into account and thereby accentuate the uniqueness of each child's circumstances, thus belying in some measure the categorical aspects of "childhood." However, even if the category "children" breaks into its age-related components within the family, it remains intact when children compare themselves with friends and neighbors of similar age. In typical situations of this kind, children inform their parents that friends of the same age have greater privileges or fewer responsibilities than they. Parents, if they cannot actually equalize the circumstances, often explain or justify the disparity by pointing to the special situation of the neighbor family; they have more money, fewer children, a bigger house. Whatever the reason, that is, parents point out the uniqueness of family circumstances and thereby emphasize the particularities of each child's situation. The school, in contrast, provides the requisite circumstances for making comparisons among pupils in categorical rather than particular terms.

Another school experience fostering the establishment of social categories is the re-equalization of pupils by means of the high school track system after they have differentiated themselves through academic achievement in the lower grades, a mechanism that minimizes the likelihood of teachers having to deal with special cases. Teachers with a variegated batch of pupils must adopt more individualized methods of instruction than those whose pupils are similar in their level of achievement. In so doing, they partially recreate a kinship-type of relationship with pupils, treating segments of the class differently according to differences in capacity, much as parents treat their children differently according to age-related capacities.

As far as level is concerned, the high school is a better place to acquire the principle of universalism than the lower school levels because pupils within each track, who are of roughly similar capacity, move from classroom to classroom, in each one receiving instruction in a different subject area by a different teacher. They discover that over a range of activities, they are treated alike and that relatively uniform demands and criteria of evaluation are applied to them. Thus they learn which differences in experience are subordinated to the principle of categorization. The elementary classroom, oriented more to instruction in different subjects by a single teacher, does not provide the necessary variations in persons and subjects for a clear-cut demonstration of the categorical principle.

Persons and Positions

Although the idea of categorization is central to the norm of universalism, it has additional and derivative aspects. One is the crucial distinction, widely relevant in industrial societies, between the person and the social position he occupies. Individuals are often expected to treat one another according to their social position, rather than according to their individual identity. Schooling contributes to the capacity to make the distinction (and to the obligation to do so) by making it possible for pupils to discover that different individuals occupying a single social position often act in ways that are attached to the position rather than to the different persons filling it. Even though all members of a given classroom find themselves in the same circumstances (they are about equal in age and roughly resemble each other in social characteristics related to residence), they still differ in many respects: sex, race, religion, ethnicity, and physical characteristics being among the most obvious. Their situation, therefore, provides the experience of finding that common interests and shared circumstances are assigned a priority that submerges obvious personal differences. The same contention holds for adults. Male and female adults are found in both school and family settings; in school, pupils can discover that an increasingly large number of different adults of both sexes can occupy the same position, that of "teacher." This discovery is not as easily made in the family because it is not possible to determine definitively whether "parent" represents two positions, one occupied by a male, the other by a female, or a single position with two occupants differing in sex. Children are not left completely without clues in this matter since they do have other adult relatives who can be seen as distinct persons occupying the same position: aunts, uncles, grandparents, and the like. Yet even extended families do not provide the frequent and systematic comparisons characteristic of the schools. Schooling, in other words, enables pupils to distinguish between persons and the social positions they occupy (a capacity crucially important in both occupational and political life) by placing them in situations in which the membership of each position is varied in its composition and the similarities between persons in a single position are made evident.

Specificity

The school provides structural arrangements more conducive to the acquisition of the norm of specificity than does the family. First, since the number of persons and the ratio between adults and nonadults is much larger in classrooms than in the household, the school provides large social aggregates in which pupils can form many casual associations (in addition to their close friendships) in which they invest but a small portion of themselves. As both the size and heterogeneity of the student body increase at each successive level, the opportunities for these somewhat fragmented social contacts increase and diversify. The relative shallowness and transiency of these relationships increase the likelihood that pupils will have experiences in which the fullness of their individuality is *not* involved, as it tends to be in their relationships among kin and close friends.

Second, on leaving the elementary school and proceeding through the departmentalized secondary levels, pupils form associations with teachers who have a progressively narrowing and specialized interest in them. (This comes about both because of subject matter specialization itself and because the number of pupils each teacher faces in the course of a day grows larger.) Although it is true that children, as they grow older, tend to form more specific relationships with their parents (symptomatically, this trend manifests itself in adolescents' complaints of parental invasions of privacy), the resources of the school far exceed those of the family in providing the social basis for the establishment of relationships in which only narrow segments of personality are invested.

Equity

An additional facet of universalism is the principle of equity, or fairness (I use the terms interchangeably). When children compare their lot—their gains and losses, rewards and punishments, privileges and responsibilities—with that of others and express dissatisfaction about their own, they have begun to think in terms of equity; their punishments are too severe, chores too onerous, allowance too small compared to those of siblings and friends. Children's comparisons with siblings, who are almost always different in age, usually prompt parents to try to resolve the sensed inequities by equalizing age hypothetically. "If you were as young as he, you wouldn't have to shovel the walk either." "He is only a child and doesn't know any better." The pained questions to which these statements are replies are familiar enough.

Writers who have discussed problems of equity and inequity have usually done so in order to identify indicative expressions of them (e.g., indignation, dissatisfaction with job, joking relationships, disputes over payment, etc.) and to discover the conditions under which such expressions originate (e.g., status inconsistency, relative deprivation, frequency of supervision, etc.).[15] My concern here is not with these two questions, but with the nature of family and school experiences in which problems of equity and inequity are defined as such, and in which the underlying principles become established in children's minds.

Among children in a family, age is critical in determining what is fair and unfair.[16] In a sense, it is the clock by which we keep developmental time, changing constantly though not periodically. The gains and losses of life are inextricably tied to age; memory reminds us of what we once had, and the experiences of others inform us of our present standing and of what the future holds. The personal significance of age is heightened among young children because the younger they are, the more significant any given age difference between them. Thus the difference between a four-year old and an eight-year old is greater than that between a fourteen-year old and an eighteen-year old because, on the average, there are greater developmental changes occurring during the earlier four year span than during the later one. When the circumstances of life change rapidly; when one is still in the process of learning what is one's due and what is due others; and when the younger children do not have to fight the battles that the older ones have

already won, it is difficult to determine whether one is being treated fairly on any given occasion.

In the family, except for the sense of unity and similarity that comes from experience in a small, solitary group whose members are reciprocally affectionate and supportive, behavior *within* the setting is governed to a considerable extent by the unique personal characteristics of the members. Among children, as I have argued, age is one of the most important of these characteristics. Except in families with one child or multiple-birth children, age alone is sufficient to distinguish them, although it is certainly not the only distinguishing characteristic. Because of the developmental importance of age, it constitutes one basis according to which parents act toward their children and siblings act toward each other. There are, of course, occasions on which parents can and do treat their children as if they were alike, but where questions of responsibility, accountability, privilege, and the like are involved, the differences between children must be taken seriously. *In this sense*, and in the context of the earlier qualification about family unity, each child exists in his own set of circumstances and is treated accordingly. This statement does not deny that parents may in fact ignore the differences among their children. It does imply, though, that if they do so over the long run, there can be disruptive consequences for the children and for the family unit. As cases in point, there are well-known situations involving overdemandingness (treating children as if they were older), and overindulgence (treating them as if they were younger).

Questions of equity, always comparative, are tied to situations. As children grow older, their circumstances and those of siblings change. The basis on which they determine what is fair and unfair also changes both absolutely and relatively. Because age is a unique personal attribute, and because there are unique constellations of events and personal characteristics associated with small age spans, there are always variables at the root of equity problems. Inequities among young children can only be set straight in the relatively short run because circumstances in the short run change steadily over time.

The contrast between age as a constant and as a variable in questions of equity is evidenced clearly in Homans' treatment of age: " . . . *one of the ways in which two men may be 'like' one another is in their investments [age being one]. Accordingly the more nearly one man is like another in age, the more apt he is to expect their net rewards to be equal and to display anger when his own are less.*"[17] In the context of this statement, age is the criterion for assessing the fairness of rewards as one man compares his gain with that of another.

In the context of the transition between childhood and adulthood, two children *within the same family* (unless they are twins) cannot easily settle a question of equity by referring to their ages (they may acknowledge that the older child is entitled to more, but not how much more) because they differ in age, because the meaning of age differences changes, and because there can be disagreement over the coefficient for converting age units into units of gain and loss. Such a conversion is unnecessary in the case described by Homans because the two men are alike in age.

The problem families have of settling equity questions attributable to age variations does not arise in school classrooms, since the age of class members is nearly constant. Teachers cannot treat all pupils identically, but they can use age similarity as a guide for assigning similar instructional tasks to all members of a class and to communicate, implicitly or explicitly, that they are all in the same boat.

Even without age differences, problems of fairness and unfairness do arise in classrooms, originating when pupils who are supposed to be treated similarly are not so treated. Grades, for example, according to the usual procedure, must be assigned according to the quality of work completed, and equivalent products should receive the same grade. Marking similar work

differently, or unequal work the same, represents unfair grading. A similar principle holds for the punishment of offenses (the punishment should fit the crime, and similar forms of misbehavior should be treated alike[18]) and for the assignment of tasks and responsibilities according to difficulty and onerousness. But there are secondary considerations that enter the process of evaluating performance: how hard pupils work and how much they have improved. These criteria cannot readily replace quality of performance unless teachers, pupils, and parents are willing to acknowledge the justice of various anomalies (so defined, at least, within the scope of American values), as when pupils who do excellent work with little effort receive lower grades than pupils who produce mediocre work through feverish activity; or when pupils who do not pull their weight in a cooperative project receive the high grade assigned to the project.

As argued earlier, equity involves a comparative assessment of one's circumstances: gains and losses, rewards and punishments, rights and obligations, privileges and responsibilities. To determine whether the circumstances in a given situation are equitable, an individual must learn to make comparisons by which he can discover whose circumstances resemble his own and whose do not, who is treated like him and who is not; he must also discover the relationships between his circumstances and the way he is treated.

Schooling, then, through the structural properties of classrooms at each school level and the treatment of pupils by teachers, provides opportunities for making the comparisons relevant to defining questions of equity far more effectively than does the family. The process is similar to that (above described) of learning the norm of universalism in general. Both within the classroom and within each grade, age (and, to a lesser extent, other personal and social characteristics) provides a basis for discovering both similarities and differences in categorical terms. The existence of grade levels distinguished primarily by the demandingness of work and demarcated by the device of yearly promotion, and the progression of pupils through them year by year, make it possible for children to learn that, *within the context of the school*, certain qualities that determine their uniqueness as persons become subordinated to those specific characteristics in which they are alike. Thus, fourth and fifth graders, despite their individuality, are judged according to the specific criterion of achievement, and the content and difficulty of their assigned tasks are regulated according to developmental considerations symbolized by grade. The fourth grader, having completed the third grade, can grasp the idea that he belongs to a category of persons whose circumstances differ from those of persons belonging to another category.

Family relationships are not organized on a group basis, nor do they entail anything comparable to the systematic step-by-step progression of grades in which the boundaries between one category and another are clearly demarcated. Although a child knows the difference between family members and nonmembers, his experiences in a kinship setting do not allow him to distinguish clearly whether his circumstances are uniquely his own or are shared. In other words, these relationships are not structured in such a way as to form a basis for making the categorical comparisons basic to the universalistic norm. Moreover, since parents treat their children in terms of the full range of personal characteristics; that is, according to the norm of diffuseness rather than that of specificity, the family setting is conducive to the special rather than the categorical treatment of each child (since the boundaries of a category are more clearly delineated if one characteristic, not many, constitutes the basis of categorization).

A CONCEPTUAL CAVEAT

The argument of this volume rests on the assumption that schools, through their structural arrangements and the behavior patterns of teachers, provide pupils with certain experiences largely unavailable in other social settings, and that these experiences, by virtue of their peculiar characteristics, represent conditions conducive to the acquisition of norms. I have indicated how pupils learn the norms of independence, achievement, universalism, and specificity as outcomes of the schooling process. A critical point, however, is how the relationship between experience and outcome is formulated.

There is no guarantee that pupils will come to accept these four norms simply because these experiences are available, nor should one conclude that these experiences contribute to the learning of only the four discussed here; for example, the pupils may lack the necessary social and psychological support from sources outside the school or sufficient inner resources to cope with the demands of schooling. These are reasons external to the school situation and may be sufficient to preclude both the instructional and normative outcomes. However, forces inherent in the schooling process itself may be equally preclusive, since the same activities and sanctions from which some pupils derive the gratification and enhancement of self-respect necessary for both kinds of outcome may create experiences that threaten the self-respect of others. Potentialities for success *and* failure are inherent in tasks performed according to achievement criteria. Independence manifests itself as competence and autonomy in some, but as a heavy burden of responsibility and inadequacy in others. Universalistic treatment represents fairness for some, cold impersonality to others. Specificity may be seen as situational relevance or personal neglect.

Within industrial societies where norms applicable to public life differ markedly from those governing conduct among kin, schools provide a sequence of experiences in which individuals, during the early stages of personality development, acquire new principles of conduct in addition to those already accepted during childhood. For reasons earlier enumerated in detail, the family, as a social setting with its characteristic social arrangements, lacks the resources and the competence[19] to effect the psychological transition. This is not to say that only the school can produce the necessary changes, but of those institutions having some claim over the lives of children and adolescents (e.g., the family, child labor, occupational apprenticeship, tutoring, the church, the mass media[20]), only the schools provide adequate, though not always effective, task experiences and sanctions, and arrangements for the generalization and specification of normative principles throughout many spheres of public life.

It is conceivable, of course, that families (and those other institutions as well as some yet to be invented) can provide the experiences necessary for the acquisition of these norms; family life provides opportunities for achievement, for assuming individual responsibility, and for categorical and specific treatment. Yet the family is more likely than schools to provide experiences that also undermine the acquisition of these norms. Similarly, the impact of the experiences that schooling provides may prove insufficient and inappropriate for their acquisition, and even if they are acquired, their acceptance is not necessarily of equal or great importance in all segments of public life. One thing that makes schooling effective is the relevance of the school's contribution to subsequent participation in public institutions. Another is the relationship between structural arrangements and activities in determining whether one setting or another is more conducive to producing a given outcome, for if two or more activities interfere with each other, or if the situation is inappropriate to the performance of an activity, the desired outcome is unlikely to appear.

AN IDEOLOGICAL CAVEAT

Although I have treated them as norms, independence and achievement have been regarded by many observers of the American scene as dominant cultural themes or values, general standards of what is desirable.[21] In view of this, it is important that the argument of this book not be taken

as a defense of national values, although it should not surprise anyone that the normative commitments of individuals who have passed through American schools are generally (though not invariably) consistent with national values. The main purpose of this analysis is to present a formulation, hypothetical in nature, of how schooling contributes to the emergence of certain psychological outcomes, and not to provide an apology or justification for those outcomes on ideological grounds. I have avoided calling universalism and specificity cultural values even though both are norms, since few, if any, observers include them among the broad moral principles considered desirable in American life. Their exclusion from the list of values should further confirm the nonideological intent of this discussion.

Having the means to produce a desired result is not the same as an injunction to use them in producing it. Of the many considerations entering into the decision to employ available resources in creating even widely valued outcomes, the probable costs involved should give pause. For the norms in question here, whose desirability can be affirmed either on ideological grounds or in terms of their relevance to public life in an industrial society, conditions conducive to their development are also conducive to the creation of results widely regarded as undesirable. Thus, a sense of accomplishment and mastery, on the one hand, and a sense of incompetence and ineffectualness, on the other, both represent psychological consequences of continuously coping with tasks on an achievement basis. Similarly with independence: self-confidence and helplessness can each derive from a person's self-imposed obligation to work unaided and accept individual responsibility for his actions. Finally, willingness to acknowledge the rightness of categorical and specific treatment may indicate the capacity to adapt to a variety of social situations in which only a part of one's self is invested, or it may indicate a sense of personal alienation and isolation from human relationships.

From the viewpoint of ideological justification, the process of schooling is problematic in that outcomes morally desirable from one perspective are undesirable from another; and in the making of school policy the price to be paid must be a salient consideration in charting a course of action.

NOTES AND REFERENCES

1. William J. Goode, *World Revolution and Family Patterns*, p. 11, Free Press of Glencoe, New York (1963).

2. See, for example, Ruth Benedict, "Continuities and Discontinuities in Cultural Conditioning," in Clyde Kluckhohn, Henry A. Murray, and David M. Schneider (eds.), *Personality*, pp. 522–531, Alfred A. Knopf, New York (1953); Talcott Parsons, "The School Class as a Social System: Some of its Functions in American Society," *Harvard Educational Review* 29, No. 4, 297–318 (1959); and S. N. Eisenstadt, *From Generation to Generation*, pp. 115–185, Free Press, Glencoe, Ill. (1956).

3. S. N. Eisenstadt, *ibid.*, p. 164.

4. My emphasis here differs from Parsons' in that he views independence primarily as a personal resource: " . . . it may be said that the most important single predispositional factor with which the child enters the school is his level of *independence*," Talcott Parsons, *op. cit.*, p. 300. Although independence is very likely such a predisposition—whether it is the most important single one is debatable—it is part of the school's agenda to further the development of independence to a point beyond the level at which family resources become inadequate to do so.

5. Winterbottom, for example, lumps independence and mastery together; the indices she uses to measure them, however, involve ostensibly different phenomena in that the mastery items refer to tendencies toward activity rather than to independence. Marian R. Winterbottom, "The Relation of Need for Achievement to Learning Experiences in Independence and Mastery," in John T. Atkinson (ed.), *Motives in Fantasy, Action, and Society*, pp. 453–478, Van Nostrand, Princeton (1958). As a definitional guideline for this discussion, I have followed the usage of Bernard C. Rosen and Roy D'Andrade, "The Psychosocial Origins of Achievement Motivation," *Sociometry* 22, No. 3, 186 (1959) in their discussion of independence training; and of McClelland and his colleagues in a study of independence training, David C. McClelland, A. Rindlisbacher, and Richard DeCharms, "Religious and Other Sources of Parental Attitudes toward Independence Training," in David C. McClelland (Ed.), *Studies in Motivation*, pp. 389–397, Appleton-Century-Crofts, New York (1955).

6. Kaspar D. Naegele, "Clergymen, Teachers, and Psychiatrists: A Study in Roles and Socialization," *Canadian Journal of Economics and Political Science* 22, No. 1, 53 (1956).

7. See, for example, Marian R. Winterbottom, *ibid.*; Bernard C. Rosen and Roy D'Andrade, *op. cit.*, pp. 185–218; and Fred L. Strodtbeck, "Family Interaction, Values, and Achievement," in David C. McClelland *et al.*, *Talent and Society*, pp. 135–191, Van Nostrand, Princeton (1958).

8. For one attempt to treat athletics condescendingly as non-intellectualism, see James S. Coleman, *The Adolescent Society*, Free Press of Glencoe, New York (1961).

9. Rupert Wilkinson, *Gentlemanly Power*, p. 21, Oxford University Press, London (1964).

10. Although Parsons considers universalism-particularism to be a dichotomy, they are distinguished on at least two dimensions: cognitive and cathectic. "The primacy of cognitive values may be said to imply a *universalistic* standard, while that of appreciative values implies a *particularistic* standard. In the former case the standard is derived from the validity of a set of existential ideas, or the generality of a normative rule, in the latter from the particularity of the cathectic significance of an object or of the status of the object in a relational system." Talcott Parsons, *The Social System*, p. 62, Free Press, Glencoe, Ill. (1951).

11. Peter M. Blau, "Operationalizing a Conceptual Scheme: The Universalism-Particularism Pattern Variable," *American Sociological Review* 27, No. 2, 169 (1962). The permission of Peter M. Blau to quote from his paper is gratefully acknowledged.

12. Peter M. Blau, *ibid.*, p. 164; my emphasis.

13. In the case of specificity, " . . . the burden of proof rests on him who would suggest that ego has obligations vis-à-vis the object in question which transcend this specificity of relevance." Talcott Parsons, *The Social System*, p. 65. In the case of diffuseness, " . . . the burden of proof is on the side of the exclusion of an interest or mode of orientation as outside the range of obligations defined by the role-expectation." Parsons, *ibid.*, p. 66.

14. For a discussion of relativity of perspective, see Daniel Lerner, *The Passing of Traditional Society*, pp.

43–75, Free Press of Glencoe, Glencoe, Ill. (1958). See also Chapter 6, below.

15. For discussions of these problems, see George C. Homans, *Social Behavior: Its Elementary Forms*, pp. 235–251, Harcourt, Brace, and World, New York (1961); Elliott Jaques, *The Measurement of Responsibility*, pp. 32–60, Harvard University Press, Cambridge (1956); and Leonard R. Sayles, *Behavior of Industrial Work Groups*, pp. 41–118, John Wiley and Sons, New York (1963). One proposition relating expressions about inequity and its conditions is the following: "The past occasions in which a man's activities have been rewarded are apt to have been occasions in which other men, in some way like him, have been rewarded too. When others like him get their reward now, but he does not, he is apt to display emotional behavior." Homans, *ibid.*, pp. 73–74.

16. There are events in family life where the explanation that renders inequities fair lies not in age but in circumstances—"Your brother could stay home from school and watch television because he was sick (and you weren't)"—and in other personal characteristics beside age, such as sex—"It isn't safe for girls to walk home alone at that hour (but it's O.K. for your brother)."

17. George C. Homans, *ibid.*, p. 75.

18. Wheeler, in his investigation of Scandinavian prisons, cites the example of two men returned to prison following a joint escape; although they had committed the identical offense, one was judged to have escaped because of claustrophobic fears, the other because of persistent psychopathic tendencies. Their subsequent treatments differed according to medical criteria—open spaces for one, maximum security for the other—even though the separate treatments violated the dictum that the punishment should fit the crime; that is, same crime, same punishment. "Both among inmates who feel that their *sentences* are just and among those who feel they are unjust, the ones housed in preventive detention institutions [centers in which the nature of prison treatment is based in part on the personality characteristics of the offender] are less likely to have a sense of justice in the *treatment* they are receiving in the institution [than inmates held in custodial settings]." Stanton Wheeler, "Legal Justice and Mental Health in the Care and Treatment of Deviance," paper presented at the Meetings of the American Orthopsychiatric Association, San Francisco, April, 1966, p. 5.

19. For a discussion of competence as an organizational characteristic, see Philip Selznick, *Leadership in Administration*, pp. 38–56, Row, Peterson, Evanston, Ill. (1957).

20. Mary Engel, "Saturday's Children: A Study of Working Boys," Cambridge, Mass.; Harvard Graduate School of Education, Center for Research in Careers, Harvard Studies in Career Development No. 51, 1966; Carl I. Hovland, "Effects of the Mass Media of Communication," in Gardner Lindzey (ed.), *Handbook of Social Psychology, II*, pp. 1062–1103, Addison-Wesley, Reading, Mass. (1954); Blanche Geer *et al.*, "Learning the Ropes: Situational Learning in Four Occupational Training Programs," in Irwin Deutscher and Elizabeth Thompson (eds.), *Among the People: Studies of the Urban Poor*, Basic Books, New York, in press.

21. For a general discussion of the concept of 'value' and of major American cultural themes, see Robin M. Williams, Jr., *American Society*, pp. 397–470, Alfred A. Knopf, New York (1960).

STUDY QUESTIONS FOR PART 3

1. If reflective teaching is a laudable goal, can teachers be taught to be reflective practitioners? What difference do you think this will make in the lives of children? Should an individual's disposition to be reflective be used as a teacher training admissions, school hiring, or promotion criterion? Why?

2. What is the relationship of Dewey's perspective on education to functionalism? What examples can you offer?

3. What are Dreeben's and Dewey's views of the role of schools in meeting the needs of an industrial society? Are these views relevant in a postindustrial information age? Why?

4. How do students who are home-schooled learn social norms? Is home-schooling in the state's or country's best interest? Why?

5. How are the ideas and issues in the readings for this section similar and different to those associated with the reforms being talked about or implemented in your state or in the whole country?

6. What is the difference between a reflective and a routine teacher? What are the pros and cons of each? If you aspire to be a reflective teacher, what do you anticipate will be the most difficult challenges of such an orientation? How would you respond to those?

7. Whose morality is to be taught in school? Why? Who might disagree with this view, and what would be their reasons?

8. How much control should a teacher exercise over a child's learning? Why?

9. Cooperative learning strategies are effective and appropriate within certain parameters. What is cheating?

10. Some would argue that the U.S. mind is being systematically closed to the heritage of the United States; that some groups are being systematically disparaged while others are being applauded. Whose legends and stories should be remembered and celebrated in schools?

PART 4

Legitimation and Reproduction

The readings thus far have examined a number of important issues and have offered several useful concepts helpful in describing and understanding essential features of the U.S. system of universal and compulsory public education. These ideas include: education as cultural transmission; the function that education plays in society's survival; universal and compulsory public schooling as a primary means by which society maintains itself and adapts to the need to change; the contribution of education to the development both of the individual being and the social being; the Deweyan ideal of the public school as a living learning community reflective of the activities and problems of social life outside the school; and the latent, but highly important, function of the school in developing the needed societal norms of independence, achievement, universalism, and specificity.

Reflecting what is termed a functionalist perspective, the foregoing conception of the U.S. system of education is broadly accepted in society. Public schools are generally viewed as society's great leveler, in striving to provide equal educational opportunities for children, regardless of gender, social class, race, language, or religion. Viewed also as important instruments of social, political, and economic policy, public schools in our country are judged both as major contributors to improving the economic and social well-being of our communities and, alternatively, as crippling our technological and industrial capacity to compete in the global economy.

Currently struggling to respond to major pressures to reform and restructure themselves to become more effective given important changes in the current economic and social environment, educators find themselves caught in the middle of a number of growing conflicts. These are reflected in the following questions:

- What should be the purpose(s) of public education?
- Should the school's curriculum be determined by professional educators, parents, or politicians?
- What is the relation of the school to the local community, the state, and the federal government, and who should set the performance standards for our schools?

These questions raise a multitude of issues for local school boards of education and state legislatures. In addition, the next century will present continuing and new challenges as we come to terms with accelerating social and technological change; an increasingly more global economic community linked by instantaneous communication networks; an increasingly urban, heterogeneous, and multicultural school-age population; a burgeoning population of aging taxpayers without school-age children; a rapidly escalating disparity between rich and poor; and a shrinking middle class.

An alternative conception to the functionalist perspective is the conflict theorist interpretation of the educational system in a capitalist society such as ours. The three selections that follow provide an overview of this Marxian perspective on schooling, and offer an example of one way public schools help maintain a sexually divided labor force (and the accompanying differentials in status, pay, and types of occupation—"men's work" and "women's work").

Marxist-oriented conflict theorists take functionalism to task, criticizing functionalism because " . . . it takes the interests and perspectives of the dominant social groups in society and elevates them to the status of universal norms. Having done this, it then uses these norms to measure the contributions of members of all other groups. In this way the interests of a particular class are misrepresented as belonging to the society as a whole, and this misrepresentation then serves to maintain the privileged position of the members of that class." (p. 46)

For conflict theorists, social class is the critical determinant of social power relations. The Marxian perspective is rooted in the idea that " . . . whenever people are related in different ways to the means of production we have a class society, and each particular class is defined in terms of this relationship" (Feinberg & Soltis, 1985, p. 49). In a capitalist society such as ours, the owners of private businesses constitute one social class, and the people who work in those businesses constitute another class. While in this contemporary time of specialized education and credentials social class distinctions are more complex than they once were, the reality is that the United States is a class society, and there are great disparities among the wealth of people in different classes and their capacity to provide for themselves and their family members.

Obviously a family that is very wealthy has many more alternatives regarding its choices of schooling for its children than does a single parent living in poverty or, for that matter, the typical middle-income wage earner.

In addition to these economic differences associated with one's relation to the means of production (owner, worker, jobless), there are other important differences connected with social class. Individuals in different classes typically have different values, beliefs (although some also are shared), and different perspectives on life in general. Class consciousness is a Marxian idea that refers to the general set of such orientations held by members of a particular social class. Two related concepts are hegemony and false consciousness. Hegemony refers to the condition wherein one class has power over another. False consciousness refers to a condition wherein members of the subordinate class " . . . express the point of view and share the values of the dominant class. . . . True consciousness of your own class is impeded by your acceptance of the values of the dominant class" (Feinberg & Soltis, 1985, p. 50).

For conflict theorists, the ideas of hegemony and false consciousness are basic Marxian concepts used to explain how a person's understanding and awareness of class consciousness can be blocked to the point where he/she actually espouses the values of the dominant class, not recognizing one's lower status as a member of the subordinate class (Feinberg & Soltis, 1985, p. 49). For example, while most people believe that public schools exist to promote the pursuit of equality, conflict theorists argue to the contrary; they believe that the real purpose of the public school system is to reproduce and maintain the existing class structure in our society, and to provide well-trained and disciplined workers for a labor force toiling to profit the owners of private enterprise (Bowles, 1972, p. 125).

As Feinberg and Soltis argue in their article, the state is an instrument of the dominant class (the rich), who in turn use public schools as a means of reproducing the existing class structure. The dominant class owns the means of production. U.S. values and beliefs promulgated by the schools are such that a false consciousness develops among the middle and lower classes, the working proletariate, which then serves to reenforce the existing class structure. This reenforcement rests on values and beliefs like: education is the great equalizer; work hard and the system will reward your efforts; everyone has an equal chance to get ahead; people make it on their own achievements.

Bowles examines this theme further, looking particularly at the connections between unequal education and reproduction of the social division of labor. His basic argument is that public schools in the United States have developed not to advance equality but to meet the needs of the rich to maintain political stability and to ensure the availability of a skilled labor force (p. 125). For Bowles, " . . . unequal education has its roots in the very class structure which it serves to legitimize and reproduce" (p. 125). In short, schools replicate social relations in the work force, thus socializing students to norms and role expectations similar to those of prospective employers: being a good subordinate, following directions, being on time, not questioning authority, and so on. Further, the schools set up the curriculum in a way that channels children into certain "tracks" based on their social class background: vocational schools and tracks on the one hand, and on the other the academic tracks for the college bound and "gifted." All of this is guided by the myth that because schooling was ostensibly equal and open to all, one's position in the social division of labor, in the class structure, was the natural result of one's own efforts and talents (p. 128). What Bowles thus illustrates is that the schooling process itself is inextricably linked to perpetuation and maintenance of the existing social class divisions.

In the final selection for this section, Linda Valli describes how schools function to transmit culture. The instance she examines is the manner in which schools systematically reinforce gender-specific cultural patterns and relations found both in the home and in the work place. She explores the experiences of young women in a cooperative office education program in which the students attended high school classes in the morning and then worked at office clerical jobs in the afternoons.

In illustrating how schools contribute to the process of cultural reproduction, in this case the perpetuation of a sexually divided labor force, she describes the messages given to the girls as they participate in the program. Messages from the school teacher and from superiors in the work place about sexual appearance and sexual behavior encouraged the girls to use their gender identities in managing their self-presentation and appearance—a reinforcement of the idea of office-worker as sex object. Further, Valli observed that a second way in which the clerical worker's office role was linked to gender identity was "either through the equation of the work with women's work in the home or through the subordination of their role in the office to their role in the home" (Valli, 1983, p. 224).

Marxist Theory and Education

WALTER FEINBERG AND JONAS SOLTIS

CONFLICT THEORY AND FUNCTIONALISM

We have seen that functionalists believe that the driving force behind the expansion of schooling is the need created by a highly industrialized, modern society to develop the skills and attitudes that are appropriate for a changing economic and social world. Functionalists like Dreeben argue that the modern school furthers the selection of individuals on the basis of merit and talent and, in so doing, discourages the distribution of income, social positions, and authority on the basis of family background, race, sex, or religion. Thus, for the functionalist, schools serve both a social and an individual purpose. On the social level they help assure that the skills and attitudes required by an industrial, urban democracy will be developed and maintained. On the individual level, they enhance the possibility that placement into jobs and the distribution of income, prestige, and authority will be fair.

While functionalism has been the dominant tradition in educational scholarship and research, it has not been without competitors. Among these, conflict theory has been the most prominent. Conflict theory derives from a number of sources. Marxist scholarship is clearly the most influential and the one that we will address most fully.

Whereas functionalists believe that the driving force behind social and educational change is the progressive movement toward technical development and social integration, conflict theorists believe the driving force in complex societies is the unending struggle between different groups to hold power and status. In modern society, they see schools as an important instrument in this struggle. They believe that schools serve the dominant privileged class by providing for the social reproduction of the economic and political status quo in a way that gives the illusion of objectivity, neutrality, and opportunity. They believe that the schools reproduce the attitudes and dispositions that are required for the continuation of the present system of domination by the privileged class.

Even though the groups that are visibly contesting for power may differ from time to time, Marxist-orientated conflict theorists believe that the basic cause of such conflict can usually be traced to differences among social classes. Thus, the direct conflict may be one among blacks and whites, males and females, or Christians and Jews, but the underlying cause will be found in something deeper—the division between the classes in a capitalist society. One important implication of this view is that while the deeper reason for a conflict involves class differences, the participants themselves may view the struggle as essentially racial, ethnic, generational, or sexual. Another implication is that there may be times when no struggle is visible and even the participants believe that harmony reigns. Yet on

Source: "Marxist Theory and Education" from *School and Society,* by Walter Feinberg and Jonas Soltis, copyright 1985. Reprinted by permission of Teachers College Press.

closer examination the seeds of conflict become visible to an outside observer. We will return to look at these and other implications shortly. First, however, it will be useful to see the different ways in which functionalism and conflict theory might view the same event.

Imagine that you are the dean of a college of education within a large state university, and you decide to increase the standards for entrance into your program. In this imaginary world, the degree in education has recently become one of the more lucrative credentials that the university is providing. Thus, your program has attracted an increasing number of applicants, and you have good evidence for believing that standards can be raised significantly without reducing the number of students entering the program. This calculation is important because the amount of resources that your school receives from the total university is partly determined by the number of students in the program. In addition, however, the university is concerned about the ranking of the teacher education program nationally, and there is a good chance that by increasing standards the national ranking of the college of education will improve. Moreover, colleges of education from other universities have been increasing their entrance standards, and unless similar steps are taken by your college, it will likely lose ground in the national rankings. An additional incentive for raising entrance standards is the competitive edge that a higher national ranking will provide your students in bidding for the better jobs in the best schools. Hence, from your own point of view, there is an overwhelming set of interrelated reasons for raising standards. To do so will enhance the position of your college within the university and will allow stronger arguments to be made for increasing your budget. At the same time a higher budget will allow you to hire more prestigious faculty, who will increase the attractiveness of your teacher education program for the better students. With both better faculty and better students, the national ranking of your program will

continue to improve, and employers will be more likely to hire students from your institution than those from competing ones.

From the functionalist point of view, the important things to see in this process are the way it actually serves to increase the talent and the technical skills that are available to the public school community and the fact that this is accomplished by instituting standards that can be applied universally to any and all applicants. Raising standards means increasing the institution's ability to discriminate on the basis of relevant criteria alone. Lower standards mean more eligible applicants and therefore more room for judgments made on the basis of less relevant factors such as in-state/out-of-state discrimination, sex, and minority quotas.

From the point of view of the conflict theorists, the situation may look quite different. They might see the result of higher standards working this way: In order to meet the new admissions requirements that have been established, students from outstanding secondary schools would clearly have the edge over those whose schools are less adequate. Since the most outstanding secondary schools are found in wealthy communities where the citizens can afford the price of high-quality education, the children of the wealthy will clearly have a marked advantage. Moreover, if a required course of study is missing from a high-school curriculum, or if a child is having difficulty with a certain subject, wealthy parents can afford to provide outside help and tutoring. Poorer parents cannot usually afford to provide this kind of help, and their children are almost completely dependent on what the public school has to offer. Thus, to raise standards for admission into the college of education is to place an added burden on the already disadvantaged. While the intent of the reform is simply to raise standards and to provide a competitive advantage to the college and its students, the effect, as seen from the conflict theorists' point of view, is to reduce the opportunities for the less advantaged youngster and to increase opportunities for the more advantaged one.

This example can be used to point out some important features of the conflict theory model. First, there is no necessary and direct relation between the intent behind an action or policy and the social effects of that action. In this case the intent of the dean was to raise standards and to increase the competitive advantage of students in the college of education. It was neither to decrease the opportunities for the less wealthy students nor to increase them for the more wealthy students. While there may be some cases in which a college policy is instituted with these goals in mind, they may also come about as the unintended consequences of other, more acceptable motives. Second, because the social effects may arise without conscious intent, there is no need to suggest that they are the result of conspiratorial action. In this case, raising entrance standards benefited the already advantaged wealthy students. It also improved the already admirable position of the college of education. It even promised benefits to the affluent schooling community, which will get more talented teachers. However, there is no reason to believe that some conscious plan or plot has been devised in order to achieve these goals. In other words, it is possible to have a system in which different members of an advantaged class decide matters independently of one another without intentionally serving the narrow interest of their own class.

The problem with functionalism, according to conflict theory, is that, consciously or not, it takes the interests and perspectives of the dominant social groups in society and elevates them to the status of universal norms. Having done this, it then uses these norms to measure the contributions of members of all other groups. In this way the interests of a particular class are misrepresented as belonging to the society as a whole, and this misrepresentation then serves to maintain the privileged position of the members of that class. In our example, certain forms of achievement, which are the values of prestigious universities and affluent school systems, become the universalized norm that keeps other groups out of teaching and maintains the affluent in the best positions. This criticism of functionalism has been developed most explicitly by that form of conflict theory known as Marxism, and it is to that perspective that we now turn. . . .

MARXIST THEORY

In order to understand Marxism, it is essential to grasp a fundamental idea about the relationship between the way we think and the way we live. For the Marxist, the way people think, perceive, and feel—that is, their "consciousness"—is related to the basic mode of economic production in their society. This means that people's fundamental ideas about the nature of truth and falsity, about goodness and beauty, can be understood by examining the way in which production is carried on at a certain point in time. It is important not to confuse Marxism with relativism. . . . Marxists are not arguing, as the relativists do, that what is true, good, or beautiful is whatever I or my culture takes to be truth, goodness, or beauty. Rather they believe that the basic concepts by which we organize our conceptual, ethical, and aesthetic worlds can be understood only if we recognize their relation to the productive possibilities of the society in which we live.

To illustrate, let us consider two of the fundamental categories through which we organize our physical world, those of *space* and *time*. These categories are a part of our "consciousness" and are fundamental to any truth claims we might make, since they allow us to locate objects and events in a way that would otherwise be impossible. Indeed, it is the conceptions of space and time that make much of our everyday conversation intelligible. If I say, "It is raining outside," or "Sally is depressed today," or "School was closed during the summer," what I am saying can be understood and its truth or falsity determined only because I share with my listener implicit conceptions of space and time. We both divide time into the same units, for example, day and night, summer and winter; and we divide space in similar ways, for example, inside and outside.

Thus, conceptions of space and time seem to be conditions for intelligibility and mutual understanding in any human society. This insight is not unique to Marxist theory. Interpretivists would also hold this view. The unique contribution of Marxist theory can be seen when we look at specific conceptions that different groups have of space and time. Take the idea of space. In our own civilization, we will often locate objects in space by using specific coordinates such as north, east, south, and west. So if it is said that "New York is south of Boston," the statement is both understandable and true. It is understandable because we each share the conception of direction, which includes the coordinates north, east, south, and west. And it is true because, given this understanding, New York is in fact south of Boston. It is important, however, to see that being "south of" indicates a relationship. To tell someone to go south is not like telling them to go to New York. The first involves an abstract notion of space, while the latter notion is concrete. There is a concrete place "New York"; "south" is not such a place.

Now imagine a society that has not yet invented the abstract concepts north, east, south, and west. Perhaps this would be a society in which directions would be given only in terms of local concrete objects: "Go to the big rock"; "look for the river"; "follow the stream"; "at the fork, look for the biggest tree"; and so forth. Here the statement that one place is south of another would be neither true nor false. It would have no meaning at all.

Truth for the Marxist is not relative in the sense that anything that one's culture deems true is true. Rather, truth is dependent on the concepts that one's culture makes available. At any given stage of our culture's development, certain concepts are made available to us that then allow us to think in new ways; and education plays a large role in ensuring that we come to share our culture's most important concepts. Now the question to be asked is: Just how do concepts such as north, east, south, and west arise? or How can we account for their development? One possible answer is that they are the inventions of very talented individuals who are able to break away from the limited forms of thought that their own civilization provides and invent new ones. The problem with this view is that it does not tell us what it is that allows such people to break the traditional boundaries of thinking (something that is very hard to do), or why the concepts of some talented people may be accepted at a certain time and become ingrained in the thinking of the population as a whole while the conceptual inventions of others are rejected.

For the Marxist, the way to address these questions properly is to explore the relationship between changes in the mode of production and changes in the characteristics of thought. In essence, the Marxist is asking us to break the traditional boundaries of our thinking and look at a new conception of how concepts and "consciousness" are formed. Let us return to our hypothetical example of the development from a concrete conception of space to an abstract one. Suppose we were to ask which was better, the concrete conception of space, where individuals are extraordinarily sensitive to immediate visual cues, or the abstract conception of space, which allows unknown areas to be charted and traveled. Given our own modern framework, where the abstract conception of space has become taken for granted and serves as an important tool, there would be little hesitation in answering the question.

Assume, however, that the material needs of the members of the earlier culture in our example are easily met; that people live quite happily and peacefully in a lush, isolated, self-contained area. Food, shelter, and other necessary items are available within the boundaries that their concrete understanding of space allows them to travel. Assume, too, that the use of a more sophisticated, abstract, and flexible notion of space could bring this group into areas where it would find itself in conflict with other groups. Given these assumptions, it is difficult to proclaim categorically that the more sophisticated conception of spatial relations is a better conception than the less sophisticated one.

Suppose, however, that certain key resources become scarce or that the environment is no longer sufficient to support a growing population. If the group is to continue to survive, means must be developed to go far afield to find new resources. Some of these means might be material ones, such as larger, more durable boats or suitable overland conveyances that could bring back the needed resources. Others would be conceptual. New ways of locating one's position in earthly space would be important to be able to travel and return successfully. The group might even invent north, east, south, and west! "Necessity is the mother of invention," but for the Marxist this does not just mean material inventions; it means conceptual ones as well, and such "inventions" are stimulated by changes in our material conditions. Therefore to say whether one way of conceiving of space is better than another way, we have to be able to view it in relation to existing material conditions and needs of a certain historical period.

While the example illustrates how conceptual differences might evolve historically within a group, it does not provide a sense of the different ways of thinking that can be found among different groups existing within the same society during the same historical period. Marxists explain this by using the concept of social class. For the Marxist, whenever people are related in different ways to the means of production we have a class society, and each particular class is defined in terms of this relationship. For example, in a capitalist society, where the means of production are privately owned, the group that owns them will constitute a different class from the group that is hired to work in their factories and plants. As we shall see, being a member of a class will entail many things that go well beyond the relation that one has to the means of produc-

tion. It will entail having certain values, a certain outlook, and a set of perceptions and concepts about the nature of social life, or, in sum, having a certain "class consciousness."

CLASS CONSCIOUSNESS, FALSE CONSCIOUSNESS, AND HEGEMONY

According to Marxism, a class can exist in two different ways—*objectively* and *subjectively*. Objectively, all of those people who must sell their labor to others in order to meet their daily needs and who do not own any significant part of the production process may be thought of as a class—the working class. Since a class is defined only in terms of the relation its members have to the means of production, a class may consist of many different kinds of individuals. For example, the working class contains people of different races, nationalities, and religions. However, because of their differences, they may fail to recognize their working-class interest as a shared one. In this instance the class would be said to have an objective existence but to lack consciousness of itself as a class. If the members of a class become aware of their common interest and are able to articulate that interest through common action and through legitimate spokespeople, then the class has not only an objective existence but also a subjective existence. At this stage it has become conscious of itself as a class. The labor union movement is sometimes an example of this. Its existence is reflected in the subjective understanding of its members. And it may be able to exert its collective power for its own interests.

The development of class consciousness may be blocked by society, and progressive social change may be impeded. Marxists use the concepts of *false consciousness* and *hegemony* to explain how this can happen. Members of the subordinate class who express the point of view and share the values of the dominant class exhibit false consciousness. True consciousness of your own class is impeded by your acceptance of the values of the dominant class. When the dominant class is successful in establishing its own mode of thinking among most members of the subordinate class, it is said to have established hegemony over the subordinate class. Hegemony means having a preponderance of influence and authority over others. This influence is expressed both in the concepts and the institutional arrangements of the social structure. False consciousness is illustrated by the slave who espouses the values of the master. The slave believes that he or she is the master's property, to do with as the master pleases. It is also illustrated by the worker who carries the values of the owner or by the concentration camp inmate who begins to think like the prison guard. Hegemony exists when one class controls the thinking of another class through such cultural forms as the media, the church, or the schools.

Orthodox Marxists believe that all social change, including changes in the way in which we think about the world around us, is rooted in the way in which people produce their goods and in the possibilities that new productive methods open up for positive human development. This means that the political, legal, religious, and educational systems must be understood dynamically in terms of whether, in any given historical period, they serve to enhance or to hinder human development. Thus, a system that, at one point in time, may have served a progressive role in a society may, because of changes in the possibilities created by new modes of production, come to serve a negative function. This means that it may be quite appropriate and functional for a certain perspective or ideology to dominate thinking at a given historical moment, while at a later time those same ideas may become unproductive expressions of false consciousness and hegemony. Let us consider a case in order to illustrate this.

Imagine a society, not unlike those in Western Europe during the Middle Ages, where there are strong moral, religious, and legal sanctions against the practice of usury, that is, the charging of high

interest rates for loans. Let us assume that this society does not have the means to accumulate capital or material goods and cannot store food and other perishable necessities for long periods of time. The production and consumption of necessities are tightly bound together in an agrarian life style. At this point in time the restrictions against usury make sense, because there is little possibility for economic growth and because the upward mobility of one person would mean the downward mobility of another. In other words, since little possibility for economic growth exists, the mutual well-being of all depends upon a smooth and stable relationship among different segments of the society. At this stage money lending is not very common, but when it occurs it is usually performed as an act of friendship. It serves to cement essential communal relations. Usury threatens to destroy those relations by turning friendship into a business. However, because there is a recognition that certain unforeseen disasters may require larger sums of money than friends can afford to lend, a special group is designated as the money-lenders-of-last-resort. These people are defined as outside of the community and generally looked down upon. The moral code that governs the members of the dominant community pictures a world of mutual service where God has given each member a specific place and role.

Suppose, however, that at another point in time new possibilities arise in the form of new knowledge about production and navigation, possibilities that, if realized, will increase the total wealth available to all. These possibilities could occur in a number of areas all at once. They might include new methods for storing food, new techniques for navigating long distances, and new ways of building larger and sturdier ships that are able to cross oceans and bring back spices to preserve foods, new kinds of fiber, gold, and exotic material goods. However, to bring these possibilities about and to realize the new wealth that they will make possible, large stores of capital must be brought together and centralized under a single project. Borrowing now becomes more businesslike and necessary.

Now the restrictions against usury would stand as an impediment to the accumulation of new wealth, and strong arguments might be developed for their elimination. As usury laws are overturned, wealth would become more centralized; large, previously unthinkable projects could be undertaken; and new territories might then be discovered, providing even more incentive for the centralization of capital. This would lead to an increase in the physical and economic mobility of individuals, in a rapid growth of cities, in new political power for a new class of merchants, bankers, and manufacturers. Moreover, in order to assure the flow of materials from recently discovered territories, a government structure attached to the homeland would have to be extended to these areas, and colonies would need to be established.

As control over different and strange people is extended, a different moral conception would be needed to justify these extended political structures. Writers might begin to develop new themes (such as the idea of the "white man's burden") for home consumption and legitimation of hegemony abroad. New educational forms would develop in order to maintain the flow of administrators needed to govern the foreign areas. Promising native students from the territories would have to be provided the opportunity to study in the homeland before returning to their own country to take up positions as subservient, middle-level administrators. And in the process, a new equilibrium would be developed between the society's productive capacities and the new social norms, legal regulations, and patterns of thought that have arisen because of the shift in relationships to the means of production.

Marxists observe that new codes are developed by and for a specific social class. They note that the development of a new code involves a struggle with other classes, which serve as the protective agents for the older, more established norms. In our example, new norms would be advanced by and for the manufacturing, banking, and merchant classes, while the older norms would be defended by the agrarian aristocracy and supported by the traditional elements of the clergy. In order to enlist the support of other classes, the new moral code would be advanced, not as serving the narrow interest of the rising classes, but as "universal principles" that promise to serve the interest of all. For example, in American history, the principles of "life, liberty, and the pursuit of happiness" were not explicitly articulated as serving the interests of only a specific class of people, even though the founding fathers had common interests as slave owners and large property holders. Rather, these ideals were formulated to appeal to as wide a range of individuals as possible. They were expressed as universal rights that would advance the position of everyone against what was seen by some as oppressive taxation and arbitrary rule by the monarchy. In general, this is a very good tactical move—it helps enlist the support of many dissatisfied elements in society. However, it also helps create a new set of standards by which even the emerging order and its newly advantaged classes may eventually be judged. In less than a hundred years a war over slavery was fought in the United States. Today freedom and equality are still elusive prizes for many blacks, other minority groups, and women.

Returning to our example, instead of a medieval society governed by the idea that God has given each and every person a specific place in life, we now would have a society in which people believed that talent should determine one's social and economic position. Of course, this principle is exactly the same as that expressed by the functionalists—that in modern society it is *achieved*, rather than *ascribed*, characteristics that are to be rewarded. However, the difference between the Marxists and the functionalists on this point must also be remembered. The functionalists believe that this principle serves as a *real* universal norm, one which evolved and governs the process of selection of talent in modern society. In contrast, the Marxists believe that the principle is best seen historically as a weapon in a class struggle used first to overcome one's assigned place in life and used later by the newly advantaged groups to maintain their gains and by the still disadvantaged ones to assert their claims to equal treatment. . . .

MARXISM, NEO-MARXISM, AND EDUCATION

There are at least two different opinions among Marxists about the role of social and educational research. Orthodox Marxists believe that their task is to discover instances of sciencelike laws that govern social movement. They believe that social research should seek to explain the way in which a particular mode of production (which includes both the means by which goods are produced and the relations of different classes to the means of production) influences and determines other forms of social life. In Marxist theory one of the fundamental laws has been the law of contradiction. This law holds that each social form contains within it the seeds of its own destruction and transcendence. In capitalist society, for example, there is an essential contradiction in the fact that while the means of production are privately owned, they are socially used. In other words, the means of production, such as factories and machinery, are owned by private individuals for their own profit, but the operation of this productive capacity requires a workforce of nonowners that is brought together in a common work place to work cooperatively. This creates the conditions required for the development of class consciousness among workers, whom the Marxists call the proletariat. With a disciplined, self-conscious proletarian work force that senses it is being exploited, the means are in place for seizing control of the productive forces and taking them from private hands through revolution. We do not need to go into detail about all of the steps that are supposed to be involved in this process. It is sufficient to note

that this development and others like it in history are seen by orthodox Marxists to have the force of a natural law about them. Orthodox Marxists believe that each social form *must* have within it the seeds of its own destruction; otherwise basic social change would not occur and the class in power would continue to sequester and use their power forever. While there are few Marxists who continue to take such a rigid and deterministic view of social change today, there are many who believe that economics and the relationship of classes to the means of production must be given primacy in understanding other institutions, including the public schools.

Newer forms of Marxism offer a challenge to the deterministic view of the orthodox position. These new forms are concerned with issues related not only to economic oppression but also to domination by classes in noneconomic social forms. These neo-Marxists still consider economic domination important, but they do not believe that the end of private ownership of the means of production is a guarantee that class domination in all its forms will come to an end. In other words, these neo-Marxists believe that there is a need to analyze critically each situation of domination on its own terms, without presupposing that the cause of injustice or inequality will always be found in the same place. Some believe that in contemporary society domination is as likely to be found in the communication structures as in the economic ones. Therefore, as much attention may need to be paid to the control of information as to the control of production. They argue that the media and the schools are as important for a Marxist critique of society as are the economic institutions and the means of production.

In recent years there has been an increasing interest in Marxist theory and an increasing application of its insights to schooling. To a large extent this renewed interest in Marxism can be understood in terms of the inability of functionalism to explain adequately some of the social effects of schooling. Randall Collins (who does not identify himself as a Marxist but as a conflict sociologist) lists a number of the failures of functionalist theory in explaining the social effects of schooling. He notes that functionalists argue that the increase in technological sophistication within society accounts for the increasing number of years required in school. However, Collins finds only a very loose relationship between years of education and any increase in the technological sophistication demanded by the job market. In reviewing the literature on this subject, he concludes that "the educational level of the U.S. labor force has changed in excess of that which is necessary to keep up with the skill requirements of jobs."[1]

The plausibility of the functionalist claim that there is a strong relationship between the increased number of years required in school and the educational level required by the technological demands of work rests on the fact that during the very early stages of industrialization, the basic skills required by the work world did undergo a change. Whereas reading and simple arithmetic were not requirements for most jobs in a preindustrial society, they are required in an industrial one. Yet functionalists have extrapolated from the relation between education and industrialization at this early stage and assumed that it holds for all stages. They then conclude that knowledge of higher-level mathematics and science is required for work in high-tech industries. Collins finds that this conclusion is not justified by the evidence. While there is likely some continuing relationship between the increasing technical sophistication of some jobs and the education requirements needed to hold them, there is little evidence suggesting that most jobs demand higher-level technical skills. If the real increase in the years of schooling cannot be explained by an increase in the technological skills needed in most jobs, then the explanation will have to be sought elsewhere. Collins's argument is supported by others. Harry Braverman, for example, presents strong evidence that the skills required for a large number of positions in society have actually decreased; owners and

managers try to squeeze more profits out of an enterprise by routinizing as much of the work as they possibly can.[2] This routinization of labor then provides them more control over the workforce by allowing the substitution of one worker for another. Thus owners are no longer dependent upon the labor of any one person or group. Moreover, according to Collins, there is little evidence that, for most jobs, the more educated the workers are, the more productive they are.[3] In fact, the opposite might be true. More education might make one less tolerant of routine and monotonous work. . . .

Functionalists argue that the newly industrializing Third-World countries need an expanded educational system to develop a workforce. Yet in many of these countries increased education seems to produce a larger unemployed urban population that is overeducated for the types of jobs available. Rather than being driven by the technical and economic needs of the society, the educational system seems to develop a momentum of its own, and the economy is unable to provide jobs for the number of educated workers that the school system produces. According to conflict theorists, the fact that functionalism cannot account for these problems suggests that a new understanding is required. Marxist theorists have attempted to provide it.

A NEO-MARXIST INTERPRETATION OF SCHOOLING IN CAPITALIST SOCIETY

Public schools are state-run educational agencies. According to Marxists, they must therefore be understood in terms of the role that the state plays as the arm of the ruling class. Marxists believe that in a capitalist society, schools will serve to reproduce the relations of production that are essential to maintaining the dominance of the capitalist class. This means that schools will produce workers who are able to work at the different levels of the capitalist enterprise. They produce managers and janitors, as well as an array of people in between. How do the schools do this? The answer is critical to Marxist educational thought, because one criticism of functionalism is based on findings that schools are relatively minor instruments for developing the technical skills required by modern, industrial society. If the schools do not reproduce the relations of production by reproducing the skills that workers need to be laborers, then what is it that schools do reproduce?

To answer this question from a Marxist point of view, we need to see the different ways in which Marxists believe that the state serves the ruling class. One of these is obvious. Through the courts, the police, and the army, the state maintains a monopoly on repressive powers. The repressive features of the state are those that involve force or the threat of force and that can be used whenever there is a direct assault on established property relations. The repressive state apparatus has limited utility, however. Its effectiveness depends upon the willingness of workers who are not members of the ruling class to intervene on behalf of the dominant group. This willingness itself can be assured only if the functionaries who staff the courts, the army, and the police can be counted on to "have the right thoughts." If they cannot be counted on to believe that what they are doing is right and justifiable, there remains the uncomfortable possibility that they will turn their weapons in the wrong direction. To put it in Marxist terms, the development of false consciousness is an essential component of maintaining the capitalist state.

Repressive force is costly, however, and an exclusive reliance on the police and the army can provide an intolerable expense for any state. In addition, while repression can be reasonably effective in preventing a population from performing acts that are directed against the ruling class, it is much less effective in forcing people to act in ways that advance the interest of the ruling class. For example, "working to rule" or to the "letter of the contract" often provides work-

ers with an effective way to protest a situation without triggering the release of repressive force. Enthusiasm and commitment cannot be legislated, even though these are important factors in maintaining a stable structure of domination.

Because the repressive apparatus of the state is not sufficient to maintain the interests of the ruling class, another mechanism is needed, and this is what Louis Althusser calls the Ideological State Apparatuses (ISAs).[4] The ISAs include the communications institutions, such as newspapers, radio, and television; the cultural institutions, such as art, literature, and sports; the religious institutions; the family; political parties; and trade unions. And, above all, the ISAs include the schools. The function of all of these institutions is to provide people with compelling reasons for doing that which they otherwise might not be inclined to do and which is essential for maintaining the current system of production relations and power.

Neo-Marxists view the schools in modern society as the most important of the ISAs. In order to understand the importance of schooling in this process, it will help to return to a fundamental claim of functionalism and see the way in which it both fits and does not fit the reality of contemporary life. That claim, you will recall, is that contemporary society exhibits a strong movement from a system of rewards based on ascribed status to one in which rewards are based on achieved status. In fact, functionalists see this movement as one of the essential features of modern society. However, a number of considerations seem to suggest that their perception is less than correct. Among these is the treatment that has been accorded to certain groups in contemporary Western societies. It is clear, for example, that in the United States, African Americans, Mexican Americans, and other minorities have not been treated in the same way as more established groups and that children from these minorities often suffer disadvantages purely because of their racial or ethnic status. In addition, in almost all advanced capitalist societies, women still function at a disadvantage simply because of their sex. The treatment of minorities and women provides strong reasons to question the functionalist view that modern society strives to reward achieved characteristics. Moreover, the steps that have been taken to correct these inequities have not arisen out of any inner tendency of advanced society. They have come from grassroots political action, from protests, sit downs, boycotts, strikes, and other such means.

The treatment of minority groups and women tells only part of the story. In analyzing data from white males in the United States, Samuel Bowles and Herbert Gintis found that economic success cannot be explained by intelligence as measured by IQ tests. An IQ-based meritocracy does not exist.[5] Moreover, they found no significant relationship between the trend toward equalizing the number of years of schooling of individuals and the equalization of income.[6] Studies like these, both in the United States and elsewhere, suggest that ascribed characteristics still play a prominent role in the distribution of economic rewards and social benefits.

However, even though the functionalist claim about the importance of achieved qualities does not hold up as a matter of fact, it does hold up as a matter of belief. In other words, people think that rewards *ought* to be distributed according to achievement and merit rather than according to family background, sex, or ethnic group. They believe that a system that does otherwise is unfair, and they judge the merits of their own social system on the basis of how well they *think* it is meeting this standard. Individuals who are unhappy with their lot in life will be more likely to endure their situation if they believe they have been given a fair chance than if they believe the cards were stacked against them. And most people believe that free public schooling gives them a fair and equal chance in life; that it is up to them. According to Bowles and Gintis and other Marxists, schools provide an important element of political stability by legitimizing existing inequalities. In other words, while the primary role of schooling under a capitalist system is to reproduce the relations of production, and thereby to reproduce the hierarchical, autocratic system of labor, it must also provide people with the belief that they have been given an equal chance to succeed. . . .

Unequal Education and the Reproduction of the Social Division of Labor

SAMUEL BOWLES

The ideological defense of modern capitalist society rests heavily on the assertion that the equalizing effects of education can counter the disequalizing forces inherent in the free-market system. That educational systems in capitalist societies have been highly unequal is generally admitted and widely condemned. Yet educational inequalities are taken as passing phenomena, holdovers from an earlier, less enlightened era, which are rapidly being eliminated.

The record of educational history in the United States, and scrutiny of the present state of our colleges and schools, lend little support to this comforting optimism. Rather, the available data suggest an alternative interpretation. In what follows I argue (1) that schools have evolved in the United States not as part of a pursuit of equality, but rather to meet the needs of capitalist employers for a disciplined and skilled labor force, and to provide a mechanism for social control in the interests of political stability; (2) that as the economic importance of skilled and well-educated labor has grown, inequalities in the school system have become increasingly important in reproducing the class structure from one generation to the next; (3) that the U.S. school system is pervaded by class inequalities, which have shown little sign of diminishing over the last half century; and (4) that the evidently unequal control over school boards and other decision-making bodies in education does not provide a sufficient explanation of the persistence and pervasiveness of inequalities in the school system. Although the unequal distribution of political power serves to maintain inequalities in education, the origins of these inequalities are to be found outside the political sphere, in the class structure itself and in the class subcultures typical of capitalist societies. Thus, unequal education has its roots in the very class structure which it serves to legitimize and reproduce. Inequalities in education are part of the web of capitalist society, and are likely to persist as long as capitalism survives.

THE EVOLUTION OF CAPITALISM AND THE RISE OF MASS EDUCATION

In colonial America, and in most pre-capitalist societies of the past, the basic productive unit was the family. For the vast majority of male adults, work was self-directed, and was performed without direct supervision. Though constrained by poverty, ill health, the low level of technological development, and occasional interferences by the political authorities, a man had considerable leeway in choosing his working hours, what to produce, and how to produce it. While great inequalities in wealth, political power, and other aspects of status normally existed, differences in the degree of autonomy in

Source: "Unequal Education and the Reproduction of the Social Division of Labor" by Samuel Bowles from *Schooling in a Corporate Society*, by Martin Carnoy, copyright 1972. Reprinted by permission of Random House, Inc.

work were relatively minor, particularly when compared with what was to come.

Transmitting the necessary productive skills to the children as they grew up proved to be a simple task, not because the work was devoid of skill, but because the quite substantial skills required were virtually unchanging from generation to generation, and because the transition to the world of work did not require that the child adapt to a wholly new set of social relationships. The child learned the concrete skills and adapted to the social relations of production through learning by doing within the family. Preparation for life in the larger community was facilitated by the child's experience with the extended family, which shaded off without distinct boundaries, through uncles and fourth cousins, into the community. Children learned early how to deal with complex relationships among adults other than their parents, and children other than their brothers and sisters.[1]

Children were not required to learn a complex set of political principles or ideologies, as political participation was limited and political authority unchallenged, at least in normal times. The only major socializing institution outside the family was the church, which sought to inculcate the accepted spiritual values and attitudes. In addition, a small number of children learned craft skills outside the family, as apprentices. The role of schools tended to be narrowly vocational, restricted to preparation of children for a career in the church or the still inconsequential state bureaucracy.[2] The curriculum of the few universities reflected the aristocratic penchant for conspicuous intellectual consumption.[3]

The extension of capitalist production, and particularly the factory system, undermined the role of the family as the major unit of both socialization and production. Small peasant farmers were driven off the land or competed out of business. Cottage industry was destroyed. Ownership of the means of production became heavily concentrated in the hands of landlords and capitalists. Workers relinquished control over

their labor in return for wages or salaries. Increasingly, production was carried on in large organizations in which a small management group directed the work activities of the entire labor force. The social relations of production—the authority structure, the prescribed types of behavior and response characteristic of the work place—became increasingly distinct from those of the family.

The divorce of the worker from control over production—from control over his own labor—is particularly important in understanding the role of schooling in capitalist societies. The resulting social division of labor—between controllers and controlled—is a crucial aspect of the class structure of capitalist societies, and will be seen to be an important barrier to the achievement of social-class equality in schooling.

Rapid economic change in the capitalist period led to frequent shifts of the occupational distribution of the labor force, and constant changes in the skill requirements for jobs. The productive skills of the father were no longer adequate for the needs of the son during his lifetime. Skill training within the family became increasingly inappropriate.

And the family itself was changing. Increased geographic mobility of labor and the necessity for children to work outside the family spelled the demise of the extended family and greatly weakened even the nuclear family.[4] Meanwhile, the authority of the church was questioned by the spread of secular rationalist thinking and the rise of powerful competing groups.

While undermining the main institutions of socialization, the development of the capitalist system created at the same time an environment—both social and intellectual—which would ultimately challenge the political order. Workers were thrown together in oppressive factories, and the isolation which had helped to maintain quiescence in earlier, widely dispersed peasant populations was broken down.[5] With an increasing number of families uprooted from the land, the workers' search for a living resulted in large-scale labor migrations. Transient, even foreign, elements came to constitute a major segment of the population, and began to pose seemingly insurmountable problems of assimilation, integration, and control.[6] Inequalities of wealth became more apparent, and were less easily justified and less readily accepted. The simple legitimizing ideologies of the earlier period—the divine right of kings and the divine origin of social rank, for example—fell under the capitalist attack on the royalty and the traditional landed interests. The general broadening of the electorate first sought by the capitalist class in the struggle against the entrenched interests of the pre-capitalist period—threatened soon to become an instrument for the growing power of the working class. Having risen to political power, the capitalist class sought a mechanism to ensure social control and political stability.[7]

An institutional crisis was at hand. The outcome, in virtually all capitalist countries, was the rise of mass education. In the United States, the many advantages of schooling as a socialization process were quickly perceived. The early proponents of the rapid expansion of schooling argued that education could perform many of the socialization functions that earlier had been centered in the family and to a lesser extent, in the church.[8] An ideal preparation for factory work was found in the social relations of the school, specifically, in its emphasis on discipline, punctuality, acceptance of authority outside the family, and individual accountability for one's work.[9] The social relations of the school would replicate the social relations of the work place, and thus help young people adapt to the social division of labor. Schools would further lead people to accept the authority of the state and its agents—the teachers—at a young age, in part by fostering the illusion of the benevolence of the government in its relations with citizens.[10] Moreover, because schooling would ostensibly be open to all, one's position in the social division of labor could be portrayed as the result not of birth, but of one's own efforts and talents.[11] And if the children's

everyday experiences with the structure of schooling were insufficient to inculcate the correct views and attitudes, the curriculum itself would be made to embody the bourgeois ideology.[12] Where pre-capitalist social institutions, particularly the church, remained strong or threatened the capitalist hegemony, schools sometimes served as a modernizing counter-institution.[13]

The movement for public elementary and secondary education in the United States originated in the nineteenth century in states dominated by the burgeoning industrial capitalist class, most notably in Massachusetts. It spread rapidly to all parts of the country except the South.[14] In Massachusetts the extension of elementary education was in large measure a response to industrialization, and to the need for social control of the Irish and other non-Yankee workers recruited to work in the mills.[15] The fact that some working people's movements had demanded free instruction should not obscure the basically coercive nature of the extension of schooling. In many parts of the country, schools were literally imposed upon the workers.[16]

The evolution of the economy in the nineteenth century gave rise to new socialization needs and continued to spur the growth of education. Agriculture continued to lose ground to manufacturing; simple manufacturing gave way to production involving complex interrelated processes; an increasing fraction of the labor force was employed in producing services rather than goods. Employers in the most rapidly growing sectors of the economy began to require more than obedience and punctuality in their workers; a change in motivational outlook was required. The new structure of production provided little built-in motivation. There were fewer jobs such as farming and piece-rate work in manufacturing in which material reward was tied directly to effort. As work roles became more complicated and interrelated, the evaluation of the individual worker's performance became increasingly difficult. Employers began to look for workers who had internalized the production-related values of the firm's managers.

The continued expansion of education was pressed by many who saw schooling as a means of producing these new forms of motivation and discipline. Others, frightened by the growing labor militancy after the Civil War, found new urgency in the social-control arguments popular among the proponents of education in the antebellum period.

A system of class stratification developed within this rapidly expanding educational system. Children of the social elite normally attended private schools. Because working-class children tended to leave school early, the class composition of the public high schools was distinctly more elite than the public primary school.[17] And as a university education ceased to be merely training for teaching or the divinity and became important in gaining access to the pinnacles of the business world, upper-class families used their money and influence to get their children into the best universities, often at the expense of the children of less elite families.

Around the turn of the present century, large numbers of working-class and particularly immigrant children began attending high schools. At the same time, a system of class stratification developed within secondary education.[18] The older democratic ideology of the common school—that the same curriculum should be offered to all children—gave way to the "progressive" insistence that education should be tailored to the "needs of the child."[19] In the interests of providing an education relevant to the later life of the students, vocational schools and tracks were developed for the children of working families. The academic curriculum was preserved for those who would later have the opportunity to make use of book learning, either in college or in white-collar employment. This and other educational reforms of the progressive education movement reflected an implicit assumption of the immutability of the class structure.

The frankness with which students were channeled into curriculum tracks, on the basis of their social-class background, raised serious doubts concerning the "openness" of the social-class structure. The relation between social class and a child's chances of promotion or tracking assignments was disguised—though not mitigated much—by another "progressive" reform: "objective" educational testing. Particularly after World War I, the capitulation of the schools to business values and concepts of efficiency led to the increased use of intelligence and scholastic achievement testing as an ostensibly unbiased means of measuring the product of schooling and classifying students.[20] The complementary growth of the guidance counseling profession allowed much of the channeling to proceed from the students' own well-counseled choices, thus adding an apparent element of voluntarism to the system.

The legacy of the progressive education movement, like the earlier reforms of the mid-nineteenth century, was a strengthened system of class stratification within schooling which continues to play an important role in the reproduction and legitimation of the social division of labor.

The class stratification of education during this period had proceeded hand in hand with the stratification of the labor force. As large bureaucratic corporations and public agencies employed an increasing fraction of all workers, a complicated segmentation of the labor force evolved, reflecting the hierarchical structure of the social relations of production. A large middle group of employees developed, comprising clerical, sales, bookkeeping, and low-level supervisory workers.[21] People holding these occupations ordinarily had a modicum of control over their own work; in some cases they directed the work of others, while themselves under the direction of higher management. The social division of labor had become a finely articulated system of work relations dominated at the top by a small group with control over work processes and a high degree of personal autonomy in their work activities, and proceeding by finely differentiated stages down the chain of bureaucratic command to workers who labored more as extensions of the machinery than as autonomous human beings.

One's status, income, and personal autonomy came to depend in great measure on one's place in the work hierarchy. And in turn, positions in the social division of labor came to be associated with educational credentials reflecting the number of years of schooling and the quality of education received. The increasing importance of schooling as a mechanism for allocating children to positions in the class structure played a major part in legitimizing the structure itself.[22] But at the same time, it undermined the simple processes which in the past had preserved the position and privilege of the upper-class families from generation to generation. In short, it undermined the processes serving to reproduce the social division of labor.

In pre-capitalist societies, direct inheritance of occupational position is common. Even in the early capitalist economy, prior to the segmentation of the labor force on the basis of differential skills and education, the class structure was reproduced generation after generation simply through the inheritance of physical capital by the offspring of the capitalist class. Now that the social division of labor is differentiated by types of competence and educational credentials as well as by ownership of capital, the problem of inheritance is not nearly so simple. The crucial complication arises because education and skills are embedded in human beings; unlike physical capital, these assets cannot be passed on to one's children at death. In an advanced capitalist society in which education and skills play an important role in the hierarchy of production, then, the absence of confiscatory inheritance laws is not enough to reproduce the social division of labor from generation to generation. Skills and educational credentials must somehow be passed on within the family. It is a fundamental theme of this essay that schools play an important part in reproducing and legitimizing this modern form of class structure.

NOTES

Many of the ideas in this essay have been worked out jointly with Herbert Gintis and other mem-

bers of the Harvard seminar of the Union for Radical Political Economics. I am grateful to them and to Janice Weiss and Christopher Jencks for their help.

1. This account draws upon two important historical studies: P. Aries, *Centuries of Childhood* (New York: Vantage, 1965) and B. Bailyn, *Education in the Forming of American Society* (Chapel Hill: University of North Carolina Press, 1960). Also illuminating are anthropological studies of education in contemporary pre-capitalist societies. See, for example, J. Kenyatta, *Facing Mount Kenya* (New York: Vintage Books, 1962) pp. 95–124. See also Edmund S. Morgan, *The Puritan Family Religion and Domestic Relations in Seventeenth Century New England* (New York: Harper and Row, 1966).

2. Aries. *Centuries of Childhood*. In a number of places, e.g., Scotland and Massachusetts, schools stressed literacy so as to make the Bible more widely accessible. See C. Cipolla, *Literacy and Economic Development* (Baltimore: Penguin Books, 1969) and Morgan, *Puritan Family*, chap. 4. Morgan quotes a Massachusetts law of 1647 which provided for the establishment of reading schools because it was "one chief project of that old deluder, Satan, to keep men from knowledge of the Scriptures."

3. H.F. Kearney, *Scholars and gentlemen: Universities and Society in Pre-Industrial Britain* (Ithaca, N.Y.: Cornell University Press, 1971).

4. See Bailyn, *Education in the Forming of American Society*. N. Smelser, *Social Change in the Industrial Revolution* (Chicago: University of Chicago Press, 1959).

5. F. Engels and K. Marx, *The Communist Manifesto* (London, England: G. Allen and Unwin, 1951); K. Marx, *The 18th Brumaire of Louis Bonaparte* (New York: International Publishers, 1935).

6. See, for example, S. Thernstrom, *Poverty and Progress: Social Mobility in a 19th Century City* (Cambridge: Harvard University Press, 1964).

7. B. Simon, *Studies in the History of Education, 1780–1870*, vol. I (London, England, Lawrence and Wishant, 1960).

8. Bailyn, *Education in the Forming of American Society*.

9. A manufacturer, writing to the Massachusetts State Board of Education from Lowell in 1841 commented

I have never considered mere knowledge . . . as the only advantage derived from a good Common School education. . . . (Workers with more education possess) a higher and better state of morals, are more orderly and respectful in their deportment, and more ready to comply with the wholesome and necessary regulations of an establishment. . . . In times of agitation, on account of some change in regulations or wages, I have always looked to the most intelligent, best educated and the most moral for support. The ignorant and uneducated I have generally found the most turbulent and troublesome, acting under the impulse of excited passion and jealousy.

Quoted in Michael B. Katz, *The Irony of Early School Reform* (Cambridge, Mass.: Harvard University Press, 1968), p. 88. See also David Isaac Bruck, "The Schools of Lowell, 1824–1861: A Case Study in the Origins of Modern Public Education in America" (Senior thesis, Harvard College, Department of Social Studies, April 1971).

10. In 1846 the annual report of the Lowell, Mass., School Committee concluded that universal education was "the surest safety against internal commotions" (*1846 School Committee Annual Report*, pp. 17–18). It seems more than coincidental that, in England, public support for elementary education—a concept which had been widely discussed and urged for at least half a century—was legislated almost immediately after the enfranchisement of the working class by the electoral reform of 1867. See Simon, *Studies in the History of Education, 1780–1870*. Mass public education in Rhode Island came quickly on the heels of an armed insurrection and a broadening of the franchise. See F. T. Carlton, *Economic Influences upon Educational Progress in the United States, 1820–1850* (New York: Teachers College Press, 1966).

11. Describing the expansion of education in the nineteenth century, Katz concludes:

A middle class attempt to secure advantage for their children as technological change heightened the importance of formal education assured the success and acceptance of universal elaborate graded school systems. The same result emerged from the fear of a growing, underschooled proletariat. Education substituted for deference as a source of social cement and social order in a society stratified by class rather than by rank (M. B. Katz, "From Voluntarism to Bureaucracy in U.S. Education," mimeograph, 1970).

12. An American economist, writing just prior to the "common school revival," had this to say:

Education universally extended throughout the community will tend to disabuse the working class of people in respect of a notion that has crept into the minds of our mechanics and is gradually prevailing, that manual labor is at present very inadequately rewarded, owing to combinations of the rich against the poor, that mere mental labor is comparatively worthless, the property or wealth ought not to be accumulated or transmitted, that to take interest on money let or profit on capital employed is unjust. . . . The mistaken and ignorant people who entertain these fallacies as truths will learn, when they have the opportunity of learning, that the institution of political society originated in the protection of property (Thomas Cooper, *Elements of Political Economy* [1828], quoted in Carlton, *Economic Influences upon Educational Progress in the United States, 1820–1850*, pp. 33–34).

Political economy was made a required subject in Massachusetts high schools in 1857, along with moral science and civic polity. Cooper's advice was widely but not universally followed elsewhere. Friedrich Engels, commenting on the tardy growth of mass education in early nineteenth-century England, remarked: "So shortsighted, so stupidly narrow-minded is the English bourgeoisie in its egotism, that it does not even take the trouble to impress upon the workers the morality of the day, which the bourgeoisie has patched together in its own interest for its own protection." (Engels, *The Condition of the Working Class in England* [Stanford, Calif,: Stanford University Press, 1968].)

13. See Thernstrom, *Poverty and Progress*. Marx said this about mid-nineteenth-century France:

The modern and the traditional consciousness of the French peasant contended for mastery . . . in the form of an incessant struggle between the schoolmasters and the priests. (Marx, *The 18th Brumaire of Louis Bonaparte*, p. 125).

14. Janice Weiss and I are currently studying the rapid expansion of southern elementary and secondary schooling which followed the demise of slavery and the establishment of capitalist economic institutions in the South.

15. Based on the preliminary results of a statistical analysis of education in nineteenth-century Massachusetts being conducted jointly with Alexander Field.

16. Katz, *Irony of Early School Reform* and "From Voluntarism to Bureaucracy in U.S. Education."

17. Katz, *Irony of Early School Reform*.

18. Sol Cohen describes this process in "The Industrial Education Movement, 1906–1917," *American Quarterly*, 20 no. 1 (Spring 1968); 95–110. Typical of the arguments then given for vocational education is the following, by the superintendent of schools in Cleveland:

It is obvious that the educational needs of children in a district where the streets are well paved and clean, where the homes are spacious and surrounded by lawns and trees, where the language of the child's playfellows is pure, and where life in general is permeated with the spirit and ideals of America, it is obvious that the educational needs of such a child are radically different from those of the child who lives in a foreign and tenement section. (William H. Elson and Frank P. Bachman. "Different Course for Elementary School," *Educational Review* 39 [April 1910] 361–63).

See also L. Cremin, *The Transformation of the School Progressivism in American Education, 1876–1957* (New York, Alfred A. Knopf, 1961), chap. 2, and David Cohen and Marvin Lazerson, "Education and the Industrial Order," mimeograph, 1970.

19. The superintendent of the Boston schools summed up the change in 1908:

Until very recently (the schools) have offered equal opportunity for all to receive *one kind* of education, but what will make them democratic is to provide opportunity for all to receive such education as will fit them *equally well* for their particular life work. (Boston, *Documents of the School Committee, 1908*, no. 7. p. 53, quoted in Cohen and Lazerson "Education and the Industrial Order")

20. R. Callahan, *Education and the Cult of Efficiency* (Chicago: University of Chicago Press, 1962), Cohen and Lazerson, "Education and the Industrial Order," and Cremin, *Transformation of the School.*

21. See M. Reich, "The Evolution of the U.S. Labor Force," in *The Capitalist System*, ed. R. Edwards, M. Reich, and T. Weisskopf (Englewood Cliffs, N.J., Prentice-Hall, Inc., 1971).

22. The role of school in legitimizing the class structure is spelled out in S. Bowles, "Contradictions in U.S. Higher Education," mimeograph, 1971.

Becoming Clerical Workers: Business Education and the Culture of Femininity

Linda Valli

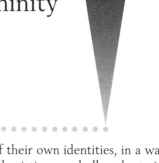

The purpose of this chapter is to map out the relation between the ideological messages of a high-school office education program regarding appropriate sex roles and gendered subjectivity, and the cultural orientations of a group of primarily working-class girls.[1] The chapter delineates the ways in which the young women acquire a basically feminine work identity, the role of the school program in strengthening that identity, and the manner in which educational practices can reinforce or contribute to the reproduction of a sexually divided labor force, in which men and women not only fill different occupations, but have different relations to wage and domestic labor as well.[2]

Since boys generally select themselves out of vocational preparation for office work before their high-school years, I was not able to study the gender-based occupational selection process.[3] I focus exclusively on the production and reproduction of gender-related meanings, behaviors, and orientations that make up the world of the office worker.

Although this chapter falls into the broad category of the study of socialization processes, I attempt to avoid a basic flaw of that approach. I do not presume that the messages that are taught or transmitted to students are the ones that are received or accepted. This assumption creates a model of the world that is far more static than reality, and produces agents who are passive recipients of their own "internalized structures." Following the models of Willis and McRobbie, I reject this concept of socialization, replacing it with a notion of cultural orientations that implies involvement by individuals and groups in the ongoing creation of their own identities, in a way that is neither mechanistic nor wholly voluntaristic, but is rooted in their social and economic pasts and in their perceived futures.[4]

Three general relations to cultural reproduction processes seem possible: acceptance, negotiation, and resistance.[5] Although it is difficult to predict which relationship will be chosen, certain factors appear to structure the choices. Acceptance of specific aspects of culture (in this situation, gender-related work aspects) tends to occur when these messages are congruent with the past and the perceived future, and when no alternatives are perceived. Negotiation and resistance, both of which imply rejection of the cultural messages and practices, occur when there is an element of incongruity, when the culture is experienced as imposed, when it does not fit with a sense of self. Negotiation will be the chosen course of action when the individual or group perceives some element of control or power over the situation, and when the struggle seems worth the effort. Resistance is chosen when, from the participants' point of view, there is no room to negotiate. In this particular context, overt resistance can take such varied forms as saying no to a directive given by a boss or teacher, entering into

Source: "Becoming Clerical Workers: Business Education and the Culture of Femininity" by Linda Valli from *Ideology and Schooling,* edited by Michael Apple and Lois Weis, copyright 1983. Reprinted by permission of Temple University Press.

argumentation, or quitting a job. Covert or hidden resistance is the chosen course of action when the person or group involved is unwilling to bear the consequences of overt resistance, consequences such as being fired. Hidden resistance looks like passive acceptance only to the outsider.

As the details of this ethnographic study suggest, the ideological messages the students received were fairly congruent with the gender-specific patterns and relations they had become accustomed to both in their homes and at school. Their primary mode of behavior, therefore, was to accept, almost to fall naturally and spontaneously into, a sexual division of labor and the subordinate roles for women it implies. In the process of elaborating their lives at work, the students utilized a fairly conventional culture of femininity that identified them not as raw labor power, but as sex objects, on the one hand, and as office wives and mothers, on the other. In so doing, they partially realized (in the dual sense of created and were aware of) their double subordination, in domestic labor and in wage labor. But because this awareness was only partial, and because they saw no alternative, they tended to fantasize an ideal future in which they worked part time and stayed home part time, regardless of the fact that this solution would only strengthen their subordination, keeping them dependent on a male provider and condemning them to low-level positions in the job market.[6]

This chapter develops by giving a brief account of the methodology employed in the study, and descriptions of the cooperative office education program, the teacher, and the students upon which it is based. The main part of the chapter is devoted to an account of those parts of the program that emphasized a work identity that was gender specific, the ways in which the students dealt with those messages, and the implications of those practices.

METHODOLOGY

The analysis presented here is based on an ethnographic study of a cooperative office education program, a vocational program in which senior high students go to school part time and work part time in an office. This methodology was selected because I was interested in analyzing the processes of cultural transmission. I focused on a group of senior high-school students who were being prepared for office work because I was primarily concerned with women's acquisition of a work identity. Since office occupations employ the largest single group of the female labor force, and since many of the areas are currently expanding, office education was the compelling choice for this study.

The data were collected during the 1980–81 school year. The site was a comprehensive, urban high school, which I will call Woodrow High, in a Midwestern city. I was present at Woodrow from September through June on approximately half the school days, scattered throughout the year. Three related techniques were used to collect the data; participant observation in the school and at work (fourteen sites in all); formal and informal interviewing, throughout the year, of significant subjects (for example, teachers, students, supervisors, alumnae and coworkers); and analysis of curricular materials and other related documents. These techniques allowed me to study the transmission of ideological messages and to understand why students accepted, negotiated, or resisted attempts to socialize them in certain ways.

In addition to sixteen students, I interviewed seventeen alumnae: ten from the previous graduating class and seven from the years 1972 to 1979. My goal was threefold: to obtain more information on family backgrounds and influences, since I had no direct contact with parents; to collect reflective accounts of their decision to take, and their experiences within, cooperative office education; and to obtain information on work life and perspectives after high school. I anticipated that these accounts would both confirm and elaborate upon the information I was gathering from my work within the school, and this expectation was realized.

THE PROGRAM

Cooperative education is a specific form of vocational education, that, unlike most educational programs, which take place primarily within school buildings, alternates work experience with school experience. Students receive help in finding career-related jobs and are to receive on-the-job, as well as classroom, training. The implicit rationale of the program is that the work site is a valuable source of learning and should be utilized as an educational tool. The stated expectation is that cooperative education will help students identify their career objectives, that this identification will lead to appropriate training in attitudes, skills, and knowledge, and that the training will lead to careers. These careers are then supposed to create a better community, a community that will "experience a productive growth of its citizens, schools and businesses."

The cooperative office education program at Woodrow High was organized in a fairly typical manner. During their senior year, students who selected the program attended classes in the morning and worked for three to four and a half hours in the afternoon. They received both one school credit and pay for their work. Both students and teacher believed that at least two credits should be given for work. In their behavior and in their conversations with me, work was a far more salient aspect of the cooperative experience than what went on in the classroom.

Students were supposed to carry three morning classes in addition to the "related" office education class, which was specifically designed to relate to their afternoon work experience. This class was scheduled to meet five times a week for forty minutes each day. Students would often miss class, excused or not, but would report for work that afternoon. Four times a year, the teacher (referred to here as Mrs. Shapiro) met with each supervisor for a student evaluation session. Within a day or two, Mrs. Shapiro would then meet with each student in her private office to discuss the evaluation.

While a full analysis of cultural reproduction mechanisms would have to take all aspects of the curriculum into consideration, it should be apparent from the above description that in this particular context too much attention to the formal corpus of knowledge would distort rather than illuminate the ideological messages actually conveyed and received. The fact is that although most of the formal syllabus was organized around the teaching of particular skills (for example, how to reconcile a checkbook, how to fill out tax forms, how to type using a dictaphone, how to proofread), in actual practice little class time was devoted to concentrated work in these areas, and the development of these skills was not the primary concern of either the teacher or the students. During interviews with the teacher, the students, and the graduates, the same refrain was consistently repeated.

I don't attempt to teach much in the class because, unlike the other city high schools, we have a junior prerequisite. I'm also less demanding in this class than in my others because the students and I spend a long time together. I'm more relaxed in here because I want to build up personal relationships. I see myself as more in a counselor's role.
—Mrs. Shapiro

The hour in school seemed wasted. We didn't discuss problems at work and what we were doing. That's what I thought it would be like—saying what problems we had at work and discussing what we could do about them.
—Kathryn '80

I don't think I'd want the class part again. I don't think it taught that much. I don't think there needs to be a class part. It doesn't help that much in the jobs most of us are in. I don't see the point of having it.
—Dorothy '81

My parents thought I was skipping when I got home early. They didn't believe she was letting us out, or that there was nothing to do.
—Jane '80

My contention is that the absence of a rigid syllabus created a gap, a space that was filled with incidental teaching and learning. The absence of an overt curriculum created a situation in which the messages students received from casual comments, relationships, school and work structures and practices were stronger than they would otherwise have been.

THE TEACHER

Mrs. Shapiro had been directing the program at Woodrow High for twelve years. She perceived herself and introduced herself as a feminist, as a person who believed in and worked toward women's equality with men, particularly in the business world. Having had parents who encouraged her to succeed just as much as they encouraged her brothers, Mrs. Shapiro belonged to numerous professional and women's organizations, and had a life history that was very much career oriented. She was married, the mother of two, and, at the time of the study, a recent grandmother.

Mrs. Shapiro was quite verbal about her feminism. On the bulletin board in her office was the saying "All discrimination against all women must be removed" and Erica Jong's poem "Woman Enough." When the principal distributed the faculty roster, she confronted him over the asterisks placed after the names of married women. A new roster was distributed the next day with the asterisks removed. During class time, she told the students she considered the term "Gentlemen" to be an inappropriate salutation since the unknown addressees could be women and, during a filing unit, she told the class that the formulation "Mrs. John Smith" was incorrect, that a woman always kept her own first name.

Because of Mrs. Shapiro's feminist orientation, this case study should be one of the strongest in testing the school's role in the reproduction of a culture of femininity in the labor force and the reinforcement of traditional, sex-typed work orientations. Since gender-related occupational training definitely and explicitly occurred in this situation, I infer that it also occurs in a large percentage of other office education programs in secondary schools across the country.

THE STUDENTS

Although an elite subdivision is within its catchment area and it draws its students from a wide range of social class backgrounds, Woodrow High is located in the industrial part of town and is basically considered a working-class high school. The seniors who elected cooperative office education did not seem any different from their female counterparts who did not. A few were unusually wealthy; a few were unusually bright. One of the graduates I interviewed was the valedictorian of her class. She went on to take the two-year Executive Secretary course at the community college. Some of the students went on to four-year universities, but the vast majority stayed in office work, occasionally supplementing their preparation with community college or on-the-job training.

Many of the students had mothers, and sometimes older sisters, who had worked in offices. This work was often done on a part-time basis, or had been returned to once families had been raised. Mothers who did not work in offices tended to be employed as sales clerks or cafeteria workers. The fathers of the students, on the other hand, generally had histories of full-time manual labor or civil-service work; most of them were loading-dock workers, mechanics, truck drivers, factory workers, or building custodians. A few students had fathers who were mail carriers or police officers; one father was a high-school teacher, and one was listed as an industrial engineer although he had never been to college.

The division of labor in the home as well as at the workplace basically followed the traditional sexual patterns. Although, for example, three students mentioned fathers who cooked for the family, in no instance did the activity flow out of a basic role identity. In one case, the mother had suffered a mental breakdown and had been institutionalized. The father, thereafter, assumed the role of housekeeper. In another instance, the father started sharing the responsibility for cooking with his high-school daughters after his wife had died. In the third instance, the father had been retired for some time because of disability. Gourmet cooking had become a hobby for him.

The usual pattern, however, was the mother-as-homemaker. Not even a working mother and retired father guaranteed that the father would partake in routine housekeeping chores. In these cases, the running of the vacuum cleaner once a week seemed to vindicate the father, in his own eyes at least.

But the fact that students came from homes with a traditional division of labor did not necessarily mean that these practices were automatically internalized. Some of the students had older sisters whose marriages did not follow the traditional pattern of their parents, others took child-development or other classes in school that raised the possibility of other marital patterns. One student, for instance, who tenaciously clung to a strict sexual division of wage labor ideology, arguing that "men are stronger than women and that's just the way it should be," simultaneously argued that men should help with everything in the house, although her own father did not, because that was the way her mother said it should be and that was what her brother-in-law did.

The reverse situation also obtained: some students envisioned a world in which women had better jobs than men without it being harmful to business or to personal relationships, and yet believed in the dominance of the man in the home. As one graduate put it,

I like men paying for my food and opening doors for me. All this stuff about keeping your own name and being equal to your husband, I don't go for. —Jane '80

To a few of the students, there seemed to be a fairly clear distinction between gender relations in wage labor and those in personal relations and domestic labor; they saw no need for congruence between the two.

Such were the sex-role orientations with which the students began the cooperative office education program. Because of these orientations, the students were predisposed to accept a work world that men and women related to in naturally different manners. Their job training and work experiences reaffirmed this basic sexual division of labor ideology.

THE OFFICE WORKER AS SEX OBJECT

Messages about sexual appearance and sexual behavior were integral elements of the students' office education training both at school and in the workplace. On the level of appearance and self-presentation, the young women were encouraged to emphasize and use their gender identities. But on the level of practice, when it came to actual behavior, they were warned to control their sexuality. The subtle message was that they would be blamed if sexual improprieties occurred at work.

In terms of their mode of self-presentation, students were informed in numerous ways of how important it was to cultivate a feminine, even provocative, appearance if they were serious about getting a job and being promoted once they had a job. Early in the school year, for instance, a woman from a job placement center spoke to the students about interviewing, stressing the importance of their appearance:

Look professional. Your best source for that is *Glamour* magazine. It regularly runs sections for the professional woman: her image, what to wear, how to get a job. Dress like you already have the job, like you would to find a boyfriend. That's a good parallel. You have to attract someone.

Later that week, Mrs. Shapiro re-emphasized how important it was for the students to sell themselves at an interview. In encouraging them to listen calmly and collect their thoughts before they answered a question in order to organize their ideas and speak intelligently she used the phrase, "just like the finalists in the Miss America contest."

This association of job with sexual attraction was graphically depicted throughout the year by an advertisement on a classroom bulletin board. Although the overt purpose of the bulletin board display was to show examples of new office machines and technology, in so doing, it also presented a certain image of women office workers.

The most striking example was the advertisement for Dictaphone's Dual Display Word Processor. In an attempt to encourage readers (presumably male managers) to purchase Dictaphone's new equipment, the creator of this advertisement cleverly equated obsolete office equipment with the Stone Age and used a photograph of a young attractive woman clad only in a leopard skin to demonstrate the point. Because this picture was displayed without comment in a business classroom of a public school, it seems that an unspoken approval or legitimation of the image was necessarily conveyed.

The issue of appearance was also regularly discussed during Mrs. Shapiro's evaluation sessions with supervisors. Appearance, was, in fact, one of the criteria on the formal student-trainee evaluation report, which included such items as quality and quantity of work, attitude, attendance, reliability. On the evaluation sheet, appearance was defined in a sex-neutral way as "neatness and personal care, appropriateness to the job." But in conversation Mrs. Shapiro often added a gender-specific element;

> You might do her a favor. She's a pretty girl. She could do a lot with herself and I don't think she's doing it. A lot of women in businesses are making appearance an important part of their day. She could capitalize on that. She puts herself together very nicely. She was wearing some very sexy shoes the other day.

While not forbidden, clogs and slacks, particularly those cut like men's, which were the fashion at the time, were frowned upon. One supervisor talked about how her student-trainee had a figure for skirts, not slacks, how slacks put twenty pounds on her, and how you could see the look of disgust on the older men's faces when young women came to work dressed casually. Appearance, she said, was a definite factor in promotability, even for a woman who was extremely capable.

The accuracy of this perception was born out in the students' experiences with job placement.

One student's difficulties in finding a job best highlight the employment obstacles some women are faced with. By the end of their first two weeks in the cooperative program all the students in the class had found jobs, except one. This student, Dorothy, stood out from the rest of the class in that she was overweight and, while always neat, dressed in old, inexpensive jeans, blouses, and shoes. Not until the end of the second month of school did Dorothy find a job. Unlike the other students, who all found afternoon jobs, Dorothy was hired for an evening shift in an assembly-line type department of a large insurance company with no public contact.

Mrs. Shapiro explained to me during those initial weeks that she was not able to place Dorothy very fast because her business background was slim and her appearance poor. In fact, however, Dorothy had more business background than many of the students in the class, had the third highest senior class rank among the cooperative office education students, and had taken a more rigorous academic program than the two students who were ranked ahead of her. In an eleventh grade standardized test, Dorothy had placed in the 99th percentile for math computation and in the 90th for math concepts. She was one of the fastest, most accurate typists in the class, and was the only student who took classroom work home to finish. The other students were apparently quick to perceive her capabilities, for they often went to her for help on their own work. It became clear that her mode of self-presentation was the only reason she was experiencing difficulty in finding a job.

One of the places to which Dorothy applied was a small bookstore, where she was turned down in favor of Cynthia, a tall, slender model-type. I was told later in the year by a graduate (a nice-looking, but plain, honor roll student who had also been rejected for the job in favor of a more attractive but less capable student) that the man in charge of hiring at the bookstore had a "penchant" for a certain type of female employee—blond and well built. Nor did this appear to be an isolated example. Mrs. Shapiro told the class that a bank employer called one day a few years back to complain that she was not sending him very pretty girls.

These examples indicate that there is not only a dual labor market, in which men and women fill different occupational categories, but that there is also a dual market within women's work. Apparently, not only are women primarily relegated to lower-level jobs, but certain types of women are excluded from the best of even these jobs.

Cultivation of a feminine appearance is only one aspect of the situation that women must deal with, for they must learn not only how to cultivate their femininity, but how to control it as well. Sheila Rowbotham makes this point in *Woman's Consciousness, Man's World*, when she says that a certain "contained sexuality" is required as part of the office worker's job.[7] Both Mrs. Shapiro and the students seemed to understand this requirement.

During a classroom discussion of a magazine article on the topic of sexual harassment this issue of "contained sexuality" arose. Mrs. Shapiro stressed the importance of an appropriate degree and type of sexual conduct on the job. While on the other occasions she had been subtly encouraging the students to present themselves with a certain amount of "sexiness," on this particular day she highlighted the importance of knowing what the limits should be if they wanted to avoid detrimental consequences. She told them they would be asking for abuse if they were too timid to control the situation or if they wore attire that was too skimpy, giving signals that they wanted to be noticed. She cautioned them to be aware of what they were communicating through their dress and bodies, indicating an awareness that their sexuality was not only something they could use to gain job benefits but was also something that could be used against them.

In order to make the most of opportunities on the job, then, young workers apparently have to be skilled not only in running typewriters and photocopiers, but in monitoring their sexuality and sexual lives as well. But in case workers do not internalize the "proper" sexual code, companies often have either formal or informal policies about social and sexual relations.

One personnel department, for example, discouraged employees from dating each other. If two employees married, one had to quit the job; that was official company policy. (The one who quit was generally the woman, of course, since she typically had the lower-paying job.)

Eleanor, a 1980 graduate, told the story of a bachelorette party for female employees held at a local bar. As part of the entertainment, a young male employee clad in bikini underwear and bow leapt out of a gift box during the course of the evening. He ended up quitting his job shortly thereafter because of the treatment he was receiving from his supervisor because of the incident, treatment that included a demotion.

Needless to say, students and employees did not always appreciate or accept attempts to control their sexual identities and practices. One student, for instance, explicitly rejected the "image of the secretary" that was conveyed to her. As she put it,

> Mrs. Shapiro had this obsession with secretaries looking gorgeous. Getting up at 5:00 in the morning to do their hair and nails. She taught us a lot about appearance, eye contact, interviews, dressing up. I thought that was good, but you don't have to put on all that make-up. Cleanliness is the important thing.
> —Jane '80

Most students, however, did not verbalize any opposition to suggestions that were made about their appearance. But in their nonverbal behavior, in the manner in which they actually dressed for work, there were indications that they, like many office workers, were not passively accepting imposed standards, but were negotiating and creating their own style. This style combined the popular men's cut slacks with open toed, spiked, "sexy" shoes. It was a definite blend of a unisex work look with a feminine social look, and appeared to be an attempt to control the issue of appearance while still emphasizing sexuality.

Resistance to company definition and control of their identities as women workers was also exemplified in a widely distributed cartoon graphic. The graphic simply added two words and a visual to the universal phone memo that is the staple of the secretary's office life. The originally staid and official memo thus read, "While you were out fucking off . . . " and displayed a naked boss "making it" with an extremely buxom nude woman. The term "fucking off" here obviously connotes both sexual intercourse and screwing around, having fun, wasting time, using company time for personal pleasure. It thus attacks both the sexual and the work identity of the boss, projecting onto him the demeaning identity women office workers feel is at times attributed to them.

But all in all, most of the students seemed to internalize definitions of themselves as women workers that took into account traditional notions of feminine appearance. Many of the reasons they could or could not imagine themselves doing certain jobs hinged on physical criteria.

I would never be a mechanic. You get messy. I really like to fly and travel and I like to meet new people, but you have to have a lot of qualifications to be a stewardess. You have to be tall and skinny. They want you to be really perfect.
—Kris '81

I'm not into all that liberated stuff. I still want to be pampered. I don't want muscles or to get dirty.
—Debbie '80

I thought of being an airline stewardess, but I weighed too much. You have to only weigh 120 or something.
—Jennifer '80

I can't imagine myself getting my hands all gooey, being sweaty and dirty all the time.
—Tanya '80

I wouldn't want to work in a garage—to be a mechanic. I wouldn't want to come home greasy.
—Priscilla '79

So, although there was some disagreement, resistance, and negotiation about the exact amount and type of "femininity" women office workers should cultivate and display, there was basic agreement on a more fundamental level. In general, a gender-specific, feminine appearance that could be contrasted to a masculine appearance was accepted and adopted.

This internalization of a gender-specific identity, an identity defined in many ways in relation to men, was strikingly evident in graffiti written on a sign posted on one of the company's bulletin boards. The sign announced "Fun and games" at a Women's Christmas Party. The graffiti responded, "How can we have fun without men?" and "Who are we going to play games with?" While obviously acting to reject what they perceived to be the company's attempt to control their social and sexual lives, the women, at one and the same time, affirmed and reinforced their dependence on men. They could not visualize an identity, or even an activity, for themselves apart from a relation to men. What they appear to object to is not their subordination to men, but to interference from the company in the way they acted out that identity.

THE OFFICE WORKER AS WIFE AND MOTHER

A second way in which office work roles were linked to the students' gender identity was through an association of office work with domestic labor, either through the equation of the work with women's work in the home or through the subordination of their role in the office to their role in the home.

The observation has often been made that the role of women in the office parallels their role in the home: picking up after men; doing the daily, repetitive, tedious housekeeping tasks; and keeping men's lives organized and undisturbed, so they can concentrate on their important work. Quoting a 1935 *Fortune* magazine article, Margery Davies claims that male bosses preferred women over "pushy young men" as office workers because, as *Fortune* stated, women "are capable of making the office a more pleasant, peaceful, and homelike place."[8] Taking on this kind of work, which has changed little in half a century, deepens women's wage labor identity as secondary and peripheral, for it patterns a gendered subjectivity already deeply etched into their day-to-day existence.

The objective structuring of these asymmetrical roles, of male leading roles and female serving roles, was already so much taken for granted in the students' lives that they were unable to even perceive it. One young graduate told me that during high school "everyone wants to be a cheerleader." She naturally presumed that in this context I would know "everyone" meant "every girl," so that she did not have to make it explicit. In much the same way, the students took the sexual division of labor they found in their offices for granted. During an interview of a graduate who had worked in the same department of the same large corporation for almost two years, I asked her to mention the types of jobs that were filled by men, by women, or by both men and women. After reflecting for a few moments, she said,

> All of the big bosses are men. I've never noticed that before, but that's the way it is. And all the secretaries are females . . . and all the key punch operators are ladies. I've never thought of that before.
> —Eleanor '80

At another workplace, a student made daily mail runs, picking up and delivering mail to every office in the building. On the desk of each employee was a name plate. The typical nameplate for a female employee read, "Beth," "Jo," "Susie," or "Pat." The typical male employee's nameplate was "Mr. Mott," "Mr. Gleeson," or "Mr. J. L. Stone." When I brought the distinction to the student's attention it was again apparent it was something she had never really noticed; she said almost in passing.

I don't think there is anything behind the difference. I think it's just a matter of preference.
—Donna '81

The relation of the woman office worker's status to that of the male worker was objectified in the structure of the workplace as well as in how the workers were addressed. Men often had offices that were private or closed off, in contrast to the public work areas of the women.[9] Even if women had their own desks, they were generally grouped together in a large, open space. About eight or nine of the places at which students worked were fairly large bureaucracies housed on more than one building level. Inevitably, when this was the case, status differentials were structured into the floor on which one's office was located. So, when referring to bosses, workers would naturally employ expressions like,

> I don't know if there are any ladies up there—up at the very top.
> —Dorothy '81
>
> One of the big bosses who sits upstairs is over him.
> —Eleanor '80

These linguistic expressions reinforce notions of superiority and inferiority that are so naturally linked with the English concepts of up/down, high/low, over/under, and top/bottom.

While the students often watched upper-level, male employees taking work home, having their work lives spill over into their home lives, so to speak, they usually saw the converse in the lives of the women with whom they worked. These women often worked only part-time so that they could see their children off to school in the mornings and be home before the school day ended. They often brought in candy or cookies to sell for their children's scout troop or hung home-made skeletons they had constructed in their role as den mother. Sometimes they had to take a temporary maternity leave or had to quit work altogether because they were no longer able to juggle working and child care, even though the family needed the money. One of the students vividly recalled how her mother was fired from her clerical job years before because she and her siblings kept walking over to her office (located just blocks from their home) to visit, ask questions, or get permissions.

In many ways, then, the identity of women office workers seems to be closely linked with their identity and work in the home. This was underscored for the students at the Appreciation Banquet given by the class in honor of their supervisors. The two main speeches were given by the teacher and by a retiring supervisor, Mrs. Carter, who was held in high esteem by coworkers, the teacher, and the numerous students whom she had supervised over the years. In both speeches, reference was made to the woman worker as mother. Mrs. Carter told the group:

> My first family was all raised and scattered around the country. I thought my parenting days were over. Then, six years ago, I began a second family. And in six years I've had forty-two offspring.

Mrs. Shapiro's speech was filled primarily with appreciative remarks to those at the banquet who had contributed to the success of the program. A special note of thanks was addressed to Mrs. Carter.

> They gained so much from being in your office. You became the mother at work that I was in school.

It is difficult to imagine male supervisors or teachers so naturally using paternal imagery in speaking about their work relationship to male apprentices.

Mrs. Shapiro also underscored her own identity as mother by knitting baby clothes during class time and used traditional notions about sex-appropriate behavior by advising the students not to express "emotionalism" if they wanted to rise up the corporate ladder, and not to shout, since "it's not ladylike." One of their texts warned them not to "chit-chat" during the workday, since it wasted their employer's dollars.

Another teaching aid, a filmstrip, similarly reinforced traditional notions of the sexual division of labor. Titled "Telephone Impressions," the filmstrip was geared to teaching students good phone techniques: courtesy, clear speaking, and promptness. Mrs. Shapiro made a point of telling the class that although the filmstrip was excellent at demonstrating good phone usage, the school system could not purchase it, because it was sexist. All the examples of the wrong way to answer the phone, she elaborated, were delivered by a male voice; all the correct examples were delivered by a female voice. Therefore, the filmstrip had an antimale bias. It should have portrayed mistakes being made equally by the man and the woman.

It appeared to me, however, that there was a deeper, more subtle sexism at work in the filmstrip. The incorrect phone manner was not just a male voice, it was an authoritative, busy, important-sounding male voice, one that was irritated that it had to be bothered by answering the phone. The female voice, on the other hand, sounded trained for the job: that was her proper work and the task for which she was perfectly suited. Far from being antimale, the filmstrip reinforced the age-old notion that men have more important things to do than answer the phone. Since women are not doing anything of value, they are the ones who should be constantly interrupted to screen and direct messages.

At some of the workplaces women workers were beginning to resist this traditional telephone role, requesting the installation of a decentralized phone system where each person would have to take his or her own messages. Mrs. Carter was one supervisor who was adamant about this. Shortly after she was hired as an executive secretary, she told her boss to take the phones away or she would leave the job. She resented the burden of answering her boss's phone, claiming that if women were relieved of that kind of task they would be freer to do "the administrative work that men won't let women do." Office workers were also starting to resist the secretary's traditional task of serving coffee. Maureen, for example, was startled when a boss asked if she had offered coffee to the men who had arrived for a business meeting. She responded in surprise, "No, was I supposed to?" Her boss replied, "You bet you are, and do it with a smile, too." Maureen characterized this attitude as chauvinistic, but when she checked with other office workers and was told it was appropriate for her to be asked to do that task, she was reluctant to say anything because she feared it would turn people against her, and affect the way she felt about working there. So, even though she thought she would "raise a ruckus" if she were an older worker, employed full time, and if the practice were habitual, because of her structural relationship to the job she ended up complying with the direction.

But, all in all, just as the students partially accept sexuality as a criterion of themselves as office workers, so do they tend to accept being defined as man's helper, as his office wife. Some students saw this as a natural division of labor, some as a social division, and some seemed unable to distinguish between the two.

> Office work is mostly for women because it's typing and a lot of guys don't like to type. Filing and receptionist, that's more for girls too, because that's secretary work and girls are secretaries, you know.
> —Kris '81

> I guess there aren't any boys in the class because the role of secretary has almost always been all women. Probably because it's traditional for the man to be the boss.
> —Katrina '81

> Women shouldn't do construction work. Men are stronger and that's just the way it should be. Secretary jobs are probably for women mostly. That's just the way things are.
> —Terri '81

> Boys don't take the class because boys aren't secretaries. They're more into manual labor. That's just today's society. Men don't sit and push pencils. Being a secretary is a girl's job.
> —Marion '80

> A guy should be the boss. I can't see a lady telling a guy what to do. He'd probably be bigger than her. . . . I'm not used to a lady boss. I mean, you don't see it on television. There a man is always the boss. And that's just the way I think it should be. Sure, there could be a lady doing Robert's job, but that wouldn't be right.
> —Cynthia '81

What "is" often became equated with what "should be" and, surprisingly enough, as late as 1981 many of these eighteen- to twenty-year-olds had not seriously considered alternatives. In fact, the ideology of the sexual division of labor remained so strong that many of the students continued to advance arguments that their everyday experiences clearly contradicted (for example, seeing men who pushed pencils, having women as bosses).

When students elaborated on the reasons why men did not or should not do women's work and why women did not or should not do men's work, a striking contrast could be heard. Generally using euphemistic language, they explained that men who ventured into what was traditionally regarded as women's work would be considered homosexual.

> I guess there weren't any boys in the class because they have the idea that it's for secretaries and they think boys aren't secretaries. I guess they think a lot of people might get the wrong idea.
> —Jessica '80

> I really can't picture a man doing a woman's job. My uncle is a nurse, but he's like this [she made a limp-wristed gesture]. That's why it would be hard for guys to have a woman's job. Because it's considered delicate and people might think they're gay.
> —Debbie '80

> Guys aren't cheerleaders because they think it's too faggy.
> —Kathryn '80

> I guess guys don't take something like the cooperative office class because they don't think it's right for them. They think they'd be laughed at—wow, what a weirdo!
> —Cynthia '81

It's only in big cities that guys are secretaries; because they're able to get lost or hide more there.
—Doris '81

Doris went on to confirm my interpretation of her statement; if men did office work it meant they were gay; and if they were gay they would naturally want to hide their identity.

On the other hand, the young women who thought that the sexual division of labor should be maintained explained that women who were after men's jobs were trying to be like men or trying to prove their (mistaken) equality.

I don't think ladies should be police or firemen either. They're just trying to show the guys they can do it and have the ability.
—Priscilla '79

On "Real People" they showed two women who were working on the docks doing loading. I'm sure they needed the job, but I think they were also proving a point.
—Debbie '80

I think jobs like construction and firefighters should go to men. Some women are trying to prove they're as equal as men, but the jobs should go to the guy.
—Cynthia '81

According to these students, then, when men do women's work, they are denying or rejecting their masculinity, their natural claim to superiority. They are becoming effeminate. When women try to do men's work, they are not accepting their natural limitations and subordination, but are trying to be as good as men, when in fact they are not.

Just as most of these students had a hard time imagining men and women doing the same wage labor jobs, so too did they find it hard to imagine men and women filling the same domestic labor roles. For them, the notion of women's work automatically meant the primary role in domestic labor. In one way or another, they made it clear that men were the primary breadwinners and they, the women, the primary homemakers and childcarers.

If I were to marry, I would still want to work part time. Otherwise I'd get bored. But I wouldn't want to work full time if my husband were bringing in a good income. There's a lot to do already with housekeeping and kids.
—Jane '80

I can't imagine not working unless I had kids. Then I might stay home until they were in school. But then I'd be bored. The perfect situation would be to work half time.
—Charlotte '77

If I had kids I would sit around the house with them. I wouldn't work. You can tell kids who have been raised by a baby sitter. I don't know if I would let John stay home with them or not. It's not what guys are supposed to do.
—Anne '80

I don't know many guys who would stay home with the kids. It's always been that it's the woman that stays home—because they're the gentle sex. Or that's what I've been told. It's just always been that way.
—Katrina '81

I would like not to be working sometimes. It's hard to come home every evening and just start to do what every housewife has to do. And I'm the one who always has to get the baby off to the sitter.
—Connie '77

I do resent having to have worked all these years, full time, while my kids were little. But there's no way I could have afforded not to. If I were able to find a part time job now, though, I would take it. In fact, I'm looking.
—Mary '71

While they might have been able to imagine themselves having full-time, interesting, or important careers when they were younger or if they were to stay single, the central force directing the students' and graduates' sense of a work identity was the expectation of eventual marriage and family. Interview material from two of the young women illustrates this underlying dynamic.

Kathryn, a 1980 graduate and an accounting student at a major university, was the most career-minded of the students I interviewed. In discussing her future she said,

I want to be independent for my own satisfaction, so I can prove to myself that I can do it, so no one has to take care of me.

She went on, however, to explain that only if she remained single would she ever attempt to be a CPA, an auditor, or the president of a credit union. That type of work, she said, was too stressful to allow other responsibilities as well. Since she definitely wanted a family, she would probably never hold those jobs, but said she would instead look for an accountant's job at a small business or credit union, which would be a good job and offer a good salary "for a woman."

Mary Jo, one of the high-school students, told much the same story from a different perspective. Reflecting on her youthful fantasies rather than her projected future, she explained how she had wanted to be an archeologist when she was in the eighth grade, how she loved to watch accounts of "digs" in various parts of the world. But even at fourteen years of age, she knew that was not practical. She knew that she had to get on with her life: to settle down, get a job, prepare for marriage and a family. So she planned to go to the community college after high school for a degree as an accountant clerk. When I asked why she had decided on a two-year rather than a four-year degree, she responded.

Why should I waste my time in school? I'd rather get going right away and get it over with.

Mary Jo said she had the old-fashioned ambition of raising a couple of children and working part time.

CONCLUSION

Experiencing office work as either secondary to or synonymous with a sexual/home/family identity further marginalized these students' work identities. The culture of femininity associated with office work made it easier for them to be less attached to their work and their workplace than

men, who stay in paid employment because they must live up to a masculine ideology of male-as-provider. Women's identities tend to be much less intrinsically linked to wage labor than are men's.

The beliefs the young women had about themselves being inferior workers were, thus, reinforced by the ideological messages in the classroom and at the work site, and by their structured experiences as office workers and became even more taken for granted as part of their everyday existence. While in some minimal ways the women may have rejected the ideology of male supremacy, at a more fundamental and persistent level, they affirmed it. They conceded legitimacy to the dominance of men in a way that appeared spontaneous and natural. By denying wage labor primacy over domestic labor, they inadvertently consented to and confirmed their own subordination, preparing themselves "for both unskilled, low-paid work and unpaid domestic service."[10]

The women used a culture of femininity to resist the impositions of wage labor, not just because work was boring and tedious—as it often is, too, for working-class men—but because it created a double work load. So they refused identities as full-time and serious workers; they resisted being subsumed into, and consumed by, capital. But this resistance did not change their primary relationships. Ultimately, the women prepared themselves to become part-time producers and part-time consumers, remaining subordinate to men in the workplace and dependent on them in the home. In this way, office women recreate their own subordinate culture, a culture they have learned to use and benefit from, since they see no way to change the material conditions from which it arises.

1. I would like to thank Michael Olneck, Michael Apple, and Vandra Masemann for their comments on the draft of this article.
2. An underlying assumption of this article is that while an advanced capitalist economy does not need a sexual division of labor in any absolute sense, a reserve labor force is used to control workers and keep wages down, and is drawn upon in times of economic expan-

sion. In a society where patriarchal practices and ideologies prevail, where it is seen as natural and right that men are the primary breadwinners and women the child-raisers and husband-supporters, the logical group to be that reserve wage labor is women. They can move in and out of the wage labor force with the least disturbance and least strain to the economy because they can be absorbed into the family where, for working class mothers at least, domestic labor is generally a full time job anyway. For detailed discussions see Annette Kuhn and AnnMarie Wolpe, eds. *Feminism and Materialism: Women and Modes of Production* (London: Routledge and Kegan Paul, 1978); and Michelle Barrett, *Women's Oppression Today: Problems in Marxist Feminist Analysis* (London: Verso Editions, 1980).

3. "Selected themselves" is the correct formulation here, since Title IX guidelines explicitly forbid sex-segregated programs in public schools and since there was some evidence of affirmative action attempts to recruit males to the cooperative office education program, at the success rate of two boys in thirteen years. Unfortunately, the term conveys an individual-voluntaristic connotation I do not wish to imply. The weight of cultural pressures on adolescents to choose traditional sex-typed classes is formidable. Generally, they do not even need the type of discouragement reported to have occurred at Woodrow High School in the form of a male counselor asking a hockey player, "What the hell do you want to take a second year of typing for?" For other accounts of the ways in which schools help orient girls and boys to occupations on the basis of gender, see Judith Stacey, Susan Bereaud, and Joan Daniels, eds., *And Jill Came Tumbling After: Sexism in American Education* New York: Dell, 1974); Rosemary Deem, ed., *Schooling for Women's Work* (London: Routledge and Kegan Paul, 1980); and Nancy Frazier and Myra Sadker, *Sexism in School and Society* (New York: Harper & Row, 1973).

4. See Paul E. Willis, *Learning to Labour: How Working Class Kids Get Working Class Jobs* (Farnborough: Saxon House, 1977), and Angela McRobbie, "Working Class Girls and the Culture of Femininity," in *Women Take Issue: Aspects of Women's Subordination*, ed. Women's Studies Group, Centre for Contemporary Cultural Studies (London: Hutchinson, 1978), pp. 96–108.

5. Similar formulations can be found in Stuart Hall and Tony Jefferson, eds., *Resistance through Rituals: Youth Subcultures in Post-War Britain* (London: Hutchinson & Co., 1975) and by Jean Anyon, "Accommodation and Resistance in Gender and Gender Development," a paper presented at the Ontario Institute for Studies in Education Conference on the *Political Economy of Gender* (Toronto, Ontario, October 30, 1981) and to be published in *Gender, Class and Education*, Len Barton, ed. (Sussex: Falmer Press, 1982).

6. This conclusion is also drawn by Madeleine MacDonald in "Cultural Reproduction: The Pedagogy of Sexuality," *Screen Education*, no. 32/33 (Autumn/Winter 1979–80): 141–53.

7. Sheila Rowbotham, *Woman's Consciousness, Man's World* (Middlesex: Penguin Books, 1973), p. 89.

8. Margery Davies, "Woman's Place is at the Typewriter: The Feminization of the Clerical Labor Force," in *Capitalist Patriarchy and the Case for Socialist Feminism*, ed., Zillah R. Eisenstein (New York: Monthly Review Press, 1979), p. 257.

9. Although this is a basic authority relation that would probably exist irrespective of gender, because gender and authority are strongly correlated in offices, hierarchical authority structures necessarily structure gender relations.

10. MacDonald, "Cultural Reproduction," p. 152.

STUDY QUESTIONS FOR PART 4

1. What are universal norms and who controls them?

2. How do schools, education, and teachers socialize students? Is that good or bad?

3. While Valli's work is a bit dated now, is the feminine work identity she describes still operating today? Give evidence that it is or is not.

4. What do the ideas of false consciousness, hegemony, acceptance, negotiation, and resistance mean, and why is it important for educators to understand these ideas and their implications for schools?

5. Do public schools really equalize educational opportunities for all students? Explain your answer.

6. What does social class have to do with schooling?

7. Do the schools benefit some groups at the expense of others? Explain.

8. Functionalists would say that schools perform an appropriate and useful sorting job in our society. Agree or disagree and explain your reasoning.

9. What connection(s) are there between schooling and achievement of the "American dream"? Explain your reasoning.

10. How will policies like "school choice" and "charter schools" mitigate or improve the equality of educational opportunity in the United States?

School Life

The three reading selections to follow provide vivid descriptions of life in an elementary school and a middle/junior high school, and include a discussion of the challenges of education in a multicultural society. While they certainly do not represent every school or classroom, the conditions and practices pictured here provoke several critical questions:

- From a student's viewpoint, what does happen in school, or in the classroom, that helps/hinders learning?
- What differences do the assumptions and expectations of teachers make for children's opportunity to learn and succeed in school?
- Should teachers and schools attempt to serve all children equally, assuming this is possible?
- What assumptions and stereotypes do teachers believe about poor children or children of color that hinder student learning?

The ethnographies of an elementary school and a junior high school in this section show how influential the teacher is and how a teacher's expectations and social inequities are imposed on children. They illustrate how teachers operate with one set of rules and expectations while students often operate with different ones. Knowledge is highly subjective. Important power relations are reflected in the teachers' pedagogical practices and in the school curriculum.

The first reading vividly describes the consequences for children of teachers' expectations for their academic performance. Rist's study of kindergarten, first grade, and second grade children in a poor, urban school confirms earlier investigations about what has been termed the "self-fulfilling prophecy" of teacher expectations. The results of Rist's study also explain in part Coleman's (1966) earlier observations, which showed that academic achievement was related to student social class, and that the gap between the academic performance of poor students increased the longer those students remained in school (Rist, 1970, p. 441).

Both Rist's and Coleman's studies suggest that one of the major effects of schooling in the United States is the perpetuation of a social class structure that relegates low-income children to a future that simply mirrors the social and economic inequality of their childhood. While schools may espouse equal opportunity for all, and while a majority of U.S. citizens may continue to believe that a major purpose of public schools is to enable those with ability to achieve and succeed in our society despite the obstacles of poor beginnings, the evidence offered by Rist suggests that children's social class and ethnic backgrounds will in large measure determine their success in school.

A major contribution of Rist's study is that it shows us how this happens. While these results have been known for more than 25 years, many schools and teachers continue practices very similar to those observed by Rist. What is especially alarming is that the kindergarten teacher observed by Rist made judgements about the academic potential of the children in her class by the eighth day of school, *using criteria that have absolutely nothing to do with academic ability or performance!* The teacher appeared to use four criteria to make this judgment:

- the child's physical appearance (quality and quantity of clothes, body odor, blackness of their skin [all children were African American, as was the teacher and the rest of the school's teachers and children], and the condition of their hair)
- their interactive behavior with each other and with the teacher
- their use of language (Standard American English or "school language" versus Black dialect)
- a set of indicators about the children's social and family conditions, suggestive of their general social status and known to the teacher prior to her decisions about their academic potential.

The teacher's decisions about the children's academic potential were reflected in the permanent seating plan she implemented on the eighth day of school. Those children she felt would be "fast learners" she seated at Table 1, closest to her. Those children who didn't appear to satisfy her image of the "ideal" student were seated further away, at Tables 2 and 3. In short, the teacher ascribed highest status to those she deemed to be fast learners, giving this group preferential treatment and essentially directing all of her attention to its members. Rist's ethnography describes in detail these actions by the teacher, and their unfortunate short- and long-term consequences for the children at the other tables. He observed a parallel set of actions by teachers in the first and second grades.

Not only were the patterns similar, but once placed in a slow group the children had no opportunity to move to a higher level, despite their real ability to do so. Similarly, children who were placed in the fast group in kindergarten were subsequently placed in the equivalent group in both the first and second grades. In terms of the self-fulfilling prophecy, those expected to do well did so, and those whom teachers deemed to be slow learners performed at the expected slow level. Teacher expectations for student performance make a difference! As you read the article by Rist, give special thought to your own image of the "ideal" student. How will this affect the way you respond to students? If a teacher doesn't consider it possible to successfully reach all of the students in a class, should the teacher focus primarily on the children most likely to succeed in school? Why? What does the Rist study say about the function of schooling in U.S. society?

The second reading is an ethnography by Robert Everhart about what life in school is like for some seventh and eighth grade boys. In this study the investigator observed several groups of boys as they made the transition from Garfield Elementary School to Harold Spencer Junior High. What Everhart's study reveals is the experience and meaning of school from the perspective of the student participants. What emerges is a portrait of the group culture that students build for themselves and through which they interpret their place in school. As will be seen in Everhart's rich description of Chris's group, having friends in school was all important. The knowledge that school offers the boys in Chris's group is not of much value to them. Much more important are the jokes, the humor, and the joking relationships that Everhart suggests form the basis of regenerative knowledge (p. 162). What Everhart illuminates for us is the large gap between the reified knowledge that the school defines as important, and the regenerative knowledge that is contextually generated through interaction in and membership in Chris's (or another's) friendship group. "Being with friends, constructing humorous incidents in class, bugging the teachers, some minimal involvement in student government—all constituted the daily routine of Chris and his group throughout the seventh and eighth grade" (Everhart, 1983, p. 157).

In describing Chris's world, Everhart helps us see the cultural processes within the group and school unfold, suggesting how these cultural processes within the school "contribute to the reproduction of the larger social structure in which they occur" (p. 157). We see in Chris's world that participation in school governance is pretty much a hollow affair from the perspectives of students, and that the topics considered by the student council were of low salience to students. They had a similar attitude toward involvement in the athletic and classroom aspects of school life. Students in general " . . . continually opposed the required activities when and where they could, given their understanding of what they opposed" (p. 155).

What Everhart's research results show us is that while schools operate on certain premises about the value of the knowledge they have to offer the students in attendance, the children themselves resist many of the regularities of school life and develop for themselves an adolescent group culture that takes on a great importance in their daily lives, and through which students oppose the very lessons the school wants them to learn about decision making in a democratic society, and about the value of " . . . knowing in the way school required knowing. . . . " (p. 163).

The third selection, by Lisa Delpit, explores the challenges for teachers of education in a multicultural society. The racial, social class, and linguistic differences among children in our communities create tremendous challenges for school teachers. The cultural clash between students and school present teachers with the necessity of being especially sensitive and responsive to a number of important factors that influence student success in school: differences in discourse styles, differences in interaction patterns and physicality of children, the influence of gender-mix on the propensity (or reluctance) to exhibit academic prowess, and other culturally grounded orientations on the part of children. Her discussion notes the effects of stereotyping by teachers and how this can result in a child not receiving the appropriate instruction. For example, Delpit discusses the " . . . widespread belief that Asian-American children are the 'perfect' students, that they will do well regardless of the academic setting in which they are placed" (p. 170). She points out how this has resulted in many teachers overlooking the needs of the majority of Asian-American students. Ignorance of community norms, stereotypes about certain ethnic or class groups, and the "labeling" of children are examined as practices among teachers that hurt children and diminish teachers as professional educators. The reading offers many specific examples of what teachers—black, white, and "other"—can do to be respectful of the cultural differences among poor children and children of color, noting that rather than expecting "less" of these children, teachers can serve them well by holding appropriately high expectations and teaching in a culturally responsive manner.

As you read these three selections, consider your own experience in school. How was it similar and different? Why? How does breaking the school day into segmented and disconnected blocks of 50-minute periods help or hinder learning and teaching? What is your image of the "ideal" student? What will you do with students who don't fit your image? What can teachers do with students who aren't interested in what schools have to offer? What cultural patterns does life in school reinforce? What cultural patterns do teachers frequently fail to recognize?

Student Social Class and Teacher Expectations: The Self-Fulfilling Prophecy in Ghetto Education

RAY C. RIST

Many studies have shown that academic achievement is highly correlated with social class. Few, however, have attempted to explain exactly *how* the school helps to reinforce the class structure of the society. In this article Dr. Rist reports the results of an observational study of one class of ghetto children during their kindergarten, first- and second-grade years. He shows how the kindergarten teacher placed the children in reading groups which reflected the social class composition of the class, and how these groups persisted throughout the first several years of elementary school. The way in which the teacher behaved toward the different groups became an important influence on the children's achievement. Dr. Rist concludes by examining the relationship between the "caste" system of the classroom and the class system of the larger society.

A dominant aspect of the American ethos is that education is both a necessary and a desirable experience for all children. To that end, compulsory attendance at some type of educational institution is required of all youth until somewhere in the middle teens. Thus on any weekday during the school year, one can expect slightly over 35,000,000 young persons to be distributed among nearly 1,100,000 classrooms throughout the nation (Jackson, 1968).

There is nothing either new or startling in the statement that there exist gross variations in the educational experience of the children involved. The scope of analysis one utilizes in examining these educational variations will reveal different variables of importance. There appear to be at least three levels at which analysis is warranted. The first is a macro-analysis of structural relationships where governmental regulations, fed-

eral, state, and local tax support, and the presence or absence of organized political and religious pressure all affect the classroom experience. At this level, study of the policies and politics of the Board of Education within the community is also relevant. The milieu of a particular school appears to be the second area of analysis in which one may examine facilities, pupil-teacher ratios, racial and cultural composition of the faculty and students, community and parental involvement, faculty relationships, the role of the principal, supportive services such as

Source: Rist, Ray C., "Student Social Class and Teacher Expectations: The Self-Fulfilling Prophecy in Ghetto Education," *Harvard Educational Review*, 40:3, pp. 411–451. Copyright 1970 by the President and Fellows of Harvard College.

medical care, speech therapy, and library facilities—all of which may have a direct impact on the quality as well as the quantity of education a child receives.

Analysis of an individual classroom and the activities and interactions of a specific group of children with a single teacher is the third level at which there may be profitable analysis of the variations in the educational experience. Such micro-analysis could seek to examine the social organization of the class, the development of norms governing interpersonal behavior, and the variety of roles that both the teacher and students assume. It is on this third level—that of the individual classroom—that this study will focus. Teacher-student relationships and the dynamics of interaction between the teacher and students are far from uniform. For any child within the classroom, variations in the experience of success or failure, praise or ridicule, freedom or control, creativity or docility, comprehension or mystification may ultimately have significance far beyond the boundaries of the classroom situation (Henry, 1955, 1959, 1963).

It is the purpose of this paper to explore what is generally regarded as a crucial aspect of the classroom experience for the children involved—the process whereby expectations and social interactions give rise to the social organization of the class. There occurs within the classroom a social process whereby, out of a large group of children and an adult unknown to one another prior to the beginning of the school year, there emerge patterns of behavior, expectations of performance, and a mutually accepted stratification system delineating those doing well from those doing poorly. Of particular concern will be the relation of the teacher's expectations of potential academic performance to the social status of the student. Emphasis will be placed on the initial presuppositions of the teacher regarding the intellectual ability of certain groups of children and their consequences for the children's socialization into the school system. A major goal of this analysis is to ascertain the importance of the initial expectations of the teacher in relation to the child's chances for success or failure within the public school system. (For previous studies of the significance of student social status to variations in educational experience, cf. Becker, 1952; Hollingshead, 1949; Lynd, 1937; Warner, *et al.*, 1944).

Increasingly, with the concern over intellectual growth of children and the long and close association that children experience with a series of teachers, attention is centering on the role of the teacher within the classroom (Sigel, 1969). A long series of studies have been conducted to determine what effects on children a teacher's values, beliefs, attitudes, and, most crucial to this analysis, a teacher's expectations may have. Asbell (1963), Becker (1952), Clark (1963), Gibson (1965), Harlem Youth Opportunities Unlimited (1964), Katz (1964), Kvaraceus (1965), MacKinnon (1962), Riessman (1962, 1965), Rose (1956), Rosenthal and Jacobson (1968), and Wilson (1963) have all noted that the teacher's expectations of a pupil's academic performance may, in fact, have a strong influence on the actual performance of that pupil. These authors have sought to validate a type of educational self-fulfilling prophecy: if the teacher expects high performance, she receives it, and vice versa. A major criticism that can be directed at much of the research is that although the studies may establish that a teacher has differential expectations and that these influence performance for various pupils, they have not elucidated either the basis upon which such differential expectations are formed or how they are directly manifested within the classroom milieu. It is a goal of this paper to provide an analysis both of the factors that are critical in the teacher's development of expectations for various groups of her pupils and of the process by which such expectations influence the classroom experience for the teacher and the students.

The basic position to be presented in this paper is that the development of expectations by the kindergarten teacher as to the differential academic potential and capability of any student was significantly determined by a series of subjectively interpreted attributes and characteristics of that student. The argument may be succinctly stated in five propositions. First, the kindergarten teacher possessed a roughly constructed "ideal type" as to what characteristics were necessary for any given student to achieve "success" both in the public school and in the larger society. These characteristics appeared to be, in significant part, related to social class criteria. Secondly, upon first meeting her students at the beginning of the school year, subjective evaluations were made of the students as to possession or absence of the desired traits necessary for anticipated "success." On the basis of the evaluation, the class was divided into groups expected to succeed (termed by the teacher "fast learners") and those anticipated to fail (termed "slow learners"). Third, differential treatment was accorded to the two groups in the classroom, with the group designated as "fast learners" receiving the majority of the teaching time, reward-directed behavior, and attention from the teacher. Those designated as "slow learners" were taught infrequently, subjected to more frequent control-oriented behavior, and received little if any supportive behavior from the teacher. Fourth, the interactional patterns between the teacher and the various groups in her class became rigidified, taking on caste-like characteristics, during the course of the school year, with the gap in completion of academic material between the two groups widening as the school year progressed. Fifth, a similar process occurred in later years of schooling, but the teachers no longer relied on subjectively interpreted data as the basis for ascertaining differences in students. Rather, they were able to utilize a variety of informational sources related to past performance as the basis for classroom grouping.

Though the position to be argued in this paper is based on a longitudinal study spanning two and one-half years with a single group of black children, additional studies suggest that the grouping of children both between and within classrooms is a rather prevalent situation within American elementary classrooms. In a report released in 1961 by the National Education Association related to data collected during the 1958–1959 school year, an estimated 77.6% of urban school districts (cities with a population above 2500) indicated that they practiced between-classroom ability grouping in the elementary grades. In a national survey of elementary schools, Austin and Morrison (1963) found that "more than 80% reported that they 'always' or 'often' use readiness tests for pre-reading evaluation [in first grade]." These findings would suggest that within-classroom grouping may be an even more prevalent condition than between-classroom grouping. In evaluating data related to grouping within American elementary classrooms, Smith (1971, in press) concludes, "Thus group assignment on the basis of measured 'ability' or 'readiness' is an accepted and widespread practice."

Two grouping studies which bear particular mention are those by Borg (1964) and Goldberg, Passow, and Justman (1966). Lawrence (1969) summarizes the importance of these two studies as "the two most carefully designed and controlled studies done concerning ability grouping during the elementary years. . . . " Two school districts in Utah, adjacent to one another and closely comparable in size, served as the setting for the study conducted by Borg. One of the two districts employed random grouping of students, providing all students with "enrichment," while the second school district adopted a group system with acceleration mechanisms present which sought to adapt curricular materials to ability level and also to enable varying rates of presentation of materials. In summarizing Borg's finding, Lawrence states:

> In general, Borg concluded that the grouping patterns had no consistent, general effects on achievement at any level. . . . Ability grouping may have motivated bright pupils to realize their achievement potential more fully, but it seemed to have little effect on the slow or average pupils. (p. 1)

The second study by Goldberg, Passow, and Justman was conducted in the New York City Public Schools and represents the most comprehensive study to date on elementary school grouping. The findings in general show results similar to those of Borg indicating that narrowing the ability range within a classroom on some basis of academic potential will in itself do little to produce positive academic change. The most significant finding of the study is that "variability in achievement from classroom to classroom was generally greater than the variability resulting from grouping pattern or pupil ability" (Lawrence, 1969). Thus one may tentatively conclude that teacher differences were at least as crucial to academic performance as were the effects of pupil ability or methods of classroom grouping. The study, however, fails to investigate within-class grouping.

Related to the issue of within-class variability are the findings of the Coleman Report (1966) which have shown achievement highly correlated with individual social class. The strong correlation present in the first grade does not decrease during the elementary years, demonstrating, in a sense, that the schools are not able effectively to close the achievement gap initially resulting from student social class (pp. 290–325). What variation the Coleman Report does find in achievement in the elementary years results largely from within- rather than between-school variation. Given that the report demonstrates that important differences in achievement do not arise from variations in facilities, curriculum, or staff, it concludes:

> One implication stands out above all: That schools bring little influence to bear on a child's achievement that is independent of his background and general social context; and that this very lack of independent effect means that the inequalities imposed on children by their home, neighborhood, and peer environment are carried along to become the inequalities with which they confront adult life at the end of school. For equality of educational opportunity through the schools must imply a strong effect of schools that is independent of the

child's immediate social environment, and that strong independent effect is not present in American schools. (p. 325)

It is the goal of this study to describe the manner in which such "inequalities imposed on children" become manifest within an urban ghetto school and the resultant differential educational experience for children from dissimilar social-class backgrounds.

METHODOLOGY

Data for this study were collected by means of twice weekly one and one-half hour observations of a single group of black children in an urban ghetto school who began kindergarten in September of 1967. Formal observations were conducted throughout the year while the children were in kindergarten and again in 1969 when these same children were in the first half of their second-grade year. The children were also visited informally four times in the classroom during their first-grade year.[1] The difference between the formal and informal observations consisted in the fact that during formal visits, a continuous handwritten account was taken of classroom interaction and activity as it occurred. Smith and Geoffrey (1968) have labeled this method of classroom observation "microethnography." The informal observations did not include the taking of notes during the classroom visit, but comments were written after the visit. Additionally, a series of interviews were conducted with both the kindergarten and the second-grade teachers. No mechanical devices were utilized to record classroom activities or interviews.

I believe it is methodologically necessary, at this point, to clarify what benefits can be derived from the detailed analysis of a single group of children. The single most apparent weakness of the vast majority of studies of urban education is

---

[1]The author, due to a teaching appointment out of the city, was unable to conduct formal observations of the children during their first-grade year.

that they lack any longitudinal perspective. The complexities of the interactional processes which evolve over time within classrooms cannot be discerned with a single two- or three-hour observational period. Secondly, education is a *social process* that cannot be reduced to variations in IQ scores over a period of time. At best, IQ scores merely give indications of potential, not of process. Third, I do not believe that this school and the classrooms within it are atypical from others in urban black neighborhoods (cf. both the popular literature on urban schools: Kohl, 1967; and Kozol, 1967; as well as the academic literature: Eddy, 1967; Fuchs, 1969; Leacock, 1969; and Moore, 1967). The school in which this study occurred was selected by the District Superintendent as one of five available to the research team. All five schools were visited during the course of the study and detailed observations were conducted in four of them. The principal at the school reported upon in this study commented that I was very fortunate in coming to his school since his staff (and kindergarten teacher in particular) were equal to "any in the city." Finally, the utilization of longitudinal study as a research method in a ghetto school will enhance the possibilities of gaining further insight into mechanisms of adaptation utilized by black youth to what appears to be a basically white, middle-class, value-oriented institution.

THE SCHOOL

The particular school which the children attend was built in the early part of the 1960's. It has classes from kindergarten through the eighth grade and a single special education class. The enrollment fluctuates near the 900 level while the teaching staff consists of twenty-six teachers, in addition to a librarian, two physical education instructors, the principal, and an assistant principal. There are also at the school, on a part time basis, a speech therapist, social worker, nurse, and doctor, all employed by the Board of Education. All administrators, teachers, staff, and

pupils are black. (The author is caucasian.) The school is located in a blighted urban area that has 98% black population within its census district. Within the school itself, nearly 500 of the 900 pupils (55%) come from families supported by funds from Aid to Dependent Children, a form of public welfare.

THE KINDERGARTEN CLASS

Prior to the beginning of the school year, the teacher possessed several different kinds of information regarding the children that she would have in her class. The first was the pre-registration form completed by 13 mothers of children who would be in the kindergarten class. On this form, the teacher was supplied with the name of the child, his age, the name of his parents, his home address, his phone number, and whether he had had any pre-school experience. The second source of information for the teacher was supplied two days before the beginning of school by the school social worker who provided a tentative list of all children enrolled in the kindergarten class who lived in homes that received public welfare funds.

The third source of information on the child was gained as a result of the initial interview with the mother and child during the registration period, either in the few days prior to the beginning of school or else during the first days of school. In this interview, a major concern was the gathering of medical information about the child as well as the ascertaining of any specific parental concern related to the child. This latter information was noted on the "Behavioral Questionnaire" where the mother was to indicate her concern, if any, on 28 different items. Such items as thumb-sucking, bed-wetting, loss of bowel control, lying, stealing, fighting, and laziness were included on this questionnaire.

The fourth source of information available to the teacher concerning the children in her class was both her own experiences with older siblings, and those of other teachers in the building related to behavior and academic performance of children in the same family. A rather strong informal norm had developed among teachers in the school such that pertinent information, especially that related to discipline matters, was to be passed on to the next teacher of the student. The teachers' lounge became the location in which they would discuss the performance of individual children as well as make comments concerning the parents and their interests in the student and the school. Frequently, during the first days of the school year, there were admonitions to a specific teacher to "watch out" for a child believed by a teacher to be a "troublemaker." Teachers would also relate techniques of controlling the behavior of a student who had been disruptive in the class. Thus a variety of information concerning students in the school was shared, whether that information regarded academic performance, behavior in class, or the relation of the home to the school.

It should be noted that not one of these four sources of information to the teacher was related directly to the academic potential of the incoming kindergarten child. Rather, they concerned various types of social information revealing such facts as the financial status of certain families, medical care of the child, presence or absence of a telephone in the home, as well as the structure of the family in which the child lived, *i.e.*, number of siblings, whether the child lived with both, one, or neither of his natural parents.

THE TEACHER'S STIMULUS

When the kindergarten teacher made the permanent seating assignments on the eighth day of school, not only had she the above four sources of information concerning the children, but she had also had time to observe them within the classroom setting. Thus the behavior, degree and type of verbalization, dress, mannerisms, physical appearance, and performance on the early tasks assigned during class were available to her as she began to form opinions concerning the capabili-

ties and potential of the various children. That such evaluation of the children by the teacher was beginning, I believe, there is little doubt. Within a few days, only a certain group of children were continually being called on to lead the class in the Pledge of Allegiance, read the weather calendar each day, come to the front for "show and tell" periods, take messages to the office, count the number of children present in the class, pass out materials for class projects, be in charge of equipment on the playground, and lead the class to the bathroom, library, or on a school tour. This one group of children, that continually were physically close to the teacher and had a high degree of verbal interaction with her, she placed at Table 1.

As one progressed from Table 1 to Table 2 and Table 3, there was an increasing dissimilarity between each group of children at the different tables on at least four major criteria. The first criterion appeared to be the physical appearance of the child. While the children at Table 1 were all dressed in clean clothes that were relatively new and pressed, most of the children at Table 2, and with only one exception at Table 3, were all quite poorly dressed. The clothes were old and often quite dirty. The children at Tables 2 and 3 also had a noticeably different quality and quantity of clothes to wear, especially during the winter months. Whereas the children at Table 1 would come on cold days with heavy coats and sweaters, the children at the other two tables often wore very thin spring coats and summer clothes. The single child at Table 3 who came to school quite nicely dressed came from a home in which the mother was receiving welfare funds, but was supplied with clothing for the children by the families of her brother and sister.

An additional aspect of the physical appearance of the children related to their body odor. While none of the children at Table 1 came to class with an odor of urine on them, there were two children at Table 2 and five children at Table 3 who frequently had such an odor. There was not a clear distinction among the children at the various tables as to the degree of "blackness" of their skin, but there were more children at the third table with very dark skin (five in all) than there were at the first table (three). There was also a noticeable distinction among the various groups of children as to the condition of their hair. While the three boys at Table 1 all had short hair cuts and the six girls at the same table had their hair "processed" and combed, the number of children with either matted or unprocessed hair increased at Table 2 (two boys and three girls) and eight of the children at Table 3 (four boys and four girls). None of the children in the kindergarten class wore their hair in the style of a "natural."

A second major criteria which appeared to differentiate the children at the various tables was their interactional behavior, both among themselves and with the teacher. The several children who began to develop as leaders within the class by giving directions to other members, initiating the division of the class into teams on the playground, and seeking to speak for the class to the teacher ("We want to color now"), all were placed by the teacher at Table 1. This same group of children displayed considerable ease in their interaction with her. Whereas the children at Tables 2 and 3 would often linger on the periphery of groups surrounding the teacher, the children at Table 1 most often crowded close to her.

The use of language within the classroom appeared to be the third major differentiation among the children. While the children placed at the first table were quite verbal with the teacher, the children placed at the remaining two tables spoke much less frequently with her. The children placed at the first table also displayed a greater use of Standard American English within the classroom. Whereas the children placed at the last two tables most often responded to the teacher in black dialect, the children at the first table did so very infrequently. In other words, the children at the first table were much more adept at the use of "school language" than were those at the other tables. The teacher utilized standard American English in the classroom and one group

of children were able to respond in a like manner. The frequency of a "no response" to a question from the teacher was recorded at a ratio of nearly three to one for the children at the last two tables as opposed to Table 1. When questions were asked, the children who were placed at the first table most often gave a response.

The final apparent criterion by which the children at the first table were quite noticeably different from those at the other tables consisted of a series of social factors which were known to the teacher prior to her seating the children. Though it is not known to what degree she utilized this particular criterion when she assigned seats, it does contribute to developing a clear profile of the children at the various tables. Table 1 gives a summary of the distribution of the children at the three tables on a series of variables related to social and family conditions. Such variables may be considered to give indication of the relative status of the children within the room, based on the income, education and size of the family. (For a discussion of why these three variables of income, education, and family size may be considered as significant indicators of social status, cf. Frazier, 1962; Freeman, *et al.*, 1959; Gebhard, *et al.*, 1958; Kahl, 1957; Notestein, 1953; Reissman, 1959; Rose, 1956; Simpson and Yinger, 1958.)

Believing, as I do, that the teacher did not randomly assign the children to the various tables, it is then necessary to indicate the basis for the seating arrangement. I would contend that the teacher developed, utilizing some combination of the four criteria outlined above, a series of expectations about the potential performance of each child and then grouped the children according to perceived similarities in expected performance. The teacher herself informed me that the first table consisted of her "fast learners" while those at the last two tables "had no idea of what was going on in the classroom." What becomes crucial in this discussion is to ascertain the basis upon which the teacher developed her criteria of "fast learner" since there had been no formal testing of the children as to their academic potential or

Table 1

Distribution of Socio-Economic Status Factors by Seating Arrangement at the Three Tables in the Kindergarten Classroom

Factors	*Seating Arrangement**		
	Table 1	*Table 2*	*Table 3*
Income			
1) Families on welfare	0	2	4
2) Families with father employed	6	3	2
3) Families with mother employed	5	5	5
4) Families with both parents employed	5	3	2
5) Total family income below \$3,000./yr**	0	4	7
6) Total family income above \$12,000./yr**	4	0	0
Education			
1) Father ever grade school	6	3	2
2) Father ever high school	5	2	1
3) Father ever college	1	0	0
4) Mother ever grade school	9	10	8
5) Mother ever high school	7	6	5
6) Mother ever college	4	0	0
7) Children with pre–school experience	1	1	0
Family Size			
1) Families with one child	3	1	0
2) Families with six or more children	2	6	7
3) Average number of siblings in family	3–4	5–6	6–7
4) Families with both parents present	6	3	2

* There are nine children at Table 1, eleven at Table 2, and ten children at Table 3.
**Estimated from stated occupation.

capacity for cognitive development. She made evaluative judgments of the expected capacities of the children to perform academic tasks after eight days of school.

Certain criteria became indicative of expected success and others became indicative of expected failure. Those children who closely fit the teacher's "ideal type" of the successful child were chosen for seats at Table 1. Those children that had the least "goodness of fit" with her ideal type were placed at the third table. The criteria upon which a teacher would construct her ideal type of the successful student would rest in her perception of certain attributes in the child that she

believed would make for success. To understand what the teacher considered as "success," one would have to examine her perception of the larger society and whom in that larger society she perceived as successful. Thus, in the terms of Merton (1957), one may ask which was the "normative reference group" for Mrs. Caplow that she perceived as being successful.[2] I believe that the reference group utilized by Mrs. Caplow to determine what constituted success was a mixed black-white, well-educated middle class. Those attributes most desired by educated members of the middle class became the basis for her evaluation of the children. Those who possessed these particular characteristics were expected to succeed while those who did not could be expected not to succeed. Highly prized middle-class status for the child in the classroom was attained by demonstrating ease of interaction among adults; high degree of verbalization in Standard American English; the ability to become a leader; a neat and clean appearance; coming from a family that is educated, employed, living together, and interested in the child; and the ability to participate well as a member of a group.

The kindergarten teacher appeared to have been raised in a home where the above values were emphasized as important. Her mother was a college graduate, as were her brother and sisters. The family lived in the same neighborhood for many years, and the father held a responsible position with a public utility company in the city. The family was devoutly religious and those of the family still in the city attend the same church. She and other members of her family were active in a number of civil rights organizations in the city. Thus, it appears that the kindergarten teacher's "normative reference group" coincided quite closely with those groups in which she did participate and belong. There was little discrepancy between the normative values of the mixed black-white educated middle-class and the values of the groups in which she held membership. The attributes indicative of "success" among those of the educated middle class had been attained by the teacher. She was a college graduate, held positions of respect and responsibility in the black community, lived in a comfortable middle-class section of the city in a well-furnished and spacious home, together with her husband earned over $20,000 per year, was active in a number of community organizations, and had parents, brother, and sisters similar in education, income, and occupational positions.

The teacher ascribed high status to a certain group of children within the class who fit her perception of the criteria necessary to be among the "fast learners" at Table 1. With her reference group orientation as to what constitute the quali-

ties essential for "success," she responded favorably to those children who possessed such necessary attributes. Her resultant preferential treatment of a select group of children appeared to be derived from her belief that certain behavioral and cultural characteristics are more crucial to learning in school than are others. In a similar manner, those children who appeared not to possess the criteria essential for success were ascribed low status and described as "failures" by the teacher. They were relegated to positions at Table 2 and 3. The placement of the children then appeared to result from their possessing or lacking the certain desired cultural characteristics perceived as important by the teacher.

The organization of the kindergarten classroom according to the expectation of success or failure after the eighth day of school became the basis for the differential treatment of the children for the remainder of the school year. From the day that the class was assigned permanent seats, the activities in the classroom were perceivably different from previously. The fundamental division of the class into those expected to learn and those expected not to permeated the teacher's orientation to the class.

The teacher's rationalization for narrowing her attention to selected students was that the majority of the remainder of the class (in her words) "just had no idea of what was going on in the classroom." Her reliance on the few students of ascribed high social status reached such proportions that on occasion, the teacher would use one of these students as an exemplar that the remainder of the class would do well to emulate.

(It is Fire Prevention Week and the teacher is trying to have the children say so. The children make a number of incorrect responses, a few of which follow:) Jim, who had raised his hand, in answer to

---

[2]The names of all staff and students are pseudonyms. Names are provided to indicate that the discussion relates to living persons, and not to fictional characters developed by the author.

the question, "Do you know what week it is?" says, "October." The teacher says "No, that's the name of the month. Jane, do you know what special week this is?" and Jane responds, "It cold outside." Teacher says, "No, that is not it either. I guess I will have to call on Pamela. Pamela, come here and stand by me and tell the rest of the boys and girls what special week this is." Pamela leaves her chair, comes and stands by the teacher, turns and faces the rest of the class. The teacher puts her arm around Pamela, and Pamela says, "It fire week." The teacher responds, "Well Pamela, that is close. Actually it is Fire Prevention Week."

On another occasion, the Friday after Halloween, the teacher informed the class that she would allow time for all the students to come to the front of the class and tell of their experiences. She, in reality, called on six students, five of whom sat at Table 1 and the sixth at Table 2. Not only on this occasion, but on others, the teacher focused her attention on the experiences of the higher status students.[3]

(The students are involved in acting out a skit arranged by the teacher on how a family should come together to eat the evening meal.) The students acting the roles of mother, father, and daughter are all from Table 1. The boy playing the son is from Table 2. At the small dinner table set up in the center of the classroom, the four children are supposed to be sharing with each other what they had done during the day—the father at work, the mother at home, and the two children at school. The Table 2 boy makes few comments. (In real life he has no father and his mother is supported by ADC funds.) The teacher comments, "I think that we are going to have to let Milt (Table 1) be the new son. Sam, why don't you go and sit down. Milt, you seem to be one who would know what a son is supposed to do at the dinner table. You come and take Sam's place."

In this instance, the lower-status student was penalized, not only for failing to have verbalized middle-class table talk, but more fundamentally, for lacking middle-class experiences. He had no actual father to whom he could speak at the din-

ner table, yet he was expected to speak fluently with an imaginary one.

Though the blackboard was long enough to extend parallel to all three tables, the teacher wrote such assignments as arithmetic problems and drew all illustrations on the board in front of the students at Table 1. A rather poignant example of the penalty the children at Table 3 had to pay was that they often could not see the board material.

Lilly stands up out of her seat. Mrs. Caplow asks Lilly what she wants. Lilly makes no verbal response to the question. Mrs. Caplow then says rather firmly to Lilly, "Sit down." Lilly does. However, Lilly sits down sideways in the chair (so she is still facing the teacher). Mrs. Caplow instructs Lilly to put her feet under the table. This Lilly does. Now she is facing directly away from the teacher and the blackboard where the teacher is demonstrating to the students how to print the letter, "O."

The realization of the self-fulfilling prophecy within the classroom was in its final stages by late May of the kindergarten year. Lack of communication with the teacher, lack of involvement in the class activities and infrequent instruction all characterized the situation of the children at Tables 2 and 3. During one observational period of an hour in May, not a single act of communication was directed towards any child at either Table 2 or 3 by the teacher except for twice commanding "sit down." The teacher devoted her attention to teaching those children at Table 1. Attempts by the children at Table 2 and 3 to elicit the attention of the teacher were much fewer than earlier in the school year.

In June, after school had ended for the year, the teacher was asked to comment on the chil-

---

[3]Through the remainder of the paper, reference to "high" or "low" status students refers to status ascribed to the student by the teacher. Her ascription appeared to be based on perceptions of valued behavioral and cultural characteristics present or absent in any individual student.

dren in her class. Of the children at the first table, she noted:

> I guess the best way to describe it is that very few children in my class are exceptional. I guess you could notice this just from the way the children were seated this year. Those at Table 1 gave consistently the most responses throughout the year and seemed most interested and aware of what was going on in the classroom.

Of those children at the remaining two tables, the teacher commented:

> It seems to me that some of the children at Table 2 and most all the children at Table 3 at times seem to have no idea of what is going on in the classroom and were off in another world all by themselves. It just appears that some can do it and some cannot. I don't think that it is the teacher that affects those that cannot do it, but some are just basically low achievers.

THE STUDENTS' RESPONSE

The students in the kindergarten classroom did not sit passively, internalizing the behavior the teacher directed towards them. Rather, they responded to the stimuli of the teacher, both in internal differentiations within the class itself and also in their response to the teacher. The type of response a student made was highly dependent upon whether he sat at Table 1 or at one of the two other tables. The single classroom of black students did not respond as a homogenous unit to the teacher-inspired social organization of the room.

For the high-status students at Table 1, the response to the track system of the teacher appeared to be at least three-fold. One such response was the directing of ridicule and belittlement towards those children at Tables 2 and 3. At no point during the entire school year was a child from Table 2 or 3 ever observed directing such remarks at the children at Table 1.

> Mrs. Caplow says, "Raise your hand if you want me to call on you. I won't call on anyone who calls out," She then says, "All right, now who knows that numeral? What is it, Tony?" Tony makes no verbal response but rather walks to the front of the classroom and stands by Mrs. Caplow. Gregory calls out, "He don't know. He scared." Then Ann calls out, "It sixteen, stupid." (Tony sits at Table 3, Gregory and Ann sit at Table 1.)

> Jim starts to say out loud that he is smarter than Tom. He repeats it over and over again, "I smarter than you. I smarter than you." (Jim sits at Table 1, Tom at Table 3.)

> Milt came over to the observer and told him to look at Lilly's shoes. I asked him why I should and he replied, "Because they so ragged and dirty." (Milt is at Table 1, Lilly at Table 3.)

> When I asked Lilly what it was that she was drawing, she replied, "A parachute." Gregory interrupted and said, "She can't draw nothin'."

The problems of those children who were of lower status were compounded, for not only had the teacher indicated her low esteem of them, but their peers had also turned against them. The implications for the future schooling of a child who lacks the desired status credentials in a classroom where the teacher places high value on middle-class "success" values and mannerisms are tragic.

It must not be assumed, however, that though the children at Tables 2 and 3 did not participate in classroom activities and were systematically ignored by the teacher, they did not learn. I contend that in fact they did learn, but in a fundamentally different way from the way in which the high-status children at Table 1 learned. The children at Table 2 and 3 who were unable to interact with the teacher began to develop patterns of interaction among themselves whereby they would discuss the material that the teacher was presenting to the children at Table 1. Thus I have termed their method of grasping the material "secondary learning" to imply that knowledge was not gained in direct interaction with the teacher, but through the mediation of peers and also through listening to the teacher though she was not speaking to them. That the children were grasping, in part, the material presented in the classroom, was indicated to me in home visits when the children who sat at Table 3 would relate material specifically taught by the teacher to the children at Table 1. *It is not as though the children at Table 2 and 3 were ignorant of what was being taught in the class, but rather that the patterns of classroom interaction established by the teacher inhibited the low-status children from verbalizing what knowledge they had accumulated.* Thus, from the teacher's terms of reference, those who could not discuss must not know. Her expectations continued to be fulfilled, for though the low-status children had accumulated knowledge, they did not have the opportunity to verbalize it and, consequently, the teacher could not know what they had learned. Children at Table 2 and 3 had learned material presented in the kindergarten class, but would continue to be defined by the teacher as children who could not or would not learn.

A second response of the higher status students to the differential behavior of the teacher towards them was to seek solidarity and closeness with the teacher and urge Table 2 and 3 children to comply with her wishes.

> The teacher is out of the room. Pamela says to the class, "We all should clean up before the teacher comes." Shortly thereafter the teacher has still not returned and Pamela begins to supervise other children in the class. She says to one girl from Table 3, "Girl, leave that piano alone." The child plays only a short time longer and then leaves.
>
> The teacher has instructed the students to go and take off their coats since they have come in from the playground. Milt says, "Ok y'al, let's go take off our clothes."
>
> At this time Jim says to the teacher, "Mrs. Caplow, they pretty flowers on your desk." Mrs. Caplow responded, "Yes, Jim, those flowers are roses, but we will not have roses much longer. The roses will die and rest until spring because it is getting so cold outside."
>
> When the teacher tells the students to come from their desks and form a semi-circle around her, Gregory scoots up very close to Mrs. Caplow and is practically sitting in her lap.

> Gregory has come into the room late. He takes off his coat and goes to the coat room to hang it up. He comes back and sits down in the very front of the group and is now closest to the teacher.

The higher-status students in the class perceived the lower status and esteem the teacher ascribed to those children at Tables 2 and 3. Not only would the Table 1 students attempt to control and ridicule the Table 2 and 3 students, but they also perceived and verbalized that they, the Table 1 students, were better students and were receiving differential treatment from the teacher.

> The children are rehearsing a play, Little Red Riding Hood. Pamela tells the observer, "The teacher gave me the best part." The teacher overheard this comment, smiled, and made no verbal response.
>
> The children are preparing to go on a field trip to a local dairy. The teacher has designated Gregory as the "sheriff" for the trip. Mrs. Caplow stated that for the field trip today Gregory would be the sheriff. Mrs. Caplow simply watched as Gregory would walk up to a student and push him back into line saying, "Boy, stand where you suppose to." Several times he went up to students from Table 3 and showed them the badge that the teacher had given to him and said, "Teacher made me sheriff."

The children seated at the first table were internalizing the attitudes and behavior of the teacher towards those at the remaining two tables. That is, as the teacher responded from her reference group orientation as to which type of children were most likely to succeed and which type most likely to fail, she behaved towards the two groups of children in a significantly different manner. The children from Table 1 were also learning through emulating the teacher how to behave towards other black children who came from low-income and poorly educated homes. The teacher, who came from a well-educated and middle-income family, and the children from Table 1 who came from a background similar to the teacher's, came to respond to the children from poor and uneducated homes in a strikingly similar manner.

The lower-status students in the classroom from Tables 2 and 3 responded in significantly different ways to the stimuli of the teacher. The two major responses of the Table 2 and 3 students were withdrawal and verbal and physical in-group hostility.

The withdrawal of some of the lower-status students as a response to the ridicule of their peers and the isolation from the teacher occasionally took the form of physical withdrawal, but most often it was psychological.

Betty, a very poorly dressed child, had gone outside and hidden behind the door. . . . Mrs. Caplow sees Betty leave and goes outside to bring her back, says in an authoritative and irritated voice, "Betty, come here right now." When the child returns, Mrs. Caplow seizes her by the right arm, brings her over to the group, and pushes her down to the floor. Betty begins to cry. . . . The teacher now shows the group a large posterboard with a picture of a white child going to school.

The teacher is demonstrating how to mount leaves between two pieces of wax paper. Betty leaves the group and goes back to her seat and begins to color.

The teacher is instructing the children in how they can make a "spooky thing" for Hallowe'en. James turns away from the teacher and puts his head on his desk. Mrs. Caplow looks at James and says, "James, sit up and look here."

The children are supposed to make United Nations flags. They have been told that they do not have to make exact replicas of the teacher's flag. They have before them the materials to make the flags. Lilly and James are the only children who have not yet started to work on their flags. Presently, James has his head under his desk and Lilly simply sits and watches the other children. Now they are both staring into space. . . . (5 minutes later) Lilly and James have not yet started, while several other children have already finished. . . . A minute later, with the teacher telling the children to begin to clean up their scraps, Lilly is still staring into space.

The teacher has the children seated on the floor in front of her asking them questions about a story that she had read to them. The teacher says, "June, your back is turned. I want to see your face." (The

child had turned completely around and was facing away from the group.)

The teacher told the students to come from their seats and form a semi-circle on the floor in front of her. The girls all sit very close to the piano where the teacher is seated. The boys sit a good distance back away from the girls and away from the teacher. Lilly finishes her work at her desk and comes and sits at the rear of the group of girls, but she is actually in the middle of the open space separating the boys and the girls. She speaks to no one and simply sits staring off.

The verbal and physical hostility that the children at Tables 2 and 3 began to act out among themselves in many ways mirrored what the Table 1 students and the teacher were also saying about them. There are numerous instances in the observations of the children at Tables 2 and 3 calling one another "stupid," "dummy," or "dumb dumb." Racial overtones were noted on two occasions when one boy called another a "nigger," and on another occasion when a girl called a boy an "almond head." Threats of beating, "whoppins," and even spitting on a child were also recorded among those at Tables 2 and 3. Also at Table 2, two instances were observed in which a single child hoarded all the supplies for the whole table. Similar manifestations of hostility were not observed among those children at the first table. The single incident of strong anger or hostility by one child at Table 1 against another child at the same table occurred when one accused the other of copying from his paper. The second denied it and an argument ensued.

In the organization of hostility within the classroom, there may be at least the tentative basis for the rejection of a popular "folk myth" of American society, which is that children are inherently cruel to one another and that this tendency towards cruelty must be socialized into socially acceptable channels. The evidence from this classroom would indicate that much of the cruelty displayed was a result of the social organization of the class. Those children at Tables 2 and 3 who displayed cruelty appeared to have learned from the teacher that it was acceptable to act in an aggressive manner towards those from low-income and poorly educated backgrounds. Their cruelty was not diffuse, but rather focused on a specific group—the other poor children. Likewise, the incidence of such behavior increased over time. The children at Tables 2 and 3 did not begin the school year ridiculing and belittling each other. This social process began to emerge with the outline of the social organization the teacher imposed upon the class. The children from the first table were also apparently socialized into a pattern of behavior in which they perceived that they could direct hostility and aggression towards those at Table 2 and 3, but not towards one another. The children in the class learned who was vulnerable to hostility and who was not through the actions of the teacher. She established the patterns of differential behavior which the class adopted.

FIRST GRADE

Though Mrs. Caplow had anticipated that only twelve of the children from the kindergarten class would attend the first grade in the same school, eighteen of the children were assigned during the summer to the first-grade classroom in the main building. The remaining children either were assigned to a new school a few blocks north, or were assigned to a branch school designed to handle the overflow from the main building, or had moved away. Mrs. Logan, the first-grade teacher, had had more than twenty years of teaching experience in the city public school system, and every school in which she had taught was more than 90 percent black. During the 1968–1969 school year, four informal visits were made to the classroom of Mrs. Logan. No visits were made to either the branch school or the new school to visit children from the kindergarten class who had left their original school. During my visits to the first-grade room, I kept only brief notes of the short conversations that I had with Mrs. Logan; I did not conduct formal observations of the activities of the children in the class.

During the first-grade school year, there were thirty-three children in the classroom. In addition to the eighteen from the kindergarten class, there were nine children repeating the first grade and also six children new to the school. Of the eighteen children who came from the kindergarten class to the first grade in the main building, seven were from the previous year's Table 1, six from Table 2, and five from Table 3.

In the first-grade classroom, Mrs. Logan also divided the children into three groups. Those children whom she placed at "Table A" had all been Table 1 students in kindergarten. No student who had sat at Table 2 or 3 in kindergarten was placed at Table A in the first grade. Instead, all the students from Table 2 and 3—with one exception—were placed together at "Table B." At the third table which Mrs. Logan called "Table C," she placed the nine children repeating the grade plus Betty who had sat at Table 3 in the kindergarten class. Of the six new students, two were placed at Table A and four at Table C. Thus the totals for the three tables were nine students at Table A, ten at Table B, and fourteen at Table C.

The seating arrangement that began in the kindergarten as a result of the teacher's definition of which children possessed or lacked the perceived necessary characteristics for success in the public school system emerged in the first grade as a caste phenomenon in which there was absolutely no mobility upward. That is, of those children whom Mrs. Caplow had perceived as potential "failures" and thus seated at either Table 2 or 3 in the kindergarten, not one was assigned to the table of the "fast learners" in the first grade.

The initial label given to the children by the kindergarten teacher had been reinforced in her interaction with those students throughout the school year. When the children were ready to pass into the first grade, their ascribed labels from the teacher as either successes or failures assumed objective dimensions. The first-grade teacher no longer had to rely on merely the presence or absence of certain behavioral and attitudinal characteristics to ascertain who would do well and who would do poorly in the class. Objective records of the "readiness" material completed by the children during the kindergarten year were available to her. Thus, upon the basis of what material the various tables in kindergarten had completed, Mrs. Logan could form her first-grade tables for reading and arithmetic.

The kindergarten teacher's disproportionate allocation of her teaching time resulted in the Table 1 students' having completed more material at the end of the school year than the remainder of the class. As a result, the Table 1 group from kindergarten remained intact in the first grade, as they were the only students prepared for the first-grade reading material. Those children from Tables 2 and 3 had not yet completed all the material from kindergarten and had to spend the first weeks of the first-grade school year finishing kindergarten level lessons. The criteria established by the school system as to what constituted the completion of the necessary readiness material to begin first-grade lessons ensured that the Table 2 and 3 students could not be placed at Table A. The only children who had completed the material were those from Table 1, defined by the kindergarten teacher as successful students and whom she then taught most often because the remainder of the class "had no idea what was going on."

It would be somewhat misleading, however, to indicate that there was absolutely no mobility for any of the students between the seating assignments in kindergarten and those in the first grade. All of the students save one who had been seated at Table 3 during the kindergarten year were moved "up" to Table B in the first grade. The majority of Table C students were those having to repeat the grade level. As a tentative explanation of Mrs. Logan's rationale for the development of the Table C seating assignments, she may have assumed that within her class there existed one group of students who possessed so very little of the perceived behavioral patterns and attitudes necessary for success that they had to be kept separate from the remainder of the class. (Table C was placed by itself on the opposite side of the room from Tables A and B.) The Table C students were spoken of by the first-grade teacher in a manner reminiscent of the way in which Mrs. Caplow spoke of the Table 3 students the previous year.

Students who were placed at Table A appeared to be perceived by Mrs. Logan as students who not only possessed the criteria necessary for future success, both in the public school system and in the larger society, but who also had proven themselves capable in academic work. These students appeared to possess the characteristics considered most essential for "middle-class" success by the teacher. Though students at Table B lacked many of the "qualities" and characteristics of the Table A students, they were not perceived as lacking them to the same extent as those placed at Table C.

A basic tenet in explaining Mrs. Logan's seating arrangement is, of course, that she shared a similar reference group and set of values as to what constituted "success" with Mrs. Caplow in the kindergarten class. Both women were well educated, were employed in a professional occupation, lived in middle-income neighborhoods, were active in a number of charitable and civil rights organizations, and expressed strong religious convictions and moral standards. Both were educated in the city teacher's college and had also attained graduate degrees. Their backgrounds as well as the manner in which they described the various groups of students in their classes would indicate that they shared a similar reference group and set of expectations as to what constituted the indices of the "successful" student.

SECOND GRADE

Of the original thirty students in kindergarten and eighteen in first grade, ten students were assigned to the only second-grade class in the main building. Of the eight original kindergarten students who did not come to the second grade from the first, three were repeating first grade while the remainder had moved. The teacher in the second grade also divided the class into three groups, though she did not give them number or letter designations. Rather, she called the first group the "Tigers." The middle groups she labeled the "Cardinals," while the second-grade repeaters plus several new children assigned to the third table were designated by the teacher as "Clowns."[4]

In the second-grade seating scheme, no student from the first grade who had not sat at Table A was moved "up" to the Tigers at the beginning of second grade. All those students who in first grade had been at Table B or Table C and returned to the second grade were placed in the Cardinal group. The Clowns consisted of six second-grade repeaters plus three students who were new to the class. Of the ten original kindergarten students who came from the first grade, six were Tigers and four were Cardinals. Table 2 illustrates that the distribution of social economic factors from the kindergarten year remained essentially unchanged in the second grade.

By the time the children came to the second grade, their seating arrangement appeared to be based not on the teacher's expectations of how the child might perform, but rather on the basis of past performance of the child. Available to the teacher when she formulated the seating groups were grade sheets from both kindergarten and first grade, IQ scores from kindergarten, listing of parental occupations for approximately half of the class, reading scores from a test given to all students at the end of first grade, evaluations from the speech teacher and also the informal evaluations from both the kindergarten and first-grade teacher.

The single most important data utilized by the teacher in devising seating groups were the reading scores indicating the performance of the students at the end of the first grade. The second-grade teacher indicated that she attempted to divide the groups primarily on the basis of these scores. The Tigers were designated as the highest reading group and the Cardinals the middle. The Clowns were assigned a first-grade reading level,

though they were, for the most part, repeaters from the previous year in second grade. The caste character of the reading groups became clear as the year progressed, in that all three groups were reading in different books and it was school policy that no child could go on to a new book until the previous one had been completed. Thus there was no way for the child, should he have demonstrated competence at a higher reading level, to advance, since he had to continue at the pace of the rest of his reading group. The teacher never allowed individual reading in order that a child might finish a book on his own and move ahead. *No matter how well a child in the lower reading groups might have read, he was destined to remain in the same reading group. This is, in a sense, another manifestation of the self-fulfilling prophecy in that a "slow learner" had no option but to continue to be a slow learner, regardless of performance or potential.* Initial expectations of the kindergarten teacher two years earlier as to the ability of the child resulted in placement in a reading group, whether high or low, from which there appeared to be no escape. The child's journey through the early grades of school at one reading level and in one social grouping appeared to be pre-ordained from the eighth day of kindergarten.

The expectations of the kindergarten teacher appeared to be fulfilled by late spring. Her description of the academic performance of the children in June had a strong "goodness of fit" with her stated expectations from the previous September. For the first- and second-grade teacher alike, there was no need to rely on intuitive expectations as to what the performance of the child would be. They were in the position of being able to base future expectations upon past performance. At this point, the relevance of the self-fulfilling prophecy again is evident, for the

---

[4]The names were not given to the groups until the third week of school, though the seating arrangement was established on the third day.

Table 2
Distribution of Socio-Economic Status Factors by Seating Arrangement in the Three Reading Groups in the Second-Grade Classroom

Factors	Seating Arrangement*		
	Tigers	Cardinals	Clowns
Income			
1) Families on welfare	2	4	7
2) Families with father employed	8	5	1
3) Families with mother employed	7	11	6
4) Families with both parents employed	7	5	1
5) Total family income below $3,000./yr**	1	5	8
6) Total family income above $12,000./yr**	4	0	0
Education			
1) Father ever grade school	8	6	1
2) Father ever high school	7	4	0
3) Father ever college	0	0	0
4) Mother ever grade school	12	13	9
5) Mother ever high school	9	7	4
6) Mother ever college	3	0	0
7) Children with pre–school experience	1	0	0
Family Size			
1) Families with one child	2	0	1
2) Families with six or more children	3	8	5
3) Average number of siblings in family	3–4	6–7	7–8
4) Families with both parents present	8	6	1

* There are twelve children in the Tiger group, fourteen children in the Cardinal group, and nine children in the Clown group.
**Estimated from stated occupation.

very criteria by which the first- and second-grade teachers established their three reading groups were those manifestations of performance most affected by the previous experience of the child. That is, which reading books were completed, the amount of arithmetic and reading readiness material that had been completed, and the mastery of basic printing skills all became the significant criteria established by the Board of Education to determine the level at which the child would begin the first grade. A similar process of standard evaluation by past performance on criteria established by the Board appears to have

been the basis for the arrangement of reading groups within the second grade. Thus, again, the initial patterns of expectations and her acting upon them appeared to place the kindergarten teacher in the position of establishing the parameters of the educational experience for the various children in her class. The parameters, most clearly defined by the seating arrangement at the various tables, remained intact through both the first and second grades.

The phenomenon of teacher expectation based upon a variety of social status criteria did not appear to be limited to the kindergarten teacher alone. When the second-grade teacher was asked to evaluate the children in her class by reading group, she responded in terms reminiscent of the kindergarten teacher. Though such a proposition would be tenuous at best, the high degree of similarity in the responses of both the kindergarten and second-grade teacher suggests that there may be among the teachers in the school a common set of criteria as to what constitutes the successful and promising student. If such is the case, then the particular individual who happens to occupy the role of kindergarten teacher is less crucial. For if the expectations of all staff within the school are highly similar, then with little difficulty there could be an interchange of teachers among the grades with little or no noticeable effect upon the performance of the various groups of students. If all teachers have similar expectations as to which types of students perform well and which types perform poorly, the categories established by the kindergarten teacher could be expected to reflect rather closely the manner in which other teachers would also have grouped the class.

As the indication of the high degree of similarity between the manner in which the kindergarten teacher described the three tables and the manner in which the second-grade teacher discussed the "Tigers, Cardinals, and Clowns," excerpts of an interview with the second-grade teacher are presented, where she stated her opinions of the three groups.

Concerning the Tigers:

Q: Mrs. Benson, how would you describe the Tigers in terms of their learning ability and academic performance?

R: Well, they are my fastest group. They are very smart.

Q: Mrs. Benson, how would you describe the Tigers in terms of discipline matters?

R: Well, the Tigers are very talkative. Susan, Pamela, and Ruth, they are always running their mouths constantly, but they get their work done first. I don't have much trouble with them.

Q: Mrs. Benson, what value do you think the Tigers hold for an education?

R: They all feel an education is important and most of them have goals in life as to what they want to be. They mostly want to go to college.

The same questions were asked of the teacher concerning the Cardinals.

Q: Mrs. Benson, how would you describe the Cardinals in terms of learning ability and academic performance?

R: They are slow to finish their work . . . but they get finished. You know, a lot of them, though, don't care to come to school too much. Rema, Gary, and Toby are absent quite a bit. The Tigers are never absent.

Q: Mrs. Benson, how would you describe the Cardinals in terms of discipline matters?

R: Not too bad. Since they work so slow they don't have time to talk. They are not like the Tigers who finish in a hurry and then just sit and talk with each other.

Q: Mrs. Benson, what value do you think the Cardinals hold for an education?

R: Well, I don't think they have as much interest in education as do the Tigers, but you know it is hard to say. Most will like to come to school, but the parents will keep them from coming. They either have to baby sit, or the clothes are dirty. These are the excuses the parents often give. But I guess most of the Cardinals want to go on and finish and go on to college. A lot of them have ambitions when they grow up. It's mostly the parents' fault that they are not at the school more often.

In the kindergarten class, the teacher appeared to perceive the major ability gap to lie between the students at Table 1 and those at Table 2. That is, those at Tables 2 and 3 were perceived as more similar in potential than were those at Tables 1 and 2. This was not the case in the second-grade classroom. The teacher appeared to perceive the major distinction in ability as lying between the Cardinals and the Clowns. Thus she saw the Tigers and the Cardinals as much closer in performance and potential than the Cardinals and the Clowns. The teacher's responses to the questions concerning the Clowns lends credence to this interpretation.

Q: Mrs. Benson, how would you describe the Clowns in terms of learning ability and academic performance?

R: Well, they are really slow. You know most of them are still doing first-grade work.

Q: Mrs. Benson, how would you describe the Clowns in terms of discipline matters?

R: They are very playful. They like to play a lot. They are not very neat. They like to talk a lot and play a lot. When I read to them, boy, do they have a good time. You know, the Tigers and the Cardinals will sit quietly and listen when I read to them, but the Clowns, they are always so restless. They always want to stand up. When we read, it is really something else. You know—Diane and Pat especially like to stand up. All these children, too, are very aggressive.

Q: Mrs. Benson, what value do you think the Clowns hold for an education?

R: I don't think very much. I don't think education means much to them at this stage. I know it doesn't mean anything to Randy and George. To most of the kids, I don't think it really matters at this stage.

FURTHER NOTES ON THE SECOND GRADE: REWARD AND PUNISHMENT

Throughout the length of the study in the school, it was evident that both the kindergarten and second-grade teachers were teaching the groups within their classes in a dissimilar manner. Variations were evident, for example, in the amount of time the teachers spent teaching the different groups, in the manner in which certain groups were granted privileges which were denied to oth-

ers, and in the teacher's proximity to the different groups. Two additional considerations related to the teacher's use of reward and punishment.

Though variations were evident from naturalistic observations in the kindergarten, a systematic evaluation was not attempted of the degree to which such differential behavior was a significant aspect of the classroom interactional patterns. When observations were being conducted in the second grade, it appeared that there was on the part of Mrs. Benson a differentiation of reward and punishment similar to that displayed by Mrs. Caplow. In order to examine more closely the degree to which variations were present over time, three observational periods were totally devoted to the tabulation of each of the individual behavioral units directed by the teacher towards the children. Each observational period was three and one-half hours in length, lasting from 8:30 a.m. to 12:00 noon. The dates of the observations were the Fridays at the end of eight, twelve, and sixteen weeks of school—October 24, November 21, and December 19, 1969, respectively.

A mechanism for evaluating the varieties of teacher behavior was developed. Behavior on the part of the teacher was tabulated as a "behavioral unit" when there was clearly directed towards an individual child some manner of communication, whether it be verbal, non-verbal or physical contact. When, within the interaction of the teacher and the student, there occurred more than one type of behavior, i.e., the teacher spoke to the child and touched him, a count was made of both variations. The following is a list of the nine variations in teacher behavior that were tabulated within the second-grade classroom. Several examples are also included with each of the alternatives displayed by the teacher within the class.

1. Verbal Supportive—"That's a very good job." "You are such a lovely girl." "My, but your work is so neat."

2. Verbal Neutral—"Laura and Tom, let's open our books to page 34." "May, your pencil is

on the floor," "Hal, do you have milk money today?"

3. Verbal Control—"Lou, sit on that chair and shut up." "Curt, get up off that floor." "Mary and Laura, quit your talking."

4. Non-verbal Supportive—Teacher nods her head at Rose. Teacher smiles at Liza. Teacher claps when Laura completes her problem at the board.

5. Non-verbal Neutral—Teacher indicates with her arms that she wants Lilly and Shirley to move farther apart in the circle. Teacher motions to Joe and Tom that they should try to snap their fingers to stay in beat with the music.

6. Non-verbal Control—Teacher frowns at Lena. Teacher shakes a finger at Amy to quit tapping her pencil. Teacher motions with hand for Rose not to come to her desk.

7. Physical Contact Supportive—Teacher hugs Laura. Teacher places her arm around Mary as she talks to her. Teacher holds Trish's hand as she takes out a splinter.

8. Physical Contact Neutral—Teacher touches head of Nick as she walks past. Teacher leads Rema to new place on the circle.

9. Physical Contact Control—Teacher strikes Lou with stick. Teacher pushes Curt down in his chair. Teacher pushes Hal and Doug to the floor.

Table 3 which follows is presented with all forms of control, supportive, and neutral behavior grouped together within each of the three observational periods. As a methodological precaution, since the categorization of the various types of behavior was decided as the interaction occurred and there was no cross-validation

Table 3

Variations in Teacher-Directed Behavior for Three Second-Grade Reading Groups During Three Observational Periods Within a Single Classroom

| Item | Variations in Teacher-Directed Behavior | | |
	Control	Supportive	Neutral
*Observational Period #1**			
Tigers	5%—(6)**	7%—(8)	87%—(95)
Cardinals	10%—(7)	8%—(5)	82%—(58)
Clowns	27%—(27)	6%—(6)	67%—(67)
Observational Period #2			
Tigers	7%—(14)	8%—(16)	85%—(170)
Cardinals	7%—(13)	8%—(16)	85%—(157)
Clowns	14%—(44)	6%—(15)	80%—(180)
Observational Period #3			
Tigers	7%—(15)	6%—(13)	86%—(171)
Cardinals	14%—(20)	10%—(14)	75%—(108)
Clowns	15%—(36)	7%—(16)	78%—(188)

* Forty-eight (48) minutes of unequal teacher access (due to one group of children's being out of the room) was eliminated from the analysis.

** Value within the parentheses indicates total number of units of behavior within that category.

checks by another observer, all behavior was placed in the appropriate neutral category which could not be clearly distinguished as belonging to one of the established supportive or control categories. This may explain the large percentage of neutral behavior tabulated in each of the three observational periods.

The picture of the second-grade teacher, Mrs. Benson, that emerges from analysis of these data is of one who distributes rewards quite sparingly and equally, but who utilizes somewhere between two and five times as much control-oriented behavior with the Clowns as with the Tigers. Alternatively, whereas with the Tigers the combination of neutral and supportive behavior never dropped below 93 percent of the total behavior directed towards them by the teacher in the three periods, the lowest figure for the Cardinals was 86 percent and for the Clowns was 73 percent. It may be assumed that neutral and supportive behavior would be conducive to learning while punishment or control-oriented behavior would not. Thus for the Tigers, the learning situation was one with only infrequent units of control, while for the Clowns, control behavior constituted one-fourth of all behavior directed towards them on at least one occasion.

Research related to leadership structure and task performance in voluntary organizations has given strong indications that within an authoritarian setting there occurs a significant decrease in performance on assigned tasks that does not occur with those in a non-authoritative setting (Kelly and Thibaut, 1954; Lewin, Lippitt, and White, 1939). Further investigations have generally confirmed these findings.

Of particular interest within the classroom are the findings of Adams (1945), Anderson (1946), Anderson, *et al.* (1946), Preston and Heintz (1949), and Robbins (1952). Their findings may be generalized to state that children within an authoritarian classroom display a decrease in both learning retention and performance, while those within the democratic classroom do not. In extrapolating these findings to the second-grade

classroom of Mrs. Benson, one cannot say that she was continually "authoritarian" as opposed to "democratic" with her students, but that with one group of students there occurred more control-oriented behavior than with other groups. The group which was the recipient of this control-oriented behavior was that group which she had defined as "slow and disinterested." On at least one occasion Mrs. Benson utilized nearly five times the amount of control-oriented behavior with the Clowns as with her perceived high-interest and high-ability group, the Tigers. For the Clowns, who were most isolated from the teacher and received the least amount of her teaching time, the results noted above would indicate that the substantial control-oriented behavior directed towards them would compound their difficulty in experiencing significant learning and cognitive growth.

Here discussion of the self-fulfilling prophecy is relevant: given the extent to which the teacher utilized control-oriented behavior with the Clowns, data from the leadership and performance studies would indicate that it would be more difficult for that group to experience a positive learning situation. The question remains unanswered, though, as to whether the behavior of uninterested students necessitated the teacher's resorting to extensive use of control-oriented behavior, or whether that to the extent to which the teacher utilized control-oriented behavior, the students responded with uninterest. If the prior experience of the Clowns was in any way similar to that of the students in kindergarten at Table 3 and Table C in the first grade, I am inclined to opt for the latter proposition.

A very serious and, I believe, justifiable consequence of this assumption of student uninterest related to the frequency of the teachers' control-oriented behavior is that the teachers themselves contribute significantly to the creation of the "slow learners" within their classrooms. Over time, this may help to account for the phenomenon noted in the Coleman Report (1966) that the gap between the academic performance of the disadvantaged students and the national norms increased the longer the students remained in the school system. During one of the three and one-half hour observational periods in the second grade, the percentage of control-oriented behavior oriented toward the entire class was about 8 percent. Of the behavior directed toward the Clowns, however, 27 percent was control-oriented behavior—more than three times the amount of control-oriented behavior directed to the class as a whole. Deutsch (1968), in a random sampling of New York City Public School classrooms of the fifth through eighth grades, noted that the teachers utilized between 50 and 80 percent of class time in discipline and organization. Unfortunately, he fails to specify the two individual percentages and thus it is unknown whether the classrooms were dominated by either discipline or organization as opposed to their combination. If it is the case, and Deutsch's findings appear to lend indirect support, that the higher the grade level, the greater the discipline and control-oriented behavior by the teacher, some of the unexplained aspects of the "regress phenomenon" may be unlocked.

On another level of analysis, the teacher's use of control-oriented behavior is directly related to the expectations of the ability and willingness of "slow learners" to learn the material she teachers. That is, if the student is uninterested in what goes on in the classroom, he is more apt to engage in activities that the teacher perceives as disruptive. Activities such as talking out loud, coloring when the teacher has not said it to be permissible, attempting to leave the room, calling other students' attention to activities occurring on the street, making comments to the teacher not pertinent to the lesson, dropping books, falling out of the chair, and commenting on how the student cannot wait for recess, all prompt the teacher to employ control-oriented behavior toward that student. The interactional pattern between the uninterested student and the teacher literally becomes a "vicious circle" in which control-oriented behavior is followed by

further manifestations of uninterest, followed by further control behavior and so on. The stronger the reciprocity of this pattern of interaction, the greater one may anticipate the strengthening of the teacher's expectation of the "slow learner" as being either unable or unwilling to learn.

THE CASTE SYSTEM FALTERS

A major objective of this study has been to document the manner in which there emerges within the early grades a stratification system, based both on teacher expectations related to behavioral and attitudinal characteristics of the child and also on a variety of socio-economic status factors related to the background of the child. As noted, when the child begins to move through the grades, the variable of past performance becomes a crucial index of the position of the child within the different classes. The formulation of the system of stratification of the children into various reading groups appears to gain a caste-like character over time in that there was no observed movement into the highest reading group once it had been initially established at the beginning of the kindergarten school year. Likewise, there was no movement out of the highest reading group. There was movement between the second and third reading groups, in that those at the lowest reading table one year are combined with the middle group for a following year, due to the presence of a group of students repeating the grade.

Though formal observations in the second-grade class of Mrs. Benson ended in December of 1969, periodic informal visits to the class continued throughout the remainder of the school year. The organization of the class remained stable save for one notable exception. For the first time during observations in either kindergarten, first or second grade, there had been a reassignment of two students from the highest reading group to the middle reading group. Two students from the Tiger group were moved during the third week of January, 1970 from the Tiger group to the Cardinal group. Two Cardinal group students were assigned to replace those in the Tiger group. Mrs. Benson was asked the reason for the move and she explained that neither of the two former Tiger group students "could keep a clean desk." She noted that both of the students constantly had paper and crayons on the floor beside their desks. She stated that the Tigers "are a very clean group" and the two could no longer remain with the highest reading group because they were "not neat." The two Cardinals who were moved into the Tiger reading group were both described as "extremely neat with their desk and floor."

POOR KIDS AND
PUBLIC SCHOOLS

It has been a major goal of this paper to demonstrate the impact of teacher expectations, based upon a series of subjectively interpreted social criteria, on both the anticipated academic potential and subsequent differential treatment accorded to those students perceived as having dissimilar social status. For the kindergarten teacher, expectations as to what type of child may be anticipated as a "fast learner" appear to be grounded in her reference group of a mixed white-black educated middle class. That is, students within her classroom who displayed those attributes which a number of studies have indicated are highly desired in children by middle-class educated adults as being necessary for future success were selected by her as possessing the potential to be a "fast learner." On the other hand, those children who did not possess the desired qualities were defined by the teacher as "slow learners." None of the criteria upon which the teacher appeared to base her evaluation of the children were directly related to measurable aspects of academic potential. Given that the I.Q. test was administered to the children in the last week of their kindergarten year, the results could not have been of any benefit to the teacher as she established patterns of organization within

the class.[5] The I.Q. scores may have been significant factors for the first- and second-grade teachers, but I assume that consideration of past performance was the major determinant for the seating arrangements which they established.[6]

For the first-grade teacher, Mrs. Logan, and the second-grade teacher, Mrs. Benson, the process of dividing the class into various reading groups, apparently on the basis of past performance, maintained the original patterns of differential treatment and expectations established in the kinder-

---

[5]The results of the I.Q. Test for the kindergarten class indicated that, though there were no statistically significant differences among the children at the three tables, the scores were skewed slightly higher for the children at Table 1. There were, however, children at Tables 2 and 3 who did score higher than several students at Table 1. The highest score came from a student at Table 1 (124) while the lowest came from a student at Table 3 (78). There appear to be at least three alternative explanations for the slightly higher scores by students at Table 1. First, the scores may represent the result of differential treatment in the classroom by Mrs. Caplow, thus contributing to the validation of the self-fulfilling prophecy. That is, the teacher by the predominance of teacher time spent with the Table 1 students, better prepared the students to do well on the examination than was the case for those students who received less teaching time. Secondly, the tests themselves may have reflected strong biases towards the knowledge and experience of middle-class children. Thus, students from higher-status families at Table 1 could be expected to perform better than did the low-status students from Table 3. The test resulted not in a "value free" measure of cognitive capacity, but in an index of family background. Third, of course, would be the fact that the children at the first table did possess a higher degree of academic potential than those at the other tables, and the teacher was intuitively able to discern these differences. This third alternative, however, is least susceptible to empirical verification.

[6]When the second-grade teacher was questioned as to what significance she placed in the results of I.Q. tests, she replied that "They merely confirm what I already know about the student."

garten class. Those initially defined as "fast learners" by the kindergarten teacher in subsequent years continued to have that position in the first group, regardless of the label or name given to it.

It was evident throughout the length of the study that the teachers made clear the distinctions they perceived between the children who were defined as fast learners and those defined as slow learners. It would not appear incorrect to state that within the classroom there was established by the various teachers a clear system of segregation between the two established groups of children. In the one group were all the children who appeared clean and interested, sought interactions with adults, displayed leadership within the class, and came from homes which displayed various status criteria valued in the middle class. In the other were children who were dirty, smelled of urine, did not actively participate in class, spoke a linguistic dialect other than that spoken by the teacher and students at Table 1, did not display leadership behavior, and came from poor homes often supported by public welfare. I would contend that within the system of segregation established by the teachers, the group perceived as slow learners were ascribed a caste position that sought to keep them apart from the other students.

The placement of the children within the various classrooms into different reading groups was ostensibly done on the promise of future performance in the kindergarten and on differentials of past performance in later grades. However, the placement may rather have been done from purely irrational reasons that had nothing to do with academic performance. The utilization of academic criteria may have served as the rationalization for a more fundamental process occurring with the class whereby the teacher served as the agent of the larger society to ensure that proper "social distance" was maintained between the various strata of the society as represented by the children.

Within the context of this analysis there appear to be at least two interactional processes that may be identified as having occurred simultaneously within the kindergarten classroom. The first was the relation of the teacher to the students placed at Table 1. The process appeared to occur in at least four stages. The initial stage involved the kindergarten teacher's developing expectations regarding certain students as possessing a series of characteristics that she considered essential for future academic "success." Second, the teacher reinforced through her mechanisms of "positive" differential behavior those characteristics of the children that she considered important and desirable.

Third, the children responded with more of the behavior that initially gained them the attention and support of the teacher. Perceiving that verbalization, for example, was a quality that the teacher appeared to admire, the Table 1 children increased their level of verbalization throughout the school year. Fourth, the cycle was complete as the teacher focused even more specifically on the children at Table 1 who continued to manifest the behavior she desired. A positive interactional scheme arose whereby initial behavioral patterns of the student were reinforced into apparent permanent behavioral patterns, once he had received support and differential treatment from the teacher.

Within this framework, the actual academic potential of the students was not objectively measured prior to the kindergarten teacher's evaluation of expected performance. The students may be assumed to have had mixed potential. However, the common positive treatment accorded to all within the group by the teacher may have served as the necessary catalyst for the self-fulfilling prophecy whereby those expected to do well did so.

A concurrent behavioral process appeared to occur between the teacher and those students placed at Tables 2 and 3. The student came into the class possessing a series of behavioral and attitudinal characteristics that within the frame of reference of the teacher were perceived as indicative of "failure." Second, through mechanisms of reinforcement of her initial expectations as to the future performance of the student, it was made evident that he was not perceived as similar or equal to those at the table of fast learners. In the third stage, the student responded to both the definition and actual treatment given to him by the teacher which emphasized his characteristics of being an educational "failure." Given the high degree of control-oriented behavior directed toward the "slower" learner, the lack of verbal interaction and encouragement, the disproportionally small amount of teaching time given to him, and the ridicule and hostility, the child withdrew from class participation. The fourth stage was the cyclical repetition of behavioral and attitudinal characteristics that led to the initial labeling as an educational failure.

As with those perceived as having high probability of future success, the academic potential of the failure group was not objectively determined prior to evaluation by the kindergarten teacher. This group also may be assumed to have come into the class with mixed potential. Some within the group may have had the capacity to perform academic tasks quite well, while others perhaps did not. Yet the reinforcement by the teacher of the characteristics in the children that she had perceived as leading to academic failure may, in fact, have created the very conditions of student failure. With the "negative" treatment accorded to the perceived failure group, the teacher's definition of the situation may have ensured its emergence. What the teacher perceived in the children may have served as the catalyst for a series of interactions, with the result that the child came to act out within the class the very expectations defined for him by the teacher.

As an alternative explanation, however, the teacher may have developed the system of caste segregation within the classroom, not because the groups of children were so dissimilar they had to be handled in an entirely different manner, but because they were, in fact, so very close to one another. The teacher may have believed quite strongly that the ghetto community inhib-

ited the development of middle-class success models. Thus, it was her duty to "save" at least one group of children from the "streets." Those children had to be kept separate who could have had a "bad" influence on the children who appeared to have a chance to "make it" in the middle class of the larger society. Within this framework, the teacher's actions may be understood not only as an attempt to keep the slow learners away from those fast learners, but to ensure that the fast learners would not be so influenced that they themselves become enticed with the "streets" and lose their apparent opportunity for future middle-class status.

In addition to the formal separation of the groups within the classroom, there was also the persistence of mechanisms utilized by the teacher to socialize the children in the high reading group with feelings of aversion, revulsion, and rejection towards those of the lower reading groups. Through ridicule, belittlement, physical punishment, and merely ignoring them, the teacher was continually giving clues to those in the high reading group as to how one with high status and a high probability of future success treats those of low status and low probability of future success. To maintain within the larger society the caste aspects of the position of the poor *vis a vis* the remainder of the society, there has to occur the transmission from one generation to another the attitudes and values necessary to legitimate and continue such a form of social organization.

Given the extreme intercomplexity of the organizational structure of this society, the institutions that both create and sustain social organization can neither be held singularly responsible for perpetuating the inequalities nor for eradicating them (cf. Leacock, 1969). The public school system, I believe, is justifiably responsible for contributing to the present structure of the society, but the responsibility is not its alone. The picture that emerges from this study is that the school strongly shares in the complicity of maintaining the organizational perpetuation of poverty and unequal opportunity. This, of course, is in contrast to the formal doctrine of education in this country to ameliorate rather than aggravate the conditions of the poor.

The teachers' reliance on a mixed black-white educated middle class for their normative reference group appeared to contain assumptions of superiority over those of lower-class and status positions. For they and those members of their reference group, comfortable affluence, education, community participation, and possession of professional status may have afforded a rather stable view of the social order. The treatment of those from lower socio-economic backgrounds within the classrooms by the teachers may have indicated that the values highly esteemed by them were not open to members of the lower groups. Thus the lower groups were in numerous ways informed of their lower status and were socialized for a role of lower self expectations and also for respect and deference towards those of higher status. The social distance between the groups within the classrooms was manifested in its extreme form by the maintenance of patterns of caste segregation whereby those of lower positions were not allowed to become a part of the peer group at the highest level. The value system of the teachers appeared to necessitate that a certain group be ostracized due to "unworthiness" or inherent inferiority. The very beliefs which legitimated exclusion were maintained among those of the higher social group which then contributed to the continuation of the pattern of social organization itself.

It has not been a contention of this study that the teachers observed could not or would not teach their students. They did, I believe, teach quite well. But the high quality teaching was not made equally accessible to all students in the class. For the students of high socio-economic background who were perceived by the teachers as possessing desirable behavioral and attitudinal characteristics, the classroom experience was one where the teachers displayed interest in them, spent a large proportion of teaching time with them, directed little control-oriented behavior

towards them, held them as models for the remainder of the class and continually reinforced statements that they were "special" students. Hypothetically, if the classrooms observed had contained only those students perceived by the teachers as having a desirable social status and a high probability of future success outside the confines of the ghetto community, the teachers could be assumed to have continued to teach well, and under these circumstance, to the entire class.

Though the analysis has focused on the early years of schooling for a single group of black children attending a ghetto school, the implications are far-reaching for those situations where there are children from different status backgrounds within the same classroom. When a teacher bases her expectations of performance on the social status of the student and assumes that the higher the social status, the higher the potential of the child, those children of low social status suffer a stigmatization outside of their own choice or will. Yet there is a greater tragedy than being labeled as a slow learner, and that is being treated as one. The differential amounts of control-oriented behavior, the lack of interaction with the teacher, the ridicule from one's peers, and the caste aspects of being placed in lower reading groups all have implications for the future life style and value of education for the child.

Though it may be argued from the above that the solution to the existence of differential treatment for students is the establishment of schools catering to only a single segment of the population, I regard this as being antithetical to the goals of education—if one views the ultimate value of an education as providing insights and experience with thoughts and persons different from oneself. The thrust of the educational experience should be towards diversity, not homogeneity. It may be utopian to suggest that education should seek to encompass as wide a variety of individuals as possible within the same setting, but it is no mean goal to pursue.

The success of an educational institution and any individual teacher should not be measured by the treatment of the high-achieving students, but rather by the treatment of those not achieving. As is the case with a chain, ultimate value is based on the weakest member. So long as the lower-status students are treated differently in both quality and quantity of education, there will exist an imperative for change.

It should be apparent, of course, that if one desires this society to retain its present social class configuration and the disproportional access to wealth, power, social and economic mobility, medical care, and choice of life styles, one should not disturb the methods of education as presented in this study. This contention is made because what develops a "caste" within the classrooms appears to emerge in the larger society as "class." The low-income children segregated as a caste of "unclean and intellectually inferior" persons may very well be those who in their adult years become the car washers, dishwashers, welfare recipients, and participants in numerous other un- or underemployed roles within this society. The question may quite honestly be asked, "Given the treatment of low-income children from the beginning of their kindergarten experience, for what class strata are they being prepared other than that of the lower class?" It appears that the public school system not only mirrors the configurations of the larger society, but also significantly contributes to maintaining them. Thus the system of public education in reality perpetuates what it is ideologically committed to eradicate—class barriers which result in inequality in the social and economic life of the citizenry.

REFERENCES

Adams, R. G. "The Behavior of Pupils in Democratic and Autocratic Social Climates." Abstracts of Dissertations, Stanford University, 1945.

Anderson, H. Studies in Teachers' Classroom Personalities. Stanford: Stanford University Press, 1946.

Anderson, H.; Brewer, J.; and Reed, M. "Studies of Teachers' Classroom Personalities, III. Follow-up Studies of the Effects of Dominative and Integrative Contacts on Children's Behavior." Applied Psychology Monograph. Stanford: Stanford University Press, 1946.

Asbell, B. "Not Like Other Children." Redbook, 65 (October, 1963), pp. 114–118.

Austin, Mary C. and Morrison, Coleman. The First R; The Harvard Report on Reading in Elementary Schools, New York: Macmillan, 1963.

Becker, H. S. "Social Class Variation in Teacher-Pupil Relationship." Journal of Educational Sociology, 1952, 25, 451–465.

Borg, W. "Ability Grouping in the Public Schools." Cooperative Research Project 557. Salt Lake City: Utah State University, 1964.

Clark, K. B. "Educational Stimulation of Racially Disadvantaged Children." Education in Depressed Areas. Edited by A.H. Passow, New York: Columbia University Press, 1963.

Coleman, J. S., et al. Equality of Educational Opportunity. Washington, D.C.: United States Government Printing Office, 1966.

Deutsch, M. "Minority Groups and Class Status as Related to Social and Personality Factors in Scholastic Achievement." The Disadvantaged Child. Edited by M. Deutsch, et al. New York: Basic Books, 1967.

Eddy, E. Walk the White Line. Garden City, N.Y.: Doubleday, 1967.

Frazier, E. F. Black Bourgeoisie. New York: The Free Press, 1957.

Freeman, R.; Whelpton, P.; and Campbell, A. Family Planning, Sterility and Population Growth. New York: McGraw-Hill, 1959.

Fuchs, E. Teachers Talk. Garden City, N.Y.: Doubleday, 1967.

Gebhard, P.; Pomeroy, W.; Martin, C.; and Christenson, C. Pregnancy, Birth and Abortion. New York: Harper & Row, 1958.

Gibson, G. "Aptitude Tests." Science, 1965, 149, 583.

Goldberg, M.; Passow, A.; and Justman, J. The Effects of Ability Grouping. New York: Teachers College Press, Columbia University, 1966.

Harlem Youth Opportunities Unlimited. Youth in the Ghetto. New York: HARYOU, 1964.

Henry, J. "Docility, or Giving the Teacher What She Wants." Journal of Social Issues, 1955, 11, 2.

_____, "The Problem of Spontaneity, Initiative and Creativity in Suburban Classrooms." American Journal of Orthopsychiatry, 1959, 29, 1.

_____, "Golden Rule Days: American Schoolrooms." *Culture Against Man*, New York: Random House, 1963.

Hollingshead, A. *Elmtown's Youth*. New York: John Wiley & Sons, 1949.

Jackson, P. *Life in Classrooms*. New York: Holt, Rinehart & Winston, 1968.

Kahl, J. A. *The American Class Structure*. New York: Holt, Rinehart & Winston, 1957.

Katz, I. "Review of Evidence Relating to Effects of Desegregation on Intellectual Performance of Negroes." *American Psychologist*, 1964, *19*, 381–399.

Kelly, H. and Thibaut, J. "Experimental Studies of Group Problem Solving and Process." *Handbook of Social Psychology*, Vol. 2. Edited by G. Lindzey, Reading, Mass.: Addison-Wesley, 1954.

Kohl, H. *36 Children*. New York: New American Library, 1967.

Kozol, J. *Death at an Early Age*. Boston: Houghton Mifflin, 1967.

Kvaraceus, W.C. "Disadvantaged Children and Youth: Programs of Promise or Pretense?" Burlingame: California Teachers Association, 1965. (Mimeographed.)

Lawrence, S. "Ability Grouping." Unpublished manuscript prepared for Center for Educational Policy Research, Harvard Graduate School of Education, Cambridge, Mass., 1969.

Leacock, E. *Teaching and Learning in City Schools*. New York: Basic Books, 1969.

Lewin, K.; Lippitt, R.; and White, R. "Patterns of Aggressive Behavior in Experimentally Created Social Climates." *Journal of Social Psychology*, 1939, *10*, 271–299.

Lynd, H. and Lynd, R. *Middletown in Transition*. New York: Harcourt, Brace & World, 1937.

MacKinnon, D. W. "The Nature and Nurture of Creative Talent." *American Psychologist*, 1962, *17*, 484–495.

Merton, R. K. *Social Theory and Social Structure*. Revised and Enlarged. New York: The Free Press, 1957.

Moore, A. *Realities of the Urban Classroom*. Garden City, N.Y.: Doubleday, 1967.

Notestein, F. "Class Differences in Fertility." *Class, Status and Power*. Edited by R. Bendix and S. Lipset. New York: The Free Press, 1953.

Preston, M. and Heintz, R. "Effects of Participatory Versus Supervisory Leadership on Group Judgment." *Journal of Abnormal Social Psychology*, 1949, *44*, 345–355.

Reissman, F. *The Culturally Deprived Child*. New York: Harper and Row, 1962.

_____, "Teachers of the Poor: A Five Point Program." Burlingame: California Teachers Association, 1965. (Mimeographed.)

Reissman, L. *Class in American Society*. New York: The Free Press, 1959.

Robbins, F. "The Impact of Social Climate upon a College Class." *School Review*, 1952, *60*, 275–284.

Rose, A. *The Negro in America*. Boston: Beacon Press, 1956.

Rosenthal, R. and Jacobson, Lenore. *Pygmalion in the Classroom*. New York: Holt, Rinehart & Winston, 1968.

Sigel, I. "The Piagetian System and the World of Education." *Studies in Cognitive Development*. Edited by D. Elkind and J. Flavell, New York: Oxford University Press, 1969.

Simpson, G. and Yinger, J. M. *Racial and Cultural Minorities*. New York: Harper and Row, 1958.

Smith, L. and Geoffrey, W. *The Complexities of an Urban Classroom*. New York: Holt, Rinehart & Winston, 1968.

Smith, M. "Equality of Educational Opportunity: The Basic Findings Reconsidered." *On Equality of Educational Opportunity*. Edited by F. Mosteller and D. P. Moynihan. New York: Random House, 1971 (In Press).

Warner, W. L.; Havighurst, R.; and Loeb, M. *Who Shall Be Educated?* New York: Harper and Row, 1944.

Wilson, A. B. "Social Stratification and Academic Achievement." *Education in Depressed Areas*. Edited by A. H. Passow. New York: Teachers College Press, Columbia University, 1963.

The World of Chris's Group

ROBERT EVERHART

I was not surprised to see Chris's name on the list of students nominated by sixth-grade teachers to be above average in academic ability. I had heard that he was an outstanding student as well as sixth-grade class president, and the little I knew of him indicated he was popular among other students, a fact confirmed by the sociometric measures.

Chris attended the same elementary school as Don and Steve, and Chris counted them as his good friends, but he also told me that he associated with Phil, Barry, and especially John, who all lived nearby. All were part of a nucleus who had been together for most of their days in elementary school and who had shared many good times together. All were good students at Garfield, all interested in sports, all rather clean-cut kids, well respected among their peers, both boys and girls. The next year at Spencer, Marty, who had come from a different elementary school, joined the coalition, which remained inviolate through the seventh grade and part of the eighth.

THE PEOPLE

Chris was a good student while at Garfield Elementary School and continued to be a good stu-dent while at Spencer. He was well known by all students at Harold Spencer, the brains as well as the "weirdos" and the troublemakers, and got along well with everyone. Not only was he articulate, but he had a good sense of humor. Most teachers, with the exception of Von Hoffman, enjoyed having him in their class.

Chris was rather small in height when I first met him, but grew rapidly over the two years of the study. In other respects, Chris was pleasing in appearance with somewhat long but well-kept hair (it was shorter in the eighth grade after his father insisted that he have a haircut) and a well-kept manner with regards to clothing. Chris's closest companion during the seventh grade was John, who was nicknamed "Choo-choo" or "Railroad tracks" by his friends because of the braces he wore on his teeth. John was less outgoing than Chris, and did not participate in class work as actively as Chris. He was content to "get by," but

Source: "The World Of Chris's Group" from *Reading, Writing, and Resistance* by Robert Everhart, copyright 1983. Reprinted by permission of Routledge Publishing Services.

he got by quite well in that he was a "B" student for the two years I knew him.

Barry, another member of the group, was short and chunky, and appeared in the seventh grade as if he should have been in fifth grade. Barry's last name was Simmons so he was, at some time before I knew him, dubbed "couch"—the name he was called by Chris, John, and others who knew him well. More academically oriented than the others in the group, Barry did what was expected of him in class, yet seemed to do it more promptly and regularly than either John or Chris, and was not as prone to goofing off in class. Barry too liked sports, and in fact he went out for the eighth-grade football team although he rarely played. He and Chris enjoyed talking about one of their favorite sports, hockey, and often made friendly wagers on the "Peter Puck" games shown on national TV at the week-ends.

It is useful here to mention two other individuals who, while not members of the group for the duration of my time at Spencer and while not as closely linked to the coalition, were still important "significant others." The first of these was Phil who, while fairly intimate with the group in the early part of the seventh grade, was obviously, purposefully, and slowly ostracized from the group by the end of the year. Phil too was quite interested in sports and, like the rest of the group, spent considerable time in school discussing athletic activities. Phil talked as if he was a very good athlete, and he always criticized others whom he thought could not match up to his athletic ability. Phil too was a good student, and while he had a greater propensity to goof off than Barry, he did not "act up" as consistently as either Chris or John.

Marty was the only member of the group to come from an elementary school other than Garfield. Unknown to the group in the early part of the seventh grade, he did not share in their collective experiences until later in the year and into the eighth grade. Nevertheless, he became important, especially to Chris who said that Marty was one of his closest friends during that

year. Marty maintained the lowest GPA (Grade Point Average) over the two-year period, a C average. Marty too was a "sportaholic," and was in the school wrestling team for two years (one of the years, the first, with Gordon). Marty, in some respects, was a cross between a typical member of Chris's group and Don's group for, especially in the eighth grade, he talked more and more about his involvement with marijuana and his ability to get supplies of beer and occasionally liquor.

Chris discussed his family life more than any other member of the group but, here again, these discussions were rare and came about only as a result of talking about something else wherein the characteristics of home life would be brought out. I knew Chris's father worked for the state in the area of fiscal analysis while his mother worked as a clerk in one of the state agencies.

Barry, who lived near Harold Spencer in a modest one-story ranch house, once mentioned to me that his father worked for a small "food place" in one of the nearby shopping centers. By checking the records, I found that his occupation was listed as being a "sales clerk" at a nearby delicatessen which had a reputation for selling quality meats and seafoods. While he did not mention it himself, I also found out that his mother was not employed outside the home. Phil, who lived within a few blocks of Barry in a similar home, was like Chris in that both of his parents worked. His father was a civilian electronics technician for a nearby military installation and his mother worked as a clerk for the military base. John lived close to Chris in a newer tract of homes. John's father was a teacher in one of the adjoining school districts, a fact that John never mentioned until late in the study. Marty lived with his aunt, who worked as a machine operator for a local wood products firm. I did not know why he lived with his aunt and never asked; nobody else did either. Once Chris told me that Marty could not have much money as he was eligible for a free lunch program for students from low-income families. Because of this, Marty was popular at lunch, especially during wrestling season when he had to restrict his food intake. Often Marty would simply get a lunch and then give it free or at reduced cost to anyone who wanted it.

The family characteristics of Chris's group were not significantly different from those of Don's group. The women worked in three of the families, and the father's occupation, with the exception of John's father, tended toward skilled technical work or semi-skilled operative work. All families, with the exception of Barry's who had moved to the district when he was in the third grade, had resided in the area since the boys were born and all had relatives living in the area. In that these characteristics represented features of most families in the area who sent their children to Spencer, the group and its origin was fairly typical.

ACTIVITIES AND PERSPECTIVES

Seventh Grade

"What's the score?"

"You have zero."

"I thought I had one point."

"Come on, Bob, that one didn't count, I moved my thumbs on that one."

"That's your problem, not mine," I replied.

"Poor sport," John interjected.

"Come on, line up, I'm ready," Barry said impatiently.

Chris placed his two index fingers parallel to each other on the desk and touched his thumbs to the desk so that the parallel fingers served as an upright. Barry spun the quarter, waited for it to stabilize, then attempted to flick it over Chris's outstretched hands. The quarter zinged over the bar and struck Chris on the chin.

"A George Blanda special," Barry said emphatically, "I'm even with you now, Chris, the score's three to three." Just then the bell rang, signaling the beginning of the first period.

The year had begun at Harold Spencer. More specifically, the year with Chris and his group had begun and, in their case, every day began with math class first period. The few moments before math class often began with the omnipresent "coin games" among Chris, John, Phil, Barry, and myself, wherein we kept a running score, often used to determine who would buy milk shakes in the cafeteria after lunch. The year also began as it had for every year that any teacher in the school could remember—with a magazine drive.

At about 8:50 the loudspeaker came on: "All students in building B should now proceed to the cafeteria for the assembly." Books were slammed shut and we all waited for the signal to proceed to the cafeteria. "Sit in your assigned seats," yelled Mr. Charles as we moved out through the door.

"Wonder what this thing is all about," Barry said innocently as we moved down the halls filled with noisy students. "I KNOW what it's about," John said confidently, "my brother told me some old dude tries to get you to hustle magazines and you get some dinky prizes if you sell the most. Big deal."

I sat between Chris and John about half-way from the front of the auditorium, and we waited for the assembly to begin while students from other classes continued to pour into the auditorium. Following the "pledge of allegiance," Mr. Pall introduced an elderly man who had been running these magazine drives for a long time. He began his presentation with some jokes (few people laughed) and some salutary comments about how he always liked to come to Harold Spencer every year because the student body was so energetic and responsible (almost everybody, especially the eighth- and ninth-graders, laughed). The salesman then proceeded into his speech, designed to convince the students on the art of selling. After providing directions on the procedures of how to fill out the subscription forms, and rattling off the list of prizes (the top room, on any given day, received free ice cream cones at the school cafeteria; the top individual seller, for any one day, was eligible for a drawing on one of the three ten-speed bikes; anyone selling at least three subscriptions could choose from a variety of large posters), the class was excused and we all returned to math class.

"Told you, Barry," John said as we entered the room. "Did you see those neat prizes, a poster of Captain Kangaroo for your very own. Just sell three magazines."

"Big deal," Don added from across the room, "I'm not selling any of their baby magazines."

"Bet you do," Chris shot back jokingly.

"Bet," Don answered, extending his hand as if to bet. "Naw, you probably won't" Chris replied, taking his seat. Mr. Glenn then came in with a big stack of subscription forms and gave them to Chris.

"Well," he said, as he handed Chris the forms, "You're the representative to the student government from this room, so I guess it's your job to hand these out and collect the money every day." He turned to the class and gave the instructions that people were to get the forms from Chris and that the first five to ten minutes of every class from now until the end of the magazine drive (one week) were to be used to hand the money in to Chris. Chris thus began his first obligations commensurate with his newly elected post as class representative to the student government.

The student government at Harold Spencer was a body elected by the students. Any student running for school-wide office had to have a 2.5 average. There were no grade requirements for room representatives, although if students elected what any one teacher thought was a "goof off," (meaning a person who would not handle the responsibilities of the office) teachers did their best to dissuade the class and, if necessary, used their authority to veto the decision. The school-wide council—president, vice-president, secretary, and treasurer—was elected in the spring and thus consisted of eighth- and ninth-graders. Room representatives were elected early in the Fall and seventh-, eighth-, and ninth-graders were equally represented.

The first meeting of the year was held early in October. As was to be the case for the two years I attended these meetings, few, if any, students knew before the meeting what was to transpire. Chris and I entered the room where the meeting was to be held and sat in the rear near the window

where some of the other seventh-graders were sitting (since seventh-graders often did not know many of the older students, they tended to cluster together for security until the middle of the year when they felt more comfortable). Mrs. Patterson, the adviser to the student council, began the meeting by introducing a gentleman "who has a product you may be interested in buying with your student body funds." The man had a large case which he placed on the table before him. Before proceeding, he asked a girl sitting in front for the name of the school mascot. Upon being told it was a stallion, the salesman taped a large piece of paper to the chalkboard behind him, took out a stencil of a horse from his sales kit, placed it on the paper, then, with a can of spray paint he took from his kit, sprayed an outline of a red horse on the paper.

The students watched attentively as the salesman continued with his demonstration.

"OK, who do you guys have your next football game with?"

"Stonebrook," the football players and cheerleaders said in unison.

"OK, then here we go," he said, taking some large letters from his kit and beginning to spray the letters G-O- S-T-A-L-L-I-O-N-S B-E-A-T S-T-O-N-E-B-R-O-O-K.

"Hey, far out," said one of the cheerleaders.

"Yeah, better than those crummy signs we have now," one of the football players added.

"Shut up, Jackson," the cheerleader said in jest. "We work hard on those signs, just so you guys might win a game once in a while."

"My kid sister makes better signs," a football player added.

"My kid brother plays football better," the cheerleader retorted. The salesman laughed at all this while continuing his pitch on the versatility of the sign kit, its use for athletic events, dances, holiday signs, special events and the like. "It's guaranteed too, if any of these rubber stencils break we'll replace it free," he added.

Chris raised his hand. "How much does it cost?"

"We'll get to that in a minute," he said as he dragged out umpteen bottles of spray paint to show all the different colors. He began spraying a new sign, demonstrating how different colors could be combined. Taking Chris's cue, another student asked how much the paint cost.

"Twenty-four dollars for a case of 12 . . . "

"What!" a student interrupted, "I can get it for one dollar and thirty-nine cents at Red Front [a local discount store]." The salesman appeared a little unnerved by this comment, so he extolled how this was a special paint and that it would last longer. Another student raised his hand to ask him how much the whole kit cost. "Let me show you one thing and then we'll get to that," the salesman replied.

Chris leaned over and said to me, "Sure sounds like he's stalling on that price."

"That, my boy, is the art of salesmanship," I replied. By now it was 9:15 and the period was almost finished. The salesman finally got to the discussion of price. "These kits range in size, with the small portable kit like this one [holds kit up] costing one ninety-five, to the large kit which has everything you could possibly want. Plus, with this large kit we'll throw in sixty dollars worth of extra silhouettes or paint free."

"How much?" Chris said impatiently from the rear of the room.

"For the large kit, three forty-five."

"You mean a dollar ninety-five for that little one and three forty-five for the big one? Heck, that's not bad."

"Yeah, we ought to get it," the talkative cheerleader added.

The salesman smiled. "No, it's one hundred ninety-five dollars for the portable one and three hundred forty-five dollars for the large kit." The gasp in the room was loud and clear. "Three hundred forty-five dollars for THAT?" someone said. Chris said loudly, "What a rip-off."

Mrs. Patterson looked embarrassed, but just then the bell rang to end the period. "Can you come back tomorrow so we can make a decision on this?" she asked the salesman. He said he could not as he had to be out of town. "OK," Mrs. Patterson said as the group filed out of the room, "we'll have another meeting first period tomorrow to make a decision on this."

The next day a meeting was held to decide whether to buy the sign kit. Terry, the president of the student council, had not been at the meeting the previous day, so Mrs. Patterson took a few moments to fill him in. While we were waiting, Chris told Jim, another seventh-grade representative, that the whole thing was a waste of money. Jim shrugged his shoulders but was preoccupied with copying John's English paper for an assignment due that afternoon. After a few more moments Terry asked if there was any discussion on the purchase.

"Wait a minute," said Chris, "how do we know we have enough money to buy this thing?" People in the front turned around, somewhat surprised that someone should ask such a question, especially a seventh-grader. The treasurer of the class, busily talking to one of her friends, looked up and said in a very matter-of-fact manner, "Oh, shoot, that's not a problem, we have a couple of thousand bucks."

"Well, let's vote on it then," prompted Terry. "How many want to buy this thing?" Led by the cheerleaders and the football players, who were urging everyone to get their hands up, the vast majority of the student council voted to purchase the super stencil kit for $345. Chris was one of the few who did not raise his hand.

I did not get an opportunity to see Chris again until the next period when I saw him in music class.

"Well, what'd you think of your first student council meeting?" I asked while we were waiting for Hackett who was, as usual, late to class.

"It was a waste."

"Did you vote to buy the sign kit?"

"Are you kidding," he replied emphatically. "They could have made that thing in the shop for half that price. I'm pissed!"

I did not doubt Chris's frustration at what had transpired in the meeting. However, as I attended similar meetings over the two years I remained in touch with the school, I became convinced that the school-based domination of meeting agendas was not the most significant issue in the operation of the student council. Instead, what seemed most clear was the over-all lack of concern most students had for the business conducted within the council or indeed the very presence of the council itself. Thus while students who were elected usually attended the meetings and often dealt with the agendas presented to them, the business of the council seemed little different from the business conducted in most of the classes. The reasons for this are complex, but are not unrelated to the very culture students built and through which they came to interpret their place in the school. A description of some of the recurrent activities of Chris and his group will illuminate this point.

The games before class, as noted earlier, typified the routine of Chris and his group. So too did a general accommodation to classroom requirements. There was, however, one notable exception. Chris and his friends had great difficulties with one teacher, Mr. Von Hoffman, and it was here that the group developed the reputation of being troublemakers.

Von Hoffman was perceived by students and teachers alike to be a poor teacher. He had been teaching for over fifteen years, and although the administration would have liked to have him fired, this was difficult. Chris, John, and Barry tried their best, however, to drive him out of teaching but Von Hoffman seemed able to outlast them.

One day it seemed Von Hoffman could not take it any more. John, Chris, and Barry had been goofing for the entire period, despite frequent admonitions from Von Hoffman. But they kept getting up, walking around, talking to each other.

Suddenly, Von Hoffman stomped to the rear of the room. "You, you, you, you and you," he said pointing to Chris, John, Mark, and two other boys, "you five come with me; we're going down to the office right now."

"ME?" Chris responded incredulously, smiling as he said it.

"I didn't do anything," John added.

"How about Barry?" Mark said, pointing to Barry who was in his seat doubled over in laughter. "He ain't been in his seat at all."

"Don't say 'ain't' in this class," Von Hoffman said almost automatically. Chris looked over at Barry in his seat. "Hey, don't flip Mr. Von Hoffman the bird," he exclaimed. By this time Von Hoffman was visibly upset and he marched the five to the office for a conference with Mr. Pall. Sitting down outside Mr. Pall's office, I could catch glimpses of the conversation inside.

"I'm sick and tired of these hoodlums disrupting things. . . . I want them all transferred."

"But Mr. Von Hoffman, you know I'm doing better, better than I was doing before." It was Chris, using his PR skills as usual.

"I guess so, but I want the rest of them transferred . . ." The conversation went on for about five more minutes. Finally they came out and returned to the room. I poked my head in Pall's office.

"What happened?" I asked.

"I transferred three of them," he sighed. "They should have gotten rid of that idiot years ago, but nobody has the guts."

John was not transferred, and the group was fairly well behaved for the next few days. Soon, however, they reverted back to their original form. Chris and John began discussing (as they had in the past) how they thought that Von Hoffman was "crazy" and that he had been in a mental institution at one time. They concocted games of looking at his habits and idiosyncrasies and "typing" them as being the characteristics of someone who is a little bit unbalanced.

Little incidents continued to build up, with Chris, John, and Barry in the middle. The next day Chris and John, sitting next to the window, happened to look out at the nearby road and saw some students strolling by.

"Hey, those are Spencer kids," said John in a loud voice. Von Hoffman looked up from his desk. "Knock it off and get to work," he said, pointing a pencil at John.

Chris ignored Von Hoffman's warning and continued, "Yeah, that's Jon Smith and he's in my science class. Wonder what he's doing out there?" The whole class was peering toward the road by this time, and Von Hoffman too had been lured over to the window.

"Must be playing hookey or skipping," John said nonchalantly. By this time Von Hoffman had swallowed the bait.

"Are those kids really from Spencer?" he asked.

"Sure," Chris replied, "one of them is in my science class." Von Hoffman turned around abruptly and headed for the door, which he opened half-way before pausing. Apparently thinking twice about leaving the room unsupervised, he re-entered it and flipped on the loudspeaker switch to the office.

"Office."

"Yes, this is Mr. Von Hoffman, would you [in the meantime, controlled and almost uncontrolled laughter from Chris and John, covering their mouths, looking out the window, doing everything they could to keep from giving the whole thing away] tell Mr. Pall that there are some boys out front trying to skip school."

"OK."

It was a well-executed trick and Chris and John had pulled it off perfectly.

Within the week, events in the class reached their lowest point of the year. John, Chris, and Barry had been especially persistent in their bugging of Von Hoffman to the point where some of the girls were even picking up on the activities (a fairly rare occurrence). On Thursday, Von Hoffman tired of the two girls near the back talking, so he sent one of them out of the room. The other girl pleaded to be sent out too, saying she promised that she would not get in any trouble, but he refused. Chris and Barry, sitting near the window and the heater, were plopping small objects down the vents, causing a "bing-bing" sound when the objects hit the fan blades.

"Knock that off over there," Von Hoffman yelled. "You boys get away from that heater." The two of them slowly moved their desks, being careful in the process to scrape them as loud as possible on the tile floors. Von Hoffman turned his back to the window to talk to the girl again.

Meanwhile, the girl in the hall was looking in the window of the door, pointing to people, laughing, and trying to make them read her lips through the window. Chris, watching the girl in the window, suddenly called out, "Hey, quit flipping Mr. Von Hoffman the bird."

That did it. Von Hoffman was back at Chris's desk in a flash, standing above him. "You little smart guy," he said in an emotional tone, "it's about time you start learning some respect," whereupon he grabbed Chris by the shoulder and began shaking him.

"Oh, my shoulder. I'm dying," Chris moaned.

"Sue him, Chris," John said, continuing to flip paper into the heater.

"I'll sue," he said.

"Get up in your seat," Von Hoffman ordered, "and start your assignment." Chris got up and sat in his chair while Von Hoffman continued to glare at him. Finally, Chris picked up his pencil and poised it on the paper, as if ready to write. He looked at Von Hoffman and asked quietly, "What's the date?"

The juxtaposition of the irate Von Hoffman and Chris's refusal to take the incident seriously was too much. "Out-out." Von Hoffman shouted and Chris walked out the door, banned to the hall for the remainder of the period.

The next day Chris told me that his penalty was to go to the library to write "I will not talk in class" 500 times, and that he could not return to class until the sentences were finished. All of which was just fine for Chris because he spent the next two weeks in the library writing fifty sentences a day and reading books most of the time. He told me that he was thinking of getting a transfer, but that since it was already the second semester it was probably too late. "Besides," he said, "Barry and John miss me. They say the class is boring and that there's nobody else to goof off with."

Von Hoffman's class was both hated and loved by the members of Chris's group, and through this contradiction we can see the manner in which they came to interpret their presence in it.

In the first place, the class was nothing but "work" to the students in it. . . . Students did what they were told to do, were provided little if any flexibility in controlling the formal basis of their work, and were given tasks the purpose of which quite often seemed more related to filling up the time than to the achievement of any specified instrumental end. Yet the personality of Von Hoffman as an authority figure was something students found incongruous as well. Here was an individual who was supposed to be "a boss" because of his age and experience, yet he seemed unable to carry out the imperatives of his position. In this sense, then, students found not only the work they did to be alienative, but found themselves estranged from the individual in authority who parceled out the work to carry out.

Given this context, they created their own knowledge system, permitting control over the dynamics within the classroom as well as the person who had authority in the classroom. This system of knowledge was based upon the mutuality of shared experience as perceived by students removed from meaningful work and from appropriate understanding of the nature of work they did. Thus, going to Von Hoffman's class became a game—one that proved to be somewhat entertaining—that Chris and his group played whenever they felt it appropriate. To the extent they controlled the game, its rules, its outcome, and understood the basis on which it was played, the class was somewhat enjoyable, and the perspective students created within it proved to be another constitutive element of their culture within the junior high school.

As with Don and his friends, Chris's group spent significant amounts of time actively comparing themselves to other students in the school. The process of and results from this comparative process constituted another dynamic in the creation of the group's distinctive belief system.

Picking on other students (usually "weirdos") occupied much of the group's time, not only outside but also within class. Sam was one boy who was the constant target of both Chris's group and

Don's. Sam was apt to be ridiculed in the lunch line, as he walked down the hall, in class, in virtually any place he went. Typically, Sam was teased for the clothes he wore, the food he ate, the motor cycle he could not fix—actually everything. Sam's typical response was to try to ignore these taunts and hope the perpetrators would tire and leave.

The group made it a practice of joking with girls with equal fervor. Usually, this was accepted with equanimity, but occasionally it was not and the good-natured joking then backfired. One day the group was in science class with nothing in particular to do (it was a day to "catch up" on assignments, meaning, for most, a time to sit around and talk). Sitting behind us was a girl named Kathy who wore braces on her teeth, as well as a cumbersome neck brace. I overheard one of her friends saying to her, "Did you ever fly on an airplane with that thing on [motioning to the brace]?"

"No, why?"

"Well, I could imagine that if you tried to go through the security gate, the metal brace would make the buzzer go off and you'd probably have to take your shirt off so they could see it was really a brace and not a bomb you were carrying."

Chris and John, who had been talking to Don, overheard the same conversation and turned around to Kathy and the girls with whom she had been talking.

"You couldn't get on anyway," Chris remarked, "they don't allow dogs to ride on airplanes."

"Or if they do they have to ride in the luggage compartment," John added.

"That's all right, there are plenty of dogs back there to keep you company."

"Yeah, especially if girls from this school are riding the plane," Don said from the front. "Kathy looks like an X-15 space pilot!"

"Why don't you boys turn around and mind your own business." one of the girls said.

"Yeah, buzz off, you creeps," another added.

John and Chris finally turned around but five minutes later Andy, one of the boys in the class, came over to John. "What'd you guys do to Kathy?"

"What do you mean what did we do?"

"Look," he said, pointing to the back of the room where Kathy had her head down on the desk, sobbing loudly. All her friends were around her trying to console her, telling her not to take it all so seriously.

"What's she bawling about?" John asked, unimpressed by all the dramatics.

"She says that she's tired of being picked on because of the way she looks," Andy said.

"She ought to," Chris said, looking into his microscope. "Hey, look at this worm here!"

All of this banter and ridiculing accentuated the minimal discussion among group members about classwork, grades, or intellectual pursuits. I knew that group members did well in class, and especially compared to Don's group, and I expected to hear the group mention classroom-related experiences more than they did. Yet they didn't and this puzzled me.

I explored this situation one day at lunch with Chris, Phil, John, and Barry.

"Barry, you told me a few weeks ago that you didn't like one of your classes because you didn't have any friends in there and that there was nothing to do. How important is it to have people to hang around with here in school?"

"Well, if you don't have anybody to be friends with, you get done and there is nothing to do because there is nobody to talk to. If you have somebody to talk to in class, even if it means getting in trouble, at least you have friends to pass the time with and to sit by in the lunch-room. If you don't have many friends, what are you going to do here except sit around and do nothing all day. Just being by yourself, sitting at lunch all by yourself every day, not being able to talk to anybody, it just wouldn't be any fun."

"So, you're saying that if you guys didn't hang out together that . . . "

"School would be a bore," John interjected.

Chris added, "That's really what this place is all about, you know the social bit. I mean, that's what I look forward to every day, the little dumb things we do, telling jokes, goofing off in Von Hoffman's class, catching up on the latest gossip, bumming money from you, Bob. By the way, got a dime for an ice cream?"

"Get lost, will you," I laughed. "How about grades, isn't that important? What if you had the choice between getting a D or F on a test and being with your friends in class or at lunch, which would be more important?"

"I wouldn't care," Chris answered immediately. He continued, "If you have friends you don't need that good of a report card and all that. You could have a 4.0 average and still not be able to talk to anybody, but you could have a zero average and have friends, good friends and that is more important, that's what I think."

To a large extent, it was. Most in the group had the internal motivation to do passing work in school. But such work was not important for group membership and thus was not a topic of conversation within the group. Classroom instruction pertained to individuals and was not a factor in social relations. The group reaffirmed this point time and time again.

The low level of student involvement in academic matters was reaffirmed even in school-based agendas that would seem to be of interest to students. This fact has been noted in the episode with the sign kit described earlier. After this, the student council lay dormant until late November (meetings were usually called by some member of the administration in order to settle one issue or another). The purpose for the November meeting was to pass out instructions to room representatives for taking orders for class and individual pictures. After Pall spent about ten minutes describing the procedures for taking orders on pictures, the meeting was open to discuss any issue of concern to the students. A few questions were raised about the use of the sign kit, but little interest seemed evident about it.

Little else related to student council affairs (or the lack of them) occurred until late in the winter when there was some talk about holding a school dance (only the second one of the year). There were preliminary plans to hire a band from outside the school at a cost of about $150, but those plans were in the process of being vetoed by Mr. Edwards because he felt the students should not spend that much money. The next actual student council meeting was in March and was called by Mr. Edwards in order to make some announcements to the council. We all waited a few moments but somebody called over the loudspeaker to announce that Edwards would be a few moments late. Tony decided to open up the floor for both old and new business. It turned out to be one of the few times when the council expressed any collective displeasure with what they had and had not been doing.

"Let's appoint a new dance committee," someone said immediately.

"Yeah, maybe we can get some decent dances at last."

"I think that the dances have been turned over to Mr. Pall now," Tony announced, looking cautiously at Mrs. Patterson in the back, "so maybe we can get some decent dances for once."

"How about a new committee?" the original spokesman reiterated.

"OK, let's have a vote," Tony said. "How many want a new committee? [two hands] How many don't ? [four hands] How many don't care? [the most hands] OK, we'll keep the same committee."

Another girl then raised her hand. "If we're going to keep the same dance committee, how about scheduling some noonies [informal dances held at lunchtime]?"

"The last time we asked Edwards, he said no," Tony replied.

"We asked Mr. Pall and he said it was OK," the girl responded.

"Yeah, except that everything has to go through Mr. Edwards."

"Typical," a girl replied.

"Figures," Chris added.

"How come we can't have one?" one of the cheerleaders asked.

Tony was put on the spot but he did not have the answers. "I don't know, he just won't go along with it. I've talked to him a couple of times and we just can't get anything going."

"What if we get up a petition," Chris offered.

"They won't accept it."

"Let's talk to Pall."

"He's out of town until Monday," Mrs. Patterson offered.

"So what, we don't have to have the dance until Monday." That sparked a small amount of laughter.

One of the cheerleaders had an idea. "Hey, what if we got a petition and had all of our parents sign it, then they'd really have trouble turning us down."

"You'll never get all the parents to sign it and they wouldn't listen to that either."

"Why not?"

"Because it has to be certified."

"Certified? What's that?"

"A lawyer has to sign it and say it was a real petition. If you can get a lawyer to certify it, then it's a real petition."

"Where'd you learn that, in history class?" someone from across the room asked.

A person in his history class replied, "No, he sleeps in there."

It was clear that students were displeased over what they saw to be the high-handed manner in which Edwards controlled the funds and decisions pertinent to the council. Yet it was also evident that their displeasure was readily displaced into the usual general apathy that characterized much of student life in school. Out of this apathy arose the bantering and joking that smoothed out the rough edges of the apathy and provided the students with some sense of control and direction. But this too wore off and frustration, intermittently connected with humor and resignation, all worked together to reveal the core of the students' internalization of Edwards controlling even the very funds that they raised for themselves in the annual magazine drive.

The meeting then continued.

"Tony, let's get this thing going before Mr. Edwards gets here," said Mrs. Patterson from the back of the room. Tony said that the dance committee would try again and asked if there was any other old business.

"No."

"Good, let's get out of here."

"No," said Tony, "that's all the old business. We still have the new business."

"Crap."

"Hurry up."

Tony went on. "OK, new business. You know those signs some of the schools have in front of their buildings, like Stonebrook Wildcats or Woodtown Red Devils? Well, some people think that we ought to have something like that in front of our school so people will know what school it is. Is there any discussion on that?"

"Yeah, I can just see it. Spencer Stallions. Big deal."

"Who wants a stallion?"

"Hey, I have an idea," said a girl in the back of the room. "How about putting a stuffed horse in front of the school. That would really be different."

"Yeah, Stonebrook has a wildcat in front of their school, how come we can't get a stuffed horse?"

"Come on you guys, get serious," remarked Tony impatiently, but to no avail.

"Sure, I can see a stuffed horse in this place; where would we put it?"

"In the cafeteria, it would fit the food."

Bill, one of Chris's friends, said bitterly, "This meeting sucks."

"Is that what it is?" Chris replied.

"Hey, I got another idea," suggested the girl who offered the idea of a stuffed horse in the first place, "How about a work horse, one of those really big ones you know."

"He'd have to be big all over," one of the football players replied.

"What do you mean?" asked the girl.

"Just big ALL over, ha, ha."

"Tough to take."

"Hey, that's what I'd expect coming from you, Bruce," the girl replied as her face turned slightly red.

"Come on, you guys, you're out of order; you're all out of order." Tony was getting impatient.

"Order? Yeah, I'll take a Big Mac."

"Two fries and a vanilla shake—to go."

Tony kept on trying. "Any more discussion?"

"Yeah, how much is all this going to cost?"

"I don't know," Tony replied, "I'll have to find out."

"How can we vote if we don't know how much it's going to cost?"

"Yeah, where's all the money going to come from?"

"Where do you think?" Chris said out loud.

"Never mind, I know," the girl replied, slouching down in her seat.

Tony continued his attempts to keep the conversation moving. "We have over one thousand dollars in the students treasury and Mrs. Patterson said we're supposed to leave something for the school."

"La-de-dah."

"I hate these meetings," shouted a ninth-grade boy. "Three years of sitting in these stupid things and it's always the same old . . . "

"Shit."

"Hey, quiet you guys," called out a boy near the door. "Here comes Edwards."

Mr. Edwards walked in and said that he had a few announcements. First, he had been talking with a representative from a copy machine company who wanted to place a copy machine in the library. The student body would derive $30 a month in rental fees, so Edwards said that he had accepted the machine on behalf of the student council and asked if there were any objections. There were none. Next he announced that he had arranged with a scrap paper company to place a large container in the rear of the school, and that there would be an all-school paper drive the last week of the month, proceeds going to the girls' athletic program. He asked if there were any objections to that and there were not. With that he left. Mrs. Patterson remained.

As soon as he walked out of the door one of the cheerleaders raised her hand. "New question," she said. "Why can't we use some of this money to buy trash containers and picnic benches so we can eat out on the patio when the weather's nice?"

"They'll get ripped off at night," a student responded.

"Chain them down, they do that in all the parks."

"Listen guys," Tony said with a sigh. "I've already gone through that, too. Mr. Edwards doesn't think that would be a good idea. He doesn't think the kids would use the trash cans and there would be paper lying all over the patio."

"How does he know; he hasn't tried it yet."

"He doesn't trust us, that's all."

"Why can't we have a chance?"

"Yeah, they bring in that xerox machine on a trial basis like it's a big deal, but they never ask us until after they've decided. Why can't we have picnic tables on a trial basis?"

"I've already told you, man," Tony replied, "I talked to him on this and it's not going anywhere. Some of the teachers have asked him too and he won't go along with it."

"I hate this place and I hate these meetings," the same boy reiterated. "I can't wait to get out of here this year."

"Lucky."

"Let's go in there again and talk to him about it."

"Look," Tony reiterated, "you could send 30–40 kids to work him over and it wouldn't convince him."

"Wanna bet."

By this time the period was over. Tony announced that they would have two meetings the following week, one on dances and one on "nooners" (they were never held). As we walked out of the room Chris complained how nothing ever got done in the meetings. Bill suggested that they put a statue of a horse on the front of the school, only they make it a dead horse.

The council never resolved the issue of the horse, the picnic tables never got past Edwards, and the council only met one more time that year. And although there was more grumbling about the absence of noonies and picnic tables, most students soon forgot about it and went back to hanging out, making jokes and bugging Von Hoffman. Expecting the students to be indignant, I found that they were, but got over it and soon were more blasé about the situation than anything else. At first I was bothered by such a lack of concern, but I came to understand it as I realized that control over issues such as a horse on the front lawn or picnic tables did not matter to most of the students anyway because few of them shared much of an institutional loyalty. After all, the schooling process rarely placed much credence on the intrinsic nature of student labor, so student presence in the school was based more on the exchange-value of their labor than the value of the work. Certainly picnic tables and the like had little intrinsic significance to students because they knew that Edwards would ultimately control their use. As far as the effort placed into raising the money, that money was raised almost totally by the seventh-graders, who sold magazines for Led Zeppelin posters and free ice cream cones as prizes. The eighth- and ninth-graders had long since seen through the shallowness of such prizes, and expended little effort over selling subscriptions. That maybe already they knew that they would have little proprietary rights over the fruit of their own labor which existed outside the school was, it seems, a very telling lesson they had learned.

Eighth Grade

Chris's and Marty's favorite class this year was history. The class seemed relatively enjoyable for them, as usually there was considerable discussion on issues such as the death penalty, world famine, and race relations. With few exceptions, however, Chris and his circle of colleagues continued to place more emphasis on the creation and sustaining of their own system of meaning in the class than they did on the discussion of salient issues. For example, for one week in the course, the class had been working on a unit on worldwide hunger. One day the discussion centered on the obligation of the developed nations to help out those who were less fortunate. As always, Chris and Marty were in the thick of it with their witticisms. After taking roll and dispensing with the preliminary formalities, the teacher, Mrs. Paul, began the discussion. "All right, class, let me have your opinions on the obligation that we as citizens of a wealthy country have to help those less fortunate than we."

"Let them starve." Tom laughed.

"Right on," commented Linda, "we've worked hard for what we have so why can't everyone else?"

"Linda," Chris exclaimed in surprise, "Where's your charity, your sense of concern for your fellow man?"

"Shut up, will you, Chris," Linda retorted.

Sally raised her hand and volunteered that "the people in India all had a chance to come here at one time; they knew about this place; why didn't they come?"

Chris added a very uncharacteristic comment, "The only reason that all the blacks came here was that they were strong and stupid."

Melvin, the only black in the class, did not like it either. "I'll get the Panthers after you," he said half jokingly, but obviously upset as well. "Besides," he went on, "blacks weren't dumb; it was a black that invented the cotton gin and a white guy stole it away from him."

A girl commented that all the people in India deserved to starve when they had all those cows around but still did not eat them.

"Yeah, but cows are sacred in India," argued a girl.

"If you were starving and a cow walked in front of you, you'd eat it, wouldn't you?"

"Would you eat an eagle?" Chris asked.

"An eagle! What's that got to do with it?"

"Well, the eagle is sacred to us, isn't it? Religions teach you certain things and that's why the people of India act the way they do. Our family is Catholic and there used to be this thing about eating meat on Fridays so that if you did eat meat you felt real bad inside."

"I didn't know you were Catholic," Marty said across the room to Chris. "What do you do, eat Romans?" That comment brought loud ripples of laughter from across the room. Mrs. Paul attempted to keep the conversation going, but by this time the humor and plays on words had become contagious and things were deteriorating. In my subsequent discussions with Mrs.

Paul, she said that she knew better than to expect more, but still was frustrated when students such as Chris, "good students" (as she said), did not take the class seriously but instead "make light of everything." I could see how that could be frustrating, but on the other hand those such as Chris and John had learned to depend upon their group-generated behaviors to make sense of their mostly subservient role within the school. The fact that Mrs. Paul's class was one of the few classes in which student dialogue on academic issues was actually encouraged was not an easy point for most students to recognize. Daily attendance in classes such as Richards's and Von Hoffman's had a cumulative and dulling effect, almost overpowering those few instances where reified knowledge was somewhat de-emphasized. Chris's group agenda setting and Mrs. Paul's frustration were clear indications that the segmentation of knowledge as it existed at Spencer was so pervasive that individual efforts by a few teachers were simply swallowed by the cultural process created by students as they interacted in the material world of the school.

The new president of the student council had been elected at the end of seventh grade; new room representatives had been elected as well and Chris had been elected to represent first period PE. After the first meeting of the year he told me, "You know, those meetings are the same old shit over and over again. Just like where we left off last year. Nothing happens, just a complete waste of time."

The next student council meeting was in October. This meeting, like all others, was called by the administration specifically to (a) elect two representatives to go to a leadership conference sponsored by the Red Cross, (b) to ask the student council to authorize spending $50 for the school-wide openhouse to be spent that week. The tone of the meeting was not all that different either, except that now I realized that the dynamics of student council meetings were little different than those in most classrooms. That is, there existed an obvious underlife continuing on and running both parallel and in opposition to the formal agenda of the meeting. Again, the underlife was illustrative of the separate culture that students created within the organizational context of the meeting.

Patterson opened the meeting, explained the leadership conference, and then turned the meeting over to Steve, the president.

"OK, who do you guys want to have go to this leadership conference?"

"Who wants to go?"

"Big deal."

"Are you going to Thespians tonight?" (Chris, overheard talking to a ninth-grade girl.)

"Yes, are you?"

"Let's send Yates [the school brain who had almost been elected secretary of the student council last year as a joke]."

"Send Yates!"

"Did you hear that Marie and Jimmie broke up?" (Overheard behind where I was sitting.)

"Yes, I couldn't believe it. Is she here today?"

"I don't know, I haven't seen her yet."

"We want Yates to go."

"How embarrassing."

"Why not, he'd like to go, then one of us won't have to go."

Patterson stepped in front of the group with the letter from the Red Cross in her hand. "The letter encourages you to send people who are in leadership positions in student government. Now, that is the intent of the letter and, of course, if you want to violate the intent, that's up to you."

"I hear they might not do the play they had been thinking of for the Interim." (Overheard between Chris and the girl he had been talking to.)

"Why not?"

"Not enough people and the wrong kind of people for the parts."

"What are they going to do?"

"I'm not sure. I heard Calamity Jane."

"Who broke it off?" (The girl behind me continued to talk about Jimmie and Marie.)

"Marie; Jimmie was acting like an ass and she just grew tired of it."

"I'm glad. I never liked him that much myself; thinks he's a super stud."

They then voted on who would go to the leadership conference. Yates came in third. Steve, the student body president, and one of the cheerleaders were chosen to go.

"New business?" Steve asked.

"I've got a super idea," queried a ninth-grade girl. "Why don't we have a slave auction like the high school does? We could auction off people to do a certain thing and then give the money for some cause or something."

"Hey that sounds like a super idea," was a response, and the excitement built.

"Yeah, why not, we could auction off Yates."

"Better yet," said one of the football players, "we could auction off Janson [a well-endowed ninth-grade girl of 'questionable' reputation]."

"For sure, I'll go for that." This was followed by general laughter and conversation among a group of boys sitting together.

"Come on, you guys, get serious," said the girl who brought up the idea of an auction.

"We are," one of the boys replied laughing, making a panting noise.

Steve tried to get the group on target again, "Well, I'll talk to Mr. Edwards about it," he said, pausing to think for a moment. "But I don't think he'll let us do it."

"Why not?" asked the girl.

"Cause he just won't."

The girl behind me leaned over toward her friend. "Fuck him," she said, and then continued her conversation. "If we don't see Marie today, let's call her after school . . ."

I had talked to Chris during the two years about his feelings regarding the student government. In the spring of the seventh grade, I asked for his thoughts after a year as a room representative in the student council. He told me: "I don't think it has really done as much as it should do but even if we do get together there's not that much we can do without having some kind of trouble from the administration. Like with that dance thing, it really worked out crummy because Edwards would only give us thirty-five dollars to hire a band so what are you going to do? They say you can have a live band and everyone gets all excited, like we have a real opportunity to do all this but then he says, 'Oh, wait a second, I forgot to tell you, you can hire a live band but you only have thirty-five dollars to do it with . . . ' We have money we could do things with but we just can't do it."

The next year, near the end of the eighth grade, he was equally as displeased. Chris had mentioned throughout the year that he was going to run for student council president in order to rectify some of those issues. I asked him what he would do if he were elected. His reply was that his main goal should be to keep the administration from controlling the student council. After this conversation I thought Chris was all fired up to run for office. Yet I had overlooked his comments that he did not know what he would do if he had to confront Edwards on some major issue, and that there was probably little he could do. I also had forgotten that most students really did not care that much about the student council and that there would be little support from Chris's peers for such a confrontation. When petitions were being circulated for the student council president, I felt sure I would see one bearing his name. The deadline passed: no petition.

The next day I saw Chris in PE class. I walked up to him, obviously a little irritated (but more importantly, disappointed) that he had not run. "Damn it, Chris," I said, "from all that talk a few weeks ago, I thought for sure you were going to run for student council president. What happened?"

"Yeah, Chris," John said jokingly, "we need some LEADERSHIP."

Don stopped bouncing the basketball for a moment. "Mr. President," he said, turning to Chris, "I vote for a vending machine for joints."

"I chickened out," Chris replied to my original question while trying not to be too serious amid all the joking. "I guess I figured that if I had been elected and said what I said I would, I'd be kicked out of school." He grabbed the ball from

Don, went for a lay up (missed) and the three of them took a few shots as if the student council was the furthest topic from their minds.

It's useful here to pick up on the activities of some people who have "disappeared" from our story this year, that is, individuals who were close friends for most of the seventh grade but who became involved in different activities and interests during the eighth grade. I'm talking of John, Barry, and Dave (from Don's group) in particular. To discover what happened to them in the eighth grade, we enter, if only for a brief time, the "athletic group."

When I first began eating lunch with this group, early in the eighth grade, most of them were involved in eighth-grade football. About a month into the season one common understanding, a dislike of the coach, Mr. Jerald, served as a common point of discussion. The team members constantly complained about him and blamed him for the team's first two losses.

"Did you hear what he said at practice yesterday?" Dave said to Harry, "What a dumb thing to say."

"What did he say?" I asked.

"Called us 'shitheads,'" Dave replied. "He said we were all shitty players and he didn't care how we played because he was getting paid to coach so it didn't make any difference to him whether we won or lost."

The next week they were actually able to say something funny about the coach and at the same time knock Phil, who was Chris's and John's old friend. As Rick told the story, one of the players had dropped a pass and Jerald sent Phil in at end to replace him. Rick said he was standing along the sidelines and said to a teammate, "He's sending Palmer [Phil] in, the coach really is a dumb bastard." The coach, overhearing this, turned around and wanted to know who had said that; of course, nobody owned up. But, on the way to losing 18–0, Rick and John said they had a good time on the sidelines laughing about calling Jerald dumb.

Athletics, then, were not much different from classes and the student council. Students continually opposed the required activities when and where they could, given their understanding of what they opposed. In class, the athletic group was not much different from other groups of students with regard to their posture toward classes. Most did what they were told and got by, some better than others. I once asked Wally how he did in his classes, since I had never heard him (or anyone else at the table for that matter) discuss grades.

"I do all right," was his reply.

"What's that mean?"

"It means I get by, you know, screw up once in a while but I'm not going to get uptight about it." I asked him what he thought he was getting out of Spencer in terms of things that interested him, and his only reply was that he liked to be there with Rick and Dale and Chuck and John, that they had a good time together "in a lot of ways" and "what else is there? I got a B on my English essay yesterday, that's not slackin' now, is it?" Wally showed me the essay, titled "The Funniest Thing I Ever Saw."

Last night we went to play basketball at the barn. When we got there somebody lit up a joint. There was [red penciled with a "were"] two cows in the barn at the time, one mother and one baby. They kept watching us toke away on it, so we were feelin' good and we gave the cows nose hits. They got stoned, so did we.

We started playing basketball and we played for a while. Then both cows started mooing and we went to see what the matter was. The cow had stuck his head in the door. It yelled and yelled, and we got him out and he was chasing us around the barn. We ran down to the store to get some munchies, then we went to Chuck's house to play poker.

"That's really great, Wally," I said.

Toward the end of basketball season, I heard increasing discussion abut the drinking parties and the smoking of pot over the week-ends. Not everyone was equally involved (I rarely heard Dave or John mention much about their participation) but it seemed, nevertheless, that at least Wally, Dale, and Clint discussed cases of beer

and "nickel bags" with increasing regularity. Clint said it did not affect his game performance because he usually tipped a few only on weekends. Their involvement and interest in drinking and marijuana appeared small compared to that of Don and some of his group.

Barry disappeared from my observations during the eighth grade, despite my attempts to keep track of him by keeping track of Chris, John, Bill, and the others with whom he associated in the seventh grade. His lunch schedule was altered a few times, so I don't think I ate lunch with him more than once during the entire eighth grade. He tried to hang around with the athletes but, because he did not have the skills to play, he never fitted in. The last I heard of him was during basketball season, when I saw him at a basketball game as the scoreboard operator.

SUMMARY AND CONCLUSIONS

Chris's group, consisting of Chris, John, and Barry and, to some degree, Phil (in the seventh grade) and Marty (in the eighth grade) was somewhat "straighter" than Don's group. Yet like those in Don's group, the members saw themselves in a relatively nondescript fashion—as a group trying to fit into the social fabric of the school. Being with friends, constructing humorous incidents in class, bugging the teachers, some minimal involvement in student government all constituted the daily routine of Chris and his group throughout the seventh and eighth grade.

The everyday behavior of Chris's group is important because it illustrates, although in a qualitatively different fashion, the process whereby social groups give rise to regenerative knowledge through cultural processes present among junior high school adolescents. The cultural processes evident with Chris and his friends reveal that, even among the more "mainstream" students, resistance to the regularities of organized school life are common and that oppositional forms to formal organizational procedures arise. Such opposition can and often does develop as a contradiction to school knowledge. The complexities of this process become more clear as we re-examine the nature of student involvement in school government, the purpose of humor and joking relations for students, the import of these conditions for student cultures, and the manner by which these cultural processes contribute to the reproduction of the larger social structure in which they occur.

Toward the end of my second year at Spencer, a colleague working in the same project attended a meeting of a Jefferson citizens' advisory board which served as a liaison between the school board and the larger community. The next day he told me that the vice-president of the student council at Harold Spencer had attended the meeting and complained quite vociferously about how Edwards controlled the students' money in the school and how he constantly vetoed their every request. The board discussed this with her for about twenty minutes and a district official in attendance promised he would look into the situation. To the best of my knowledge, the subject was not raised again.

I was somewhat puzzled by this student's willingness to express herself so openly before such high-ranking officials, especially since this rarely was done within the school itself. I questioned her at lunch one day as to what had prompted her to raise the issue and what (if anything) she knew about any outcome. She and the friends sitting with her laughed at my question. The whole incident, they told me, came about as the result of "a bet" which her friends had made as to whether or not she had the "guts" to go before the advisory board and express her views. Because the father of one of the boys sitting at the lunch table happened to be the president of the advisory board, the whole incident was viewed with irony in that the girl indicated how the father pulled out various regulation books to support the stand on why students could not have certain activities. In the final analysis, the confrontation, while connected with complaints that the students had articulated over the past few years, was not motivated by any

seething resentment on the part of the student council vice-president. Rather, it was seen as a joke and in that sense represented another form students created based upon their interpretation of their interaction in the material world of Harold Spencer.

I suppose that I placed much more faith in the involvement of students in student governance than could reasonably be expected. First, one could see that school officials rarely were facilitative in their attempts to get students involved in a viable policy forum. Given the circumstances, then, I had to agree with Chris in his decision not to run for student body president. What was there he could do? Teachers had confronted Edwards on his dominance of student council activities and funds and to no avail, and it was certainly not reasonable to expect that Chris or any other student, for that matter, would meet with any greater degree of success.

Yet how involved could the majority of students ever be in a forum such as the student council? The creation and operation of such a body assumes that the topics to be dealt with are of high saliency to the students in the school; it was obvious that most were not. Few students cared about putting a stallion on the front lawn and only the cheerleaders (supported by the athletes) pushed for buying the sign machine. Even though school dances were discussed and summarily vetoed by Edwards, it was only a small group (again the cheerleaders and some of their friends) who ever pushed for dances, "nooners," or picnic tables on the outside patio. Most did not care one way or the other. When Chris told Karen and Linda in art class that Edwards would not permit much money to be spent on dances or parties the girls appeared ambivalent and reacted more strongly to the fact that Tony (the student council president) "kissed like a fish" than the fact that the money was being expropriated from them.

Yet the minimal involvement of students in school governance can be examined as still another organizational regularity based upon reified knowledge. The governance of school activities, indeed the definition of who has power over what, is preselected within defined parameters through tradition, and attempts at maintenance are made by those in control. Issues that do emerge or are allowed to emerge in student government are not salient to the vast majority of students because such issues have more to do with the ongoing history of the school organization (such as the stallion) or the image of the school to outside agents (the sign machine, sending a representative to the leadership seminar), and these are not of particular concern to most students because, since they pass through the school in three years, they have little stake in institutional permanency or image. Still, the fact that issues and processes of school governance are predefined, absolute, and treated as "real" indicates that reified knowledge can and does occur through more forms than those pertaining to the academic instruction of students. Rather, such knowledge is an integral part of a school organization that reproduces a specific system of social relations in a hierarchically oriented society, predicated on unequal access to control of the means of production. This is more than Marxian rhetoric, for limited access to the means of production signifies, in the case of the production of political power, that student government is little more than a reconfirmation and re-creation of an ideology that political decision-making is done within the limits that others have defined as the scope of legitimate political action. This ideology is important, pervasive, and dominant as the young become adults.

This is why such minimal control by students is so critical even though the students themselves appear largely unconcerned about it. It points to the manner in which activities that play such a small role in the lives of most students in schools come to take on such a great importance. We need ask ourselves what it is that is being learned here, and how students are being taught about political decision-making in an ostensibly democratic society. For it seems they are learning at minimum that there is no useful role for them, that their involvement has been established and regulated, and thus that their apathy is a reasonable accommodation. Consequently, the fact that students seem so unconcerned (and that "no harm" has come to them) is, in fact, the wrong observation. In a democratic society, depending as it must on the active participation of its citizens, we should be concerned that the students are so resigned to this condition.

In the absence of critical involvement in school-based knowledge, the play on words during student council meetings, the jokes about the Spencer stallion, and other forms through which cultural processes work make more "sense," given the organizational and institutional context within which they are created. The telling of stories and jokes was a trademark of Chris's group and provided them with an identity unavailable to other coalitions of students. There was no doubt that Chris, Marty and, later, Pete were very good at telling jokes. Communicating these jokes served three purposes in so far as a group identity was concerned. First, it meant that members had to have access to new and funny jokes, a point about which there was some pride. Second, joke telling required a certain dramatic skill and there was no doubt that Chris and Pete had the skills to tell good jokes. Finally, and perhaps most importantly, the telling of certain types of jokes symbolized an understanding of group membership—who would understand certain types of jokes and who would counter with equally complex and sometimes obscure lines. I remember once, in math class, that Chris told a joke to Ralph, a rather immature student, who did not even understand the joke. Later, in history class, Chris told the same joke to Pete and Marty who doubled up in laughter and Marty immediately countered with an Italian joke. Such jokes required a certain level of sophistication and not everyone could counter with jokes equally as sophisticated and novel. Thus most joke telling usually was carried on within the group or between groups of equal understanding.

Wisecracking in class, while it served many purposes. . . . was a demonstration of superior perceptiveness or creativity, and a creative wisecracker was one who had a higher social standing among his peers. Ordering a "Big Mac" in the student council meeting, Marty asking Chris if he "ate Romans," Chris asking Mr. Von Hoffman what the date was while Von Hoffman was standing above him in a state of rage—all these served to demonstrate the wit and craftiness of the perpetrator. I clearly remember the awe in which Wally, one of the athletes, was held in the eighth grade as a result of his wisecracking in English class. The class had been studying poetry and their assignment was to bring a short poem to class, read it, and tell what type of poem it was. That day, poems by Wordsworth, Keats, Browning—all the "classic" poets—were read before the class. Then it was Wally's turn.

"What type of poem are you going to read, Wally?" asked Mr. Vincent.

"Uh, this will be blank, uh, blank, whatever it is."

"Blank verse, Wally," Vincent filled in.

"Yeah, that's what it will be."

"OK, we're ready, you may go ahead."

Wally stood before the class, smiled slightly, and then rattled off in perfect style: "Two all beef patties, special sauce, lettuce, cheese, pickles, onions, on a sesame seed bun." He then sat down amid roars of laughter.

"What was THAT?" asked Vincent.

"My poem," replied Wally, "in blank verse."

"You've got to be kidding," replied Vincent, "how can that be a poem?"

"I don't know," Wally said in a straight voice. "All I know is that McDonald's had this contest and if you went in and could say the ingredients of a 'Big Mac' without making a mistake, you got a free shake. I did it and the guy said it was poetic." The whole eighth grade talked about Wally for the next two days.

All in all, then, humor and its uses served to establish and reinforce social identities, demonstrate social acceptance, and to provide a means of boundary maintenance between and within the social group. Rather than just being "something that junior high kids do," it became something they did for a specific purpose although it was not always an immediately recognizable purpose. Perhaps Chris summarized it best when I asked him what held him, Mike, Marty, and Pete together during the eighth grade. Speaking of Mike, he said: "We hang around together because we can goof off together and if I say something funny, he thinks it's funny; if he says something funny, I think it's funny. It's mostly just the relationship between a bunch of guys goofing off and having a good time."

In humor, jokes, and joking relationships we see the very forms that are the basis of regenerative knowledge. These cultural forms are extended by students against the school's control of time, space, and organizational outcome. In the process, students appropriate for themselves a commodity over which they have full control—the ability to joke, interject, and to interpret as humorous the most mundane of activities. The importance of humor and its dimensions lies in the fact that it is the group out of which humor is generated and defined that decides what is funny and what is not, what can be taken to be irreverent and what is sacred. In this respect, Don, Roger, and Gary decided when throwing "jello" was funny and when it was not; and Chris and his friends gained a sense of pride, almost as if they possessed a secret code, because teachers thought that rough-housing was violent when in fact it often symbolized intimacy. That only participants, out of context and through communication and interpretation, could define such incidents and build upon them is critical, and anchors firmly what often appears to be the "squirliness" of junior high social life.

So, with Chris and his group we see, as with Don and his friends, existence of opposition and resistance to the pervasive nature of reified knowledge and the forms in which it is transmitted in the school. This resistance occurs in part because of the exclusion of students from crucial decisions about the nature of their labor, from their failure to see their labor as much beyond labor power that has exchange-value, and from their lack of understanding about the very "value" of the commodity that they had produced through their labor. Clearly, even for those students who did moderately well in school, the demands of the institution were relatively minimal and sporadic. Time was something that students "filled in" because the school could not fill much of it in and, even when it did, the value of the requirement was questionable to the students. That Wally could get a "B" for his story abut the cows then symbolized both the ritualistic manner in which students viewed work and the limits to which the institution would go to accept anything for the sake of legitimizing the demands it made of the students and having students accept those demands.

In schools, then, that are the backbone of formal education in modern capitalistic societies, the knowledge of youth—that interpretive, contextually generated knowledge of community or subcommunities—is built up through social forms that are largely unrecognized, indeed even separate, from those official channels through which reified knowledge is transmitted. There is then a disjuncture—a chasm—between the assumptions of reified and regenerative knowledge systems, and it is the extent of the interface between the two that is particularly crucial. This is so because it is the content of regenerative knowledge (as well as its structure), as it increasingly contradicts the content of reified knowledge, that serves as a discriminator between and among students and school knowledge, thereby "allocating" students ultimately to particular organizational patterns. Note that I am talking about the cultural process of knowledge generation, and not the determining factors of school structure in and of itself. The degree of disjuncture is well illustrated in the case of John and Chris. In Chris's instance, his father spent considerable time discussing politics and "philosophy" with him; with John, his father was a teacher and one could assume certain predispositions there. These factors contributed to a closer integration between the knowledge system demanded by the school and the content of the regenerative knowledge that grew out of their interpretive setting. Thus the activities of John and Chris, unlike many of those of Don and his friends, skirted around and teased the predominance of reified knowledge but did not reject or transcend it. Chris and his friends resisted to a considerable extent but, in the end, adapted to the imperatives of reified knowledge. Even Chris, in his opposition to Von Hoffman's inane procedures, realized the ultimate importance of "knowing" the way the school required knowing and the proper social relations to "know" in that way.

In the case of Don and his friends, that opposition took on a more "anti-school" form, despite the adequate grades that group members received. Certainly Don and Steve "got by," but it was obvious to me that both were finding it more difficult to make that accommodation in eighth grade than they had in seventh. To them, the reconciliation between the reified knowledge of the school and the regenerative knowledge they created as they interpreted their existence in school was more difficult because they had little or no additional sources (parents or families) to make them believe that the reified knowledge and its attendant behavioral dispositions had any value to them. Thus their own participation in the school became increasingly self-determined, which in turn alienated them even more from whatever value there might be in accepting the premises of school knowledge.

We begin now to get the glimmerings of how schools contribute to the reproduction of social differentiation in a class-based society. This happens not so much in a deterministic, "knee-jerk" fashion but rather through the constitutive process by which knowledge is produced, used, and modified, and the nexus of knowledge systems. It is, again, a materialist process—a process that occurs as actors create their history in a material world, in ongoing systems of labor and exchange. It is also in a materialist world that students come to form their understandings and interpretations of these forces of production and their place in those forces. . . .

Education in a Multicultural Society: Our Future's Greatest Challenge

Lisa Delpit

In any discussion of education and culture, it is important to remember that children are individuals and cannot be made to fit into any preconceived mold of how they are "supposed" to act. The question is not necessarily how to create the perfect "culturally matched" learning situation for each ethnic group, but rather how to recognize when there is a problem for a particular child and how to seek its cause in the most broadly conceived fashion. Knowledge about culture is but one tool that educators may make use of when devising solutions for a school's difficulty in educating diverse children.

THE CULTURAL CLASH BETWEEN STUDENTS AND SCHOOL

The clash between school culture and home culture is actualized in at least two ways. When a significant difference exists between the students' culture and the school's culture, teachers can easily misread students' aptitudes, intent, or abilities as a result of the difference in styles of language use and interactional patterns. Secondly, when such cultural differences exist, teachers may utilize styles of instruction and/or discipline that are at odds with community norms. A few examples: A twelve-year-old friend tells me that there are three kinds of teachers in his middle school: the black teachers, none of whom are afraid of black kids; the white teachers, a few of whom are not afraid of black kids; and the largest group of white teachers, who are *all* afraid of black kids. It is this last group that, according to my young informant, consistently has the most difficulty with teaching and whose students have the most difficulty with learning.

I would like to suggest that some of the problems may certainly be as this young man relates. Yet, from my work with teachers in many settings, I have come to believe that a major portion of the problem may also rest with how these three groups of teachers interact and use language with their students. These differences in discourse styles relate to certain ethnic and class groups. For instance, many African-American teachers are likely to give directives to a group of unruly students in a direct and explicit fashion, for example, "I don't want to hear it. Sit down, be quiet, and finish your work NOW!" Not only is this directive explicit, but with it the teacher also displays a high degree of personal power in the classroom. By contrast, many middle-class European-American teachers are likely to say something like,

---

"Would you like to sit down now and finish your paper?", making use of an indirect command and downplaying the display of power. Partly because the first instance is likely to be more like the statements many African-American children hear at home, and partly because the second statement sounds to many of these youngsters like the words of someone who is fearful (and thus less deserving of respect), African-American children are more likely to obey the first explicit directive and ignore the second implied directive.

The discussion of this issue is complex, but, in brief, many of the difficulties teachers encounter with children who are different in background from themselves are related to this underlying attitudinal difference in the appropriate display of explicitness and personal power in the classroom.

If teachers are to teach effectively, recognition of the importance of student perception of teacher intent is critical. Problems arising from culturally different interactional styles seem to disproportionately affect African-American boys, who, as a result of cultural influences, exhibit a high degree of physicality and desire for interaction. This can be expressed both positively and negatively, as hugging and other shows of affection or as hitting and other displays of displeasure. Either expression is likely to receive negative sanction in the classroom setting.

Researcher Harry Morgan documents in a 1990 study what most of us who have worked with African-American children have learned intuitively: that African-American children, more than white, and boys more than girls, initiate interactions with peers in the classroom in performing assigned tasks. Morgan concludes that a classroom that allows for greater movement and interaction will better facilitate the learning and social styles of African-American boys, while one that disallows such activity will unduly penalize them. This, I believe, is one of the reasons that there recently has been such a movement toward developing schools specifically for African-American males. Black boys *are* unduly penalized in our regular classrooms. They *are* disproportionately assigned to special education. They do not have to be, and would not be, if our teachers were taught how to redesign classrooms so that the styles of African-American boys are accommodated.

I would like to share with you an example of a student's ability being misread as a result of a mismatch between the student's and teacher's cultural use of language. Second-grader Marti was reading a story she had written that began, "Once upon a time, there was an old lady, and this old lady ain't had no sense." The teacher interrupted her, "Marti, that sounds like the beginning of a wonderful story, but could you tell me how you would say it in Standard English?" Marti put her hand on her hip, raised her voice and said, "But this old lady ain't had *no* sense!" Marti's teacher probably did not understand that the child was actually exhibiting a very sophisticated sense of language. Although she clearly knew the Standard English form, she chose a so-called nonstandard form for emphasis, just as world-class writers Charles Chesnutt, Alice Walker, Paul Laurence Dunbar, and Zora Neale Hurston have done for years. Of course, there is no standardized test presently on the market that can discern that level of sophistication. Marti's misuse of Standard English would simply be assessed as a "mistake." Thus, differences in cultural language patterns make inappropriate assessments commonplace.

Another example of assessment difficulties arising from differences in culture can be found in the Latino community. Frequently, Latino girls find it difficult to speak out or exhibit academic prowess in a gender-mixed setting. They will often defer to boys, displaying their knowledge only when in the company of other girls. Most teachers, unaware of this tendency, are likely to insist that all groups be gender-mixed, thus depressing the exhibition of ability by the Latino girls in the class.

A final example involves Native Americans. In many Native American communities there is a prohibition against speaking for someone else. So strong is this prohibition that to the question, "Does your son like moose?", an adult Native American man responded to what should have been asked instead: "*I like moose.*" The consequence of this cultural interactional pattern may have contributed to the findings in Charlotte Basham's study of a group of Native American college students' writing. The students appeared unable to write summaries and, even when explicitly told not to, continued to write their opinions of various works rather than summaries of the authors' words. Basham concludes that the prohibition against speaking for others may have caused these students considerable difficulty in trying to capture in their own words the ideas of another. Because they had been taught to always speak for themselves, they found doing so much more comfortable and culturally compatible.

STEREOTYPING

There is a widespread belief that Asian-American children are the "perfect" students, that they will do well regardless of the academic setting in which they are placed. This stereotype has led to a negative backlash in which the academic needs of the majority of Asian-American students are overlooked. I recall one five-year-old Asian-American girl in a Montessori kindergarten class. Cathy was dutifully going about the task assigned to her, that of placing a number of objects next to various numerals printed on a cloth. She appeared to be thoroughly engaged, attending totally to the task at hand, and never disturbing anyone near her. Meanwhile, the teacher's attention was devoted to the children who demanded her presence in one form or another or to those she believed would have difficulty with the task assigned them. Small, quiet Cathy fit neither category. At the end of work time, no one had come to see what Cathy had done, and Cathy neatly put away her work. Her behavior and attention to task had been exemplary. The only problem was that at the end of the session no numeral had the correct number of objects next to it. The teacher later told me that Cathy, like Asian-American students she had taught previously, was one of the best students in the class.

Yet, in this case, a child's culturally influenced, nondisruptive classroom behavior, along with the teacher's stereotype of "good Asian students," led to her not receiving appropriate instruction.

Another example of stereotyping involved African-American girls. Research has been conducted in classroom settings which shows that African-American girls are rewarded for nurturing behavior while white girls are rewarded for academic behavior. Though it is likely true that many African-American girls are excellent nurturers, having played with or helped to care for younger siblings or cousins, they are penalized by the nurturing "mammy" stereotype when they are not given the same encouragement as white girls toward academic endeavors.

Another example of stereotyping concerns Native American children. Many researchers and classroom teachers have described the "nonverbal Indian child." What is often missed in these descriptions is that these children are as verbal and eager to share their knowledge as any others, but they need appropriate contexts—such as small groups—in which to talk. When asked inappropriate questions or called on to talk before the entire class, many Native American children will refuse to answer, or will answer in as few words as possible. Thus, teachers sometimes refrain from calling on Native American students to avoid causing them discomfort, and these children subsequently miss the opportunity to discuss or display their knowledge of the subject matter.

A primary source of stereotyping is often the teacher education program itself. It is in these programs that teachers learn that poor students and students of color should be expected to achieve less than their "mainstream" counterparts.

CHILD-DEFICIT ASSUMPTIONS THAT LEAD TO TEACHING LESS INSTEAD OF MORE

We say we believe that all children can learn, but few of us really believe it. Teacher education usually focuses on research that links failure and socioeconomic status, failure and cultural difference, and failure and single-parent households. It is hard to believe that these children can possibly be successful after their teachers have been so thoroughly exposed to so much negative indoctrination. When teachers receive that kind of education, there is a tendency to assume deficits in students rather than to locate and teach to strengths. To counter this tendency, educators must have knowledge of children's lives outside of school so as to recognize their strengths.

One of my former students is a case in point. Howard was in first grade when everyone thought that he would need to be placed in special education classes. Among his other academic problems, he seemed totally unable to do even the simplest mathematics worksheets. During the unit on money, determining the value of nickels and dimes seemed hopelessly beyond him. I agreed with the general assessment of him until I got to know something about his life outside of school. Howard was seven years old. He had a younger sister who was four and afflicted with cerebral palsy. His mother was suffering from a drug problem and was unable to adequately care for the children, so Howard was the main caretaker in the family. Each morning, he would get his sister up, dressed, and off to school. He also did the family laundry and much of the shopping. To do both those tasks, he had become expert at counting money and knowing when or if the local grocer was overcharging. Still, he was unable to complete what appeared to his teachers to be a simple worksheet. Without teachers having knowledge of his abilities outside of school he was destined to be labeled mentally incompetent.

This story also exposes how curriculum content is typically presented. Children who may be gifted in real-life settings are often at a loss when asked to exhibit knowledge solely through decontextualized paper-and-pencil exercises. I have often pondered that if we taught African-American children how to dance in school, by the time they had finished the first five work-

books on the topic, we would have a generation of remedial dancers!

If we do not have some knowledge of children's lives outside of the realms of paper-and-pencil work, and even outside of their classrooms, then we cannot know their strengths. Not knowing students' strengths leads to our "teaching down" to children from communities that are culturally different from that of the teachers in the school. Because teachers do not want to tax what they believe to be these students' lower abilities, they end up teaching less when, in actuality, these students need *more* of what school has to offer. This is not a new concept. In 1933 Carter G. Woodson discussed the problem in *The Mis-Education of the Negro:*

> The teaching of arithmetic in the fifth grade in a backward county in Mississippi should mean one thing in the Negro school and a decidedly different thing in the white school. The Negro children, as a rule, come from the homes of tenants and peons who have to migrate annually from plantation to plantation, looking for light which they have never seen. The children from the homes of white planters and merchants live permanently in the midst of calculation, family budgets, and the like, which enable them sometimes to learn more by contact than the Negro can acquire in school. Instead of teaching such Negro children less arithmetic, they should be taught much more of it than white children.

Teaching less rather than teaching more can happen in several ways. Those who utilize "skills-based" approaches can teach less by focusing solely on isolated, decontextualized bits. Such instruction becomes boring and meaningless when not placed in any meaningful context. When instruction allows no opportunity for children to use their minds to create and interpret texts, then children will only focus on low-level thinking and their school-based intellect will atrophy. Skills-oriented approaches that feature heavy doses of readiness activities also contribute to the "teaching less" phenomenon. Children are typically assigned to these activities as a result of low scores on some standardized test. However, they end up spending so much time matching circles and triangles that no one ever introduces them to actually learning how to read. Should anyone doubt it, I can guarantee you that no amount of matching circles and triangles ever taught anyone how to read. Worse, these activities take time away from real kinds of involvement in literacy such as listening to and seeing the words in real books.

Teaching less can also occur with those who favor "holistic" or "child-centered" approaches. While I believe that there is much of value in whole language and process writing approaches, some teachers seem almost to be using these methodologies as excuses for not teaching. I am reminded of a colleague who visited a classroom in California designed around the state-mandated whole language approach. My colleague witnessed one child in a peer reading group who clearly could not read. When she later asked the teacher about this child, the teacher responded that it was "OK" that this fourth-grader could not read, because he would understand the content via the subsequent discussion. While it is great that the child would have the opportunity to learn through a discussion, it is devastating that no one was providing him with what he also needed—explicit instruction in learning how to read.

In some "process writing" classrooms, teachers unfamiliar with the language abilities of African-American children are led to believe that these students have no fluency with language. They therefore allow them to remain in the first stages of the writing process, producing first draft after first draft, with no attention to editing or completing final products. They allow African-American students to remain at the level of developing fluency because these teachers do not understand the language competence their students already possess. The key here is not the kind of instruction but the attitude underlying it. When teachers do not understand the potential of the students they teach, they will underteach them no matter what the methodology.

IGNORANCE OF COMMUNITY NORMS

Many school systems have attempted to institute "parent training" programs for poor parents and parents of color. While the intentions of these programs are good, they can only be truly useful when educators understand the realities with which such parents must contend and why they do what they do. Often, middle-class school professionals are appalled by what they see of poor parents, and most do not have the training or the ability to see past surface behaviors to the meanings behind parents' actions.

In a preschool I have often visited, four-year-old David's young mother once came to his class to provide a birthday party for her son. I happened to hear the conversation of the teachers that afternoon. They said she came to school in a "bum costume" yelling, "Let's party!" and running around the room. She had presents for all the children and a cake she or someone else had baked for the occasion. The teachers were horrified. They said they could smell alcohol on her breath, that the children went wild, and that they attempted to get the children out to recess as quickly as possible.

From an earlier conversation, I happened to know that this woman cares deeply for her son and his welfare. She is even saving money to put him in private school—a major sacrifice for her—when he enters kindergarten. David's teachers, however, were not able to see that, despite her possible inappropriateness, his mother had actually spent a great deal of effort and care in putting together this party for her son. She also probably felt the need to bolster her courage a bit with a drink in order to face fifteen four-year-olds and keep them entertained. We must find ways for professionals to understand the different ways in which parents can show their concern for their children.

Another example of a cultural barrier between teacher understandings and parental understanding occurred at a predominantly Latino school in

Boston. Even though the teachers continually asked them not to, the parents, primarily mothers, kept bringing their first graders into their classroom before the school day officially began. The teachers wanted all children to remain on the playground with a teacher's aide, and they also wanted all parents to vacate the school yard as soon as possible while the teacher readied the classrooms for the beginning of the day. When the parents continued to ignore the request, the teachers began locking the school doors. Pretty soon feelings escalated to the point of yelling matches, and the parents even approached the school board.

What the teachers in this instance did not understand was that the parents viewed six-year-olds as still being babies and in need of their mother's or their surrogate mother's (the teacher's) attention. To the parents, leaving children outside without one of their "mothers" present was tantamount to child abuse and exhibited a most callous disregard for the children's welfare. The situation did not have to have become so highly charged. All that was needed was some knowledge about the parents and community of the children they were teaching, and the teachers could have resolved the problem easily—perhaps by stationing one of the first-grade teachers outside in the mornings, or by inviting one of the parents to remain on the school grounds before the teachers called the children in to class.

INVISIBILITY

Whether we are immediately aware of it or not, the United States is surely composed of a plethora of perspectives. I am reminded of this every time I think of my friend Martha, a Native American teacher. Martha told me how tired she got of being asked about her plans for Thanksgiving by people who seemed to take no note that her perspective on the holiday might be a bit different than their own. One year, in her frustration, she told me that when the next questioner asked, "What are you doing for Thanksgiving?",

she answered, "I plan to spend the day saying, 'You're welcome!'"

If we plan to survive as a species on this planet we must certainly create multicultural curricula that educate our children to the differing perspectives of our diverse population. In part, the problems we see exhibited in school by African-American children and children of other oppressed minorities can be traced to this lack of a curriculum in which they can find represented the intellectual achievements of people who look like themselves. Were that not the case, these children would not talk about doing well in school as "acting white." Our children of color need to see the brilliance of their legacy, too.

Even with well-intentioned educators, not only our children's legacies but our children themselves can become invisible. Many of the teachers we educate, and indeed their teacher educators, believe that to acknowledge a child's color is to insult him or her. In her book *White Teacher*, Vivian Paley openly discusses the problems inherent in the statement that I have heard many teachers—well-intentioned teachers—utter, "I don't see color, I only see children." What message does this statement send? That there is something wrong with being black or brown, that it should *not* be noticed? I would like to suggest that if one does not see color, then one does not really see children. Children made "invisible" in this manner become hard-pressed to see themselves worthy of notice.

ADDRESSING THE PROBLEMS OF EDUCATING POOR AND CULTURALLY DIVERSE CHILDREN

To begin with, our prospective teachers are exposed to descriptions of failure rather than models of success. We expose student teachers to an education that relies upon name calling and labelling ("disadvantaged," "at-risk," "learning disabled," "the underclass") to explain its failures, and calls upon research study after research study to inform teachers that school achievement is intimately and inevitably linked with socioeconomic status. Teacher candidates are told that "culturally different" children are mismatched to the school setting and therefore cannot be expected to achieve as well as white, middle-class children. They are told that children of poverty are developmentally slower than other children.

Seldom, however, do we make available to our teacher initiates the many success stories about educating poor children and children of color: those institutions like the Nairobi Day-School in East Palo Alto, California, which produced children from poor African-American communities who scored three grade levels above the national average. Nor do we make sure that they learn about those teachers who are quietly going about the job of producing excellence in educating poor and culturally diverse students: teachers like Marva Collins of Chicago, Illinois, who has educated many African-American students considered uneducable by public schools; Jaime Escalante, who has consistently taught hundreds of Latino high school students who live in the poorest *barrios* of East Los Angeles to test their way into advanced-placement calculus classes; and many other successful unsung heroes and heroines who are seldom visible in teacher education classrooms.

Interestingly, even when such teaching comes to our consciousness, it is most often not by way of educational research but via the popular media. We educators do not typically research and document this "power pedagogy" (as Asa Hilliard calls it), but continue to provide, at worst, autopsies of failure and, at best, studies in minimalist achievement. In other words, we teach teachers rationales for failure, not visions of success. Is there any wonder that those who are products of such teacher education (from classroom teachers to principals to central office staff) water down the curriculum for diverse students instead of challenging them with more, as Woodson says, of what school has to offer?

A second reason problems occur for our culturally diverse students is that we have created in most schools institutions of isolation. We foster the notion that students are clients of "professional" educators who are met in the "office" of the classroom where their deficiencies are remediated and their intellectual "illnesses" healed. Nowhere do we foster inquiry into who our students really are or encourage teachers to develop links to the often rich home lives of students, yet teachers cannot hope to begin to understand who sits before them unless they can connect with the families and communities from which their students come. To do that, it is vital that teachers and teacher educators explore their own beliefs and attitudes about non-white and non-middle-class people. Many teachers—black, white, and "other"—harbor unexamined prejudices about people from ethnic groups or classes different from their own. This is partly because teachers have been so conditioned by the larger society's negative stereotypes of certain ethnic groups, and partly because they are never given the opportunity to learn to value the experiences of other groups.

I propose that a part of teacher education include bringing parents and community members into the university classroom to tell prospective teachers (and their teacher educators) what their concerns about education are, what they feel schools are doing well or poorly for their children, and how they would like to see schooling changed. I would also like to see teacher initiates and their educators go out to community gatherings to acquire such firsthand knowledge. It is unreasonable to expect that teachers will automatically value the knowledge that parents and community members bring to the education of diverse children if valuing such knowledge has not been modelled for them by those from whom they learn to teach.

Following a speech I made at a conference a few years ago, I have been corresponding with a very insightful teacher who works at a prestigious university lab school. The school is staffed by a solely European-American faculty, but seeks to maintain racial and cultural balance among the student body. They find, however, that they continue to lose black students, especially boys. The teacher, named Richard, wrote to me that the school often has problems, both behavioral and academic, with African-American boys. When called to the school to discuss these problems, these children's parents typically say that they do not understand, that their children are fine at home. The school personnel interpret these statements as indications of the parents' "being defensive," and presume that the children are as difficult at home as at school, but that the parents do not want to admit it.

When Richard asked for some suggestions, my first recommendation was that the school should work hard to develop a multicultural staff. Of course, that solution would take a while, even if the school was committed to it. My next and actually most important suggestion was that the school needed to learn to view its African-American parents as a resource and not as a problem. When problems arise with particular African-American children, the school should get the parents of these children involved in helping to point out what the school might do better.

Richard wrote back to me:

> The change though that has made me happiest so far about my own work is that I have taken your advice and I am asking black parents about stuff I never would have brought up before. . . . We do a lot of journal writing, and with the 6- to 8-year-olds I teach, encourage them to draw as well as write, to see the journal as a form of expression. I was having a conference with the mother of one black boy. . . . We looked at his journal and saw that he was doing beautiful intricate drawings, but that he rarely got more than a few words down on the page. I talked to his mother about how we were trying to encourage C. to do the writing first, but that he liked to draw.
>
> During the conversation I started to see this as something like what you were talking about, and I asked C.'s mom how she would handle this at home. I only asked her about how she herself might deal with this, but she said, "In black fami-

lies, we would just tell him write the words first." I passed that information on to C.'s reading teacher, and we both talked to him and told him he had to get the words down first. Suddenly he began making one- and two-page entries into his journal.

> While this is pleasing in and of itself, it is an important lesson to us in terms of equity. C. is now getting equal access to the curriculum because he is using the journal for the reasons we intended it. All we needed was a culturally appropriate way to tell him how to do it.

I am not suggesting that excellent teachers of diverse students *must* be of their students' ethnicity. I have seen too many excellent European-American teachers of African-American students, and too many poor African-American teachers of African-American students to come to such an illogical conclusion. I do believe, however, that we should strive to make our teaching force diverse, for teachers who share the ethnic and cultural backgrounds of our increasingly diverse student bodies may serve, along with parents and other community members, to provide insights that might otherwise remain hidden.

The third problem I believe we must overcome is the narrow and essentially Eurocentric curriculum we provide for our teachers. At the university level, teachers are not being educated with the broad strokes necessary to prepare them properly for the twenty-first century. We who are concerned about teachers and teaching must insist that our teachers become knowledgeable of the liberal arts, but we must also work like the dickens to change liberal arts courses so that they do not continue to reflect only, as feminist scholar Peggy McIntosh says, "the public lives of white Western men." These new courses must not only teach what white Westerners have to say about diverse cultures, they must also share what the writers and thinkers of diverse cultures have to say about themselves, their history, music, art, literature, politics, and so forth.

If we know the intellectual legacies of our students, we will gain insight into how to teach them. Stephanie Terry, a first-grade teacher I have recently interviewed, breathes the heritage of her students into the curriculum. Stephanie teaches in an economically strapped community in inner-city Baltimore, Maryland, in a school with a 100 percent African-American enrollment. She begins each year with the study of Africa, describing Africa's relationship to the United States, its history, resources, and so forth. As her students learn each new aspect of the regular citywide curriculum, Stephanie connects this knowledge to aspects of their African ancestry; while covering a unit about libraries she tells them about the world's first libraries, which were established in Africa. A unit on health presents her with the opportunity to tell her students about the African doctors of antiquity who wrote the first texts on medicine. Stephanie does not replace the current curriculum; rather, she expands it. She also teaches about the contributions of Asian-Americans, Native Americans, and Latinos as she broadens her students' minds and spirits. All of Stephanie's students learn to read by the end of the school year. They also learn to love themselves, love their history, and love learning.

Stephanie could not teach her children the pride of their ancestry and could not connect it to the material they learn today were it not for her extraordinarily broad knowledge of the liberal arts. However, she told me that she did not acquire this knowledge in her formal education, but worked, read, and studied on her own to make such knowledge a part of her pedagogy.

Teachers must not merely take courses that tell them how to treat their students as multicultural clients, in other words, those that tell them how to identify differences in interactional or communicative strategies and remediate appropriately. They must also learn about the brilliance the students bring with them "in their blood." Until they appreciate the wonders of the cultures represented before them—and they cannot do that without extensive study most appropriately begun in college-level courses—they cannot appreciate the potential of those who sit before them, nor can they begin to link their students' histories and worlds to the subject matter they present in the classroom.

If we are to successfully educate all of our children, we must work to remove the blinders built of stereotypes, monocultural instructional methodologies, ignorance, social distance, biased research, and racism. We must work to destroy those blinders so that it is possible to really see, to really know the students we must teach. Yes, if we are to be successful at educating diverse children, we must accomplish the Herculean feat of developing this clear-sightedness, for in the words of a wonderful Native Alaskan educator: "In order to teach you, I must know you." I pray for all of us the strength to teach our children what they must learn, and the humility and wisdom to learn from them so that we might better teach.

STUDY QUESTIONS FOR PART 5

1. Given that teacher expectations and social interactions are strong forces within classrooms, what are the ways that they can have positive consequences for students? What are some examples where these forces might diminish a child's success in the classroom?

2. Even though many school drop-outs usually do not physically "leave" until high school, the seeds for that destiny seem to be planted much earlier. What can teachers do to reduce the number of children inclined to leave school?

3. The first teacher in the Rist article believed it was going to be very tough for her students to "make it" because of their ethnicity and poverty. Because she felt as an individual that she couldn't help all of her children succeed, she decided to focus on the students with the most potential and pump them up by building their skills and self-esteem. In her view, rather than giving just a little bit to everyone, she gave a lot to a few. She felt she was simply trying to give every advantage to the best of the group in the hopes that these few could make it and return one day as teachers, social workers, doctors, lawyers, and so forth to help in the community. Is this a defensible position for a teacher? Why? Was she a reflective teacher? What would Lisa Delpit say about this attitude?

4. How would a functionalist explain the scenario described by Rist? What would Lisa Delpit say about what Rist described? How would a conflict theorist explain the scenario described by Rist?

5. If the teachers in the schools described by Rist and Everhart had followed the principles advocated by Delpit, how might things have been different for the children? What might have been some differences in the orientations of teachers to their students?

6. What qualities would enable a middle/junior high school teacher to build on children's natural inclinations to learn regenerative forms of knowledge?

7. How would you explain the observation that a vast majority of teachers emphasize the learning of reified knowledge at the expense of regenerative knowledge?

8. What changes in our expectations for the role of teachers might enable teachers to more adequately serve the diverse range of learners in contemporary classrooms? What changes in our expectations for the role of students might enable teachers to more adequately serve more students?

9. Should the ideas espoused by Delpit be applied in a school serving primarily middle-class white children? Why? How? In a school like this, what are teachers' responsibilities as educators in a multicultural society?

10. The tools available to students and teachers have changed considerably over the last decade, and the emerging advances in electronic technology promise even greater possibilities than have heretofore been imaginable. In what ways might teaching and learning be enhanced by these new tools; and in what ways might these new tools change the roles of students and teachers?

PART 6

Education and Societal Inequality: Race, Gender, Class, and Ethnicity

It is tempting to think in this day and age, given our nation's resources and everything we've learned about effective schooling, that the harmful practices of the past have by now been "fixed" in education. That is, that sufficient federal and state laws have been enacted and public awareness has been raised to the level where schools are truly equitable places in which all students can learn.

This, unfortunately, is not the case. Despite the tremendous strides that have been made since the inception of a system of free public schooling in this country some 100 years ago, much remains to be done. The readings selected for this section prompt these questions:

- Do Americans want equity in schools; if so, why?
- Given the reality of limited resources to support public education, what aspects of schooling would you be willing to forego to achieve educational equity, and why?
- In what ways are some children privileged over others in public schools, and why is this differentiation tolerated in a society espousing democratic ideals?

Our communities and hence our schools are becoming more and more heterogeneous, and these conditions severely complicate the challenges for classroom teachers. The growing cultural diversity in our nation's schools and the increasingly broad band of ability levels among the children attending school make the teacher's job ever more complicated, and this is particularly so in the face of dwindling resources and public support for education.

As you will recall from the readings in Part 1, we looked at the connections between education and cultural transmission and the impact of schools on shaping and sustaining such values as humanitarianism, equality, and the effort and optimism associated with productivity and problem-solving. One of the beliefs we hold most dear is that a good part of what it means to be American is that each individual has an equal opportunity to get ahead, to make the most of his or her abilities.

Related to this central value of equality is the belief in *equal educational opportunity*, that is, that every member of society has an equal chance to receive an appropriate education. However, as Spring reminds us in the next reading, many groups of U.S. citizens have historically been denied the opportunity to attend public schools, and even when the legal right to attend has been won, the education received often is of poor quality, or at least inadequate to enable recipients to compete on a level playing field with members of more advantaged groups.

The reading by Spring chronicles the struggles many groups in U.S. society have experienced in securing basic civil rights for their members, in particular the right to equality of educational opportunity. The obstacles to equal educational opportunity affect many different social groups and come in many different forms. While we might initially think of the historical disenfranchisement of African Americans and their struggle for civil rights and equality of educational opportunity, many other groups have had similar struggles. These include Native Americans; Mexican Americans; Asian Americans; Americans with physical, mental, and emotional disabilities; young girls and women; and many children from families who do not speak English in their homes or communities. Beyond these groups, and unfortunately the largest and most rapidly expanding groups, are the urban and rural poor. While federal and state laws now for the most part provide special opportunities for members of these groups, the available resources are inadequate to serve their needs. As schools and classrooms become increasingly diverse in terms of the ability range and cultural complexity of the groupings of children served in the public schools, teachers and communities face unprecedented challenges to be responsive and to provide an education suited to the economic, social, and political challenges that children face in the world today, as they enter the workplace and take on the responsibilities of adulthood and citizenship in a democratic society.

While basic access to educational opportunity is now available to the great majority of U.S. citizens, the educations received are by no means equal for many reasons beyond the limitations of resources to support public education. Among these are unequal treatment *within* schools, for boys and girls, for poor and middle-class children, for white and people of color, and for native and non-native English speakers. Teachers' and administrators' prejudices, school textbooks and other aspects of the curriculum, and local community values all influence the quality, extent, and nature of the education provided in public schools. Although there are many good examples of public schools that demonstrably meet these challenges head-on and do their very best to provide equal educations to all who enter their doors, we should not be deluded into thinking this is typical practice. It is not; it is *still* the exception in many schools and communities.

While educators struggle to overcome their prejudices and strive to implement effective instructional practices, states and local communities continue to debate how public schools are funded. As Ward so aptly illustrates in the second reading in this section, public school finances can have a tremendous impact on the quality of education. The quality and amount of education our children receive depends heavily on the level of one's family's social strata, and on the community in which one lives (Ward, 1992, p. 242).

Most public schools are funded through local property taxes, and thus the amounts available to support education vary substantially between wealthy and poor communities. While there have been numerous efforts to redress the inequities caused by the nature of funding for education, the "politics of privilege and exclusion" (Ward, 1992, p. 246) and the historically rooted belief by communities in local control of education have hampered initiatives to equalize funding across school communities.

Ward suggests a number of policies and strategies states could adopt that would end these disparities in funding. Without such efforts, U.S. public schools will, as they have historically, tend to reproduce and maintain many of the inequalities evident in society. As discussed earlier in Part 4, without measures such as those proposed by Ward, schools will reproduce and continue to legitimize the current inequities in U.S. society. While public schools are but one ingredient in a very complex web of influences on children, they undoubtedly are a critical ingredient and one well within our grasp to effect. We currently spend on average about $5,000 annually per child to support public schools. The average cost to incarcerate a person for one year exceeds $25,000 and is increasing.

Perhaps the biggest challenge we face is helping the public understand the benefits and the opportunities of a system of public education that truly yields an equally well-educated citizenry. Schooling and democracy are critically intertwined, and the nature and quality of schooling bear directly on the capacity of citizens to govern themselves well and to preserve the traditions of a democratic society.

Equality of Educational Opportunity

JOEL SPRING

At the heart of education-related discussions about gender, race, and ethnicity is the issue of *equality of educational opportunity*. Simply defined, equality of educational opportunity means that everyone has an equal chance to receive an education. In the United States, as I will discuss later, women and racial and ethnic minorities have been deprived of this opportunity and continue to struggle for an equal chance to receive an education. This sorry chapter in the history of the American school illustrates how education can be a source of freedom or a tool of oppression.

Throughout the world, educational systems that are designed to enslave women and racial and ethnic minorities can be found. This is done by either denying these groups access to an education or providing an education that teaches them that they are inferior. But there are also educational systems that serve as a means for ensuring equality of opportunity and for cultivating pride in being a woman or a member of a racial or ethnic minority.

When defined as an equal chance to attend publicly supported schools, equal educational opportunity is primarily a legal issue. In this context, the provision of equal educational opportunity can be defined solely on the grounds of justice: If government provides a service like education, all classes of citizens should have equal access to that service.

But legal equality of opportunity to attend public schools does not guarantee that education will be a source of freedom. As mentioned earlier, public schools can be structured to deny equal educational opportunity. This is illustrated by events in Selma, Alabama, in the early 1990s. During the 1950s and 1960s, Selma was a center of violent civil rights protests to demand equal voting rights and integrated education. As a result, by the time of the school protests of 1990, legislation guaranteed African American children equal educational opportunity to attend publicly supported schools. But this right of attendance was undermined by a system of tracking students into different curricula. The dispute in 1990 centered on the racial distribution in advanced placement and college preparatory courses offered in Selma's public high school.

Selma, like many other communities in the South, separates races within the public schools by placing them in different curriculum tracks, such as college preparatory and advanced placement. The racial bias underlying the placement of students in such tracks is clearly evident in Selma's high school. In Selma 90 percent of all white students were placed in college preparatory and advanced-placement tracks, while only 3 percent of all African American students were placed in those tracks. According to Phyllis McClure, an education specialist with the Legal Defense and Education Fund of the National Association for the Advancement of Colored People (NAACP), this form of racial segregation through tracking is common throughout southern states.

When Dr. Norward Roussell, Selma's first African American school superintendent, tried to

---

Source: "Equality of Educational Opportunity" from *American Education*, 7E, by Joel Spring copyright 1996. Reprinted by permission of McGraw-Hill, Inc.

correct this racial imbalance by increasing the percentage of African American students in college preparatory and advanced-placement tracks to 10 percent, he was notified by the white-dominated school board that he was being dismissed. Dr. Roussell stated that the school system was violating students' rights by tracking them primarily on the basis of teachers' recommendations. "And of course, as you might imagine, the majority of students in the bottom levels were black," he said in an interview in the February 21, 1990, issue of *Education Week*, "despite the fact that many had standardized-test scores as high or higher than those in the upper level." It required a school boycott by African American students before he was reinstated. White parents reacted with threats to remove their children from the public schools and send them to private institutions.

Therefore, equality of educational opportunity requires more than just an equal chance to attend a publicly supported school. It also requires equal treatment within schools. Inequality of treatment in school can be a result of other factors as well. For many years handicapped students were denied equal access to an education because of the lack of provisions to accommodate their special needs. Entry into buildings and movement between floors were difficult for many handicapped students because they could not negotiate stairs, and neither ramps for wheelchairs nor elevators were provided. Equal educational opportunity for handicapped people has meant making physical changes in buildings.

In addition to providing equal treatment in placement in curricular tracks and physical access to buildings, equality of educational opportunity requires positive recognition of the gender, race, and ethnic background of the student. Equality of educational opportunity has little meaning if students gain equal access to an education and then are taught they are inferior.

Inequality of treatment can occur in very subtle ways. This is particularly evident in the history of discrimination against women in education. For instance, while doing research on the history of education during World War II, Felecia Briscoe encountered a reproduction of a poster of which the National Education Association had distributed 50,000 copies in 1944 as part of its "teacher-recruiting and morale-building campaign." Titled "The Teacher," the poster depicts a female teacher and an elementary-school-age boy and girl standing around a world globe. The little girl is wearing a neat dress and her hair is perfectly groomed. She is staring passively at the globe with a blank expression on her face, and her empty arms dangle beside her. The teacher is seated between the two children. Her head is turned away from the girl and she gazes with approval at the boy. The boy clutches a book in one hand and points to a place on the globe with the other. Unlike the girl, his hair is rumpled and his face is animated. The poster clearly conveys an impression that males are active learners and intellectually superior to females, whereas girls are passive and intellectually dull.

Equality of educational opportunity can be denied also to children from homes where English is not the spoken language, when no special provision for this language problem is made by the schools. Courts have ruled that children who do not fully comprehend the language of the school are being denied equal access to instruction. Equality of educational opportunity in this situation means that the schools must provide special help for children with non-English-speaking backgrounds.

In summary, the concept of equal educational opportunity covers a broad spectrum of educational issues including equal opportunity to attend public supported schools, educational practices within schools, the content of curriculum and textbooks, and recognition of the cultural and language background of the student.

EQUALITY OF EDUCATIONAL OPPORTUNITY AND EQUALITY OF OPPORTUNITY

There is an important distinction between equality of opportunity and equality of educational opportunity. . . . Equality of opportunity means that everyone has the same chance to compete for positions in society. Equality of educational opportunity means that everyone has the same chance to receive an education. Equal educational opportunity does not guarantee equal opportunity in the labor market. It can be argued that equality of educational opportunity is essential for equality of opportunity in society. But this argument can be maintained only if there is proof that education does in fact provide equality of opportunity, and, as shown in the previous chapter, the ability of education to provide equality of opportunity is still debatable.

One important role education can play in aiding equal opportunity for women and racial and ethnic minorities is the eradication of prejudices and stereotypes. Prejudices and stereotypes often hinder the advancement of these groups in the economic system. From this standpoint, educating students to tolerate diverse groups can be one of the most important contributions of schools to equal opportunity. This opinion was expressed with regard to Native Americans by Joseph Abeyta, superintendent of the Santa Fe Indian School, at a 1990 conference on Native American education. As reported in the February 21, 1990, issue of *Education Week*, Abeyta declared that the greatest educational challenge is to "help change the attitudes of this country regarding Native-American students."

Highlighting the importance of eliminating prejudices and stereotypes to ensure equal opportunity are recent findings on promotion opportunities for women working in corporations. Despite greater educational opportunities for women and corporate programs designed to keep women in the work force, such as on-site day care and parental leave, women continue to have difficulty moving up the corporate ladder. In 1990, Cindy Skrzycki, a *Washington Post* staff writer, reported that in interviews conducted with fifty professional and managerial women who left major American corporations after five or more years of employment, their primary rea-

son for leaving was a feeling of being "dead-ended" in their jobs. She found that corporate chief executives admitted the existence of a "glass ceiling" that prevented women from reaching top corporate positions. Interviews with two hundred top corporate leaders revealed that the major stumbling blocks to the advancement of women are stereotyping and preconceptions about female abilities.

These findings suggest that an important role for education in providing equality of opportunity is the elimination of prejudices and stereotypes. As will be discussed in the next section, the historic struggle for civil rights includes the fight against prejudice and a struggle for both equality of opportunity and equality of educational opportunity.

THE STRUGGLE FOR CIVIL RIGHTS

American history is the story of the steady struggle for increased civil participation in society. Usually the term *civil rights* means the right to an equal opportunity to gain economic and social advantages, and equal treatment by the law. Since the founding of the republic, groups have struggled to remove barriers that deny equal access to economic opportunities, institutions, and political power. It is important to understand that an increase in civil rights occurred only because of active participation and struggle by citizens. The reason improving civil rights requires struggle is that it usually results in reducing the advantages held by one class of citizens over another class of citizens.

The two most important struggles for equal civil rights have been by women and by racial minority groups. For both groups the struggle was for equal political power, equal access to economic opportunities, equal treatment and access to social institutions, and equality of educational opportunity. One important struggle for women in the United States was for the right to vote. Although the suffrage movement was international, in the United States its final resolution was the adoption in 1920 of the Nineteenth Amendment to the Constitution.

Another important struggle for women is gaining equal access to economic opportunities. Historically, women were relegated to certain sectors of the labor market. In the nineteenth century, the primary sources of employment for women outside the home were as domestic help, teachers, factory workers, and in other service occupations. These employment opportunities were usually occasions for economic exploitation. For instance, women and children comprised a large sector of industrial employment in the nineteenth century because they were a cheap form of labor. . . . Women were allowed to enter the ranks of teaching primarily because they were viewed as a cheap and steady work force. In the latter part of the nineteenth and early part of the twentieth centuries, women came to dominate the professions of nursing and social work, which are often referred to as the helping professions. Again, the wage scales of these professions were considerably below those in professions dominated by men.

With the growth of white-collar occupations in the twentieth century, women became the major source of workers for office positions such as secretaries, typists, and clerks. In the twentieth century, schools played an important role in assuring the perpetuation of women in these occupations. One of the most successful vocational education programs has been in business and secretarial skills. These programs tend to enroll women primarily. This means that a sex-segregated curriculum contributes to the maintenance of a sex-segregated sector of the labor market.

Educational institutions are central to the struggle by women for equal access to occupations. First, although women have composed a majority of the teaching force since the nineteenth century, they do not hold an equivalent number of administrative positions in public schools, nor have they held an equivalent number of positions on university faculties. Second,

educational training is the primary means of entering many professions, such as law and medicine. Gaining equal access to these educational programs is an important part of women's struggle for equality of opportunity.

One important gain for women was the passage by the federal government of the Higher Education Act of 1972. Title IX of this legislation provided both for sexual equality in employment in educational institutions and for sexual equality in educational programs. The legislation applied to all educational institutions, including preschool, elementary and secondary schools, vocational and professional schools, and public and private undergraduate and graduate institutions. A 1983 U.S. Supreme Court decision, *Grove City College v. Bell*, restricted Title IX in its application to specific educational programs within institutions. In the 1987 Civil Rights Restoration Act, Congress overturned the Court's decision and amended Title IX to include all activities of an educational institution receiving federal aid. . . .

Like oppressed women, minority groups have struggled for equal civil rights. For African Americans, the major problem has been struggling against the legacy of slavery. After the Civil War, two amendments to the Constitution promised to give African Americans equal political status. The Fourteenth Amendment to the Constitution, ratified in 1868, guaranteed equality before the law. This amendment is extremely important in arguments for equality of educational opportunity. It will be discussed and mentioned throughout this chapter. . . . The Fifteenth Amendment to the Constitution, ratified in 1870, guaranteed that the right to vote would not be denied on account of race, color, or previous condition of servitude.

The promise of equality before the law was denied to African Americans in southern states in the latter part of the nineteenth century with the passage of "Jim Crow" laws. These laws made it extremely difficult for African Americans to vote, and mandated segregation in public schools and other public institutions. The abolition of these restrictive laws was a major focus of the African American community's civil rights struggle, beginning in the late nineteenth century and continuing through the 1960s, when Congress passed legislation protecting civil rights and the right to vote for African Americans.

The African American community in the United States believed ending racial segregation in schools was a means of improving equality of opportunity, because desegregation would help to remove the stigma of racial inferiority and would provide greater opportunities for upward occupational mobility. This is why educational aspirations are high in the African American community. Historically, much of the hope of the African American community centered on gaining equality of educational opportunity.

Like women, minority groups found themselves relegated to low-wage sectors of the labor force. In fact, there is a direct relationship between segregation in education and economic exploitation. One clear example is found in the state of California, which at different periods in history segregated Chinese, Japanese, Chicanos, Indians, and African Americans. Segregation of these groups coincided with their exploitation as workers. For instance, Chinese were segregated in California during the period when they were brought into the country as inexpensive labor to work on the railroads; Japanese were segregated at the time they were being brought in as agricultural workers. In the South, African Americans were segregated during a period when their labor was considered necessary for the building of the new industrial South.

Problems of employment discrimination continue in the 1990s. For instance, according to a 1990 study by the National Science Foundation, African Americans accounted for 2.5 percent and women accounted for 15 percent of all employed scientists and engineers. While African Americans showed gains from a 1.6 percent figure in 1976, the numbers still did not reflect the fact African Americans represented 10 percent of the work force. The percentage of women scientists and

engineers was also up from 9 percent from 1976. For Hispanic Americans, only 2 percent were scientists and engineers while they constituted 7 percent of all workers. The National Science Foundation was particularly disturbed by these figures because within the next thirty years about 70 percent of those entering the work force will be women, immigrants, and those now considered minority members.

As discussed earlier in the chapter, segregation carries with it the stigma of racial inferiority. The belief in the racial inferiority of one group allows other groups to rationalize its place at the bottom of the labor market. In other words, one can justify placing racial groups in positions of economic exploitation by claiming that they are inferior and unsuitable for other positions. Historically, segregated education in the United States and other countries was a means of perpetuating myths of racial superiority and inferiority.

Institutional racial discrimination occurs in the same form in which social-class discrimination occurs. There is a tendency for white school teachers and principals to have lower expectations for African American students than for white students. This is not necessarily an example of overt racism but is primarily a result of the cultural isolation of the white community from the African American community and the lack of awareness by the white community of the high educational aspirations of African American parents and students. In addition to the problem of teachers' low expectations, there is a tendency in large school systems for younger and less experienced teachers to be placed in schools that are predominantly nonwhite.

The greatest impact of civil rights struggles on schools is the process of desegregation. Desegregation helped to fulfill the promise of equal educational opportunity and changed the organizational structure of education by fostering the development of magnet schools. This chapter will next explore the process of desegregation, the problems of institutional segregation and racism, and the effects of the struggle of women for equal rights.

DESEGREGATION OF AMERICAN SCHOOLS

The historic 1954 Supreme Court school desegregation case, *Brown v. Board of Education of Topeka*, gave legal meaning to the idea that segregated education means unequal education. Until 1954, segregated schools in the United States operated under a ruling given by the Supreme Court in 1895, *Plessy v. Ferguson*, that segregation did not create a badge of inferiority if segregated facilities were equal and the law was reasonable. The decision in both cases centered around the meaning of the Fourteenth Amendment to the Constitution. This amendment was ratified in 1868, shortly after the close of the Civil War. One of its purposes was to extend the basic guarantees of the Bill of Rights into the areas of state and local government. The most important and controversial section of the Fourteenth Amendment states: "No State shall make or enforce any law which shall abridge the privileges or immunities of citizens . . . nor . . . deprive any person of life, liberty, or property, without due process of law; nor deny to any person within its jurisdiction the equal protection of the laws."

The 1895 decision, *Plessy v. Ferguson*, involved Homer Plessy, who was one-eighth African American and seven-eighths white. He was arrested for refusing to ride in the colored coach of a train, as required by Louisiana state law. The Supreme Court's decision in this case, that segregated facilities could exist if they were equal, became known as the "separate but equal" doctrine.

The 1954 desegregation decision, *Brown v. Board of Education of Topeka*, overturned the "separate but equal" doctrine by arguing, on the basis of the findings of social science, that segregated education was inherently unequal. This meant that even if school facilities, teachers, equipment, and all other physical conditions were equal between two racially segregated schools, the two schools would still be unequal because of the fact of racial segregation.

In 1964 Congress took a significant step toward speeding up school desegregation by passing the important Civil Rights Act. In terms of school desegregation, Title VI of the 1964 Civil Rights Act was most important because it provided a means for the federal government to force school desegregation. In its final form, Title VI required the mandatory withholding of federal funds from institutions that practiced racial discrimination. Title VI states that no person, because of race, color, or national origin, could be excluded from or denied the benefits of any program receiving federal financial assistance. It required all federal agencies to establish guidelines to implement this policy. Refusal by institutions or projects to follow these guidelines was to result in the "termination of or refusal to grant or to continue assistance under such program or activity."

Title VI of the 1964 Civil Rights Act was important for two reasons. First, it established a major precedent for federal control of American public schools, by making explicit that the control of money would be one method used by the federal government to shape local school policies. . . . Second, it turned the federal Office of Education into a policing agency with the responsibility of determining whether or not school systems were segregated, and if they were, of doing something about the segregated conditions.

One result of Title VI was to speed up the process of school desegregation in the South, particularly after the passage of federal legislation in 1965 that increased the amount of money available to local schools from the federal government. In the late 1960s southern school districts rapidly began to submit school desegregation plans to the Office of Education.

In the North prosecution of inequality in educational opportunity as it related to school segregation required a different approach from that used in the South. In the South, school segregation existed by legislative acts that required separation of the races. In the North there were no specific laws requiring separation of the races. But even without specific laws, racial segregation existed. Therefore, it was necessary for individuals bringing complaints against northern school districts to prove that the existing patterns of racial segregation were the result of purposeful action on the part of the school district. It had to be proved that school officials intended racial segregation to be a result of their educational policies.

The conditions required to prove segregation were explicitly outlined in 1974, in the Sixth Circuit Court of Appeals case *Oliver v. Michigan State Board of Education.* The court stated, "A presumption of segregative purpose arises when plaintiffs establish that the natural, probable and foreseeable result of public officials' action or inaction was an increase or perpetuation of public school segregation." This did not mean that individual motives or prejudices were to be investigated, but that the overall pattern of school actions had to be shown to increase racial segregation. In the language of the court: "the question whether a purposeful pattern of segregation has manifested itself over time, despite the fact that individual official actions, considered alone, may not have been taken for segregative purposes. . . ."

MAGNET SCHOOLS AND CHOICE

As school desegregation proceeded across the country it caused a fundamental change in the organization of school curricula, with the introduction of magnet, or alternative, schools. Magnet, or alternative, schools are designed to provide an attractive program that will have wide appeal throughout a school district. Theoretically, magnet schools will attract enough students from all racial backgrounds to achieve integrated schools. For instance, a school district might establish a school for creative and performing arts that would attract students of all races from all areas of the district. If one criterion in selecting students is the maintenance of racial balance, then that school becomes a means of achieving integration.

The great attraction of magnet schools, and a major reason why they are widely supported, is that they provide a means of voluntary desegregation. Also, they are supported because it is believed they will reduce the flight of middle-class and white families from school districts undergoing desegregation. It is hoped that by providing unique and attractive programs, school districts will stabilize their populations as voluntary desegregation takes place.

The concept of magnet schools also received support from the federal government, which aided in their rapid adoption by school districts. The 1976 amendments to the Emergency School Aid Act (ESAA) provided financial support specifically for magnet school programs. In addition, President Ronald Reagan's administration in 1984 used magnet-school plans as its method of achieving out-of-court settlements of desegregation cases. . . .

Some school districts developed elaborate plans for magnet schools. In Houston, Texas, magnet schools were established ranging from Petro-Chemical Careers Institute to a High School for Law Enforcement and Criminal Justice. In most school districts, magnet schools are introduced by first offering a program in creative and performing arts. For example, both Philadelphia and Cincinnati established a School of Creative and Performing Arts as their early magnet-school offering. In Philadelphia, school-desegregation plans resulted in schools offering programs that range from the study of foreign affairs to community-based education. In many cases, special programs already in existence, particularly for academic excellence and vocational training, were classified as magnet schools.

In evaluating the desegregation aspect of magnet schools, a distinction must be made between mandatory and voluntary desegregation plans. According to Mark Smylie in a 1983 article for *Urban Education,* "Districts implementing mandatory plans achieved over three times the racial balance among schools achieved by districts implementing voluntary plans." In some situations, magnet-school programs established as a part of involuntary desegregation plans are viewed as a means of reducing the potential hostility of parents. In these situations, the choice is not between a segregated neighborhood school and a desegregated magnet school, but a choice among

(1) forced reassignment to a desegregated school, (2) leaving the school system, or (3) selecting a desegregated magnet school. Christine Rossell in a 1979 article in *Urban Education* reported that in Boston, where magnet schools were part of a court-ordered desegregation plan, they "reportedly have long waiting lists . . . and were perhaps the only 'successful' aspect of the plan despite greater busing distance and numbers bused."

By the 1990s, the magnet school movement was incorporated into the concept of "choice" in education. Conservative and Republican political leaders in the 1980s argued that public schools would improve if they were forced to compete for students. A free marketplace idea of quality through competition was introduced into education. If schools were unable to attract students in a school district, they would either have to improve or close their doors.

During the 1992 presidential campaign, both George Bush and Bill Clinton supported the idea of choice. The difference between their positions was that Bush supported choice between private and public schools, while Clinton wanted choice between public schools. By 1992, eight states had passed laws allowing students to choose any public school in the state. These states were Arkansas, Idaho, Iowa, Minnesota, Nebraska, Ohio, Utah, and Washington.

By the early 1990s, in a reversal of previous thinking on the issue, choice was being attacked as a cause of segregation, as reflected in the title of an article by Isabel Wilkerson in *The New York Times*, "Des Moines Acts to Halt White Flight after State Allows Choice of Schools." In the case of Des Moines, the Iowa state legislature passed a choice law with the assumption that poor and minority students would choose to go to suburban schools to receive a better education. But just the opposite happened. Rather than poor or minority students taking advantage of the law, white parents began to send their children to suburban schools. The result was a decline in the number of white students and, as a further result, an increase in segregation.

THE RESULTS OF DESEGREGATION

While the civil rights struggle held out the hope for greater equality of educational opportunity for many groups that were traditionally oppressed in American society, its actual results regarding desegregation have been rather dismal. On the positive side, there no longer exist state laws requiring school segregation. On the negative side, segregated schools continue to exist around the country. In 1992, the following figures (see Table 1) were reported regarding the

Table 1

Segregation of African Americans and Hispanics by State

(Percentage attending schools with 50 to 100 percent minority population)

AFRICAN AMERICANS	
Illinois	88.8%
New York	85.7
Michigan	84.6
New Jersey	79.6
California	78.7
Maryland	76.1
Wisconsin	75.3
Texas	67.9
Pennsylvania	67.5
Connecticut	65.9

HISPANICS	
New York	86.1
Illinois	85.0
Texas	84.3
New Jersey	84.1
California	79.1
Rhode Island	77.8
New Mexico	74.4
Connecticut	72.4
Pennsylvania	66.9
Arizona	56.9

Source: This table was adapted from Kern DeWitt, "The Nation's Schools Learn a 4th R: Resegregation," *New York Times* (19) January 1992): E5.

percentage of African Americans and Hispanics attending segregated schools. As Table 1 indicates, Illinois, New York, Michigan, New Jersey, California, and Texas now lead the nation in the extent of segregation.

While actual segregation of students by race is increasing in some areas, the courts are beginning to rule that some school systems are not "legally" desegregated. In 1994, federal judges declared school systems in Savannah, Georgia, and Dallas, Texas, to be legally desegregated. These decisions ended court supervision of the school systems. To accomplish desegregation, the Savannah school system spent $57 million since 1988 which, in part, was spent on creating 22 magnet schools. The Dallas school system spent $20 million on a "supermagnet" school to house six existing magnet high schools.

While "legal" segregation has ended in some school systems, many schools are experiencing second generation segregation.

SECOND GENERATION SEGREGATION

Second generation segregation refers to forms of racial segregation that are a result of school practices such as tracking, ability grouping, and the misplacement of students in special education classes. Unlike segregation that existed by state laws in the South prior to the 1954 *Brown* decision, second generation forms of segregation can occur in schools with balanced racial populations. In schools with balanced racial populations, students can be segregated by, for instance, placing all white students in one academic track and all African American or Hispanic students in another track.

In some cases, second generation segregation is not accidental, but the result of conscious school policies. The situation in Selma, Alabama, in 1990 is a perfect example of consciously planned second generation segregation.

As I discussed in the first part of this chapter, the boycott of Selma schools was prompted by

the school board's attempt to fire the African American superintendent who tried to increase the percentage of African American students in the upper-ability tracks of the high school from 3 to 10 percent. The obvious purpose of the tracking system was to segregate white from African American students. This segregation paralleled the economic segregation existing in the community.

The continuing economic segregation in Selma is highlighted in an interview with Professor William Bernard of the University of Alabama, conducted by Ronald Smothers for *The New York Times*. Bernard describes what he considers to be the "dual view of great change and no change." In this case, "the great change" is the appearance of African Americans on the city councils and school boards of the South and the "no change" is the continuation of a segregated social order and white domination of economic power. Professor Bernard provides the following description of the economic order of the South:

> Like Sinclair Lewis's "Main Street," there is a group of real estate, banking and other professional people who are the power in town, and much of the way people live is more affected by the decision of the banker than of the City Council. You don't have black bankers, but neither do you have white bankers from the wrong side of the tracks.

In reporter Smothers' interviews, African Americans refer to the "white elite" and whites refer to the "blue bloods" who controlled the town's economy and political system. Aspiring African American business people spoke of their inability to get loans to start new businesses because of the economic elite working behind the scenes. Obviously, new African American businesses would compete with existing white businesses. This white power elite controls Selma's city council which includes four African Americans among nine members. In Selma, the school board is appointed by the city council and includes five African Americans among eleven members. Thus, the city council and school board reflect Professor Bernard's statement about the "dual view of great change and no change." The great change is the presence of African Americans on the city council and school board, and the no change is the continuing economic power of a white elite.

Also, tracking in the Selma high school reflects the "dual view of great change and no change." The great change is the integration of the school building and the 3 percent of African Americans placed in the high-ability tracks with 90 percent of the white students. The no change is the racial segregation that continues with the tracking system. The segregation resulting from the tracking systems reflects the economic differences in the community. Tracking is a method of closing the door to equal economic opportunity for African Americans in Selma.

Nationally, a number of studies examine the process of great change and no change as integration of schools results in segregation within schools. One collection of studies can be found in Ray Rist's *Desegregated Schools: Appraisals of an American Experiment*. The studies describe the subtle forms of segregation that began to occur as white and African American students were placed in integrated schools for the first time. For instance, in one recently integrated school, African American students were suspended for committing the same offenses for which white students received only a reprimand. A teacher in the school complained that, unlike African American students, when white students were sent to the principal's office, they were immediately sent back to class. In this school, equal opportunity to attend the school did not result in equal treatment within the school.

Unequal treatment of different races within the same school is one problem in integrated schools; the establishment of racial boundaries among students creates another. One study in the Rist book describes how racial boundaries were established in a high school in Memphis, Tennessee, after the students of an all-African-American school were integrated with the students of

an all-white school. Here, white students maintained control over most student activities. Activities in which African American students began to participate after integration were athletics and cheerleading. When this occurred, the status of these activities was denigrated by white students. On the other hand, whites were able to maintain control of the student government, ROTC, school clubs, and the staff of the yearbook.

This division of control among student activities reflected the rigid social boundaries that existed in the high school between the two groups. Individuals who crossed these social boundaries had to adapt to the social customs of those on the other side. For instance, African American students changed their style of dress and social conduct in order to be accepted by white students. African American students who crossed racial lines by making such changes found themselves accused by other African American students of "acting white" and were subsequently rejected by "unchanged" African American students. The same was true of white students who crossed racial boundaries.

The racial boundaries that continue to exist in high schools after integration reflect the racial barriers that continue in the larger society. The social life of a school often reflects the social world outside the school. Integration of a school system can help assure equality of educational opportunity, but it cannot break down society's racial barriers. Although schools attempt to deal with this problem, its solution requires a general transformation of racial relationships in the larger society.

The following story of "Black Suburbia" exemplifies the different forms racism can take in a school district. The story also shows the complicated set of factors that put a school system on the path of discrimination and the tragedy that often strikes minorities in their quest for equal educational opportunity.

BLACK SUBURBIA

One particular suburban community of about 40,000 people is on the border of a major midwestern industrial city. Prior to the 1960s, the majority of the population was white; family incomes were primarily in the lower middle and middle range. During the mid-1960s, the population of the community began to shift rapidly from a majority of white residents to a majority of African American residents. This was dramatically reflected in the school enrollments. In 1965, the percentage of African American students enrolled in the school system was 10 percent. By 1970, the percentage of African American students was 87 percent, and in 1974 it was 97 percent. By the middle of the 1970s the few remaining white children were in one elementary school in the more affluent section of the suburb.

The African American population that moved into Black Suburbia was primarily in the middle income range and very concerned about the quality of the educational system. When income figures from the 1960 and 1970 censuses for this suburban area are compared and 1960 dollars are adjusted to 1970 dollars, it is revealed that the African American population moving into Black Suburbia in the 1960s had slightly higher incomes than the whites moving out of the community. The bulk of the African American population moving into the area during this period was in the middle income range and could be viewed as a group interested in upward mobility.

A study of the community in the late 1960s showed the mobility concerns and educational aspirations of the new African American population. The study provided profiles of nine different social groups, including old and new white residents at different income and age levels and new African American residents at different income and age levels. The study found that both middle-aged and young middle-class African American residents had high expectations of upward mobility and believed that quality schools were a major element in a quality community. The population group labeled "new, middle-aged, black middle-class residents" was earning more than $10,000 a year and was employed as managers, proprietors, and profes-

sionals. This group was found to have an "extraordinarily high degree" of expectations for continuing upward mobility and a concern about the quality of schools. The same expectations and concerns were held by the "new, young, black middle class," who were earning between $6,000 and $9,000 per year and also were employed as managers, proprietors, and professionals. (It should be remembered that the incomes quoted are in 1960 dollars, which were worth considerably more than current dollars.)

The middle-aged and young African American working class described in the study evidenced varying degrees of concern about the quality of schooling. For the middle-aged, African American working-class family, schools were not an important reason for moving to Black Suburbia. This group comprised unskilled workers earning between $6,000 and $7,000 per year. On the other hand, the quality of schools was important to the young African American working-class residents, who were earning between $5,000 and $9,000 per year and were employed primarily in skilled and semiskilled jobs.

During the early 1970s the high mobility and the educational aspirations of African American residents who arrived in Black Suburbia in the 1960s were threatened by the rapid influx of a poor African American population. The introduction of a large group of low income African American families was reflected in the percentage of children from welfare families in the school system. Between 1965 and 1970 the percentage of children from welfare families in Black Suburbia increased from 6 to 16 percent as the racial composition of the population changed. Between 1970 and 1973 the percentage of children from welfare families increased dramatically, from 16 to 51 percent. The migration of upwardly mobile middle-class African Americans was followed by the rapid migration of African American welfare families.

The educational aspirations of those in the early African American migration were frustrated both by the response of the local school system to these new residents, and by the later migration of poor African Americans. One of the first things to happen was that the educational expectations of the mainly white teachers and administrators in the school system began to fall. This seemed to be caused by the assumption of the white school staff that the African Americans moving into the community were not interested in education and would create major problems in the school system. This assumption is most clearly shown when the educational expectations of elementary school principals are compared with the educational expectations of the African American community.

In the early 1970s, a local government survey of Black Suburbia included a question dealing with the level of educational aspirations. The survey asked parents how far they would like their sons or daughters to progress in school. Seventy-three percent of the parents wanted their sons to complete college, and 71 percent had that goal for their daughters. More important, when asked how far they believed their sons or daughters would actually go in school, 60 percent believed their sons would complete college, and 62 percent believed their daughters would do the same.

The contrast between the educational aspirations of the parents and the expectations of the elementary school principals illustrates the problems and frustrations encountered by African American residents. When I asked elementary school principals what percentage of the students in their schools they felt would go to college, the responses from three of the principals were 3 percent, 12 percent, and 10 percent. Two elementary school principals evaded the question and claimed it had nothing to do with their work in the elementary school, and one elementary school principal gave a figure of 50 percent.

One of the important things about these responses is that the 50-percent figure was given by a new African American elementary principal, who clearly was closer to understanding the values of the local community. All the other principals

were white, and were principals in the school system before the racial change occurred. The educational expectation levels of these principals not only were considerably below those of the community, but were also below those of the teachers. A survey of elementary school teachers found that they thought that 29 percent of their students would graduate from college. Although this figure was still lower than the figure for the community, it was at least closer to community expectations than were the principals' estimates. One of the reasons for this might be that the teaching staff changed more than the elementary administrative staff and there was a recent effort by the school district to recruit African American teachers.

Several examples can be used to show how the lower expectations of school staff translated into practice. When I interviewed the head of the local community library, he informed me that in the years prior to the racial change, scholarly and professional journals were heavily used by high school students. This was not because the students read these journals for pleasure, but because teachers gave homework assignments in the journals. After the racial change, teachers stopped giving homework assignments in these advanced journals. The African Americans who moved to the community because of its relatively high educational standards suddenly found those standards being lowered as their children entered the system.

The director of the local YMCA stated that a person who really wanted to know what was going on in the local school system should park his car outside the high school at closing time and count the number of students carrying books home from school. The director claimed that only a few students carried books, and this was another indication that teachers were no longer giving homework assignments and had given up trying to teach.

Complaints about teachers not teaching were echoed by students in the tenth and twelfth grades of the high school. I interviewed a random sample of the tenth graders and asked about their future plans and if they had any complaints about the school system. Fifty-eight percent of the tenth-grade students who were interviewed had expectations of attending and graduating from college. The major complaint of the students was the quality of the teaching staff.

Twelfth-grade students were chosen to be interviewed from a list of those students designated by the school administration as the "best." Sixty percent of these students expressed concern and even bitterness about the teaching staff. Their major complaint was that certain teachers made no effort to teach and wasted most class periods. One student stated that he had teachers who probably accomplished one day's worth of teaching out of every five days in the classroom. Another student stated that many teachers did not seem to care whether or not students did the work or learned. No attempt was made to make students want to come to class. One student argued that the reason teachers did not care was because they were so upset at trying to control "rowdy" students.

The issue of rowdy students entered almost every discussion about the quality of education in the local high school. There seemed to be an underlying assumption in any conversation with a community member that the rowdy students came from low income African American families. This reflected a tension between the middle-class African Americans who moved into the community in the 1960s and the low income African Americans who moved into the community in the 1970s. Low income families represented a threat to the aspirations and status of the middle-class residents of Black Suburbia.

One example of this was an African American member of the local school board who pounded the table and exclaimed that all he wanted was to live a middle-class existence and provide a home and future for his family. This, he stated, was why he moved to the community. Now he felt his dreams were not being realized, as crime increased in the community, and he feared that his children were not receiving an adequate edu-

cation at the local school. He complained that every time his children left the house, he worried that they would get involved with the rowdy youths of the community. Currently he was sending his daughter to a private school, but his son went to the local high school. He worried constantly that his son would get in with the "wrong" group in the school.

This particular school board member led a group in the community that demanded a strict dress code. The reason for this was that those students identified as rowdy very often wore large hats and high-heeled shoes. The community members demanding the dress code saw it as a means of controlling and disciplining rowdy students. One result of this campaign were signs throughout the high school restricting the wearing of hats.

That the community related rowdiness with low income background was evident from discussions with other community members. One leader of a community welfare organization claimed that rowdy juveniles were organized into natural street groupings, with one street in rivalry with another street. These street groupings, he argued, were primarily based on economic differences; kids from better streets put down kids from poorer streets. The community social-welfare worker saw rowdy juveniles as a product of poverty who were characterized by their lack of a sense of direction, which easily led them to drift into a life of stealing, drugs, and gambling. Another social-welfare worker, who dealt directly with cases of juvenile delinquency, described middle-class youth in the community as walking a thin line where, at any time, pressures from this delinquent subculture could persuade the student to join the rowdy culture. This was very much the fear expressed by the school board member.

Students at the high school tended to see the issue of rowdy students as one of the problems with the teaching staff. Teachers generalized from the misbehavior of a few students to all students. One of the common complaints of tenth graders was the way teachers handled discipline problems. The majority of students felt that teachers were unable to control students in a just and fair manner. The problem was compounded, students believed, because teachers did not know how to control rowdy students and, consequently, acted "mean" toward all students.

The process of generalizing from a few students to all students might be one of the factors contributing to the failure of teachers in the school system to understand or attempt to respond to the educational aspirations of the middle-class African American community. Perhaps the delinquent subculture reinforced existing stereotypes held by white teachers and administrators about the way African American students acted and learned. This would influence the levels of teacher expectations, as reflected in not assigning homework or not expecting students to use the community library.

For middle-class African Americans who entered the community in the 1960s with high aspirations for upward mobility and quality education for their children, the school system became a source of frustration and disillusionment. Teachers did not provide the instruction parents hoped for and, in addition, they came to fear that their children might enter a delinquent subculture. For the more affluent African American residents, the solution was a rejection of the public school and the transfer of their children to private schools.

African American families and students who were not interested in college but hoped that the school could provide some form of immediate job training also were frustrated in attaining their goals, as a direct result of racial discrimination. In the early 1970s the school system in Black Suburbia built a new vocational high school directly connected to the traditional high school. The vocational school was the product of a state master plan for vocational education, which mandated the establishment of joint vocational-school districts or individual vocational schools within each district. The problems of the vocational school in Black Suburbia were directly related to the discriminatory policies of the surrounding white suburban communities.

The story of Black Suburbia's vocational school came from the local superintendent and his staff, as well as a superintendent in the district next to Black Suburbia. After the resolution of the vocational-school issue, these superintendents were no longer on speaking terms. The problem began when a meeting of all the superintendents in one suburban area of this metropolitan area was called to discuss the formation of a joint vocational-school district as a method of complying with state requirements. The suburbs in this area were mostly white, except for three integrated suburban communities and Black Suburbia. Before the actual meeting, the superintendents of the predominantly white suburbs agreed by telephone to form their own vocational district, which would exclude the three integrated school districts and Black Suburbia. When the four school superintendents representing the suburbs having sizable African American populations arrived at the meeting, they found that all decisions had been made and that they would be forced to work together in establishing a separate vocational district.

There is no agreement on what happened after this meeting. The superintendent of Black Suburbia claimed that the three integrated suburbs were hesitant about working with his school district, because those three communities had a higher income population. Consequently, the superintendent of Black Suburbia was forced to build a vocational high school next to the one regular high school in the community. The superintendent of the adjoining integrated community claims the whole situation was a misunderstanding and that his community was willing to work on a joint vocational-school district.

The establishment of a separate vocational school in Black Suburbia had the effect of increasing the degree of segregation between white and African American suburban schools. A joint vocational school covering the entire eastern area would have made a major contribution to school integration. The segregation of Black Suburbia's vocational school assured that its training programs would be inferior to the joint vocational school's programs, because an all-African-American school faced major problems in establishing links with unions, which traditionally excluded African Americans, and with white businesses. Because it was difficult for an all-African-American school to establish these contacts, it was very hard to place students graduating from the vocational program.

This problem was highlighted in a conversation with the head of the vocational high school. In his vocational training programs he could claim the placement of only three welders in the last three years. The superintendent admitted conducting his own telephone survey to determine the problems in placement of the graduates in cosmetology. He found that only a few African American graduates were able to get jobs in beauty parlors, and those jobs were at very low wages. Even those who got jobs found they lasted only a short time, because beauty parlors depend on a high turnover of personnel.

Another problem now faced by the Black Suburbia school system was that it had a vocational building that had to be filled and a teaching staff that needed to protect their jobs by attracting students. The size of the vocational school required that almost half the students in the eleventh and twelfth grades enroll in its programs. In the tenth grade the students were shown through the school and given a choice between entering the vocational program the following year or continuing in an academic program. From the perspective of the staff of the vocational school, it was important to persuade students to enter their programs.

When the guidance counselor in the vocational school was asked what methods were used to persuade students to enter programs that could not promise jobs, his response was that they lied to the students. He justified this in terms of needing students to build good programs in the future, and said that even though jobs would be difficult to find for the students, the training they would be receiving in the vocational program would be more useful than that received in the traditional academic program. From his perspective, very few of the students in the secondary school were capable of going on to college.

A different interpretation was given by the African American director of the local YWCA. She felt that the vocational school was keeping students from going to college. When she was asked what percentage of local high school students she felt would go on to college, she stated that before the vocational high school was established, about 70 percent of the girls attending the YWCA planned on attending college. After the establishment of the vocational school, the number dropped to 30 or 40 percent. She argued quite strongly that if the community were all white, the vocational school never would have been built. It was, she felt, a racist institution designed primarily to give African American students an inferior education. Another observer referred to the vocational program as "education for welfare."

The story of Black Suburbia highlights some fundamental problems encountered by minority groups in the United States. The fact that the expectations of teachers and school administrative staffs can be far below the aspirations of the minority group can cause a major decrease in the quality of education. In addition, the school staff can generalize from the behavioral problems of children from low income families to all members of the minority group. In this case study, students directly felt this process of generalization. The tension in Black Suburbia between middle-class and lower-class African Americans highlights the importance of social class as a factor in discussions of segregation.

NATIVE AMERICANS

While African Americans are at the forefront of the struggle for equal educational opportunity, Native Americans, Mexican Americans, and Asian Americans joined the civil rights movement with complaints that government schools were destroying their cultures and languages, and that they were subject to segregation. In particular, Native Americans wanted to gain control of the education of their children and restore their cultural heritage and languages to the curriculum. The demand for self-determination by Native Americans received consideration in government decisions after the election of John F. Kennedy in 1960. The Kennedy administration advocated Indian participation in decisions regarding federal policies. Kennedy's secretary of interior, Stewart Udall, appointed a Task Force on Indian Affairs which, in its 1961 report, recommended that Native Americans be given full citizenship and self-sufficiency.

One of the results of the drive for self-determination was the creation of the Rough Rock Demonstration School in 1966. Established on a Navajo reservation in Arizona, the school was a joint effort of the Office of Economic Opportunity and the Bureau of Indian Affairs. One of the major goals of the demonstration school was for Navajo parents to control the education of their children and to participate in all aspects of their schooling.

Besides tribal control, one of the important features of the Rough Rock Demonstration School was the attempt to preserve the Navajo language and culture. In contrast to the attempts to destroy Native cultures and languages that took place in the nineteenth and early twentieth centuries, the goal of learning both Navajo and English was presented as a means of preparing children to live in both cultures.

The struggle for self-determination was aided by the development of a pan-Indian movement in the United States. The pan-Indian movement was based on the assumption that Native American tribes shared a common set of values and interests. Similar to the role played by CORE and SCLC among African Americans, pan-Indian organizations, such as the American Indian Movement (AIM) and the Indians of All Tribes, led demonstrations demanding self-determination. In 1969, members of the Indians of All

Tribes seized Alcatraz Island in San Francisco Bay as a means of calling attention to the plight of Native Americans and demanding that the island, which Indians had originally sold to the federal government for $24 worth of beads, be made an Indian cultural and education center. In 1972, AIM organized a march on Washington, D.C., called the Trail of Broken Treaties. Members of the march seized the Bureau of Indian Affairs and hung a large sign at its entrance declaring it the American Indian Embassy.

It was in this climate of civil rights activism and political support for Indian self-determination that the U.S. Senate Committee on Labor and Public Welfare issued in 1969 the report, *Indian Education: A National Tragedy—A National Challenge*. The report opened with a statement condemning previous educational policies of the federal government: "A careful review of the historical literature reveals that the dominant policy of the Federal Government toward the American Indian has been one of forced assimilation . . . [because of] a desire to divest the Indian of his land."

After a lengthy review of the failure of past educational policies, the report's first recommendation was for "maximum participation and control by Indians in establishing Indian education programs." In its second recommendation, the report called for maximum Indian participation in the development of educational programs in federal schools and local public schools. These educational programs were to include early childhood education, vocational education, work-study, and adult literacy education.

The Congressional debates resulting from the report eventually culminated in the passage of the Indian Education Act in 1972. The declared policy of the legislation was to provide financial assistance to local schools to develop programs to meet the "special" educational needs of Native American students. In addition, the legislation created a federal "Office of Indian Education."

In 1974, the Bureau of Indian Affairs issued a set of procedures for protecting student rights and due process. In contrast to the brutal and dictatorial treatment of Indian students in the boarding schools of the late nineteenth and early twentieth centuries, each Indian student was extended the right "to make his or her own decisions where applicable." And, in striking contrast to earlier deculturalization policies, Indian students were granted "the right to freedom of religion and culture."

The most important piece of legislation supporting self-determination was the 1975 Indian Self-Determination and Education Assistance Act which gave tribes the power to contract with the federal government to run their own education and health programs. The legislation opened with the declaration that it was "an Act to provide maximum Indian participation in the Government and education of Indian people; to provide for the full participation of Indian tribes in programs and services conducted by the federal government. . . . "

The Indian Self-Determination and Education Assistance Act strengthened Indian participation in the control of education programs. The legislation provided that a local school district receiving funds for the education of Indian students which did not have a school board composed of a majority of Indians had to establish a separate local committee composed of parents of Indian students in the school. This committee was given the authority over any Indian education program contracted with the federal government.

The principles embodied in the Indian Self-Determination and Education Assistance Act of 1975 were expanded upon in 1988 with the passage of the Tribally Controlled Schools Act. In addition to the right to operate schools under federal contract as provided in the 1975 legislation, the Tribally Controlled Schools Act provided for outright grants to tribes to support the operation of their own schools.

MEXICAN AMERICANS

Similar to African Americans, Mexican Americans experienced many years of segregation in schools throughout the Southwest and attempted to redress their grievances through the courts. In Ontario, California, in 1945, Mexican American parents demanded that the school board grant all requests for transfer out of segregated Mexican schools. When the board refused this request, Gonzalo Mendez and William Guzman brought suit for violation of the Fourteenth Amendment to the Constitution. The school board responded to this suit by claiming that segregation was not based on race or national origins but on the necessity of providing special instruction. In other words, the school district justified segregation on the basis that Mexican American children required special instruction because they came from homes where Spanish was the spoken language.

In 1946 a U.S. District Court ruled in *Mendez et al. v. Westminster School District* of Orange County that the only possible argument for segregation was the special educational needs of Mexican American children. These needs centered around the issue of learning English. Completely reversing the educational justification for segregation, the judge argued that "evidence clearly shows that Spanish-speaking children are retarded in learning English by lack of exposure to its use by segregation. . . . " Therefore, the court ruled segregation was illegal because it was not required by state law and because there was no valid educational justification for segregation.

Heartened by the *Mendez* decision, the League of United Latin American Citizens (LULAC), the Mexican American equivalent of the NAACP, forged ahead in its legal attack on segregation in Texas. With support from LULAC, a group of parents in 1948 brought suit against the Bastrop Independent School District charging that local school authorities had no legal right to segregate children of Mexican descent and that segregation was solely because the children were of Mexican descent. In *Delgado v. Bastrop Independent School District*, the court ruled that segregating Mexican American children was illegal and discriminatory. The ruling required that the local school district end all segregation. The court did give local school districts the right to separate some children in the first grade, only if scientific tests showed that they needed special instruction in English and the separation took place on the same campus.

In general, LULAC was pleased with the decision. The one point they were dissatisfied with was the provision for the separation of children in the first grade. This allowed local schools to practice what was referred to in the latter part of the twentieth century as second generation segregation. Second generation segregation refers to the practice of using educational justifications for segregating children within a single school building. In fact, many local Texas school districts did use the proviso for that purpose.

While the *Mendez* and *Delgado* decisions did hold out the promise of ending segregation of Mexican Americans, local school districts used many tactics to avoid integration, including manipulation of school district lines, choice plans, and different forms of second generation segregation. For instance, the California State Department of Education reported in 1966 that 57 percent of the children with Spanish surnames were still attending schools that were predominantly Mexican American. In 1973 a civil rights activist, John Caughey, estimated that two-thirds of the Mexican American children in Los Angeles attended segregated schools. In *All Deliberate Speed: Segregation and Exclusion in California Schools, 1855–1975*, Charles Wollenberg estimates that in California by 1973 more Mexican and Mexican American children attended segregated schools than in 1947.

In 1970, Mexican Americans were officially recognized by the federal courts as an identifiable dominated group in the public schools in a MALDEF case, *Cisernos v. Corpus Christi Independent School District*. A central issue in the case was whether or not the 1954 school desegregation decision could be applied to Mexican Americans. The original *Brown* decision dealt specifically with African Americans who were segregated by state and local laws. In his final decision, Judge Owen Cox ruled that blacks and Mexican Americans were segregated in the Corpus Christi school system and that Mexican Americans were an identifiable dominated group because of their language, culture, religion, and Spanish surnames.

Despite years of struggle, many Mexican Americans still feel their demands for equality of educational opportunity have not been met. In the fall of 1994, the Latino Education Coalition in Denver, Colorado, threatened to call a student strike if the school district did not hire more bilingual education teachers, . . . involve Latino parents in policy decisions, and increase the number of Latino students going on to college. The threat was reminiscent of 1969, when 3,000 Latino students went on strike against the Denver school district because of high drop-out rates, low academic achievement, and the failure to be sensitive to cultural differences. It would appear that only steady political pressure can assure equality of educational opportunity.

ASIAN AMERICANS

Also suffering a history of discrimination in U.S. schools, Asian Americans are often viewed by others as the model minority group. And, until the publication of Ronald Takaki's *Strangers from a Different Shore: A History of Asian Americans*, Asian Americans were usually invisible in standard U.S. history texts.

Ironically, the stereotype of model minority student has caused many educators to overlook the educational problems encountered by many Asian American students in U.S. schools. Part of the problem is the tendency for non-Asians to lump all Asian Americans together. In fact, Asian Americans represent a broad spectrum of different cultures and nations including, as Valerie Ooka Pang indicates in her article "Asian-American Children: A Diverse Population," "Cambodian, Chinese, East Indian, Filipino, Guamian, Hawaiian, Hmong, Indonesian, Japanese, Korean, Laotian, Samoan, and Vietnamese . . . [and]

smaller Asian-American groups within the category of all other Asians." According to U.S. Census classification there are sixteen of these smaller Asian American groups.

The diversity of Asian Americans also reflects a wide range of adjustment to conditions in the United States. Most non-Asians think of Asian Americans as successful entrepreneurs and professionals who were model students while in school and quickly moved up the economic ladder after graduation. In fact, a report issued in 1994 by the Asian Pacific American Public Institute and the Asian American Center suggests that many Asian Americans face a difficult economic life in the United States. For instance, according to the report, while 8 percent of households nationally received public assistance in 1991, 77 percent of Cambodian and Laotian households in California received public assistance. The report states that Cambodians, Vietnamese, and Laotians have the highest rate of welfare dependency of any racial or ethnic group in the United States. For all Asian Americans the per capita income in 1990 was $10,500 which was less than the $12,000 per capita income for non-Hispanic whites. Or, another way of viewing the economic differences in the Asian American community, according to the report, is to consider that for every Asian American family earning more than $75,000 there is an Asian American family earning less than $10,000 a year. While a third of Asian Americans have college degrees, 23 percent of those Asian Americans over 25 have less than a high school diploma. A quarter of all families in Chinatown in New York City are living below the poverty line.

While economic figures highlight the plight of many Asian Americans, history points out the educational discrimination encountered by Asian American students. In *All Deliberate Speed*, Charles Wollenberg tells the story of the denial of equal educational opportunity to Asian Americans in California schools. With cries of "yellow peril" coming from the European American population, the State Superintendent of Public

Instruction in California, William Welcher, pointed out in 1884 that the state constitution referred to Chinese as "dangerous to the well-being of the state" and, therefore, argued that San Francisco did not have "to undergo the expense of educating such people." Denied a public education for his daughter, Joseph Tape, an Americanized Chinese, challenged the decision in court. Judge Maguire of the municipal court ruled that since the daughter, Mamie, was an American citizen she could not be denied equal educational opportunity according to the Fourteenth Amendment to the U.S. Constitution. In addition, Judge Maguire argued that it was unjust to tax Chinese for the support of a school system which excluded Chinese children. State Superintendent Welcher reacted angrily to the decision, declaring it a "terrible disaster" and asked, "Shall we abandon the education of our children to provide that of the Chinese who are thrusting themselves upon us?"

In reaction to the court decision, the California State Assembly passed legislation allowing school districts to establish segregated schools for "Mongolians." This legislation empowered the San Francisco Board of Education to establish a segregated school for Asians. The courts affirmed this action in 1902, when Wong Him challenged the requirement of attending a segregated institution. Eventually, pressure from the Chinese American community brought an end to segregation. In 1921, Chinese American educator, Mary Bo-Tze Lee, challenged the segregation policy by showing that Chinese students scored as well as white students on I.Q. tests. As the Chinese population dispersed through the city, traditionally white schools were forced to open their doors to Chinese students. A study in 1947 found that formal school segregation had ended but that the original segregated Commodore Stockton school was still 100 percent Chinese.

Asian American students are currently discriminated against because of the stereotype of "model minority" student. Asian American students with educational problems are often neglected because teachers assume they will do well in school. On the other hand, many non-Asian educators resent the achievement of some Asian Americans. In 1987, *Time* magazine called Asian Americans the "new whiz kids." *Time* reported that Asian Americans comprised 25 percent of the entering class at the University of California at Berkeley, 21 percent at the California Institute of Technology, and 14 percent at Harvard. *Time* magazine, in 1987, also reported that as a result of quota systems many qualified Asian Americans were being refused admission to major universities.

The largest number of complaints centered on the admission policies of the University of California at Berkeley. *Time* quotes the cochairperson of the Asian American Task Force on University Admissions, Alameda County Superior Court Judge Ken Kawaichi, that university administrators envision a campus that "is mostly white, mostly upper class with limited numbers of African Americans, Hispanics and Asians. One day they looked around and said, 'My goodness, look at this campus. What are all these Asian people doing here?' Then they started tinkering with the system."

The political actions taken by Asian Americans, Mexican Americans, and Native Americans to gain equal educational opportunity highlight the recent research findings that second generation segregation can be reduced by the exercise of effective political power. As the next section suggests, there is evidence of a relationship between decreasing second generation segregation, the election of Hispanics and African Americans to school boards, and the hiring of Hispanics and African Americans as teachers and school administrators. These findings are applicable to situations of segregation encountered by Native Americans and Asian Americans.

SECOND GENERATION SEGREGATION AND POLITICAL POWER

Two important books—Kenneth Meier, Joseph Stewart, Jr., and Robert England, *Race, Class,*

and Education: The Politics of Second-Generation Discrimination, and Kenneth Meier and Joseph Stewart, Jr., *The Politics of Hispanic Education*—focus on the relationship between political involvement and second generation segregation. The two books are concerned with political organizations that promote segregative practices in schools and deny certain groups equality of educational opportunity. In addition, they link segregative practices with student achievement. They consider student achievement to be dependent on equal access to educational opportunities.

The main conclusion of their studies is that segregative practices in schools are reduced by the presence on boards of education and in educational bureaucracies of representatives from affected groups such as Hispanics and African Americans. Therefore, their suggested reforms focus on ways to increase representation from dominated groups.

In their research, they found that schools still practice segregation through academic grouping, such as placement in special education classes, ability grouping, curriculum tracking, and segregated bilingual education. In addition, they found that discipline is applied in different ways to different ethnic and racial groups. For instance, Hispanic and African American students might be suspended or expelled from school at different rates than white students. And finally, they concluded that all of these segregative practices have a negative effect on high school graduation rates.

With regard to Hispanic Americans, they conclude that the larger the number of Hispanic representatives in an educational system the less chance of second generation segregation. In their study, representation includes boards of education, educational bureaucracies, and teachers. In other words, there will be less second generation segregation if there are more Hispanics on boards of education, and working as school administrators and teachers.

In addition, Meier and Stewart found an interrelationship between representation on boards of education, and representation in the bureaucracy and teaching ranks. The higher the level of representation of Hispanics on boards of education, the higher the level of representation of Hispanics in the school administration. In other words, Hispanic representation on boards of education creates a greater than normal possibility that the board will choose Hispanic administrators. In turn, they found, the higher the representation of Hispanics in the bureaucracy, the higher the number of Hispanic teachers.

These findings suggest a chain reaction. Hispanics are elected to the board of education and they select more Hispanic administrators, who in turn select more Hispanic teachers, which results in a decline in second generation segregation and greater equality of educational opportunity. Specifically, they found that greater Hispanic representation is associated with proportionately fewer Hispanic students in special education classes and larger numbers of Hispanic students in gifted programs. Also, higher rates of Hispanic representation are related to less disparity in discipline. And finally, a higher representation of Hispanics is related to a higher proportion of Hispanics graduating from high school.

Policy recommendations follow logically from these conclusions. Of course, Meier and Stewart recommend greater representation of minority populations on school boards. They recommend greater federal scrutiny of second generation forms of discrimination and that school districts hire more Hispanic administrators and teachers. They recommend the elimination of most academic grouping.

In the final analysis, the most important message in their research is that political power is the key to having a school system serve a group's educational interests. And in the case of Hispanics, African Americans, and Native Americans, this political power is essential to ending forms of inequality of educational opportunity. Just as African Americans in the South had to organize to stop segregation, other groups must exercise political muscle to stop second generation forms of segregation.

RACIAL OR SOCIAL-CLASS DIFFERENCES?

School people must remain sensitive to the possibility of racial differences being translated into socioeconomic differences. Sparking this debate is sociologist William J. Wilson's book, *The Declining Significance of Race: Blacks and Changing American Institutions*. Wilson argues that as a result of the civil rights movement racial differences are less important in explaining social differences between African Americans and whites; socioeconomic differences are now more important than differences of race.

To support his argument, Wilson cites statistics on the changing pattern of the occupational structure in the African American community and the increasing gap in social conditions between middle- and lower-class African Americans. Wilson notes a dramatic change in African American social mobility during the 1950s and 1960s. In 1950, 16.4 percent of African American males were employed in middle-class occupations. In 1960, this percentage reached 24 percent, and in 1970, it rose to 35.3 percent. These changes reflect the dramatic increase in civil rights for minority groups during these two decades.

But during the 1970s, Wilson argues, the gap between middle-class and poor African Americans began to increase, thus making it more difficult for African Americans born into a state of poverty to experience social mobility. He notes the steady decrease in the number of African Americans below the poverty line, from 48.1 percent in 1959 to 29.4 percent in 1968; in the 1970s, however, this percentage did not undergo any significant change, with the percentage of African Americans below the poverty line persisting at 27 to 28 percent.

Not only has the percentage of African Americans below the poverty line remained about the same since the 1960s, but the gap in income between middle-class and lower-class African Americans has been increasing. The unemployment rate for young African Americans from poor families also has been increasing, and many have given up looking for work. In addition, there has been a steady increase in single-parent families among poor African Americans, which has a direct effect on family income. What all this adds up to, according to Wilson, is deteriorating social and economic conditions for poor African Americans.

Wilson's findings were supported in a 1989 report of the National Research Council titled *A Common Destiny: Blacks and American Society.* A primary concern of the report was that the economic status of African Americans relative to whites deteriorated from 1970 to the 1980s. Particularly worrisome was the growing gap between middle income and low income African Americans. The report stated that between 1970 and 1980 the proportion of African American families with incomes above $35,000 increased from 18 to 22 percent, while the proportion of incomes below $10,000 also increased from 26 to 30 percent. In addition, in 1985 the number of African American families headed by single females was 50 percent and these families received only 25 percent of total African American family income.

The deteriorating conditions for many African Americans were reflected in the findings of a study conducted by Deborah Carter and Reginald Wilson for the American Council of Education on the decline in college enrollments among middle and low income minorities. Based on census figures, they found that there was a drop in the number of African American high school graduates attending college between 1976 and 1988 from 30.8 percent to 30.3 percent. In addition, during this time the number of African Americans receiving college degrees declined by 4.3 percent. For Hispanic Americans the drop was even more dramatic—from 50.4 percent to 35.2 percent during the same period. On the other hand, the percentage of low income white high school graduates attending college rose slightly during the same period, from 36.9 percent to 38.8 percent. For all races and incomes,

college enrollment increased to 57.5 percent in 1988 from 53.4 percent in 1976.

The authors of the report conclude that the main reason for the decline in minority college attendance is the decline in student financial aid. Without economic resources and with the continuing increase in college costs, low income minority students are finding it difficult to attend college. The report states, "comprehensive and sustained efforts are needed at the institutional level to recruit, retain, and graduate larger numbers of minority students."

Thus, teachers and administrators must not only be aware of racial barriers but also socioeconomic barriers. It would be relatively easy for school people to integrate student activities and classrooms with middle-class African Americans, without giving consideration to social-class differences within the African American community. Integration of middle-class students could only give teachers or administrators a false sense of having solved racial problems when, in fact, they might be contributing to the development of a permanent underclass.

A major problem that could result from the accomplishment of equal educational opportunity among races is increased inequality in educational opportunity among social classes. For instance, magnet schools might bring about racial balance but also might result in a social-class stratification in particular schools. It is not beyond the realm of possibility that white and African American children of working-class parents both might receive counseling that sends them to vocational schools, while upper- and middle-class children are counseled to select academic programs. Although the high aspirations of middle-class African American parents might be satisfied, there would be a danger of increased segregation between social classes.

This is particularly important when we consider the relationship between education and social mobility.... The high educational aspirations held by the African American community are related to a belief that schooling is a means of social mobility. It is also true that segregated education has been a means of maintaining a stratified society by keeping African American people separated from the career routes available to the majority of the population. Integrated education will be a means of moving the African American population into the mainstream of occupational mobility in the United States. This could be one of the important consequences of integration.

On the other hand. . . . receiving equal education does not guarantee social mobility, which is not directly related to the school but to the job market. In addition, there is some evidence that the school's role includes a combination of facilitating the movement of people into new occupations as they occur and maintaining stratification between social classes. It is certainly good that poor African American people receive equal education, but the frustrations now felt by poor whites in using the school as a means of social mobility might well be shared by poor African Americans as the middle-class African American population reaps the rewards of integration.

RACISM AND EDUCATION

While social class must be considered as a factor in the provision of equal educational opportunity, racism still appears to be a major factor. The concept of *race* is socially and historically constructed, and its meaning is full of ambiguity. Discussions of racial issues are often emotionally charged and, in the context of racism in the United States, cause a crisis in white identity. Consequently, I will link my discussion of race and racism to the guilt and anger expressed by some white students when they are confronted with issues of racism.

Racism refers to acts of oppression of one racial group toward another. Often, *racism* is defined as prejudice plus power. This definition of racism distinguishes between simple feelings of hostility and prejudice toward another racial group and the ability to turn those feelings into some form of oppression. For instance, black

people might have prejudicial feelings toward white people, but they have little opportunity to express those prejudicial feelings in some form of economic or political oppression of white people. On the other hand, prejudicial feelings that white people might have towards blacks can turn into racism when they become the basis for discrimination in education, housing, and the job market. Within this framework, racism becomes the act of social, political, and economic oppression of another group.

When discussions of racism occur in my multicultural education classes, white students complain of a sense of hostility from black students and, consequently, accuse black students of racism. Black students respond that their feelings represent prejudice and not racism because they lack the power to discriminate against whites. The troubling aspect of this response is the implication that if these black students had the power they would be racist. One black student pointed out that there are situations where blacks can commit racist acts against whites. The black student used the example of recent killings of white passengers by a black man on a commuter railroad. The evidence seemed to indicate that the killer was motivated by extreme hatred of whites which the newspapers labeled "black rage." This was a racist act, the black student argued, because the gun represented power.

Racism is often thought of as "whites" oppressing "people of color." Of course, there are many problems with this definition. If one parent is black and another white are their children considered black or white? Can one white-skinned child of this marriage be considered white while one dark-skinned child is considered black? Jake Lamar recalls how the confusion over skin color sparked the development of his racial consciousness at the age of three. Jake was sitting at the kitchen table when his Uncle Frank commented "about how obnoxious white people were." Jake responded, "But Mommy's white." His uncle replied that his mother was not white but was "just light-skinned." Jake then said that he thought his father, brother, and himself were black while his sister and mother were white. His mother then explained that they had many white ancestors which caused the variation in skin color, but they were still "all Negroes." Thinking back on this incident, Jake Lamar reflected, "Black and white then meant something beyond pigmentation . . . so my first encounter with racial awareness was at once enlightening and confusing, and shot through with ambiguity."

While the social and historical construction of the meaning of race is full of ambiguity, the United States still remains a society divided by race. Just as racial concepts were used to justify economic exploitation, racial divisions continue to reflect economic differences. The major racial division in the United States is between black and white, which also reflects major economic differences. According to the 1990 census, the average white family income was $36,915 while the average black family income was $21,423. But even more indicative of economic differences based on race were the differences in the economic value of education. On the average, black men earned 20 percent less than white men when they had the same level of education. For instance, a black man without a high school education earned on the average 20.3 percent less than a white man without a high school education. A black man with a high school diploma earned on the average 23.6 percent less than a white man with a high school diploma. A black man with 4 years of college earned 20.2 percent less than a white man with a similar education, and a black man with more than 5 years of college earned 22.9 percent less than a white man with a similar education. Therefore, despite similar educational opportunities there are still sharp economic differences along racial lines. In 1990, the average unemployment rate for whites was 4.1 percent while for blacks it was 11.3 percent. There are also major racial divisions in the labor force, with blacks being overrepresented in many occupations and underrepresented in others.

In his 1992 book, *Two Nations: Black and White, Separate, Hostile, Unequal*, Andrew Hacker describes how he had his white students attempt to determine the economic value of being white by presenting them with a fictional account of a white person being visited by representatives of an unnamed institution. The white person is informed that a terrible mistake was made and that he should have been born black. Consequently, the person was now going to be given a black skin and facial features but his memory and ideas would remain the same. Since this was a mistake, the person would be offered financial compensation for being made black. The white students were then asked to name what they felt should be the compensation for becoming black. Their answer was $1 million yearly for the rest of the person's life.

Discussions of concepts of race often make white students feel guilty and this guilt can quickly turn into hostility and resentment. Educator and African American activist Beverly Tatum worries about the loss of white allies in the struggle against racism and the hostility she feels from white college students when teaching about racism. Reflecting on her teaching experiences, she writes, "White students . . . often struggle with strong feelings of guilt when they become aware of the pervasiveness of racism. . . . these feelings are uncomfortable and can lead white students to resist learning about race and racism." Part of the problem, she argues, is that seeing oneself as the oppressor creates a negative self-image which results in a withdrawal from a discussion of the problem. What needs to be done, she maintains, is to counter the guilt by providing white students with a positive self-image of whites fighting against racism. In other words, a self-image of whites being allies with blacks in the struggle against racism.

One of the most popular antiracist curricula for preschool children is the National Association for the Education of Young Children's *Anti-Bias Curriculum: Tools for Empowering Young Children*. This curriculum and related methods of instruction are designed to reduce prejudice among young children regarding race, language, gender, and physical ability differences. The premise of the method is that at an early age children become aware of the connection between power and skin color, language, and physical disabilities. Cited as examples are a 2½-year-old Asian child who refuses to hold the hand of a black classmate because "It's dirty" and a 4-year-old boy who takes over the driving of a pretend bus because "Girls can't be bus drivers."

According to the *Anti-Bias Curriculum*, research findings show that young children classify differences between people and they are influenced by bias toward others. By the age of 2, children are aware of gender differences and begin to apply color names to skin colors. Between ages 3 and 5, children try to figure out who they are by examining the differences in gender and skin color. By 4 or 5 years old, children engage in socially determined gender roles and they give racial reasons for the selection of friends. Based on these research findings, the advocates of the curriculum believe that prejudice can be reduced if there is conscious intervention to curb the development of biased concepts and activities.

Another antiracist education program is the Teaching Tolerance Project which began after a group of teenage skinheads attacked and beat to death an Ethiopian man on a street in Portland, Oregon, in 1988. After this incident, members of the Southern Poverty Law Center decided it was time to do something about teaching tolerance. Dedicated to pursuing legal issues involving racial incidents and denial of civil rights, the Law Center sued, on behalf of the man's family, the two men who were responsible for teaching violent racism to the Portland skinheads. These two teachers, Tom Metzger, the head of the White Aryan Resistance, and his son, became symbols of racist teachings in the United States. In a broad sense, the Teaching Tolerance Project is designed to provide information about teaching methods and materials that will counter the type of racist teachings represented by Metzger and his son.

Similar to the *Anti-Bias Curriculum*, the Teaching Tolerance Project primarily defines racism as a function of economic exploitation. On the inside cover of its magazine, *Teaching Tolerance*, *tolerance* is defined as "the capacity for or the practice of recognizing and respecting the beliefs or practices of others." Within the context of this definition, the project members "primarily celebrate and recognize the beliefs and practices of racial and ethnic groups such as African Americans, Latinos, and Asian Americans."

The primary purpose of the Teaching Tolerance Project is to provide resources and materials to schools to promote "interracial and intercultural understanding between whites and nonwhites." While this is the primary focus of the project, there have been decisions to include material dealing with cultural tolerance, homelessness, and poverty.

The Teaching Tolerance Project is only one of many educational attempts to end racism in the United States. The end of racism is essential for the full provision of equality of opportunity and equality of educational opportunity in U.S. society.

SEXISM AND EDUCATION

While racial differences are one source of inequality of educational opportunity, gender differences are another source. Historically, equality of educational opportunity was to provide equal access to occupations. However, women tend to dominate certain professions while finding it difficult to enter other professions. In their 1994 book, *Failing at Fairness: How America's Schools Cheat Girls*, Myra and David Sadker summarize current research on educational discrimination against girls.

One of the surprising results of their research and analysis of other data was that girls are equal to or ahead of boys in most measures of academic achievement and psychological health during the early years of schooling, but by the end of high school and college girls have fallen behind boys on these measurements. On entrance examinations to college, girls score lower than boys, particularly in science and mathematics. Boys receive more state and national scholarships. Women score lower than men on all entrance examinations to professional schools.

One of the explanations for the decline in test scores is that girls suffer a greater decline than boys in self-esteem from elementary school to high school. (Of course, an important general question about the following statistics is why *both* boys and girls decline in feelings of self-esteem.) As a measure of self-esteem, the Sadkers rely on responses to the statement, "I'm happy the way I am." The Sadkers report that in elementary school 60 percent of girls and 67 percent of boys responded positively to the statement. By high school these positive responses declined to 29 percent for girls and 46 percent for boys. In other words, the decline in self-esteem for girls was 31 percentage points as compared to 21 percentage points for boys. Why is there less self-esteem and a greater decline in self-esteem among girls as compared to boys?

As a method of getting an answer to the question, the Sadkers asked students how their lives would be different if they suddenly were transformed into members of the opposite sex. In general, girls responded with feelings that it wouldn't be so bad and that it would open up opportunities to participate in sports and politics. In addition, girls felt they would have more freedom and respect. With regard to self-esteem, girls expressed little regret about the consequences of the sex change. In contrast boys expressed horror at the idea and many said they would commit suicide. They saw themselves becoming second-class citizens, being denied access to athletics and outdoor activities, and being racked with physical problems. With regard to self-esteem, and in contrast to girls, boys expressed nothing but regret about the consequences of the sex change.

Contributing to the lack of self-esteem among girls, the Sadkers argue, are modes of classroom interaction, the representation of women in textbooks and other educational materials, and the dis-

criminatory content of standardized tests. In one of their workshops with classroom teachers, the Sadkers illustrate classroom sex bias by asking four of the participants—two men and two women—to act like students in a middle school social studies classroom. The lesson is about the American Revolution and it begins with an examination of homework. Acting as the teacher, David Sadker perfunctorily tells one woman that two of her answers are wrong and comments to the group on the neatness of the other woman's homework. He tells one of the men that two of his answers are wrong and, unlike his response to the woman with wrong answers, he urges the man to try harder and suggests ways of improving his answers. David then states to the other man that he failed to do his homework assignment. In contrast to the woman with the neat paper, this man illustrates what the Sadkers call the "bad boy role."

David Sadker then continues the lesson by discussing battles and leaders. All of the revolutionary leaders are, of course, male. During the course of the lesson he calls on the males twenty times each while only calling on one woman twice and completely ignoring the other woman. The one woman that is called on misses her questions because she is given only half a second to respond. When questioning the men, David Sadker spends time giving hints and probing. At the end of this demonstration lesson, the Sadkers report, one woman commented that she felt like she was back in school. She often had the right answer, but was never called on by the teacher.

What this workshop demonstration illustrates, based on the Sadkers' findings on classroom interaction, is that boys receive more and better instruction. Boys are more often called upon by the teacher and boys interact more with the teacher than girls. In a typical classroom situation, if both boys and girls have their hands raised to answer a question, the teacher is most likely to call on a boy. A teacher will spend more time responding to a boy's question than to a girl's question. In other words, girls do not receive equal educational opportunity in the classroom.

In addition, women are not as well represented as men in textbooks. The Sadkers found in 1989 elementary school language arts textbooks that there were from two to three times as many pictures of men as women. In one elementary history text, they found four times as many pictures of men as women. In one 1992 world history textbook of 631 pages they found only seven pages related to women. Two of those pages were devoted to a fifth-grade female student who made a peace trip to the Soviet Union.

It is most likely that the treatment received by girls in the classroom and in textbooks contributes to their low self-esteem and to their decline, as compared to boys, in performance on standardized tests from elementary school to high school. It would seem logical that if less instructional time is spent with girls than boys that boys would more rapidly advance academically. In addition, without equal representation in textbooks, girls might value themselves less and have less incentive to achieve. Instructional time and representation in textbooks contribute to the glass ceiling of the classroom.

The lowering of self-esteem and content bias may contribute to the significant gender gap in scores on standardized college entrance examinations and entrance examinations to professional schools. For instance, on the widely used Scholastic Aptitude Test (SAT) males score 50 points higher on the math section and up to 12 points higher on the verbal section. It is important to understand that discrimination in standardized testing involves the denial of economic rewards. These economic rewards are in the form of scholarships and career opportunities.

The content bias and economic value of standardized tests was recognized in a 1989 ruling by a federal judge in New York. The judge ruled that the awarding of New York State scholarships using the SAT discriminated against female students. The case was brought to court by the Girls Clubs of America and the National Organization for Women. The court argued that the scholarships were to be awarded on the basis of academic achievement in high school and that the SAT was not constructed to test achievement but to determine college performance. The court's decision states, "The evidence is clear that females score significantly below males on the SAT while they perform equally or slightly better in high schools."

In this court case, academic achievement was defined according to grades received in high school courses. Interestingly, the Sadkers argue that this apparent paradox between girls' high grades and low standardized test scores is a result of grade inflation. This grade inflation results from female passivity and their willingness to follow classroom rules. Often, teachers formally and informally incorporate evaluations of student behavior in their academic grading practices. For girls, good behavior can result in good grades.

But the issue of grade inflation still doesn't solve the puzzle of lower performance by girls on tests like the SAT. One possible answer is that the content of standardized tests is biased. The Sadkers suggest that this is one possible reason for the differences in scores between males and females. Boys are more familiar with organized sports, financial issues, science, wars, and dates. Consequently, test items referring to these areas tend to favor boys. As an example, the Sadkers describe a gifted high school girl who lost her concentration on the Preliminary SAT when she encountered an analogy question comparing a "football and a gridiron." The analogy baffled her because she had little knowledge of football.

One possible solution to teacher bias in classroom interaction, the Sadkers suggest, is to have an observer code classroom interactions so that the teacher becomes aware of any possible bias. If teachers are unconsciously favoring boys, then this observation provides the opportunity for them to change their behavior. One teacher told the Sadkers that she distributed two chips to all students. When students want to comment or ask a question they have to give up one chip. Before the class is over, all students must use their two chips. This guarantees equal participation of all students and assures that classroom interaction is not dominated by only a few students.

In addition, the Sadkers recommend that teachers consciously search for books portraying strong female characters in a variety of occupational and social roles. They point to the work of the National Women's History Project which since the 1970s has published materials emphasizing women's roles in history. In addition, the Sadkers recommend the use of workshops to heighten teachers' awareness of their own possible sexist behavior and to understand how to find nonsexist educational material for the classroom.

One possible solution is single-sex education. This would eliminate the problem of female students having to compete with male students for teachers' attention. In classrooms of only girls, teachers would not tend to push girls aside and focus their instructional efforts on boys. In an all-girls school or classroom, female students might receive the equal educational opportunity denied to them in a coed classroom.

Writing in favor of girls' schools, Susan Estrich, professor of law and political science at the University of Southern California, notes that 60 percent of the National Merit Scholarship finalists are boys. Echoing the Sadkers' findings, she reports from a 1992 study of the American Association of University Women, "that even though girls get better grades (except in math), they get less from schools." While she does not dismiss efforts to equalize opportunities for girls in coed schools, she argues that currently single-sex education is working. For instance, in all-girls schools 80 percent of girls take four years of math and science, while in coed schools the average is two years of math and science. In Fortune 1,000 companies, one-third of the female board members are graduates of women's colleges even though graduates of women's colleges represent only 4 percent of all female college graduates. In addition, graduates of women's colleges earn 43 percent of the math and 50 percent of engineering doctorates earned by all women, and they outnumber all other females in *Who's Who*.

Estrich does see the possibility of offering single-sex classes within a coed institution. She cites the example of the Illinois Math and Science Academy which experimented with a girls-only calculus based physics class. Instead of sitting meekly at their desks while boys command all the attention, girls are actively asking and answering questions. In an all-girls algebra class in Ventura, California, the teacher reports spending time building self-confidence along with teaching math. For Estrich, at least at this point in time, all-girls schools are a means for ending sexism in education.

Of course, for an all-girls school or classroom to completely overcome the problems of sexism it would require the maintenance of the same educational expectations as there are for boys and the use of textbooks and other educational materials that provide strong female role models. As I discussed previously in this chapter, one of the problems with segregated female education in the nineteenth century was the belief that women did not have the physical and mental stamina to undergo the same academic demands as men. Consequently, to avoid sexism, there should be no watering down of the curriculum in female schools and classrooms. In addition, sex-segregated education would have to avoid the pitfalls of tracking women into a sex-segregated labor market. One of the problems in the development of the high school in the early twentieth century was that it tended to track women into certain occupations. For an all-girls school or classroom to avoid this form of discrimination there would have to be an emphasis on opening up all career opportunities for women.

There are many critics of proposals for all-female schools. One University of Michigan researcher, Valerie Lee, found that many all-girls classrooms still contained high levels of sexist behavior on the part of the teacher. In one case, a history teacher assigned a research paper and told students that she would provide "major hand-holding" to help the students. Lee argued that the offer of major hand-holding would not occur in a boys' school. In addition, she found "male bashing" taking place in some all-female schools.

In addition, Lee found boys in all-male schools engaging in serious sexist comments about women. In other words, all-female schools do not do anything about the sexist attitudes of men. In fact, all-male schools might reinforce male sexist behavior. For instance, in a 1994 court case involving a suit by Shannon Faulkner to gain entrance to the all-male military college, The Citadel, one of the witnesses, a 1991 graduate of the school, reported that the word *woman* was used on campus in a derogatory manner "every day, every minute, every hour [it was] a part of the life there."

Therefore, there is the possibility that single-sex education might result in greater academic achievement for girls while doing nothing about sexist attitudes among men. The academic gains made by women might mean little in a world dominated by sexist males. Also, the courts may not approve of single-sex public schools, because of a decision regarding all-boys African American schools in Detroit. The court argued that the all-boys schools were a violation of the 1954 *Brown* decision which declared as unconstitutional "separate but equal" schools that were racially segregated. In the Detroit case, separate but equal all-boys schools were declared unconstitutional.

STUDENTS WITH SPECIAL NEEDS

By the 1960s, the civil rights movement encompassed students with special needs, including students with physical handicaps; special mental, emotional, and behavioral needs; and hearing and visual impairments. Within the context of equality of educational opportunity, students with special needs could only participate equally in schools with other students if they received some form of special help. Since the nineteenth century, many of the needs of these students have been neglected by local and state school authorities because of the expense of special facilities and teachers.

The political movement for federal legislation to aid students with special needs followed a path similar to the rest of the civil rights movement. First, finding themselves unable to change educational institutions by pressuring local and state governments, organized groups interested in improving educational opportunities for students with special needs turned to the courts. This was the path taken in the late 1960s by the Pennsylvania Association for Retarded Children (PARC).

PARC was one of many associations organized in the 1950s to aid citizens with special needs. These organizations were concerned with state laws that excluded children with special needs from educational institutions because they were considered ineducable and untrainable. State organizations like PARC and the National Association for Retarded Children campaigned to eliminate these laws and to demonstrate the educability of all children. But, as the civil rights movement discovered throughout the century, local and state officials were resistant to change and relief had to be sought from the judicial system.

In *Pennsylvania Association for Retarded Children (PARC) v. Commonwealth of Pennsylvania*, a case that was as important for the rights of children with special needs as the *Brown* decision was for African Americans, PARC objected to conditions in the Pennhurst State School and Hospital. In framing the case, lawyers for PARC focused on the legal right to an education for children with special needs. PARC, working with the major federal lobbyist for children with special needs, the Council for Exceptional Children (CEC), overwhelmed the court with evidence on the educability of children with special needs. The state withdrew its case, and the court enjoined the state from excluding children with special needs from a public education and required that every child be allowed access to an education. Publicity about the PARC case prompted other lobbying groups to file thirty-six cases against different state governments. The CEC prepared model legislation and lobbied for its passage at the state and federal levels.

In 1975, Congress passed Public Law 94–142 (Education for All Handicapped Children Act) which guaranteed equal educational opportunity for all children with special needs. One of the issues confronting Congress during the debates over the legislation was that of increased federal control over local school systems. One way that Congress decided to resolve this issue was to require that an individual education plan (IEP) be written for each student with special needs. This avoided direct federal control by requiring that each student's IEP be developed at the local level.

IEPs are now a standard part of education programs for children with special needs. Public Law 94–142 requires that an IEP be developed for each child jointly by the local educational agency and the child's parents or guardians. This gives the child or the parents the right to negotiate with the local school system about the type of services to be delivered.

Another concern regarding the education of children with special needs is their isolation from other students and lack of access to the educational opportunities of a regular classroom. Federal legislation called for placing students in the "least restrictive environment." The result was the practice of *mainstreaming*. The basic idea of mainstreaming is that students with special needs will spend part of their day in a special education classroom and part of the day in regular classrooms. Obviously, the arrangement requires the classroom teacher to have some knowledge of the requirements of students with special needs. Working together, special education teachers and regular classroom teachers plan the mainstreaming of students with special needs into regular classrooms.

Many parents of students with special needs and many special education professionals felt that mainstreaming did not go far enough in providing a "least restrictive environment." They demanded full inclusion. Full inclusion is different from mainstreaming because students with special needs spend all their time in a regular classroom. The basic argument for full inclusion is that even

with mainstreaming, students with special needs spend a majority of their time segregated from regular students. Similar to any form of segregation, the isolation of children with special needs often deprives them of contact with other students and denies them access to equipment found in regular classrooms, such as scientific equipment, audiovisual aids, classroom libraries, and computers. Full inclusion, it is believed, will improve the educational achievement and social development of children with special needs.

In 1990, advocates of full inclusion received federal support with the passage of the Americans with Disabilities Act. This historic legislation bans all forms of discrimination against the disabled. The Americans with Disabilities Act played an important role in the 1992 court decision, *Oberti v. Board of Education of the Borough of Clementon School District*, which involved an 8-year-old classified as educable mentally-retarded: Rafael Oberti. U.S. District Court Judge John F. Gerry argued that the Americans with Disabilities Act requires that people with disabilities be given equal access to services provided by any agency receiving federal money, including public schools. Judge Gerry decided that Rafael Oberti could manage in a regular classroom with special aides and a special curriculum. In his decision, Judge Gerry wrote, "Inclusion is a right, not a privilege for a select few."

In 1992, the National Association of State Boards of Education gave its support to the idea of full inclusion with the issuance of its report, "Winners All: A Call for Inclusive Schools." The report calls for a fundamental shift in the provision of services of students with special needs. As the report envisions the full inclusion process, rather than teaching in a separate classroom, special education teachers would provide their services in regular classrooms by team-teaching with the regular teacher or providing other support.

The idea of inclusion is resisted by some parents who believe that separate special education classrooms provide important benefits for their children. For instance, twenty parents of children with special needs attending the Vaughn Occupational High School in Chicago carried signs at the board of education meeting on September 7, 1994, reading "The board's inclusion is exclusion." The parents were protesting the board's decision to send their children to neighborhood schools for inclusion in regular classrooms. Traditionally, Vaughn provided vocational training for students with special needs. The students would hold low-level jobs at McDonald's, an airline food service company, and a glass-installation business.

The board's actions regarding the Vaughn students was the result of a 1992 complaint by the Illinois state board that Vaughn students were not spending time with nondisabled peers. The state board threatened to remove all federal and state funds from the school district if the students were not included in regular classrooms. Martha Luna complained about the decision because it denied her 15-year-old son, Tony, vocational training to meet his needs. Ms. Luna stated, "I know Tony won't go to college so I don't expect that, just for him to learn everyday living and work skills."

The Education for All Handicapped Children Act, IEP, mainstreaming, the Americans with Disabilities Act, and full inclusion highlight the extent to which the civil rights movement reached out to include concerns for equal educational opportunity for all children, including children with special needs. It is a matter of justice that if all citizens are taxed to support schools, then all citizens should have an equal opportunity to attend school and benefit from an education.

CONCLUSION

Unequal educational opportunities continue to plague American schools. Even though the civil rights movement was able to overturn laws requiring school segregation, racial segregation between schools and second generation segregation in schools continue to be problems. And . . . the differences between school districts in expenditures

per student tend to increase the effects of segregation. Many Hispanic, African American, and Native American students attend schools where per student expenditures are considerably below those of elite suburban and private schools. These reduced expenditures contribute to unequal educational opportunity which, in turn, affects a student's ability to compete in the labor market.

It is possible . . . that unequal school expenditures, segregation, and second generation segregation will result in the vast majority of Hispanics, African Americans, and Native Americans being confined to boring and tedious jobs in routine production services and inperson services. Of course, large numbers of low income whites will also fill the ranks of these occupations. If education remains the key to advancement to high paying and interesting work, and if present inequalities and forms of segregation continue, then it is possible that the children of routine production and inperson services workers will be trapped in the occupations of their parents. If the promise of America is that hard work will lead to social mobility, then these conditions might foretell the end of the American Dream.

SUGGESTED READINGS AND WORKS CITED

Ballantine, Jeanne. *The Sociology of Education.* Englewood Cliffs, N.J.: Prentice-Hall, 1983. Chapter 4 is devoted to a discussion of sexism in education.

Borman, Kathryn M., and Joel Spring. *Schools in Central Cities.* White Plains: Longman, 1984. Chapter 6 analyzes the impact of desegregation on the curriculum.

Committee on Labor and Public Welfare, U.S. Senate 91st Congress, 1st Session. *Indian Education: A National Tragedy—A National Challenge.* Washington, D.C.: U.S. Government Printing Office, 1969. This is the report that set the stage for recent efforts in Indian education.

DeWitt, Karen. "The Nation's Schools Learn a 4th R: Resegregation." *New York Times* (19 January 1992): E5. This article provides statistics on the degree of segregation in the United States.

Dunn, Ashley. "Southeast Asians Highly Dependent on Welfare in U.S." *New York Times* (19 May 1994): 1, 23. This article summarizes report of the Asian Pacific American Public Policy Institute and the Asian American Studies Center on the economic conditions of Asian Americans.

Estrich, Susan. "For Girls' Schools and Women's Colleges, Separate Is Better." *New York Times Magazine* (22 May 1994): 39. Estrich argues against coeducation.

Hacker, Andrew. *Two Nations: Black and White, Separate, Hostile, Unequal.* New York: Charles Scribner's Son, 1992. A study of racial divisions in the United States.

Heller, Carol, and Hawkins, Joseph. "Teaching Tolerance: Notes from the Front Line." *Teachers College Record* (Spring 1994): 1–30. A history and description of the Teaching Tolerance Project.

Kluger, Richard. *Simple Justice.* New York: Random House, 1975. A good history of *Brown v. Board of Education* and the struggle for equality.

Krsycke, Cindy. "Efforts Fail to Advance Women's Jobs: 'Glass Ceiling' Intact Despite New Benefits." *Compuserve Executive News Service Washington Post* (20 February 1990). This article summarizes studies of difficulties encountered by women in trying to climb the corporate ladder.

Lamar, Jake. *Bourgeois Blues: An American Memoir.* New York: Plume Books, 1992. An autobiography dealing with the racism encountered by an upper-middle-class African American.

Levine, Daniel, and Robert Havighurst. *Society and Education.* 6th ed. Boston: Allyn and Bacon, 1984. Chapter 18 is devoted to women in education.

Manegold, Catherine. "'Save the Males' Becomes Battle Cry in Citadel's Defense Against Woman." *New York Times* (25 May 1994): A4. Story of female student's struggle to enter an all-boys school.

Meier, Kenneth, and Joseph Stewart, Jr. *The Politics of Hispanic Education.* Albany: State University of New York Press, 1991. This is an important study of the relationship between second generation segregation and Hispanic political power.

Meier, Kenneth, Joseph Stewart, Jr., and Robert England. *Race, Class, and Education: The Politics of Second-Generation Discrimination.* Madison: University of Wisconsin Press, 1989. This book studies the politics of second generation segregation.

"Mid- and Low-Income Minorities in Decline on College Rolls." *New York Times* (15 January 1990):

A13. This article reports on a study by the American Council of Education on the decline in minority college attendance.

Neal, David, and David Kirp. "The Allure of Legalization Reconsidered: The Case of Special Education." In David Kirp and Donald Jensen, eds., *School Days, Rule Days: The Legalization and Regulation of Education.* Philadelphia: Falmer Press, 1986. This is an important study of the evolution of court cases and laws affecting students with special needs.

O'Reilly, Patricia, and Kathryn Borman. "Sexism in Education: Documented Biases, Destructive Practices and Some Hope for the Future." *Theory into Practice* 23, no. 2 (Spring 1984). A good summary of information on institutional sexism in education.

Orfield, Gary. *The Reconstruction of Southern Education: The Schools and the 1964 Civil Rights Act.* New York: Wiley-Interscience, 1969. A study of the desegregation of southern schools following the passage of the 1964 Civil Rights Act.

Pang, Valerie Ooka. "Asian American Children: A Diverse Population." *The Educational Forum* (Fall 1990): 49–66. This is a good discussion of diversity in the Asian American population in the United States.

Prucha, Francis Paul. *Documents of United States Indian Policy.* Lincoln: University of Nebraska Press, 1990. This volume contains reprints of all the important laws, court cases, and reports affecting Indian education.

Reyhner, Jon, and Jeanne Eder. *A History of Indian Education.* Billings: Eastern Montana College, 1989. This book provides a history of Indian education to present times. It discusses recent Native American civil rights actions and recent legislation.

Rist, Ray. *Desegregated Schools: Appraisals of an American Experiment.* New York: Academic Press, 1979. This book provides many examples of second generation segregation.

Rossell, Christine. "Magnet Schools As a Desegregation Tool." *Urban Education* 14, no. 3 (October 1979). A study of the role of magnet schools in desegregation plans.

San Miguel, Jr., Guadalupe. *"Let All of Them Take Heed": Mexican Americans and the Campaign for Educational Equality in Texas, 1910–1981.* Austin: University of Texas Press, 1987. This is a good history of the events and court cases surrounding efforts by Mexican Americans to end segregation.

Schmidt, Peter. "Outlook Is Bleak for Many Blacks Study Concludes." *Education Week* (2 August 1989): 1, 29. Summary of report by the National Research Council titled *A Common Destiny: Blacks and American Society.*

Schnaiberg, Lynn. "Chicago Flap Shows Limits of 'Inclusion,' Critics Say." *Education Week* (5 October 1994): 1, 12. Article describes parent protest about inclusion in Chicago.

Sims, Calvin. "The Overlooked." *New York Times* (18 February 1990). Article reports on studies of the decline in minority college attendance.

_____. "Frustrated Hispanics Call for School Boycott in Denver." *Education Week* (21 September 1994): 3. A report on the threatened Latino student strike in Denver.

Smothers, Ronald. "In Pupil 'Tracks,' Many See a Means of Resegregation." *New York Times* (18 February 1990): E5. A report on how the use of tracking as a means of second generation segregation caused a school boycott in Selma, Alabama.

_____ "In School Conflict, Selma Discovers Old Racial Tensions Are Unresolved." *New York Times* (20 February 1990): A12. A report of student boycotts caused by second generation segregation.

Smylie, Mark. "Reducing Racial Isolation in Large School Districts: The Comparative Effectiveness of Mandatory and Voluntary Strategies." *Urban Education* 17, no. 4 (January 1983). A good analysis of the different types of school desegregation plans.

Snider, William. "Schools Are Reopened in Selma amid Continuing Racial Tension." *Education Week* (21 February 1990): 1, 14. A report of the school boycott and second generation segregation in Selma, Alabama.

Takaki, Ronald. *Strangers from a Different Shore: A History of Asian Americans.* New York: Penguin Books, 1989. An excellent history of Asian Americans.

Tatum, Beverly Daniel. "Teaching White Students about Racism: The Search for White Allies and the Restoration of Hope." Paper presented at the American Educational Research Association annual Meeting, April 5, 1994. Discussion of methods of creating positive antiracist models for white students.

Viadero, Debra. "'Full Inclusion' of Disabled in Regular Classes Favored." *Education Week* (30 September 1992): 11. This is a report on the court case, *Oberti v. Board of Education of the Borough of Clementon School District*, involving full inclusion.

_____. "NASBE Endorses 'Full Inclusion' of Disabled Students." *Education Week* (4 November 1992): 1, 30. This article discusses the report supporting full inclusion of students with special needs. The report, "Winners All: A Call for Inclusive Schools," was issued by the National Association for State Boards of Education.

_____. "Va. Hamlet at Forefront of 'Full Inclusion' Movement for Disabled." *Education Week* (18 November 1992): 1, 14. This article describes the implementation of a full inclusion plan in a community in Virginia.

Walsh, Mark. "Judge Finds Bias in Scholarships." *Education Week* (15 February 1989): 1, 20. This article describes the court ruling that found the awarding of scholarships using test scores to be biased against female students.

West, Peter. "Interior Dept. Sets 4 Objectives for Indian Education: Tribal Leaders Asked to Help Shape Goals." *Education Week* (21 February 1990): 1, 22. A report on some of the new plans for the education of Native Americans.

Wilkerson, Isabel. "Des Moines Acts to Halt White Flight After State Allows Choice of Schools." *New York Times* (16 December 1992): B9. This article briefly describes choice plans instituted by states and focuses on the issue of choice plans resulting in white flight from urban areas.

Wilson, William J. *The Declining Significance of Race: Blacks and Changing American Institutions.* Chicago: University of Chicago Press, 1979. This book argues that social class is a more important factor than race in determining equality of opportunity among African Americans.

Wollenberg, Charles. *All Deliberate Speed: Segregation and Exclusion in California Schools, 1855–1975.* Berkeley: University of California Press, 1976. This is a good history of segregation in California. It includes a discussion of the important court decision regarding Mexican Americans, *Mendez et al. v. Westminster School District of Orange County*, and of the segregation of Asian Americans.

Schools and the Struggle for Democracy: Themes for School Finance Policy

JAMES GORDON WARD

. . . U.S. schools are becoming more racially and culturally diverse. Another way of saying this is that the differences among children are increasing, raising issues of pedagogy, community building, and financing as well as issues relating to governance and political support. Many of these differences relate to different experiences prior to formal schooling. U.S. public schools will see more children whose home language is not English, more children who were not born or whose parents were not born in the United States, more children who were born and are growing up in poverty, and more children who have home lives that differ significantly from the traditional American dream. Many of these children will live and go to school in communities that are geographically and socially isolated from "middle-class America." Poverty and culturally diverse populations are not evenly spread across the landscape and tend to be concentrated in urban enclaves as well as in certain self-contained suburban and rural communities.

At the same time, economic and political power in the United States is more and more concentrated in an elite that has seceded from the rest of society in much of their daily lives (Reich, 1991). This elite is well educated, affluent, and not likely to live near those different from themselves. This elite uses private transportation to travel between a home in an urban high-rise building, trendy town house, or lush suburban community to a secure and opulent office building in the city center or suburban office park, rarely seeing the rest of the world

along the way. Class and race have a lot to do with the cultural differences that exist in the United States, and these factors all have a major impact on education and school finance. The quality of schooling received and the amount of money spent on that schooling differ greatly depending on where one lives and in what social strata one's parents reside. This has provided an enduring dilemma for public school finance specialists and for public policymakers, and demographic changes are likely to worsen the situation. What is emerging is a situation where, more than ever before in the history of our nation, the acquisition of economic and political power is dependent on access to high-quality education. As a scarce resource, high-quality education is carefully allocated, and it is no accident that those who have economic and political power allocate it to their own children, either through private schools or excellent public schools, and the rest of society makes do with the leftovers. Demographic trends in the United States set the stage for a situation where economic and political power will be held by a maturing, affluent middle class who will tend to live in the suburbs, while the greatest educational needs will be

Source: "Schools and the Struggle for Democracy: Themes for School Finance Policy" by James G. Ward from *Who Pays for Student Diversity? Population Changes and Educational Policy*, edited by James G. Ward and Patricia Anthony. Copyright 1992 by American Education Finance Association. Reprinted by permission of Corwin Press, Inc.

257

among poor and often minority children in the inner city or in rural ghettoes. Will the former pay higher taxes to properly educate the latter?

SCHOOLS AND DEMOCRACY

This question raises the question of what schools are likely to be like as organizations. Greenfield (1984, p. 145) has written that "organizations are manifestations of culture and we may understand them with only so much ease or difficulty as we can understand the culture in which they are embedded." Recent social and economic analysis has indicated that the rich are getting richer and the poor are getting poorer in the United States, and the implication is that two distinctly different cultures can be associated with the affluent and the needy in this country (Phillips, 1990; Reich, 1991). Reich (1991) argues that the affluent are part of a global culture, based on information and the ability to engage in symbolic analysis. Those performing routine production services or in-person services are less mobile, have fewer life opportunities, and earn much less money. This social analysis would suggest that these two different cultures will produce two different kinds of school organizations, which will in turn produce educational experiences that will vary greatly in nature and quality through the process of cultural reproduction (Bowles & Gintis, 1989).

The nature and quality of schooling not only are important for economic reasons, such as career preparation, but are politically important as well. The political aspects of education may have been stated best by Cremin (1990, p. 85) when he wrote that "education has always served political functions insofar as it affects, or at least is believed or intended to affect, the future character of the community and the state." Giroux and McLaren (1989, p. xxi) remind us that "American schooling becomes a vital sphere for extending civil rights, fighting for cultural justice, and developing new forms of democratic public life within a life-affirming public culture." These issues suggest the development of a community with common cultural values and argue for an approach to public schooling that prepares children for living through common experiences. Values form the basis for public policy decisions about schooling and for school finance policy decisions (Guthrie, Garms, & Pierce, 1988; Ward, 1987). It is fundamental to a democracy that public institutions will represent democratic values. Gutman (1987, p. 14) argues that

> a democratic theory of education recognizes the importance of empowering citizens to make educational policy and also of constraining their choices among policies in accordance with these principles—of nonrepression and nondiscrimination—that preserve the intellectual and social foundations of democratic deliberations.

The issue of nondiscrimination must be raised concerning the differing nature and quality of education among different schools and school districts. When different cultures produce different school organizations that support very different kinds of educational services, questions of discrimination arise because of the economic, social, and political consequences of those educational services. This is the essence of the issue of student equity in school finance. The question is not fundamentally one of finance, however, but one of governance and control. Gutman (1987, p. 16) goes on to say that "the central question posed by democratic education is: Who should have authority to shape the education of future citizens?"

THE CONTROL AND FINANCING OF SCHOOLS

The traditional view of public education in the United States is that it is the responsibility of the states but is delivered through local agencies under state supervision. Therefore the systems of governance and finance for U.S. public schools have been mixed state-local systems. This very fact has produced much discontent, because different individuals and groups have had different views on what the relative responsibilities of each party should be in differing circumstances. Much of this has had to do with differences in values and interests. This poses a dilemma, which has been described as follows:

> Education for citizenship and self-government . . . affirmatively obligates the state to provide all citizens with the quality and character of education appropriate for participation in political and community affairs. The state must provide an education that conforms to the level of participation self-governing communities expect from the citizenry. (Hubsch, 1989, p. 99)

The precise nature of the dilemma concerns what constitutes a community for purposes of self-governing. The implication in much of the school governance and school finance literature is that the community is a local community, such as a city, town, or village and its hinterlands. This is embodied in the traditional idea of local control, which has had a long and healthy life in public education in the United States. While not predicting its demise, Alexander (1990) makes a powerful argument that local control is a powerful mechanism for fostering discrimination and perpetuating privilege in public schooling. What then might constitute the proper community?

In his classic work, Morrison (1930) argues that the state is the community. After careful and exhaustive analysis of the history and functions of the U.S. public school system, he concluded that

> the several states themselves are the appropriate fiscal and administrative units in the support and conduct of the citizenship school which has long been held to be the cornerstone of our policy as a self-governing State. (Morrison, 1930, p. 214)

To the extent that the affluent and the less than affluent live in the same state, although not in the same local community, by regarding the self-governing community as the state, we can move toward removing some of the repression and discrimination that may now exist in public school-

ing. If the "quality and character" of education is determined at the state level, and that quality and character are assured for all children, then progress is being made. The critical issues become the definition of the quality and character of public education and the enforcement of that definition across school districts. Local community control, just as parental or family control, will undermine attempts to ensure a high level of quality and character for all children. Local communities will lose much of their ability to be enclaves for the protection of privilege or as places to which the "successful have seceded" from the rest of society (Reich, 1991).

POLICY MECHANISMS FOR ATTAINING EQUALITY OF OPPORTUNITY

Following the early intellectual leadership of Cubberley (1905), school finance policymakers have used state equalization formulas as one mechanism for providing some standardization of education quality among communities. There is a broad literature in this area, and there is no need to examine it here. State equalization formulas, however, have generally failed to accomplish their purposes for two reasons: They are seldom funded at a high enough level by the state to be effective, and they continue to allow local communities discretion in setting local property tax rates for school purposes. The politics of privilege and exclusion prevent either of these from being changed. Affluent local school districts can support a high level of education without a great deal of assistance from the state. Any increase in state taxes to assure this level of education for all children in the state would produce a heavy tax burden on the residents of these affluent districts with the economic benefit flowing to other districts in the state. Affluent communities also want no restrictions on their tax levying ability because they fear that state controls may reduce their ability to maintain their position of privilege. In many states, the growing political power of suburban legislators, representing areas where most of the affluent districts are located, prevent any resolution of this problem.

Another policy mechanism that has been used to address this problem is petition to the courts for redress for alleged discrimination or failure to provide quality education. This approach has had varying popularity with particularly heavy periods of judicial activity in the early 1970s and since 1989 (Thro, 1990). While there is ample evidence that such legal suits have altered state school finance formulas in states where the plaintiffs have been successful in court, the evidence is much less clear on whether there have been any significant gains in overall funding levels as a result of school finance reform suits, and there is scant evidence that the quality and character of the education of children of the poor have been significantly improved (Salmon & Alexander, 1990; Ward, 1990).

Outside of the realm of school finance policy, a variety of policy interventions have been attempted to solve the problem through attempts at the alleviation of poverty, income distribution, and local community economic development. Williams (1989) has documented the extreme difficulties inherent in indigenous neighborhood organizing for urban school reform, while Wilson (1987) has analyzed the persistence of urban poverty and the difficulties of maintaining high-quality social institutions and services in the midst of urban decay. The problems of rural poverty and maintaining viable social institutions under conditions of rural decline have been well established by Davidson (1990). Finally, the classic work of Ogbu (1978) has discussed the issues of race and education and documented the caste-like rigidity of race-based barriers to educational and economic success. The politics of redistribution have also met with little success in alleviating urban poverty and the low quality of social services in declining urban areas (Peterson, 1981). These all call into question the effectiveness of various social policy interventions in moving our society toward quality education for all children.

What can be some avenues for freeing U.S. public schools from being antidemocratic instruments of social reproduction that support the perpetuation of privilege among our political and economic elite and fail to properly serve many of our children?

SOME THEMES FOR POLICY RESEARCH AND DEVELOPMENT

I do not propose that I have the answer to the question I just posed, but I do want to suggest some areas for the redirection of our current policy research and development activities in education finance and governance that I think will move us toward answering the question.

The connections between educational outcomes and results and spending and governance patterns need additional exploration. The weak link in much of the educational research and in the factual base for school finance reform cases is the relationship among governance systems, expenditures per pupil, and educational outcomes. Traditional production function studies are limited methodologically and present few useful outcomes. Their error factors are too large to be of any explanatory value. Many of the school finance reform lawsuit complaints claim a direct relationship between spending per pupil and educational results, but upon careful scrutiny, they fail to prove the case. We need more studies that show the relationship between the way schools are organized and the way they are financed and the results they produce. Outcome variables are needed to make these studies useful; process variables are of much less value. If commentators like Reich and Phillips are correct, we should be able to discern the relationship between the dollars spent on education and the qualitative outcomes of that education.

We need to rethink the state's role in specifying educational outcomes and results for local schools. While states have constitutional responsibility for public education, they allow tremendous latitude in what they permit local school districts to do in the name of curriculum and instructional programs. As a result, the quality of education varies greatly across districts according to patterns described in this chapter. We need to give greater consideration to state standards and state expectations without constraining local districts in their ability to innovate and experiment. Accountability measures need to focus on outcomes and results rather than processes.

The federal role in education also needs reexamination. If some consistency of quality and character of education within states is important, then a similar degree of consistency among states is also a critical issue. The traditional federal role of funding programs for special needs students will require expansion. States do not have the fiscal resources, in many cases, to provide sufficient funding for programs for those with special needs. In a global economy, based on information and symbolic analysis, there is sufficient national interest in high-quality educational services for all children to justify a much larger federal role in education.

We need to rethink the program content and curriculum of our public schools. Some schools offer the kind of curriculum that allows students to succeed in an information-based society; many do not. One of the problems of local control is that the preferences of many communities do not include the quality and character of education that is needed for success in contemporary society. While parents have a responsibility to do what is best for their children, they should not have the right to intellectually handicap their children for life. In these instances, the responsibility of the state should take precedence over the rights of the parents. Local control is often a stalking-horse for educational mediocrity.

We need to institute systems of full-state funding and statewide school systems to protect the rights of all children. The current state-local system of public schools fails many children. Only a system where the state assumes responsibility for the quality and character of education for all children will ensure equal educational opportunities. It has been known for more than 60 years

that current systems of school finance and school governance are inadequate to the task, but we are not willing to change. Until we are willing to do so, little if any progress will be made.

We need to engage in a public dialogue about why all these innovations are necessary. We cannot underestimate the power of public discourse in convincing the citizens of our states that major systemic changes need to take place to ensure the equal educational opportunity for all children for the future of our society. Public conversations can be a powerful device to arrive at social consensus.

All of these ideas require additional research and development work. They should help set the research agenda for school finance specialists for the next decade or so. We have a moral imperative to make sure that they do.

REFERENCES

Alexander, K. (1990). Equitable financing, local control, and self-interest. In J. K. Underwood & D. A. Verstegen (Eds.), *The impacts of litigation and legislation on public school finance: Adequacy, equity, and excellence* (pp. 293–309). New York: Harper & Row.

Bowles, S., & Gintis, H. (1989). Can there be a liberal philosophy of education in a democratic society? In H. A. Giroux & P. McLaren (Eds.), *Critical pedagogy, the state, and cultural struggle* (pp. 24–31). Albany: State University of New York Press.

Cremin, L. A. (1990). *Popular education and its discontents.* New York: Harper & Row.

Cubberley, E. P. (1905). *School funds and their apportionment.* New York: Columbia University, Teachers College.

Davidson, O. G. (1990). *Broken heartland: The rise of America's rural ghetto.* New York: Free Press.

Giroux, H. A., & McLaren, P. (1989). Introduction: Schooling, cultural politics, and the struggle for democracy. In H. A. Giroux & P. McLaren (Eds.), *Critical pedagogy, the state, and cultural struggle* (pp. xi–xxxv). Albany: State University of New York Press.

Greenfield, T. B. (1984). Leaders and schools: Willfulness and nonnatural order in organizations. In T. J. Sergiovanni & J. E. Corbally (Eds.), *Leadership and organizational culture* (pp. 142–169). Urbana: University of Illinois Press.

Guthrie, J. W., Garms, W. I., & Pierce, L. C. (1988). *School finance and education policy: Financing educational efficiency, equality, and choice.* Englewood Cliffs, NJ: Prentice-Hall.

Gutman, A. (1987). *Democratic education.* Princeton, NJ: Princeton University Press.

Hubsch, A. W. (1989). Education and self-government: The right to education under state constitutional law. *Journal of Law and Education, 18*, 93–140.

Morrison, H. C. (1930). *School revenue.* Chicago: University of Chicago Press.

Ogbu, J. U. (1978). *Minority education and caste: The American system in cross-cultural perspective.* New York: Academic Press.

Peterson, P. E. (1981). *City limits.* Chicago: University of Chicago Press.

Phillips, K. (1990). *The politics of rich and poor.* New York: Random House.

Reich, R. B. (1991). *The work of nations: Preparing ourselves for 21st-century capitalism.* New York: Knopf.

Salmon, R. G., & Alexander, M. D. (1990). State legislative responses. In J. K. Underwood & D. A. Verstegen (Eds.), *The impacts of litigation and legislation on public school finance: Adequacy, equity, and excellence* (pp. 249–271). New York: Harper & Row.

Thro, W. F. (1990). The third wave: The impact of the Montana, Kentucky, and Texas decisions on the future of public school finance reform litigation. *Journal of Law and Education, 19*, 219–250.

Ward, J. G. (1987). An inquiry into the normative foundations of American public school finance. *Journal of Education Finance, 12*, 463–477.

Ward, J. G. (1990). Implementation and monitoring of judicial mandates: An interpretive analysis. In J. K. Underwood & D. A. Verstegen (Eds.), *The impacts of litigation and legislation on public school finance: Adequacy, equity, and excellence* (pp. 225–248). New York: Harper & Row.

Williams, M. R. (1989). *Neighborhood organizing for urban school reform.* New York: Teachers College Press.

Wilson, W. J. (1987). *The truly disadvantaged: The inner city, the underclass, and public policy.* Chicago: University of Chicago Press.

STUDY QUESTIONS FOR PART 6

1. Does equal access to education produce equal results for students? Why?

2. Have changes in the law produced "real" changes in opportunities for those who have historically not been advantaged by education (ethnic minorities, poor people, women, linguistic minorities, and the physically challenged)? Explain your reasoning.

3. Within your academic specialty (literature, mathematics, science, music, etc.) can you talk about five famous women and five famous ethnic minorities who have contributed to your discipline? If this is hard, why is that? What can you do in the classroom to be more inclusive of diversity within the curriculum?

4. If laws, rules, and policies are not making sufficient positive changes in the lives of students, what needs to be done to make improvements? How can individual teachers help?

5. Who deserves to receive schooling in our society? Why?

6. What knowledge (whose?), skills, values, etc. should be taught in public schools? What are your reasons?

7. How should this knowledge and these skills and values be taught in our schools? Why should teaching occur this way?

8. How should learning in schools be assessed? Is some knowledge more valuable than other knowledge? What performance standards will apply, and who gets to decide? Explain your thinking in answering these questions.

9. What might be some reasons to fund education for the children of undocumented immigrants?

PRACTICUM
EXPERIENCES

Suggested Guidelines for Students and Instructors

A major purpose of this collection of readings is to introduce teachers to the many facets of teaching beyond the child or the subject to be taught. A teacher's work life is influenced by a multitude of factors, ranging from the clarity of the school's curriculum and the availability of the needed instructional resources to the politics of the local community, the cultural and socioeconomic diversity of the children to be taught, and the degree of parental involvement in the classroom or school, to name but a few.

There are many influences on the quality, amount, and focus of a teacher's classroom instruction. A practicum that provides some insight into these various influences can help the veteran as well as the inexperienced or prospective teacher understand the complexity and the challenges faced by the classroom teacher. Too often, teachers enter their first teaching assignment with little understanding of all the forces shaping what occurs in a classroom or school. And frequently, experienced teachers work for years with little else to guide them but their subject-matter expertise and the little they might recall of their preservice class in human growth and development. While many teachers have taken the initiative to keep up with the latest theory and research about good teaching and child development practices, few veterans have been encouraged to explore the bigger picture—the school and community beyond their classroom.

The purpose of the suggested practicum experiences is to enable beginners as well as veteran teachers develop their awareness of these factors influencing their work, and to give them opportunities to reflect upon their effects in the classroom and to consider courses of action they might take to ameliorate, insulate, or build upon those forces to help them be more effective as a teacher. Being a good teacher involves a lot more than knowledge about child development, teaching methods, and subject matter.

The best practicum for a prospective teacher is one that allows the individual extended opportunities to work directly with school-age children in a school, although it does not have to be limited to a traditional classroom or school setting.

There are any number of opportunities to work with children in other community contexts that will introduce individuals firsthand to the myriad forces shaping the teaching and learning that occur in schools. Some suggestions for students in a preservice teacher education program include working with teen parents, Head Start, English as a Second Language (ESL) programs, the Urban League, migrant education programs, youth development programs in the community, a youth outreach center, children with disabilities, 4H youth programs, or a juvenile treatment center. Every community will offer a number of opportunities for individuals to volunteer for one or more programs serving children.

For the experienced teacher, a practicum can take a number of forms, including "trading" assignments for a day or week with a teacher colleague working at a different grade level or in a socioeconomically, linguistically, racially, or culturally different school or community. While such an experience will require extra effort by the teachers involved, it frequently proves to be both a refreshing and an inspiring experience. Veterans taking advantage of such opportunities often find themselves making major changes in their regular classroom practices; changes that reflect their new understanding of the assumptions they'd been making about children, about teaching, and about the purposes of public education. Sometimes the practicum for a veteran teacher can simply take the form of "shadowing" another teacher, a school administrator, or perhaps a special education specialist or ESL teacher.

The practicum experience for a preservice teacher can occur in a school or in some other setting. A 30-hour experience is recommended. Whatever the nature of the practicum, each individual should be asked to take responsibility for sharing their observations and reflections on their experience with other members of the class, and perhaps to prepare a brief report describing their experience and discussing its implications for their future work as a classroom teacher.

A practicum has a number of additional benefits, depending on the audience it serves: It can

- inform admission decisions in a teacher education program
- help experienced teachers gain fresh insights
- help individuals determine whether teaching really is for them
- foster community-based learning that returns something to the community
- serve as an enriching multicultural experience
- introduce the challenges of inclusion models of education
- serve as a confidence builder for the individual
- provide an early experience in teaching and working with children for the prospective teacher.

The suggested practica are a win-win situation. University or college students grow and develop as a result of their teaching experience in the practicum, and they receive additional assistance and support beyond what an individual instructor can provide. In addition, their overall learning experience is more robust and engaging because it provides opportunities for them to experience firsthand the many ideas, cultural and economic influences, and moral dilemmas they will encounter in the selected readings. For prospective teachers, a practicum experience provides a relatively efficient way to test out some of their understandings of what being a teacher might be like. For veteran teachers, a practicum can be the means for providing insights about the efficacy of their current perspective as a teacher, or about the promises and challenges of teaching in a manner that reflects a deeper understanding of the functions of schools and how schools perpetuate inequalities among children and, ultimately, in our society. For the veteran teacher, a practicum experience can serve as a catalyst for change that results in greater educational equity for all children, particularly for those not well-served by current practices.

FIELD EXPERIENCES

Suggested Guidelines for
Students and Instructors

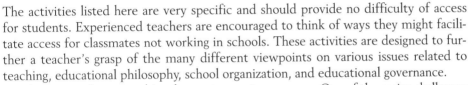

The activities listed here are very specific and should provide no difficulty of access for students. Experienced teachers are encouraged to think of ways they might facilitate access for classmates not working in schools. These activities are designed to further a teacher's grasp of the many different viewpoints on various issues related to teaching, educational philosophy, school organization, and educational governance.

As veterans know, teaching does not occur in a vacuum. One of the major challenges of teaching involves developing a personal perspective on schooling, teaching, and learning that is at once rooted in what the profession knows about good practice, while at the same time being responsive to the diversity of views within the profession and the school community and providing a *realistic* sense of how schools and classrooms actually work. It is not always clear what is right or good. Judgments must be made, and in the course of making such judgments many different elements need to be considered. Part of what enables due consideration is the ability to anticipate the viewpoints or possible responses of others to a particular decision or course of action. What helps one do this is the breadth and depth of formal learning and experience one brings to the situation.

The field experiences described here can provide the preservice student with an initial glimpse of the diversity of perspectives held by others regarding teaching, learning, schooling, and educational governance, among other concerns. Experienced teachers can also benefit from these experiences, particularly if the school or community context of the interviewee is linguistically, racially, culturally, or socioeconomically different from one's current situation. Even if the experienced teacher must observe or interview others in their own school, the learning to be achieved by this activity can be enhanced to the extent that the person observed or interviewed is someone unfamiliar, or someone with whom you don't normally interact.

The following activities are recommended:

- Interview a teacher.
- Interview a school principal or assistant principal.

269

- Attend a school faculty meeting.
- Attend a site council or PTA meeting.
- Attend a school board meeting.

Interview questions or guides for observation should be developed by the individual students based on class readings and conversations. A general guideline is to ask questions that require either a description or an explanation; try to stay away from questions calling for a yes/no response. Reassure the person with whom you are talking that his or her name and the name of the school and district will not be revealed to anyone. Plan for an interview that will last 30–60 minutes. Do your best to make an appointment with the person and set the interview up to be held at a time and in a location convenient for the subject and unlikely to be interrupted by noise or intrusions (people, telephone, etc). Introduce yourself as a student, and tell the subject that your major purpose is to understand things from his or her viewpoint.

Suggested interview questions:

- Tell me about your first year as a teacher. What was your greatest frustration; your greatest accomplishment?
- How are things different (or the same) for you now?
- What do you do when you have children with a very broad range of academic abilities?
- What do you like (don't like) about your school; why?
- What are your greatest sources of reward as a teacher/administrator?
- Tell me what you think about the following: multicultural education, cooperative learning, career or vocational education, bilingual education, school prayer schools, nongraded primary schools, gender bias in curricula, instructional technology, AIDS education, parental involvement, site-based decision making that involves teachers and parents, student internships, (a topic of your choosing).
- What are your beliefs about student grouping for instruction?
- We hear a lot about equal educational opportunity. What does that mean in your classroom/school? What would you change, if anything, and why?
- What is the role of school in society?
- Some people argue that local school boards should be abolished. What do you think?
- What are your thoughts about education funding? What are your thoughts about full-state funding for education?
- What do you look for when hiring a new teacher?

There are many purposes to be served by completion of these field activities. While the general outcome will be a broadening of the individual's perspective, some particular outcomes can include

- exposure to various influences on teachers

- gaining a better understanding of how your colleagues view their work
- hearing firsthand from teachers and administrators about their jobs
- getting a better understanding of who controls the schools
- seeing what role parents and community members play in education
- enabling career exploration and helping students decide if teaching is the *right fit* for them
- gaining a glimpse of the larger reality of teaching—that it's *not* just you and the kids in your classroom, it's other teachers, parents, administrators, school board members (with all of them having somewhat disparate and frequently conflicting views)
- broadening your perspective as a veteran teacher; seeing how others might be successfully responding to many of the challenges raised by the readings

A field experience like those listed above can be very helpful in broadening an individual's view of what *being a teacher* is all about. The more such experiences an individual can get, be that person a veteran or a prospective teacher, the more complete will be his or her understanding of what it means to be a teacher. The insights gained will enable teachers to be more reflective about their practice, and to be more deliberate and informed in deciding the what, how, and why of their work as a teacher.

Suggested Readings

Aronowitz, S., and Giroux, H. 1993. *Education still under siege.* Westport, CT: Bergin & Garvey.

Banks, J., and Banks, C. (Eds.). 1995. *Handbook of research on multicultural education.* New York: Macmillan.

Brown, L., and Gilligan, C. 1992. *Meeting at the crossroads: Women's psychology and girls' development.* Cambridge, MA: Harvard University Press.

Carnoy, M. 1974. *Education as cultural imperialism.* New York: Longman.

Cyrus, V. 1993. *Experiencing race, class and gender in the United States.* Mountain View, CA: Mayfield Publishing.

Darder, A. 1991. *Culture and power in the classroom.* Westport, CT: Bergin & Garvey.

Fiol-Matta, L., and Chamberlain, M. (Eds.). 1994. *Women of color and the multicultural curriculum: Transforming the college classroom.* New York: The Feminist Press.

Grusky, D. (Ed.). 1994. *Social stratification: Class, race, and gender in sociological perspective.* Boulder, CO: Westview Press.

Hakuta, K. 1986. *Mirror of language: The debate on bilingualism.* New York: Basic Books, Inc.

Kerber, L., and De Hart, J. (Eds.). 1995. *Women's America: Refocusing the past.* New York: Oxford University Press.

Kochman, T. 1981. *Black and white styles in conflict.* Chicago: University of Chicago Press.

Kuykendall, C. 1992. *From rage to hope: Strategies for reclaiming Black and Hispanic students.* Bloomington, IN: National Educational Services.

Ladson-Billings, G. 1994. *The dreamkeepers: Successful teachers of African American children.* San Francisco: Jossey-Bass Publishers.

McCarthy, C., and Crichlow, W. 1993. *Race identity and representation in education.* New York: Routledge.

Nakanishi, D., and Nishida, T. 1995. *The Asian American educational experience.* New York: Academic Press.

Ogbu, J. 1978. *American education and caste: The American system in cross-cultural perspective.* New York: Academic Press.

Orenstein, P. 1994. *School girls: Young women, self-esteem, and the confidence gap.* New York: Doubleday.

Paley, V. 1995. *Kwanzaa and me: A teacher's story.* Cambridge, MA: Harvard University Press.

Poplin, M., and Weeres, J. 1992. *Voices from the inside: A report on schooling from inside the classroom.* Part One: Naming the Problem. Claremont, CA: The Institute for Education In Transformation At the Claremont Graduate School.

Rothenberg, P. 1995. *Race, class, and gender in the United States: An integrated study.* New York: St. Martin's Press.

Shapiro, H., and Purpel, D. (Eds.). 1993. *Critical social issues in American education: Toward the 21st century.* New York: Longman Publishing Group.

Tavris, C. 1992. *The mismeasure of woman: Why women are not the better sex, the inferior sex, or the opposite sex.* New York: Simon & Schuster.

Thompson, B., and Tyagi, S. (Eds.). 1993. *Beyond a dream deferred: Multicultural education and the politics of excellence.* Minneapolis, MN: University of Minnesota Press.

Weis, L., and Fine, M. (Eds.). 1993. *Beyond silenced voices: Class, race and gender in United States schools.* Albany: State University of New York Press.

West, C. 1993. *Race matters.* Boston: Beacon Press.

Wilson, W. J. 1987. *The truly disadvantaged: The inner city, the underclass, and public policy.* Chicago: The University of Chicago Press.

Index